THE AVIATION FACTFILE

CIVIL AIRCRAFT

THE AVIATION FACTFILE

CIVIL AIRCRAFT

GENERAL EDITOR: JIM WINCHESTER

THUNDER BAY
P·R·E·S·S

San Diego, California

Thunder Bay Press
An imprint of the Advantage Publishers Group
5880 Oberlin Drive, San Diego, CA 92121-4794
www.thunderbaybooks.com

All notations of errors or omissions should be addressed to Thunder Bay Press, Editorial Department, at the above address. All other
correspondence (author inquiries, permissions) concerning the content of this book should be addressed to Amber Books Ltd., Bradley's Close,
74–77 White Lion Street, London N1 9PF, England, www.amberbooks.co.uk.

ISBN 1-59223-226-4

Library of Congress Cataloging-in-Publication Data available upon request.

Printed in Singapore

1 2 3 4 5 08 07 06 05 04

Contents

INTRODUCTION

When aircraft with any degree of carrying capacity first became available to civilians, airmail was considered more important than passengers. The first passenger service, from St. Petersburg to Tampa in Florida, ran on a trial basis only in 1912, but soon after the First World War there were enough adventurous (and wealthy) people who were prepared to travel in converted bombers to establish the first air routes and airlines. Until the mid-1930s, the biplane and the trimotor monoplane ruled the airways.

Although there are many candidates for the 'first modern airliner', the aircraft that set the standard for all to follow was the immortal Douglas DC-3. First flown in 1935, the DC-3 was built in relatively small numbers before World War II, but allowed the airlines of the USA and elsewhere to establish reliable

connections between distant cities, challenging the dominance of the railways for the first time. During the war, the DC-3 was built in huge numbers for the military as the C-47 Skytrain. Post-war, the thousands of surplus C-47 troop carriers that were converted to airliners equipped second-tier US and European airlines and connected communities in many of the remotest corners of the globe.

The immediate post-war years were the heyday of the great piston-engined airliners such as Lockheed's Constellation, Boeing's Stratocruiser and the DC-6 and DC-7 from Douglas. Britain introduced jet passenger travel to the world in 1952 with the de Havilland Comet, but a series of disasters saw the lead lost to the next American generation, the 707 and DC-8. The post-war economic boom in the US

and the return of thousands of trained pilots to civilian life saw the golden age of general aviation and flying for fun. The products of Cessna, Piper and Beech allowed many to fulfil the dream of flight. Product liability issues almost killed the US light aircraft industry in the 1980s and 1990s, but European manufacturers and producers of kits for home builders filled the demand, as did the growing popularity of microlights or ultralites.

After Lockheed's tribulations with the TriStar, this pioneering company left the airliner business. McDonnell Douglas stayed out of the medium-range mid-sized airliner market dominated by the 757/767 and Airbus A300/A310, and failed to sell the MD-11 in large numbers. Absorption by Boeing left just one maker of large airliners in the United States.

Above left: Good endurance and the safety of a twin-engined design makes the Piper Seneca ideal for 'eye in the sky' traffic information broadcasting.

Above right: The ubiquitous and versatile Boeing 747 was used by NASA to transport the Space Shuttle across the United States from Edwards AFB to Cape Canaveral.

Outside of the Boeing/Airbus battle, smaller manufacturers such as Beech, Brazil's Embraer, Germany's Dornier and Bombardier (owners of Canadair, Lear and De Havilland Canada) have found their niche in the regional airliner market. Some of these have ambitions to take on the market long dominated by the 737. Russian manufacturers have advanced technologically in recent years but have struggled to find customers for their products. Even Aeroflot has re-equipped largely with western designs.

Below: The Comet 4C was a long-range development of de Havilland's original groundbreaking design.

Left: A flying legend, the Douglas DC-3 has remained in active service more than 60 years.

Right: Designed by aviation technology pioneer Burt Rutan, the unique shape of Beech's Starship 1 was no guarantee of commercial success.

Right: An engineering marvel of the 1970s, Concorde remained in service into the 21st century, despite its economic and environmental shortcomings.

Although many supersonic airliner designs were drawn up, only the Anglo-French Concorde and the Soviet Tu-144 ever entered service. Both were built without much consideration for conventional economics and only the Concorde (eventually) achieved a measure of commercial success on transatlantic, luxury routes. The small Concorde fleet was retired in 2003 without any successor on the horizon.

The true success story in modern civil aviation has to be the Boeing 747, which has sold and sold with no direct competition for nearly 35 years. The 747's unrivalled capacity and operating economics has allowed most ordinary people a chance to experience the world. Today we are on the brink of the 800-seat airliner, a technical marvel, but one which will probably be more fun to watch take off than to travel in.

AERO SPACELINES

SUPER GUPPY

● Outsize load-lifter ● Space rocket transporter ● Airbus component carrier

Since 1961, Aero Spacelines has modified ancient piston-powered prop-driven Boeing Stratocruisers to carry outsized rocket boosters and oil derricks. Known as 'Guppies' after the bulbous fish, their most notable features are the huge extensions built into their fuselages. Old it might be, but the Guppy has done a valuable job hauling everything from Saturn V rocket stages to the components of Europe's Airbus.

▲ For an aircraft that no-one seemed to want when it was conceived, the Guppy family has been a great success. The outsized planes may still be in service for years to come.

AERO SPACELINES SUPER GUPPY

▼ **Aeromaritime**
Aeromaritime, the freight division of the UTA airline, operated Super Guppy 201s, but these were eventually replaced by modified A300s known as the 'Beluga'.

▲ **Airbus cargo**
The fin of this Airbus A300 started its flying career when a Super Guppy flew it from Hamburg to Toulouse.

◀ **Inside the Guppy**
The cavernous hold of a Guppy is almost unique in being very high. Later Guppies could swallow an entire Airbus A320 wing.

◀ **Filton visit**
Guppies have been frequent visitors to the BAe plant at Filton, England, since the 1980s. Their task was to ship Airbus A320 wings by air to the Toulouse factory.

The world's strangest plane? ▶
The massive swelling of the upper fuselage makes it hard to accept that such a bizarre aircraft could ever get off the ground. But it can fly as well as its Stratocruiser and B-29 ancestors.

FACTS AND FIGURES

➤ The first B-377PG Pregnant Guppy flew on 18 September 1962.

➤ About 15 ground runs and test 'hops' were made before that first flight.

➤ The bigger B-377SG Super Guppy, the first to use turboprop engines, is an ex-military YC-97J and serves with NASA.

➤ The original Guppy could carry three million peanuts.

➤ Other aircraft may be able to carry heavier loads, but the Guppy's forte has always been outsize cargoes.

➤ The A300-600ST 'Beluga' is a 'Guppy' version of the A300 Airbus.

PROFILE

The fattest plane ever

Aero Spacelines in the USA saw the potential of outsized aircraft to haul cargoes which were not unreasonably heavy but had enormous dimensions. In 1961, the company modified its first piston-engined Boeing B-377 Stratocruiser, the military C-97, by stretching the aircraft and creating a 'bubble' structure atop the fuselage.

Eight Guppys were built in six configurations. Four aircraft (including two Guppy 201s converted by UTA) support

Airbus in the multinational manufacture of jetliners by hauling large components from different factories to a central point for final assembly.

A Guppy being loaded is one of the most amazing sights in aviation. The whole cockpit section, complete with nosewheel, is all but detached from the aircraft and swung through 110° to leave unobstructed access to the open fuselage.

These ex-Boeing freighters have proved so practical that

The inventors of the Guppy series succeeded in creating a market of their own with these aircraft. Thirty years on, there are few aircraft capable of handling such outsize loads.

Airbus created a 'Guppy' of its own. The A300-600ST Super Transporter, or 'Beluga', is taking over carrying cargoes for the international aircraft manufacturer.

The cockpit area is much the same as a Stratocruiser, with accommodation for two pilots, a navigator and flight engineer. The cockpit is pressurised, unlike the hold.

The ancestry of the Guppy family is immediately apparent when the wing plan view is seen. It is almost identical to the C-97 Stratocruiser wing.

Despite the huge fuselage doubling the cross-sectional area of the C-97, the Guppy only required six per cent more power to maintain a given airspeed.

Super Guppy 201

Type: heavy transport

Powerplant: four 3663-kW (4,912-hp.) Allison 501-D22C turboprops

Maximum speed: 463 km/h (287 m.p.h.) at 6100 m (20,000 ft.)

Cruising speed: 407 km/h (252 m.p.h.) at 6100 m (20,000 ft.)

Range: 813 km (504 mi.)

Weights: empty 45,359 kg (99,790 lb.); loaded 77,111 kg (169,644 lb.)

Accommodation: cargo compartment length 33.99 m (112 ft.); width 7.77 m (25 ft.); height 7.65 m (25 ft.)

Dimensions:
span	47.63 m (156 ft.)
length	43.84 m (144 ft.)
height	14.78 m (48 ft.)
wing area	182.51 m² (1,964 sq.ft.)

The Super Guppy 201 is the largest member of this unique family. The aircraft have had a busy life, mainly transporting large components for Airbus.

The nose contains a small AVQ-55 weather radar.

The Super Guppy is powered by Allison 501 turboprops, mounted in the same nacelles as those fitted to the Lockheed P-3 Orion.

The huge area of the fuselage creates very little difference in the stability of the Guppy, and actually improves some aspects of the aircraft's handling.

The Guppy family have extensively modernised tail surfaces compared to the Stratocruisers from which they were derived.

AERO SPACELINES

N1038V

The wing centre section of the Super Guppy was extended by about 4 m (12 ft.), to give increased lift and improve propeller clearance.

ACTION DATA

MAXIMUM SPEED

SUPER GUPPY	463 km/h (287 m.p.h.)
An-22 ANTEI	740 km/h (459 m.p.h.)
BELFAST	544 km/h (337 m.p.h.)

Turboprop power meant that the Super Guppy was no slower than its piston-engined predecessors, even though its huge fuselage expansion created more drag. It is still much slower than other large turbo-powered transports of the 1960s, however.

PAYLOAD

SUPER GUPPY 201	An-22 ANTEI	BELFAST
24 tonnes (24 tons)	80 tonnes (80 tons)	35 tonnes (35 tons)

While the Super Guppy can lift a respectable weight of cargo, it cannot match aircraft designed to lift heavy weights such as the Belfast or the massive Soviet An-22, which for several years was the world's largest aircraft. Neither can match the Super Guppy's abilities with large-volume cargoes, however.

HOLD DIAMETER

SUPER GUPPY 201	An-22 ANTEI	BELFAST
7.7 m (25 ft.)	4.5 m (15 ft.)	3.5 m (12 ft.)

The Belfast was designed to carry three armoured cars or up to 200 troops. The An-22 was capable of operating out of rough fields while carrying a main battle tank or two huge SA-4 missile launch systems. But neither could have carried the third stage of a Saturn V moon rocket, or the entire wings or fuselage sections of a wide-body airliner, which are the Guppy's stock in trade.

King-size cargo carriers

■ **GLOBEMASTER:** Designed to carry large cargoes for the US Air Force of the 1950s and 1960s, the Douglas C-124 featured a fixed nose with clamshell loading doors.

■ **CANADAIR CL-44:** Based on the Bristol Britannia airliner, the CL-44 had a swinging tail to allow direct access to the cargo hold. But it lacked the Guppy's outsize load ability.

■ **ANTONOV'S GIANTS:** The Ukrainian concern has long specialised in large aircraft, the massive An-124 being its current workhorse. It offers yet another method of hold access.

■ **TWENTY-FIRST CENTURY GUPPY:** Based on the Airbus A300 airframe, the 'Beluga' will ensure that the Guppy concept will be around for many years to come.

AÉROSPATIALE (SUD AVIATION)

CARAVELLE

● First French jet airliner ● Rear-mounted turbojet ● 30 years' service

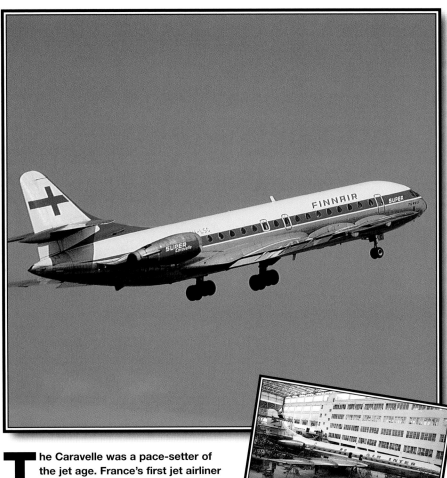

The Caravelle was a pace-setter of the jet age. France's first jet airliner was one of the earliest short- to medium-range turbojet transports, and the first with podded engines fixed to the rear fuselage. This was a successful attempt to ensure improved wing performance and to decrease cabin noise, an idea later copied by many other manufacturers. Hundreds of Caravelles were produced, and served with distinction for three decades.

▲ *The Caravelle gave French aviation a huge boost. It proved that France could compete in commercial as well as military aviation, though it relied initially on British design for engines and other components.*

PHOTO FILE

AÉROSPATIALE (SUD AVIATION) CARAVELLE

▲ Caravelle line
The Toulouse St Martin production line was busy producing these beautiful airliners between 1959 and 1973.

▲ Sterling
The Caravelle 12, as operated by Sterling Airways of Denmark, could carry up to 140 passengers. Sterling was one of 24 operators still using the Caravelle during the 1980s.

◀ Long service
Air Inter used the Caravelle for many years. It had 14 aircraft, which serviced a large French domestic route network.

Luxury liner ▶
Some aircraft were fitted out as VIP transports, their luxury interiors having full conference and business facilities which were enhanced by the Caravelle's low noise and smooth ride.

◀ New engines
The Caravelle 7 was a trials version using the General Electric CJ-805 engine. It used the 'short cowl' turbofan in an attempt to increase fuel economy.

FACTS AND FIGURES

➤ The SE 210 Caravelle prototype made its first flight on 27 May 1955.

➤ Design of the front fuselage was based on the de Havilland Comet.

➤ First flown on 3 March 1964, the Super Caravelle was a refinement of the Caravelle III and IV.

➤ Construction of the first two Caravelles was sponsored by the French government.

➤ The 'ultimate' Caravelle variant was the Caravelle 12, the biggest and most powerful model.

➤ The Caravelle 12 took to the air for the first time on 29 October 1970.

PROFILE

Rear-engine pioneer from France

The Caravelle was a product of the early 1950s. Designed by Sud Aviation (now part of Aérospatiale) as a 52-seater, it was to grow considerably after its first flight in 1955. By the time the Caravelle 12 came along in 1970, passenger capacity had increased to 140 and some 35 airlines in two dozen countries were operating the type.

The Caravelle is renowned for being much quieter inside than other first-generation jetliners like the de Havilland Comet and Boeing 707. All versions pampered passengers with a sumptuous interior, plenty of room and excellent vision. Pilots found the Caravelle a very sensible and practical machine. It was also considered a bargain by airline executives nervous about fuel prices.

In the 1980s, approaching old age, Caravelles were gradually withdrawn from most scheduled routes, but with considerable reluctance. Caravelles found other uses. Many succeeded as freighters; some were used as VIP transports, utility craft or electronic intelligence-gatherers for the military.

The Caravelle was a great design success for France. Not only did it have a relatively trouble-free entry into service, but it introduced a totally new engine layout, in rear pods, at a time when American designs used wing-mounted pods and the British persisted with engines mounted in the wingroots.

The Caravelle tailplane was mid-set on the fin to keep it clear of the engine exhaust.

A projected Caravelle 10A was designed with a leading-edge root extension and double-slotted flaps, but only one prototype was ever built.

A unique and instant recognition feature of the Caravelle was the graceful swept tail. Early aircraft also had a shallow spine from the fin to the mid-fuselage, housing radio antennas.

Caravelle 12

Type: short-/medium-range transport

Powerplant: two 64.50-kN (14,470-lb.-thrust) Pratt & Whitney JT8D-9 turbofans

Maximum cruising speed: 825 km/h (512 m.p.h.) at 7620 m (25,000 ft.)

Range: 4040 km (2,860 mi.)

Service ceiling: 10,900 m (35,750 ft.)

Weights: empty 29,500 kg (64,900 lb.); loaded 58,000 kg (127,600 lb.)

Accommodation: 52 to 64 passengers in initial versions; up to 104 passengers on Super Caravelle; up to 140 passengers on Caravelle 12

Dimensions:
span 34.29 m (112 ft. 6 in.)
length 36.23 m (118 ft. 10 in.)
height 9.02 m (29 ft. 7 in.)
wing area 146.70 m² (1,579 sq. ft.)

CARAVELLE III 'ALTAIR'

Alitalia operated one of the largest Caravelle fleets, with 21 aircraft in service by 1965. 'Altair' entered service in 1960 and was eventually sold to an Ecuadorian airline which flew it throughout the 1970s.

The forward fuselage of the Caravelle was based upon that of the British de Havilland Comet, the world's first operational jet airliner.

Over the years the fuselage of the Caravelle was 'stretched' many times. The first Caravelles seated only about 50 passengers, but the final version seated about 140 in economy-style layout.

Due to the absence of engine mountings the wing was unusually clean and efficient in design. Two fences were fitted on the outboard of the wing.

Caravelle IIIs were powered by the Rolls-Royce Avon engine, which was powerful but rather thirsty. Fuel economy was much improved with the fitting of Pratt & Whitney JT8D turbofans in the Caravelle 10B.

Only a pilot and co-pilot were usually housed in the flight deck.

The cabin windows had an unusual rounded triangular shape.

Rear-mounted engines meant that the passenger cabin of the Caravelle was quieter than any of the other first-generation jet airliners.

ACTION DATA

MAXIMUM SPEED

The Caravelle was one of the earliest jet liners, so it was marginally slower than some of its contemporaries. But it was the first short-haul jet, and it could travel twice as fast as the piston-engined twins that many airlines were using in the 1950s.

CARAVELLE III	805 km/h (512 m.p.h.)
COMET 4C	861 km/h (534 m.p.h.)
DC-9	900 km/h (558 m.p.h.)

RANGE

As a short-haul jet, a typical Caravelle route had stages ranging from 150 km (100 mi.) to around 1000 km (600 mi.). The later DC-9 was designed for the same market and has a similar layout and range. Although the Comet had a much longer range, it too was largely used on short- and medium-haul routes.

COMET 4C 7000 km (4,300 mi.)

CARAVELLE III 2300 km (1,400 mi.)

DC-9 2000 km (1,250 mi.)

PASSENGER LOAD

Although early Caravelles could carry nearly 100 passengers in a high-density layout, 64 passengers in a two-class configuration was a more usual payload. First-class passengers sat four abreast, with economy seating in rows of five.

CARAVELLE III maximum 99

COMET 4C maximum 118

DC-9 maximum 90

Constant improvement

CARAVELLE III: Tunis Air operated nine assorted Caravelles between 1961 and 1977. This was a Series III, which mated the original fuselage with more powerful Rolls-Royce Avon engines.

CARAVELLE 11R: This had a 1.93-m (6-ft. 4-in.) fuselage extension and a large cargo door. This example served in Tahiti for many years, supporting France's nuclear test range in the Pacific.

CARAVELLE 12: The Caravelle 12 was 4.23 m (13 ft. 10 in.) longer than the original. Air Inter operated Caravelles to 23 destinations in France, and this example seated 128 passengers.

AÉROSPATIALE/BAC

CONCORDE

● World's fastest airliner ● Mach 2 performance ● Supreme luxury

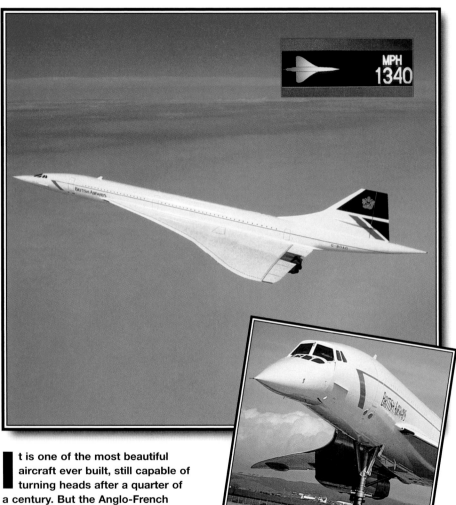

MPH
1340

I t is one of the most beautiful aircraft ever built, still capable of turning heads after a quarter of a century. But the Anglo-French Concorde is much more than a work of aeronautic art. A record breaker from the start, it proved to be highly profitable on the prestige air routes between Europe and the USA until shortly before its retirement in October 2003.

▲ Although it is a product of 1960s technology, without the benefit of multi-screen cockpits and fly-by-wire controls, Concorde is still the most futuristic airliner to be seen anywhere in the world.

AÉROSPATIALE/BAC CONCORDE

◀ Supercruise
Concorde is one of the very few aircraft able to maintain a supersonic cruise without the use of afterburners, which enables it to fly further at Mach 2 than any other aircraft.

Olympus power ▶
Concorde's engines each pour out more than 17 tons of thrust.

▼ Powerpack
To gain additional thrust at critical moments such as take-off and transition to supersonic speed, Concorde's engines are fitted with afterburners.

▲ Streamlining
Even at altitudes above 15,000 m (49,000 ft.), air friction at twice the speed of sound is a significant factor, so Concorde is polished mirror smooth to reduce drag.

AIR FRANCE

▲Elegant travelling
Concorde's aesthetically pleasing shape is matched by a standard of service more luxurious than that of any other scheduled airliner.

FACTS AND FIGURES

➤ Since Concorde entered scheduled service in 1978, British and French aircraft have carried 3,000,000 supersonic passengers.

➤ Concorde's only rival, the Soviet Tu-144, is no longer in service.

➤ During supersonic flight, Concorde's skin heats to 127°C (260°F) at the nose.

➤ Concorde gains 3000 m (9,850 ft.) as fuel is burned off during a flight.

➤ Concorde flies 16 km (10 mi.) while a passenger's champagne glass is filled.

➤ The 14 Concordes have clocked up more supersonic hours than all the fighters used by the world's air forces.

PROFILE

Mach 2 across the Atlantic

Over the past two decades a handful of Concordes have carried more people beyond the speed of sound than all the other supersonic aircraft ever built.

Since its commercial debut in 1976, Concorde has proved deservedly popular. It is the only way a businessman can cross the Atlantic for a meeting and return the same day, while his subsonic competitor faces at the very least two seven-hour flights and serious jet lag. As a result, Concorde flights are nearly always filled with high-paying passengers.

And yet Concorde has been a commercial failure. When it entered service the oil crisis had made the viability of a gas-guzzling supersonic jet question-able, and influential American environmentalists were loud in their protests over the noise its powerful engines generated. As a result, options on 70 aircraft by more than a dozen airlines were cancelled.

Nevertheless, the 14 production aircraft delivered to the national carriers in Britain and France performed splendidly, with higher than average mechanical reliability. They remained the world's only operational supersonic airliners until their retirement in October 2003.

Concorde in flight could never be confused with any other aircraft currently in service. The graceful arrow-like layout, the slender nose and unique curved double delta wing are instant recognition features.

CONCORDE

G-BOAB was the sixth production Concorde, it entered service with British Airways on 21 January 1976.

Concorde

Type: luxury supersonic airliner

Powerplant: four 169.17-kN (227-hp.) Rolls-Royce/SNECMA Olympus 593 Mk 610 turbojets with afterburning

Cruising speed: 2180 km/h (1355 m.p.h.) at 15,000 m (49,000 ft.) (Mach 2.04)

Range: 6250 km (3880 mi.) with maximum payload and reserves

Service ceiling: 18,300 m (60,000 ft.)

Weights: empty 78,700 kg (173,500 lb.); loaded 185,066 kg (408,000 lb.)

Payload: three crew, 100 passengers

Dimensions: span 25.55 m (83 ft. 10 in.)
length 62.10 m (203 ft. 9 in)
height 11.40 m (37 ft. 5 in.)
wing area 358.22 m² (3,856 sq. ft.)

Concorde's curved double delta wing is a good compromise between supersonic efficiency and low-speed controllability during landing and take-off.

During supersonic flight, the aircraft's equilibrium shifts. To compensate, fuel is pumped during flight from front to rear to ensure that the jet remains stable.

BRITISH AIRWAYS

G-BOAB

AB

Concorde's unique hydraulically-powered nose 'droops' by 12.5° to increase pilot visibility during take-off and landing. At supersonic speeds the nose is raised for streamlining, and a heat-resistant visor protects the cockpit windows.

Concorde's cabin could hold 128 passengers seated at normal airline density, but both operators restrict capacity to 100. This allows the premium-paying passengers even more room than in conventional first-class layout.

Concorde's landing gear is made by Messier Hispano. The wheels, which have to withstand higher landing speeds than normal aircraft, retract inwards towards the fuselage.

Concorde does not have a conventional tailplane. Each wing has three trailing-edge elevons, which combine the pitch control function of elevators and the roll control of ailerons.

Supersonic flight path

16000 m
MACH 2
MACH 1.7
MACH 1
10000 m

1 **TAKE-OFF:** Concorde uses afterburners for take-off, then cuts them until the aircraft is clear of land. They are engaged again to accelerate through Mach 1.

2 **SUPERCRUISE:** At Mach 1.7 the afterburners are cut, and the aircraft continues to accelerate to Mach 2 under normal power.

BOEING 747 6 hours

3 **CLIMB:** As fuel is burned and Concorde becomes lighter, the aircraft drifts upwards from 15,000 to 18,000 m (49,000 to 59,000 ft.).

CONCORDE 3 hours

MACH 2.2

MACH 1

4 **DESCENT:** Several hundred kilometres out, Concorde reduces thrust. Speed falls below Mach 1 as the aircraft descends below 11,000 m (36,000 ft.) to normal commercial flight levels and becomes just another airliner.

LONDON

NEW YORK

QUEEN ELIZABETH II 5 Days

1600 km (1,000 mi.)

3200 km (2,000 mi.)

4800 km (3,000 mi.)

AIRBUS INDUSTRIE

AIRBUS A300

● European collaboration ● Medium-range wide-body airliner

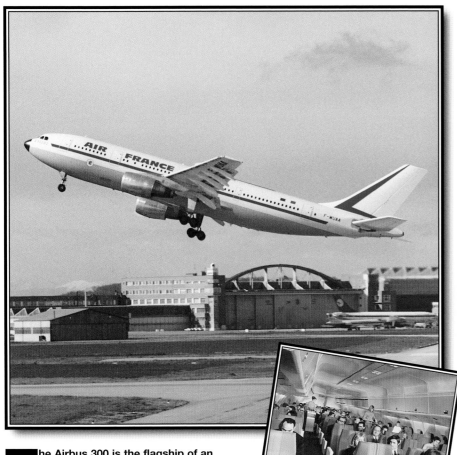

The Airbus 300 is the flagship of an international manufacturing enterprise. It was designed as an economical and efficient large jetliner for busy, medium-range routes of up to 2225 km (1,380 mi.) and carrying 250 passengers. When the A300 burst on the scene in 1973, success was far from certain. Today, the A300B model heads a family of airliners that successfully challenges American manufacturers Boeing and McDonnell Douglas.

▲ *From the start of its design, the A300 was envisaged as offering wide-body comfort in a twin-aisle arrangement. The large cabin can be readily altered to suit an individual customer's requirements, allowing for maximum density seating for charter operators or a full three-class layout for scheduled airlines.*

Modular ▶ construction
Components of the Airbus are built in several countries. These are then brought together and assembled at Toulouse in France.

▼ Global success
The A300 design was the first of the Airbus products and immediately took a large share of the world airliner market.

▲ High-tech wing
Built by British Aerospace, the A300 wing has an advanced supercritical airfoil section for maximum efficiency.

◀ European standard
Many of Europe's airlines, including Olympic, adopted the A300 for their European routes.

Ongoing ▶ development
Airbus Industrie has continued to refine the A300, with greater range and load-carrying ability.

▲ Long-range winglets
The later variants of the A300 feature triangular-shaped surfaces on the wingtips. These reduce drag, increasing range and efficiency.

FACTS AND FIGURES

➤ According to the US-based Air Transport Association, Airbus 300s have flown more than a billion revenue-miles.

➤ The Airbus 300 has its roots in the Anglo-French HBN100 design dating from 1967.

➤ Eleven ex-airline A300s are currently being converted into freighters.

➤ The A300-600ST 'Beluga' is the giant replacement for the Super Guppy used to transport Airbus parts to Toulouse.

➤ The first A300 to fly, an A300B1, took to the air on 28 October 1972.

➤ The A300 is one of the few Western designs flown by Aeroflot of Russia.

PROFILE

Airbus people carrier

Airbus Industrie launched the A300 as the first jetliner in what has become a legendary family of advanced, efficient air transports, successfully challenging America's post-war domination of the world airliner market.

One of the first medium- to long-range passenger craft to be powered by just two engines (in under-wing pods), the A300 was purpose-designed to accommodate any of several engine types. Not readily visible from outside are features of the A300 which have become a

trademark of all Airbus transports – the latest, most advanced technology in cockpit instrumentation and computers which aid the two pilots in every task from taxiing out to navigating.

Airbus has manufactured half a dozen versions of this fine jetliner, including the longer-range A300B4 introduced in 1974 and the A300-600R, which is currently in production. Around the world, nearly 400 A300s are flying in the colours of 53 airlines, with over half operating in Asia and Australasia.

Lufthansa has a large fleet of Airbus aircraft, including the A300-600 (illustrated), A310, A320, A321 and A340.

The A300 can be powered by two families of engines, depending on customer choice. One is the Pratt & Whitney JT9D/PW4000 series: the other is the General Electric CF6 series.

The nose radome covers a small weather-avoidance radar set. There is also room for a second weather radar and a ground proximity warning system.

The A300 introduced a wide range of new construction technologies. The wing skin is milled from one solid piece of metal.

Airbus A300B4

Type: medium-haul twin-engined airliner

Powerplant: two 233.54-kN (52,390-lb.-thrust) General Electric CF6-50CI advanced technology turbofan engines

Maximum cruising speed: 911 km/h (565 m.p.h.) at 7620 m (25,000 ft.)

Service ceiling: with passengers 13,000 m (42,640 ft.); empty 15,000 m (49,200 ft.)

Weights: empty 79,831 kg (175,628 lb.); loaded 165,000 kg (363,000 lb.)

Accommodation: flight deck crew of two; eight to 12 flight attendants; seating layouts for 220 to 336 passengers; maximum capacity 375

Dimensions:
span	44.84 m	(147 ft.)
length	53.62 m	(175 ft. 10 in.)
height	16.53 m	(54 ft. 3 in.)
wing area	260 m²	(279 sq. ft.)

AIRBUS A300B4

In May 1974 Air France introduced the Airbus into service, ushering in a new era of efficient, economic air travel. The A300 was designed to move large numbers of people between major population centres, perfect for the European market where it achieved great sales success. It also made small inroads into the US domestic market.

Fuel is held principally in the wings. The internal structure of the wing has two main spars with the outer skins stretched between them. This forms a very strong box, which is filled with fuel from the wingroot to the tip.

Airbus designed a very efficient wing with a supercritical section for high-speed flight. For take-off and landing, the wing deploys very powerful flaps and leading-edge slats to provide vital extra lift.

The tailplane of the Airbus has conventional elevators on the trailing edge for pitch control, but to accurately trim the aircraft the whole tailplane pivots around a central point. The diamond shape around the tailplane fixture is a sealing plate.

Just two pilots fly the A300, although there is room for two more crewmembers on the flight deck.

Under the cabin floor is a baggage hold which is designed to take standard size containers making loading easy.

The main cabin can be configured to suit customer preferences. A two-class layout would typically have around 20 seats in first class and 240 in economy, while a three-class layout would have 18 first-class, 63 business-class and 126 in economy-class seating.

A true multi-national

One of the unique characteristics of the Airbus project is the fact that parts are manufactured by aircraft companies all over Europe. After completion the individual sections are flown to the Airbus factory at Toulouse for final assembly.

WING STRUCTURE: The Airbus wing is manufactured by British Aerospace. Flaps were made by the now defunct Fokker, but later models have parts from Belgium.

ACTION DATA

PASSENGER LOAD

The modern wide-body airliners have greater capacity than old narrow-body types like the Boeing 727.

A300B4	375 passengers
L-1011 TRISTAR	315 passengers
MODEL 727	189 passengers

KEY (A300-600)

- Aérospatiale (France)
- Deutsche Aerospace (Germany)
- British Aerospace (UK)
- Casa (Spain)
- Fokker (Netherlands)
- General Electric (USA)
- Messier (France)

TAIL STRUCTURE: Deutsche Aerospace builds the vertical tail of the A300, with Casa of Spain supplying the tailplane and other small parts. Engines on the A300 series are provided by General Electric of the USA.

FUSELAGE STRUCTURE: Germany supplies the largest part of the Airbus fuselage, with France providing the cockpit section and most of the avionics, as well as the engine pylons and wingroots.

AIRBUS INDUSTRIE

AIRBUS A310

● Twin turbofan ● Medium/long range ● Advanced technology airliner

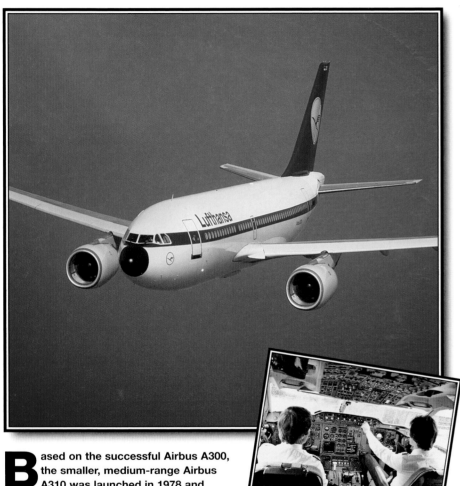

Based on the successful Airbus A300, the smaller, medium-range Airbus A310 was launched in 1978 and was first flown in April 1982. The A310's fuselage is 8.10 m (26 ft. 6 in.) shorter but has the same cross-section, and can accommodate 280 passengers. The type first entered service with Swissair and Lufthansa in April 1983, and the latter currently operates 10 of the longer range A310-300 series.

▲ The Airbus A310 has an advanced two-crew 'glass' EFIS (electronic flight instrument system) cockpit. It was one of the first airliners to dispense with the flight engineer's station.

AIRBUS INDUSTRIE **AIRBUS A310**

▲ **Toulouse assembly**
The Airbus international consortium supplies the major sections for assembly in France.

▲ **New wing**
The A310's advanced wing reduces drag and, therefore, increases fuel economy. It was designed by British Aerospace and is manufactured at the company's Chester works.

▲ **Longer range**
This Airbus A310 is one of a pair of long-range -304s operated by the Czech Republic airline CSA. The only distinguishing feature externally is the small winglets, and it has an extra fuel tank in the fin.

▲ **Good performance**
The A310's powerful engines and high-lift wing give it a good take-off performance when operating from small international airports at maximum weight.

Wide body ▶
Like the A300, the A310 was an advance on previous designs and provided wide-body capacity for medium-range routes.

FACTS AND FIGURES

➤ Announced in 1978, the A310 was first flown on 3 April 1982; by this date, 181 had already been ordered by airlines.

➤ First deliveries were made to Swissair and Lufthansa on 29 March 1983.

➤ Lufthansa introduced the aircraft on 21 April 1983, nine days after Swissair.

➤ The A310 is manufactured in France, Germany, Spain and the UK; final assembly is by Aérospatiale at Toulouse.

➤ Three versions of the A310 were planned, but only the -200 and -300 have been sold.

➤ By January 1997, 254 A310s had been delivered from total orders for 271.

PROFILE

High-technology European airliner

The success of the twin-engined, medium- to long-range Airbus A300 airliner in the 1970s highlighted the need for the European consortium to develop a smaller, medium-range version. The aircraft was first promoted as the A300B10, and became the A310 in 1978.

The new Airbus retained the wide-body cabin, but was 11 frames shorter than the A300. It had a new BAe-designed wing, a modified undercarriage and a two-crew 'glass' cockpit with the then-current state-of-the-art instrumentation.

The A310 is powered by either General Electric CF6 or Pratt & Whitney PW4152 turbofans. Two versions of the aircraft are offered to airlines: the A310-200 (range 6667 km (4,135 mi.) with General Electric engines) and the -300 (range 7963 km (4,995 mi.) with General Electric engines). The PW4152 engines give slightly greater range.

Airbus delivered the first -300, which had extra fuel capacity, maximum take-off weight increased to 150,000 kg (330,000 lb.) and winglets, to Thai Airways in 1986, after certification on 5 December 1985. The A310 remains in production and Airbus is re-proposing the short-range -100 in an updated, lighter configuration as the A310 Lite.

The Airbus A310-300, powered by Pratt & Whitney JT9D-7R4E turbofans, was first flown at Toulouse, France, on 8 July 1985.

To extend the range of the A310, Airbus developed the -300 with more powerful engines, a fuel tank in the fin and a computerised fuel trimming system.

Currently, two different turbofan engines are offered for the A310-300: the Pratt & Whitney PW4156A (249 kN (56,000-lb. thrust)) or the more powerful General Electric CF6-80C2A8 (262 kN (59,000-lb. thrust)).

Retaining the same basic structure as the A300, the A310's wing is, aerodynamically, completely new. Wingtip fences were introduced on the -300 and fitted retrospectively to earlier aircraft.

A310-300

Type: twin-engined medium- to long-range passenger airliner

Powerplant: two 262-kN (59,000-lb.-thrust) General Electric CF6-80C2A8 or 249-kN (56,000-lb.-thrust) Pratt & Whitney PW4156A turbofans

Maximum speed: 804 km/h (498 m.p.h.) at 9450 m (31,000 ft.)

Range: 8056 km with P&W engines

Service ceiling: 12,192 m (40,000 ft.)

Weights: empty 71,840 kg (158,048 lb.); maximum take-off 150,900 kg (331,980 lb.)

Accommodation: standard seating for 250 passengers; maximum 280

Dimensions: span   43.89 m (144 ft.)
length   46.66 m (153 ft.)
height   15.80 m (51 ft. 10 in.)
wing area   219 m² (2,356 sq. ft.)

A310-204

Hapag-Lloyd Fluggesellschaft has a fleet of four A310-204s and four -304/8s for use on its international scheduled and charter passenger services.

When launched in 1978 the A310 was the first Airbus airliner with a forward-facing two-crew arrangement and an electronic flight instrument system 'glass' cockpit.

Forward fuselage, upper centre fuselage and rear fuselage sections, and their associated doors, are built by Daimler-Benz Aerospace Airbus. Aérospatiale manufactures the majority of the remaining fuselage components, BAe produces the wings and CASA and Fokker construct all other sections.

The A310's wide-body fuselage has eight-abreast seating for economy-class passengers. The rear fuselage is reprofiled to allow seats to be fitted further to the rear.

The main passenger access door is situated behind the cockpit on the port side of the fuselage.

The inward-retracting, four-wheel bogie main undercarriage legs on the A310 differ from those on the A300.

More extensive use is made of carbon fibre, such as in the tail control surfaces, to lighten the structure of the A310. The tailcone houses a Garrett GTCP 331-250 auxiliary power unit.

ACTION DATA

STANDARD SEATING

Airbus has produced an airliner which offers good payload/range characteristics and which closely matches market requirements. Additional flexibility is offered with a 280-seat, high-density layout.

A310-200   250 passengers
767-200   224 passengers
Il-96-300   235 passengers

TAKE-OFF RUN

When operating from smaller airports, good take-off performance is essential if payload or range is not to be sacrificed. Both the A310 and the Boeing 767-200 are closely matched. The Il-96 has a much longer take-off run.

A310-200   1860 m
767-200   1798 m
Il-96-300   2600 m

RANGE

From this diagram it is evident that the Il-96 theoretically offers greater range than the A310. In practice, however, operators report that excessive fuel consumption limits the Il-96's range. The A310 is therefore the longest ranged of these types, with the added flexibility of being able to fly shorter sectors if required.

A310-200   6667 km (4,135 mi.)
767-200   5963 km (3,628 mi.)
Il-96-300   7500 km (4,650 mi.)

Airbus A310 variants

■ **A310-300:** More -200s have been sold than -300s, but this newer, long-range variant is gaining in popularity.

■ **A310-200F:** Federal Express converted 13 former Lufthansa -200s to freighter configuration with a large cargo loading door

■ **CC-150 POLARIS:** Six A310-300s are flown on passenger and freight transportation duties by the Canadian Armed Forces as the Polaris.

■ **A310 MULTI-ROLE TANKER TRANSPORT:** The MRTT, with a cargo door, extra fuel tanks and refuelling pods, underwent trials in 1995.

AIRBUS INDUSTRIE

AIRBUS A320

● **Revolutionary fly-by-wire airliner** ● **The aircraft that made Airbus' fortune**

Once in a generation, a new aircraft changes aviation for ever. The Airbus A320 is just such a trailblazer. It introduced such far-reaching advances in terms of technology that it stands as the first of a whole new generation of commercial transports – the 'electric' airliners. Designed and built by computers, and flown with the aid of computers, the A320 offers its passengers high-technology safety, reliability and comfort.

▲ *Passenger comfort is everything in a modern airliner. The fly-by-wire controls make the A320 one of the smoothest of modern airliners in even the roughest turbulence.*

AIRBUS INDUSTRIE AIRBUS A320

▼ **Multinational product**
Airbus airliners are built by a European consortium, each manufacturing major parts. These are shipped to the central factory at Toulouse, where all the parts are brought together in final assembly.

▲ **The glass cockpit**
The cockpit of the A320 has TV-style screens in place of the traditional dials. The pilots even have sidesticks, like the F-16 fighter, instead of a central control column.

Advanced aerodynamics ▶
All new A320s have these characteristic wingtip-mounted winglets. Most modern airliners have such additions, designed to reduce drag and so increase range.

▲ **Family member**
The A320 is just one of a whole series of jets with which Airbus Industrie has risen to challenge Boeing and McDonnell Douglas.

◀ **Thorough testing**
Today's airliners go through rigorous testing before they are allowed into passenger service. Here an A320 simulates a landing on a waterlogged runway.

FACTS AND FIGURES

➤ Airbus Industrie is a true international partnership, bringing together France, Germany, Spain and Great Britain.

➤ The A320 was the first production airliner with a digital flight control system.

➤ Since 1972, Airbus has sold over 4500 airliners to 123 customers worldwide.

➤ The stretched A321 is built in Hamburg, the first Airbus built outside France.

➤ The A320 introduced the new European multinational IAE V2500 turbofan.

➤ Boeing tried to acquire an A320 to park on its 737 assembly line to act as a motivation to its workers.

PROFILE

Europe's fly-by-wire pioneer

The dedicated plane-builders at Europe's Airbus Industrie started from behind, but learned fast to build airliners equal to the champions from Boeing and McDonnell Douglas. With the A320, Airbus have now gone further, introducing a new standard by which other short- and medium-haul airliners are measured.

The Airbus A320 is a technological marvel. Each tiny part of this aircraft is crafted with love, care and the latest in technology. The A320 flight deck uses computers and colour electronic displays in a bigger and better way than any previous airliner, and the pilot controls the aircraft with just a small stick at his side.

Sophistication in the sky is of little benefit unless it boosts business for the airline. The Airbus A320 flies superbly, but it also makes a profit. Advanced aerodynamics and electronic engine systems keep fuel-burn to a minimum, while other onboard systems allow the A320 to self-diagnose any faults as

The A320's high-technology construction and extremely efficient engines make it very economical to run. It has proved successful with small airlines, and more than 930 A320s and their derivatives have been ordered or are on option.

they happen, allowing them to be fixed easily and speedily. Less time in the hangar means more time in the air earning money for the airline.

Until recently, Airbus relied on the Aero Spacelines Super Guppy to transport its airframe components to their final assembly line at Toulouse. These elderly veterans were replaced by the Beluga – a much modified A300 cargolifter.

AIRBUS A320

One of Europe's great success stories of recent times, the Airbus company now challenges Boeing as the world's most popular planemaker. High technology is the key to the Airbus success, and the A320 spearheads the campaign.

Only two pilots are needed to fly the A320, with all the necessary information at their fingertips in the high-tech cockpit.

The A320 comes with a choice of engines – either the CFM56 or the IAE V2500. Both types develop about 115 kN (25,000 lb.) of thrust each.

The A320 has a fly-by-wire control system. This has a computer which stops the pilots putting the aircraft into dangerous flight situations.

The A320 is part of the larger Airbus family, but itself forms the lead member of a sub-group. The A319 is a slightly shorter version, while the A321 is about 6 m (20 ft.) longer. All three use the same wing and tail structures.

Large sections of the A320, including the fin and rudder, are manufactured from aramid-fibre-, carbon-fibre- or glass-fibre-reinforced plastic composites. These are stronger and lighter than aluminium.

BRITISH AIRWAYS

G-BUSC

Airlines can tailor the cabin layout to their own requirements. A typical configuration may have a business class section for about 12, and 138 in the economy class section.

A320-200

Type: twin-engine short- and medium-haul airliner

Powerplant: two 111.21-kN (20,000-lb.-thrust) IAE V2525 or two 117.98-kN (26,500-lb.-thrust) CFM56 turbofans

Operating speed: 960 km/h (600 m.p.h.)

Range: 5460 km (3,400 mi.) (V2525); 5615 km (3,500 mi.) (CFM56) with optional long-range tanks

Weights: empty 41,500 kg (91,500 lb.); loaded 73,000 kg (161,000 lb.)

Accommodation: two flight deck crew; four cabin attendants; maximum 179 passengers (single class) or 150 passengers (two classes)

Dimensions:
span	33.91 m	(111 ft. 3 in.)
length	37.57 m	(123 ft. 3 in.)
height	11.80 m	(38 ft. 8 in.)
wing area	122.40 m²	(1,318 sq. ft.)

ACTION DATA

RANGE

The A320 and its competitors are designed for short-haul, frequently-flown high-density air routes. However, the definition of 'short-haul' has changed dramatically in the last 20 years. They still fly the city to city routes for which they were designed, but such airliners can now fly the Atlantic non-stop.

A320	**5400 km (3,400 mi.)**
737-400	**5000 km (3,100 mi.)**
MD-83	**4851 km (3,000 mi.)**

PAYLOAD

The explosive growth in demand for air transport since the 1960s has seen jets at all ends of the market develop greater carrying capacity. In 1970 a typical short-haul airliner might have carried between 80 and 100 passengers; now their capacity has almost doubled.

A320	737-400	MD-83
up to 179 single class	up to 171 single class	up to 172 single class

NOISE LEVELS

Noise pollution is a major environmental hazard, and all new airliners must meet US and European noise abatement regulations. The A320 is one-tenth as noisy as first-generation jet airliners.

A320	737-400	MD-83
94-95 dB / 96-97 dB	93-95 dB / 95-96 dB	90-95 dB / 93.3 dB
MAXIMUM TAKE-OFF / LANDING	MAXIMUM TAKE-OFF / LANDING	MAXIMUM TAKE-OFF / LANDING

The Airbus family

Airbus Industrie was established in 1970 to handle the production of the Airbus range of airliners. The main companies involved are Aérospatiale (France), Daimler-Benz Aerospace (Germany), British Aerospace (UK) and CASA (Spain). Other European countries such as Belgium, the Netherlands and Italy also have a stake.

A300 (range 7408 km+/4600 mi.+) First flew 28 October 1972. Two 222.42-kN (50,000-lb.) engines. c.266 seats.

A310 (range 7963 km+/4777 mi.+) First flew 3 April 1982. Two 222.42-kN (50,000-lb.) engines. c.220 seats.

A320 (range 5300 km+/3290 mi.+) First flew 22 February 1987. Two 111.21-kN (25,000-lb.) engines. c.150 seats.

A330 (range 8900 km+/5527 mi.+) First flew 2 November 1992. Two 300.27-kN (67,500-lb.) engines. c.135 seats.

A340 (range 13612 km+/8453 mi.+) First flew 25 October 1991. Four 138.77-kN (32,000-lb.) engines. c.300 seats.

AIRBUS INDUSTRIE

AIRBUS A321/A319

● International development ● Medium range ● High capacity

AIRBUS INDUSTRIE AIRBUS A321/A319

▼ **American bird**
Entering the competitive American market, the Airbus family has proved itself to be more than capable of beating the Boeing designs.

▲ **European orders**
Swissair was the third customer for the A321, ordering 19 examples; its aircraft operate across Europe. A follow-up order has been rumoured but, at present, no more examples have entered service.

▼ **First flight**
Traditional coloured tails are a hallmark of the Airbus fleet, particularly on the prototypes.

▲ **Advanced design**
By incorporating the latest design developments, the A321 can perform flight manoeuvres that would otherwise be impossible.

Italian operations ▶
The Italian airline Alitalia chose the A321 because of the exceptional operating economy that the design offers. One of the largest operators, Alitalia has taken options on 107 A321s.

Having established the 150-seat A320 as its most successful model in terms of sales, Airbus Industrie decided to go ahead with a stretched A321 version in November 1989. By 1996 another variant, the shortened A319, had also entered service. The three aircraft can be powered by the same engines and can be maintained by the same engineers using the same stock of spare parts – yet they carry passenger loads ranging from 124 to 186 people.

▲ *With the competitive nature of the airliner industry, the unveiling of new models is often surrounded by much 'pomp and ceremony'; here, the A321 is rolled out.*

FACTS AND FIGURES

➤ The short-fuselage A319 was announced in May 1992 as the third member of the A320 Airbus 'family'.

➤ British Aerospace designed the wings, and construct them at its Filton site.

➤ Exceptionally wide fuselages are a feature of the A319/A321 designs.

➤ To produce the A321 from the various components takes only 46 days, including a full series of flight tests.

➤ Flight controls of the A319 and A321 utilise 'fly-by-wire' technology.

➤ Both aircraft have received numerous European orders.

PROFILE

Stretched to success

Like the A320, both the shortened A319 and stretched A321 use fly-by-wire flight controls. They also have cockpits which are almost identical, enabling the same pilots to fly any of the three models.

Compared with the A320, the A321 has eight additional fuselage frames forward of the wing and an extra five aft. It entered service with Lufthansa in 1994 and a second version, the A321-200, flew for the first time in December 1996. The -200 has a higher maximum take-off weight of 89,000 kg

(195,800 lb.) to accommodate a new centre-section fuel tank, extending its range from 4900 km (3,040 mi.) to 5550 km (3,440 mi.).

The A319 has seven fewer fuselage frames than the standard A320. It entered service with Swissair in April 1996 and, like the other two models in the family, comes with a choice of two engines. Both produce less noise and fewer emissions than those fitted to older airliners.

For passengers, the wide fuselage used by all three variants – with a diameter

19 cm (7 in.) bigger than that of the Boeing 737 and 757 – spells increased comfort, with room for wider seats and aisles and bigger overhead baggage bins.

Above: The prototype of the A321 visited numerous trade exhibitions and flew at air shows to demonstrate its potential.

Above: The A321 is a stretched version of the A320 and seats 185 passengers. This example operates far from European skies, flying with TransAsia Airways which has found the aircraft a major improvement over earlier types.

A319

Type: short- to medium-range airliner

Powerplant: two 97.9-kN (22,025-lb.-thrust) CFM56-5A4 turbofans, or two 104.5-kN (23,510-lb.-thrust) IAE V2524-A5 turbofans

Cruising speed: 903 km/h (560 m.p.h.) at high altitude

Take-off distance: 1829 m (6,000 ft.)

Range: 4907 km (3,040 mi.)

Cruising altitude: 9500 m (31,170 ft.)

Weights: operating empty 40,149 kg (88,328 lb.), maximum take-off 64,000 kg (140,800 lb.)

Accommodation: 124 passengers in two classes

Dimensions:
span	33.91 m	(111 ft. 3 in.)
length	33.80 m	(110 ft. 10 in.)
height	11.80 m	(38 ft. 8 in.)
wing area	122.4 m²	(1,317 sq. ft.)

A321

Alitalia was the first airline to sign a contract for the A321, and quickly followed this with an order for 20 examples. Operated on the domestic and European networks, the aircraft are proving a success.

The wide-bodied design of the aircraft has only a single central aisle, and can seat 186 passengers in typical first and economy classes. Reports indicate that the less cramped conditions are well appreciated by passengers, particularly on the medium-haul flights.

Design features found to be successful on earlier Airbus aircraft have been incorporated into the A321, so reducing the overall cost of the aircraft.

A fuel dump pipe is located in the extreme rear of the fuselage, allowing the A321 to jettison its fuel load in an emergency while not inhibiting the engines' operation.

An advanced flight deck is fitted with multi-function displays and fly-by-wire controls. Pilot conversion from the A319 to the A321 is easy because of the similarity between the two flight decks. Crews appreciate the handling qualities of the airliner.

There is a choice of engines for the A321: either the CFM 56-5 constructed jointly in the US and England, or the IAE V2500 produced by a consortium of nations including Italy, Japan and Germany. Both powerplants offer the A321 low operating costs.

An advanced wing design, featuring raised wingtips and trailing-edge flaps, affords the Airbus excellent handling. Thanks to this feature and the 'fly-by-wire' inputs, the prototype aircraft performed amazing displays of agility at air shows, creating huge interest in the design.

ACTION DATA

MAXIMUM CRUISING SPEED

Operating at a high cruising speed allows airliners to reach their destinations quicker, allowing more flights to be undertaken. The Boeing 757 is the leader in this field.

AIRBUS A319	903 km/h (560 m.p.h.)
737-500	912 km/h (565 m.p.h.)
F100	861 km/h (534 m.p.h.)

RANGE

From experience gained with earlier designs, Airbus's aircraft have grown in both size and capability. These advances have given the Airbus fleet a range advantage over their contemporaries, which has led to an increase in sales in the competition with Boeing's designs.

AIRBUS A319 4907 km (3,040 mi.)
737-500 4481 km (2,780 mi.)
F100 2956 km (1,830 mi.)

CAPACITY

Featuring the widest fuselage in current airliner production, the passenger capacity of the A319 is superior to that of the German design but inferior to that of its American competitor.

AIRBUS A319	124 PASSENGERS
737-500	132 PASSENGERS
F100	107 PASSENGERS

The smaller fleet

■ **BOEING 737-400:** Air UK Leisure was the first airline outside the USA to fly the new super-stretched Boeing. Its five aircraft were used on domestic routes.

■ **FOKKER 100:** Developed in Germany, the Fokker 100 operates as an advanced regional airliner. Variants include dedicated cargo and VIP configurations.

■ **McDONNELL DOUGLAS MD 90:** Powered by twin turbofans, the MD 90 was launched in 1989 with an order for 50 from Delta Air Lines. The design uses the latest advanced technology.

AIRBUS INDUSTRIE

AIRBUS A330

● Twin-engined wide-body airliner ● A340 variant ● 'Glass' cockpit

Developed in parallel with the four-engined A340, the A330 uses the same fuselage and wings, and has an almost identical cockpit for maximum crewing flexibility. Whereas the A340 was designed for maximum range, the A330 was intended to provide optimum flexibility at the lowest possible operating cost. Thus, a wide range of seating arrangements is possible, and the cargo hold is 60 per cent bigger than that of the Boeing 747.

▲ Commonality between the four-engined A340 and twin-engined A330 gives an airline operating both aircraft more crewing flexibility and lower training costs.

AIRBUS INDUSTRIE AIRBUS A330

▼ Mixed fleet
The 100th aircraft off the A330/340 production line was an A330-322 delivered to Malaysian Airline System in 1995. This aircraft was the 69th example.

▲ Multi-coloured tailfins
At the end of 1996, Airbus Industrie had delivered 47 of the 160 A330s ordered.

▼ Toulouse assembly
Final A330 assembly is undertaken alongside A340s at Airbus Industrie's main plant.

▲ Launch carrier
Air Inter (now Air France Europe) was the airline with which the A330 entered service in 1994. Apart from five Fokker 100s, Airbuses make up the entire fleet.

Asian fleet ▶
Seen landing at Hong Kong's busy Kai Tak airport, this Thai Airways International A330, named Bang Rashan, was one of eight operated by the airline in 1997 alongside A300s and A310s.

FACTS AND FIGURES

➤ In 1996, the annual combined A330/340 production rate was 30 to 35 units, the majority of which were A340s.

➤ F-WWKB, the first A330, flew for the first time on 3 December 1992.

➤ Airbus has been studying enlarged A330 versions, dubbed A330-400.

➤ The A330-200, which entered service in April 1998, is a direct competitor to Boeing's long-range 767-300ER.

➤ Aer Lingus flew the first ETOPS transatlantic A330 service in May 1994.

➤ A 'stretched' A330 may have seats in a forward cargo bay fitted with windows.

PROFILE

A340's twin-engined brother

Flown for the first time in December 1992, the A330 became the first aircraft in history to be certified simultaneously by both the European and US authorities. The original A330-300 entered service with launch customer Air Inter (now Air France Europe) in January 1994, carrying 412 single-class passengers.

Typical seating arrangements for the A330-300 are 295 in three classes or 335 in two. Range is 8982 km (5,140 mi.) with 335

passengers, or up to 10,200 km (6,325 mi.) with a reduced payload, though the aircraft can also operate high-density, short-haul routes with as many as 440 people aboard.

In 1998 the A330-300 was joined by the A330-200, which has a shorter fuselage but has space for 42,000 litres (11,000 gal.) more fuel than the A330-300 – to give it an extended range of 11,700 km (7,250 mi.). It will be able to carry a three-class load of 256.

Below: German scheduled, charter and cargo airline LTU was an early operator of the A330-300, from its Düsseldorf base.

Above: Hong Kong-based Cathay Pacific Airways operates a modern mixed fleet of at least 50 aircraft, including A330s and A340s and Boeing 747s and 777s.

Economic operation was a principal goal of the A330's design, and it has been achieved so successfully that at least one airline uses its A330s as freighters during the night.

A330-300

Type: twin-engined wide-body airliner

Powerplant: (typical) two 300-kN (67,500-lb.-thrust) General Electric CF6-80E1A2 turbofans

Maximum speed: Mach 0.86

Range: (longer-range variant with CF6 engines) 8982 km (5,140 mi.) with 335 passengers and baggage and fuel for 370-km (230-mi.) diversion

Weights: operating empty 120,170 kg (264,374 lb.); maximum take-off 230,000 kg (506,000 lb.)

Accommodation: two flight crew plus cabin crew and (typically) 295 (three-class) or 335 (two-class) passengers; maximum 440 passengers

Dimensions: span 60.30 m (197 ft. 9 in.)
length 63.65 m (208 ft. 9 in.)
height 16.74 m (54 ft. 11 in.)
wing area 363.10 m² (3,907 sq. ft.)

The almost identical cockpits of the A330 and A340 are also very similar to that of the A320. Six cathode ray tubes (CRTs) display engine and other vital information before the two-person crew. The aircraft is controlled via sidesticks rather than the more conventional yokes favoured by Boeing and uses fly-by-wire technology to operate the control surfaces.

As with earlier Airbus wide-body types, the construction of the A330 and A340 is divided among the Airbus consortium members. Aérospatiale is responsible for the cockpit, engine pylons and part of the centre fuselage, as well as final assembly at the Toulouse factory. British Aerospace builds the wings, Daimler-Benz Aerospace most of the fuselage, fin and interior, CASA the tailplane and Belairbus the leading-edge slats.

Six cabin crew rest beds or sleeping accommodation for passengers are available as optional equipment for the rear underfloor cargo hold. The passengers' version consists of five mini cabins, each with one or two full-length bunk beds and other equipment.

AIRBUS A330-300

In May 1997 Cathay Pacific Airways had a fleet of 11 A330-300s, with options for up to 16 others. Like some other operators, Cathay Pacific also employs a number of A340s.

An auxiliary power unit (APU) in the tail of the A330 provides power for aircraft systems when the main engines are shut down.

To manoeuvre the aircraft on the ground the A330 has nosewheel steering via the rudder pedals. This disengages automatically at speeds above 185 km/h (115 m.p.h.).

Like most modern airliners the A330 is available with a selection of engines. Apart from the latest versions of the G.E. CF6, the A330 is available with Pratt & Whitney PW4000s or Rolls-Royce Trent 700s. All are rated between 300 kN (67,5000 lb.) and 322 kN (72,440 lb.) each.

With a fuel capacity of 97,170 litres (25,670 gal.), the A330 may undertake extended-range twin-engined operations (ETOPS) on transoceanic routes.

A330 hold capacity

SMALLER HOLD THAN THE A340: Though it shares its fuselage with the A340, the A330 has a shorter forward cargo hold. Total capacity is 30 standard LD3 containers compared to 32 in the A340.

ACTION DATA

FUEL CAPACITY

Modern airliners are required to fly vast distances and consequently carry a huge weight in fuel. A larger four-engined aircraft, the A340 carries more fuel than its twin-engined brother, the A330. Boeing's 777-200 is another long-range twin-jet with a capacity of over 100,000 litres (30,000 gal.).

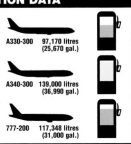

A330-300 — 97,170 litres (25,670 gal.)

A340-300 — 139,000 litres (36,990 gal.)

777-200 — 117,348 litres (31,000 gal.)

A330/A340 commonality

PARALLEL DEVELOPMENT: A major feature of the A330/A340 programme was the 85 per cent commonality of components between the two types, which helped control development costs and had benefits for operators.

ADDITIONAL CYLINDRICAL FUSELAGE ELEMENTS

COMMON LANDING GEAR

COMMON EMPENNAGE

COMMON COCKPIT

COMMON FUSELAGE

COMMON SYSTEMS (Differences limited to engine interface)

COMMON WING (Differences limited to outboard engine installation)

'UNDERFLOOR EARNING POWER': As well as the obvious passenger features, Airbus Industrie has been keen to sell the aircraft's freight-carrying abilities.

ARMSTRONG WHITWORTH

ARGOSY

● Turboprop transport design ● 30 years of service ● Limited production

W hen it came on the scene in the 1950s, the AW.650 Argosy was an advanced freighter. The company's first customer was Miami freight operator Riddle Airlines, which ordered four aircraft in 1959 for logistic support flights between USAF bases. Other airlines followed suit, including British European Airways, and 56 aircraft were delivered to the RAF. Although it was expensive to operate, the Argosy served for 30 years.

▲ While loading and unloading was accomplished with ease, thanks to the nose and rear doors, the Argosy Series 100's relatively small payload forced Hawker Siddeley to redesign the aircraft to carry larger loads. The Series 220 was the result, but it was built in even smaller numbers than the original version.

ARMSTRONG WHITWORTH ARGOSY

▼ Ex-RAF Argosy in Africa
Zairean-registered 9Q-COA was originally an RAF Argosy C.Mk 1. After being withdrawn from RAF service in 1971, it was sold and flew in Africa in the late 1970s. It was scrapped in 1981.

▲ One of the last
This Series 222 was delivered to BEA in 1965. After service in Canada and Ireland, in 1973 it was sold to Safe Air in New Zealand and named Merchant Pioneer.

Improved Series 220 ▶
BEA began flying Argosies in 1961, but needed aircraft with a greater payload capacity. Hawker Siddeley (which AW had joined in 1961) redesigned the wing and interior and fitted more powerful Dart engines with larger propellers.

◀ Australasian survivors
IPEC Aviation in Australia flew its aircraft on freight charters into the 1990s. IPEC's last Argosy was retired in 1992.

Twin-boom design ▶
The Argosy's layout was shared by other aircraft, including the twin-engined C-119 and Noratlas.

FACTS AND FIGURES

➤ The first Argosy flew at Bitteswell on 8 January 1959, less than two years after major design work got under way.

➤ BEA received the first of its Argosy Series 100 freighters in 1961.

➤ A BEA Argosy Series 222 was lost in an accident at Milan, Italy, in July 1965.

➤ After the first public appearance of the Argosy at the Paris air show in 1959, two appeared at Farnborough in 1960.

➤ A twin Rolls-Royce Tyne-engined variant, the AW.651, was proposed but not built.

➤ A short-haul version was proposed with a capacity for six cars and 30 passengers.

PROFILE

'Whistling wheelbarrows'

Taking to the sky in 1955, the Argosy was a result of the British Air Ministry's challenge to manufacturers to create a medium-range freighter for military and civilian use. Armstrong Whitworth designed an aircraft with two booms and two turboprop engines. It became the twin-boomed, four-engined Freightliner, and was renamed the Argosy in 1958.

By 1960 British and American officials had given the Argosy permission to undertake commercial operations.

This burly but attractive aircraft was fairly easy to load and unload, held a useful, but limited, amount of cargo and performed well. If it had weaknesses, they were a lack of range and capacity, which, combined with the four turboprop engines (the source of the nickname 'Whistling Wheelbarrow'), made it expensive to operate.

Sixteen civil aircraft, together with 56 C.Mk 1s transports for the RAF, were built between 1959 and 1966.

Below: Series 100 aircraft could be configured for 89 passengers, although Argosies were rarely used in passenger service.

Above: The prototype and 15 of the 16 civil Argosy aircraft built were delivered to BEA and the American operator Riddle Airlines. The Series 200 prototype was scrapped.

Argosy Series 100

Type: four-engined transport aircraft

Powerplant: four 1506-kW (2,020-hp.) Rolls-Royce Dart 526 turboprop engines

Maximum speed: 477 km/h (296 m.p.h.) at 6100 m (20,000 ft.)

Cruising speed: 451 km/h (280 m.p.h.)

Range: 885 km (550 mi.) with maximum payload and fuel

Maximum ferry range: 3660 km (2,270 mi.)

Service ceiling: 6100 m (20,000 ft.)

Weights: empty 20,865 kg (45,903 lb.); maximum take-off 39,916 kg (87,815 lb.)

Accommodation: two pilots, navigator (on some aircraft), two loadmasters, plus up to 12,700 kg (27,940 lb.) of cargo on cabin floor or on six 2.74-m (9-ft.) cargo pallets, or up to 89 passengers

Dimensions:
span	35.05 m (115 ft.)
length	26.44 m (86 ft. 9 in.)
height	8.92 m (29 ft. 3 in.)
wing area	135.45 m² (1,457 sq. ft.)

ARGOSY SERIES 222

First flown in 1965, G-ASXM was one of a number of Argosies built for BEA. It was active until a landing accident in 1990, during its last days with Safe Air in New Zealand.

Like the Bristol 170 Freighter and the Blackburn Beverley transport aircraft, the Argosy's cockpit was positioned above the main hold.

All the Argosy's fuel tanks were situated in the wings, one outboard of each engine. Total capacity was 15,454 litres (4,080 gal.).

Two small tanks held the water-methanol mixture used to boost engine power on take-off.

A major feature of the Series 220 was its redesigned wing which saved weight and thus contributed to a greater payload capacity.

Four of Rolls-Royce's pioneering and highly successful Dart turboprops powered the Argosy. Each drove a four-bladed propeller and provided 2.25 kN (506 lb.) of additional exhaust thrust.

The retractable tricycle undercarriage was hydraulically operated, with the main gears folding into the inner engine nacelle and tail boom. Dunlop Maxaret anti-skid brakes were fitted.

The rear of the Argosy's cargo bay was hinged on the starboard side and swung open for access. Military Argosies had a split 'beaver tail', the bottom half forming a ramp for vehicles. It could be opened in flight.

The tail unit, with its twin fins and rudders, was carried on elliptical-section metal tail booms. These extended rearwards from the inner engine nacelles.

ACTION DATA

ECONOMIC CRUISING SPEED

Although the Argosy was a fairly fast aircraft compared to piston-engined types, when it appeared in the late 1950s the Armstrong Whitworth aircraft was still slower than the contemporary Hercules.

ARGOSY 220	451 km/h (280 m.p.h.)
CL-44J	612 km/h (379 m.p.h.)
L-100-20 HERCULES	581 km/h (360 m.p.h.)

MAXIMUM PAYLOAD

The CL-44 was able to lift more than 29 tons of cargo, but was not able to carry the outsize loads of the Hercules and Argosy. The L-100 was able to carry 50 per cent more than the Argosy.

ARGOSY SERIES 220 14,095 kg (31,000 lb.)

CL-44J 29,200 kg (64,240 lb.)

L-100-20 HERCULES 21,132 kg (46,490 lb.)

RANGE

Designed to the USAF's exacting specification for a tactical transport, the C-130 Hercules was able to move vehicles and other loads more than 4000 km (2,980 mi.). Lockheed found a ready market for a civil version of the aircraft. The CL-44 was based on the Bristol Britannia airliner and shared its long range.

ARGOSY SERIES 220 885 km (548 mi.)

CL-44J 8460 km (5,245 mi.)

L-100-20 HERCULES 4110 km (2,550 mi.)

Armstrong Whitworth's airliners

■ **ARGOSY:** The 'Argosy' name was first used for this three-engined airliner of the mid-1920s. Seven were built and served with Imperial Airways in Europe and Africa until the mid-1930s.

■ **AW.XV ATALANTA:** Experience with the Argosy led Imperial Airways to standardise with four-engined aircraft. The first example, G-ABPI, flew in 1932. Eight of these 17-seaters were built.

■ **AW.27 ENSIGN:** Built for Imperial Airways, the Ensign of 1938 came in two versions – the 40-seat 'Empire' and the 27-seat 'European'. Many served with the RAF during World War II.

■ **AW.55 APOLLO:** Two Apollos were built to the same specification as the Vickers Viscount, and the first flew in 1949. Intended as a 30-seater, the aircraft suffered engine and other problems.

AVIATION TRADERS

CARVAIR

● Car carrier ● British DC-4 conversion ● Twenty-one delivered

▲ *The unique load-carrying capabilities of the Carvair have seen it pressed into service airlifting all manner of different cargoes. Until recent years the plentiful supply of spare parts for the DC-4 made the Carvair a cheap aircraft to operate.*

With its unique bulbous nose, the ATL.98 Carvair (a contraction of Car-via-air) filled a niche market in the United Kingdom for a cross-Channel car carrier. The Carvair was an inexpensive solution to the problem as it was not a new aircraft but a conversion of a 20-year-old airliner – the reliable Douglas DC-4. Ultimately, Carvairs served around the world, carrying all manner of outsized loads until their retirement in the 1980s.

PHOTO FILE

AVIATION TRADERS CARVAIR

▲ **British United Air Ferries**
'Chelsea Bridge', the second Carvair conversion, demonstrates the car-loading lift designed by Aviation Traders for use with the aircraft.

▲ **American export**
In the twilight of its career, N55243 was one of several Carvairs based in the United States in the mid-1980s.

▲ **Touching down**
G-AOFW first flew in 1964, one of seven Carvairs delivered to British United Air Ferries.

▲ **Carvair prototype**
The first ATL.98 in hybrid Channel Air Bridge/British United Airways colours. The open fairing for the nosewheel can be seen under the nose.

◄ **Red Cross duty**
This Norwegian-registered Carvair carries the traditional colours of the International Red Cross relief organisation.

FACTS AND FIGURES

➤ In 1966 ATL proposed a Rolls-Royce Dart turboprop-powered DC-7 conversion called the 'Carvair 7', but none was built.

➤ The 'Carvair' name was chosen after a competition was held in Southend.

➤ Carvairs have carried a wide range of cargoes, from radio transmitters to oil.

➤ The managing director of both Channel Air Bridge and ATL was Freddie Laker, later famous for his cut-price airline Skytrain.

➤ Certification of the prototype was delayed after a forklift almost severed its tail.

➤ Two early Carvairs were pure freighters with nine seats behind the flight deck.

PROFILE

From airliner to car carrier

In the late 1950s British airline Channel Air Bridge Limited needed an aircraft to replace their existing Bristol Freighter car ferries. However, with the market for such an aircraft being comparatively small the cost of a new machine was expected to be too high.

Its associated company Aviation Traders came up with an inexpensive option. Second-hand Douglas DC-4s (and ex-military C-54s) could be bought for about $110,000.

With technical help from Douglas, Aviation Traders set about designing the Carvair – a converted DC-4. Nose-loading was essential for a car carrier, therefore the redesigned cockpit was raised 2.08 metres and a hydraulically operated swing nose was fitted. A forward fuselage stretch of 2.64 metres was also carried out. A former World Airways C-54B was chosen to be the first ATL.98 and flew in June 1961. This aircraft entered service between Southend and Rotterdam the following March and was followed by 20 further conversions, the last in July 1968. Used in at least 10 countries, a handful remained in use in the early 1980s but all have now been grounded, the last being operated in America.

Below: Channel Air Bridge merged with Silver City Airways to form British United Air Ferries, later British Air Ferries (BAF). The lettering on the tailfin of this BAF Carvair advertises the aircraft's 8.5-tonne (8.5-ton) cargo capacity and BAF's telephone number.

Above: 'Big John' was part of British Air Ferries' large fleet. Carvairs retained their DC-4 cabin windows after conversion.

ATL.98 CARVAIR

G-AXAI 'Fat Albert' was the seventeenth of 21 Carvairs converted from Douglas C-54s and DC-4s. Other BAF Carvairs included 'Plain Jane' and 'Porky Pete'.

The new bulbous nose required a raised cockpit to be designed.

The initial car-carrying version of the Carvair had a rear cabin for up to 25 passengers as well as room for five cars at the front.

Internally, the floor area was increased from the DC-4's 15.19 m² (163 sq. ft.) to over 24 m² (258 sq. ft.) and the maximum useable volume from 104.5 m³ (3,690 cu. ft.) to 123.2 m³ (4,350 cu. ft.).

British Air Ferries used several colour schemes on their Carvairs, including this white and blue finish.

To offset the increased side area over the DC-4 the taller fin of the DC-7 was fitted.

BRITISH AIR FERRIES

G-AXAI

A hydraulically operated nose door and lift were installed to ease the loading of cars.

The engines were the same 1081-kW (1,450-hp.) Pratt & Whitney R-2000 Twin Wasps as those fitted to most DC-4s.

To cope with the increased weight of the aircraft the stronger brake system of the DC-6 was fitted.

The passenger cabin at the rear of the Carvair necessitated the fitting of extra windows behind the cargo door. These are not found on a DC-4.

Airliner freight conversions

■ **CANADAIR CL-44D-4:** This variant of the CL-44, itself a derivative of the Bristol Britannia, had a hinged tail to allow straight-in loading of large freight items. First flying in 1960, 27 CL-44D-4s were built.

■ **AEROSPACELINES GUPPY:** Derived from the Boeing Stratocruiser, the first Guppy appeared in 1961 to transport outsize parts for the US space programme. More were converted later, including five Super Guppies with Allison turboprops.

■ **SATIC A300-600ST 'BELUGA':** Derived from the Airbus A300 series, four Belugas will be built to replace Super Guppies transporting Airbus parts from factories around Europe to Toulouse for final assembly. They are the widest civil jets.

AVIONS DE TRANSPORT RÉGIONAL

ATR 42/ATR 72

● Regional airliner ● Best-selling turboprop ● Freighter

▲ *The ATR has many rivals with similar performance, but the marketing effort behind the French/Italian aircraft has been very effective. In particular, sales to the former French colonies and the North American market were high.*

As products of one of the most successful collaborative airliner programmes, the ATR 42 and the later ATR 72 have dominated the twin-turboprop regional airliner market. Built by Aérospatiale of France and Alenia of Italy, the ATR series has been sold worldwide. By the mid-1990s, the aircraft had achieved total sales amounting to over half the world market, with the prospect of more orders to come.

AVIONS DE TRANSPORT RÉGIONAL **ATR 42/ATR 72**

◀ **Series production**
Wing and cabin components are produced at St Nazaire and Nantes, with final assembly taking place in Toulouse.

▼ **Multi-function displays**
Cockpit technology is very advanced in the ATRs, with multi-function displays and a colour screen for the Honeywell P-800 weather radar.

▲ **American Express**
PanAm was one of a large number of North American users before the airline went bankrupt.

◀ **Air Littoral**
Linking 14 French cities and eight other European destinations, Air Littoral is typical of the airlines that appreciate the efficient operation of the ATR.

Cargo-hauling turboprop ▶
With its large fuselage cargo door the ATR 42 Cargo can be swiftly loaded with up to 4000 kg (8,820 lb.) on pallets.

FACTS AND FIGURES

➤ Air Littoral now operates a single ATR 72 and six ATR 42-300s; these serve domestic French and European destinations.

➤ Air Dolomiti operates ATR 42-500s on services like that from Geneva to Trieste.

➤ ATR 42s have been very successful in French-speaking nations of Africa.

➤ The ATR 52 is a military freighter version with a rear-loading ramp, but only one has been ordered – by Gabon.

➤ Aérospatiale manufactures the wing and flight deck and Alenia builds the tail unit.

➤ The ATR 42 Cargo can be reconfigured in just one hour to carry nine containers.

PROFILE

Best-selling turboprop airliner

An example of just how successful collaborative aircraft ventures can be, the ATR series of turboprop airliners has achieved remarkable success in only a few years. Developed by Alenia and Aérospatiale, the Avions de Transport Régional aircraft are named after their seating capacities of 42 and 72, respectively.

The prototype of the ATR 42 first flew in August 1984, and type certification followed in September 1985. The first user of the ATR 42 was Air Littoral, who received the fourth aircraft built.

Since then it has dominated the world market, being purchased almost everywhere outside the former Soviet Union.

The ATR 42-320 has improved-performance PW 121 engines for enhanced hot-and-high power, and the ATR 42-500 is powered by PW 127s. A cargo version, the ATR 42 Cargo, has a cargo door and a reconfigurable cabin.

The stretched ATR 72, powered by PW 124 engines, flew in October 1988. The first recipient was Kar-Air of Finland, and since then more than 170 have been ordered. The problems which

caused the loss of two ATRs have now been solved and the aircraft is currently selling well.

Like joint manufacturers Saab/Fairchild and IPTN/CASA, Alenia and Aérospatiale have produced a highly successful turboprop.

The nosecone is constructed of Nomex and Kevlar composite for lightness and strength. Aérospatiale are responsible for the layout of the cabin and flight deck.

Lateral control is effected by ailerons and a single spoiler ahead of each outer flap. Two-segment, double-slotted flaps are controlled by Ratier-Fiegeac hydraulic actuators.

Both rudder and elevators are horn balanced to ease control forces in flight.

The wing is a 'fail safe', two-spar design, with the leading edges being made of a Kevlar/Nomex sandwich.

ATR 42

Many airlines in former French colonial nations have purchased the ATR series. Early customers included Air Mauritius which flies to destinations in Africa.

Two pilots fly the ATR and there is a fold-away seat for an observer. The avionics fit includes a Honeywell DFZ-600 automatic flight control system, a ground proximity warning system, a radio altimeter, two radios, VOR, DME and ILS systems and a digital flight data recorder.

Highly efficient and reliable, the PW 120 turboprops drive four-bladed, constant-speed Hamilton Standard propellers.

The main baggage and cargo compartment is located between the cockpit and passenger cabin.

The toilet, galley and wardrobe are located at the rear of the cabin. An additional cargo compartment is also located in the rear fuselage.

All the flying controls are mechanically actuated, with electrically actuated trim tabs. The fin and tailplane are mainly constructed of aluminium alloys.

AIR MAURITIUS
AGALEGA
3B-NAH

ATR.42-300

Type: short-haul twin-turboprop regional airliner and cargo aircraft

Powerplant: two 1342-kW (1,800-hp.) Pratt & Whitney Canada PW 120 turboprops

Maximum speed: 463 km/h (305 m.p.h.)

Initial climb rate: 640 m/min (2,100 f.p.m.)

Range: 1946 km (1,209 mi.) with 45 passengers

Service ceiling: 3140 m (10,302 ft.)

Weights: empty 10,285 kg (22,674 lb.); loaded 16,700 kg (36,817 lb.)

Passenger capacity: up to 50 at maximum density in four abreast layout

Dimensions:
span	24.57 m (80 ft. 7 in.)
length	22.67 m (74 ft. 4 in.)
height	7.58 m (24 ft. 10 in.)
wing area	54.50 m² (543 sq. ft.)

ACTION DATA

PASSENGERS

Standard passenger loads are often less than these maxima. Saab's 2000 is a development of the smaller 340, intended to compete with the larger versions of the ATR 42 and Dash-8.

ATR 42-300 — 50 passengers
SAAB 2000 — 58 passengers
DASH-8 — 56 passengers

MAXIMUM SPEED

The larger Saab 2000 is easily the fastest of this group, because of its more powerful Allison engines. Speed, range and fuel economy are important attributes for this type of aircraft.

ATR 42-300 — 463 km/h (305 m.p.h.)
SAAB 2000 — 680 km/h (422 m.p.h.)
DASH-8 — 527 km/h (327 m.p.h.)

RANGE

The large size of the Saab 2000 gives it extra fuel capacity and therefore greater range. Although the Dash-8 has shorter range, it has superior field performance.

ATR 42-300 — 1946 km (1,209 mi.)
SAAB 2000 — 2577 km (1,598 mi.)
DASH-8 — 1540 km (955 mi.)

Airline customers for the ATR

■ **FOSHING:** One of the largest Asian ATR customers, Taipei-based Foshing has six ATR 42s and nine ATR 72s in service.

■ **HOLLAND AIR:** Based at Amsterdam Schipol, Holland Air also operated Boeing 737s and 757s on European regional services.

■ **THAI AIR:** One of Asia's finest airlines, Thai Air operates two ATR 42s and two ATR 72s, as well as many Boeing jet airliners.

■ **TRANSASIA:** Based in Taiwan, TransAsia operates three ATR 42s and 12 ATR 72s on regional services from Taipei.

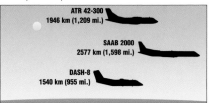

AVRO CANADA
C-102 JETLINER

● Jetliner prototype ● Rolls-Royce engines ● Only one built

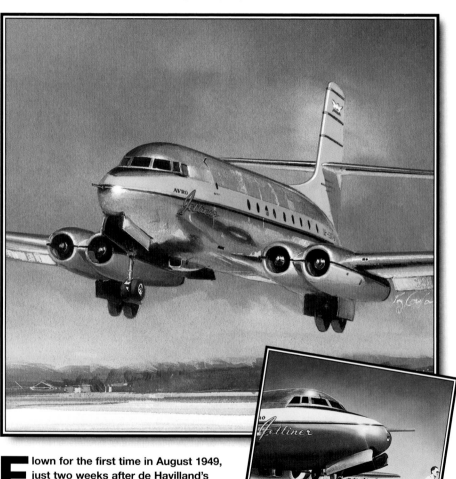

▲ Rolls-Royce
Avon development delays and the British reluctance to release the engine for civil use badly affected a Jetliner programme that was reliant on the new powerplant.

F lown for the first time in August 1949, just two weeks after de Havilland's Comet, the C-102 was an audacious attempt by A.V. Roe Canada Limited to build a jet transport with a cruising speed twice that of contemporary piston-engined types. Canadian and American airlines showed interest in the new aircraft, but the outbreak of war in Korea and the Canadian government's demand for CF-100 fighters led to the cancellation of the project.

◀ Conservative lines
Although a clean design, the C-102 retained the somewhat dated look of a piston-engined aircraft.

▼ Observation ship
After cancellation, the Jetliner spent a short time in the US before being returned to Canada for use as an observation aircraft during CF-100 tests. These included gun-pack firing and ejection seat activation.

▲ Avro Canada products
The prototype C-102 is seen alongside the CF-100 prototype. The Canadian government cancelled the C-102 in favour of accelerated CF-100 development.

▼ Trans-Canada Air Lines
After the powerplant change, TCA was released from its commitment to purchase the C-102. The re-engined aircraft needed to carry more fuel, which reduced payload.

▲ First flight
Upon its first flight on 10 August 1949, the C-102 became the first jet transport in North America to take to the air. The Boeing 707 prototype did not fly until 1954.

FACTS AND FIGURES

➤ After testing by the USAF, Avro Canada proposed a trainer variant with four Allison J-33 engines.

➤ Construction of a second C-102 prototype began, but was not completed.

➤ After cancellation, the C-102 was used as an observation platform for CF-100 tests.

➤ Flown for the last time on 23 November 1956, CF-EJD-X was scrapped in December, having flown about 425 hours.

➤ After flying the aircraft in 1952, Howard Hughes considered building the C-102.

➤ The C-102's nose is now in Canada's National Aeronautical Collection.

PROFILE

Canada's first and only jetliner

Only one C-102 was flown, although a second machine was close to completion when the programme was cancelled. The aircraft, registered CF-EJD-X, first flew on 10 August 1949, powered by four Rolls-Royce Derwent 5 turbojet engines.

However, these engines were not the ones originally intended for the new airliner. Avro Canada had hoped to install a pair of Rolls-Royce's new AJ 65 Avon turbojets, but the British government was not prepared to release them for civil use.

Intended to carry 30 to 50 passengers, the C-102 would have covered route stages of around 1750 km (1,085 mi.).

After an early landing accident, the prototype was repaired, demonstrated extensively and later re-engined with more powerful Derwent 8s and 9s (two of each). On one occasion the aircraft flew 587 km (400-plus mi.) from Toronto to New York in 59 minutes with a cargo of mail.

The C-102's launch customer was to be Trans-Canada Air Lines, although US firms were also impressed enough to propose a production order.

The RCAF and USAF also tested the aircraft, but ultimately performance shortcomings, the Korean War and the Canadian government's request that Avro concentrate on the CF-100 fighter led to cancellation in 1951.

Had development continued, the C-102 could have been the world's second jet airliner in service, an honour left to the Soviet Tupolev Tu-104.

Rolls-Royce Derwent turbojets were installed in nacelles designed with the aid of wartime German research.

The Jetliner's twin-spar wing was of conventional stressed-skin construction. Split flaps were fitted.

The elevators and rudder were in two pieces, the rear portions being manually operated and the front section power-assisted.

Had the British government released the Rolls-Royce Avon for civil use, the C-102 would have been fitted with two in single nacelles.

C-102 JETLINER

Although two prototypes were planned, only CF-EJD-X was completed and flown. The tail legend reads 'Designed and built by A.V. Roe Canada Limited, Malton, Ontario'.

Unswept vertical tail surfaces were a feature of many early jet types. Aerodynamic research later showed the benefits of a swept tail.

The Jetliner's flightdeck was of conventional layout with fully duplicated controls and seating for two pilots, plus a 'jump' seat between for an observer.

Pressurisation was a feature of the C-102's 3.05-m (10-ft.) diameter fuselage. Seating arrangements for between 30 and 50 passengers were proposed. During demonstration flights passengers were impressed by its low noise levels.

After its second flight the C-102 was unable to lower its main undercarriage and was forced to make a belly landing. It came to rest on its extended nose gear, the ends of its tail pipes and the rear fuselage.

The C-102 was fitted with tricycle undercarriage, with dual mainwheels retracting into the rear of the engine nacelles.

While the prototype was undergoing testing, Avro worked on a production version with a 1.22-m (4-ft.) forward fuselage stretch and a rear fuselage shortened by 0.53 m (nearly 2 ft.). Alternative powerplants were suggested, including Allison J-33s and Pratt & Whitney J-42s (licence-built Rolls-Royce Nenes).

C-102 Jetliner

Type: medium-range civil transport

Powerplant: four 16.01-kN (3,600-lb.-thrust) Rolls-Royce Derwent 5/17 turbojets

Maximum speed: 804 km/h (498 m.p.h.) at 9145 m (30,000 ft.)

Cruising speed: 692 km/h (429 m.p.h.) at 9145 m (30,000 ft.)

Initial climb rate: 561 m/min (1,840 f.p.m.)

Range: 2012 km (1,250 mi.)

Service ceiling: 11,368 m (37,300 ft.)

Weights: empty 15,050 kg (33,110 lb.); maximum take-off 29,510 kg (64,922 lb.)

Accommodation: (proposed) flight crew of two, plus 30 to 50 passengers in various seating configurations

Dimensions:
span	29.89 m	(98 ft.)
length	24.61 m	(80 ft. 9 in.)
height	8.06 m	(26 ft. 5 in.)
wing area	107.48 m²	(1,156 sq. ft.)

ACTION DATA

CRUISING SPEED

The de Havilland Comet flew two weeks before the Jetliner and was the first jet airliner to enter service. Powered by four de Havilland Ghosts, the aircraft had a 96 km/h (60 m.p.h.) speed advantage.

C-102 JETLINER	692km/h (429 m.p.h.)
COMET Mk 1	789 km/h (489 m.p.h.)
Tu-104 'CAMEL'	770 km/h (477 m.p.h.)

PASSENGERS

All three of these jetliners had similar capacity, although with 50 passengers aboard, the C-102 was at its upper limit. The Comet was later 'stretched' to increase seating.

C-102 JETLINER	50 passengers
COMET Mk 1	44 passengers
Tu-104 'CAMEL'	50 passengers

RANGE

In prototype form the C-102 demonstrated a range of just over 2000 km (1,250 mi.). When fitted with four Derwent engines, the Jetliner's fuel capacity was reduced and extra tankage was required to maintain range. Payload capability therefore suffered. Both the Comet and Tu-104 were larger aircraft, the latter having two engines.

C-102 JETLINER 2012 km (1,250 mi.)

COMET Mk 1 2816 km (1,745 mi.)

Tu-104 'CAMEL' 2650 km (1,645 mi.)

British jet transport prototypes

AVRO 706 ASHTON: Six of these large aircraft were built for the Ministry of Supply for research into jet operations. Four Rolls-Royce Nene turbojets were fitted.

DE HAVILLAND DH.106 COMET: First flown in July 1949, the de Havilland Ghost-powered Comet was to be the world's first jet airliner in service, just under three years later.

VICKERS NENE-VIKING: Rolls-Royce Nene turbojets were installed in a Viking airliner to create the world's first pure-jet transport aircraft. Flown in 1948, it was strictly a test aircraft.

VICKERS VISCOUNT 663: The second Viscount turboprop airliner prototype was rebuilt in 1950 as a flying engine testbed with two Rolls-Royce Tay turbojets.

BAC
ONE-ELEVEN

● Short-haul airliner ● Holidaymaker's special ● Licence-built in Romania

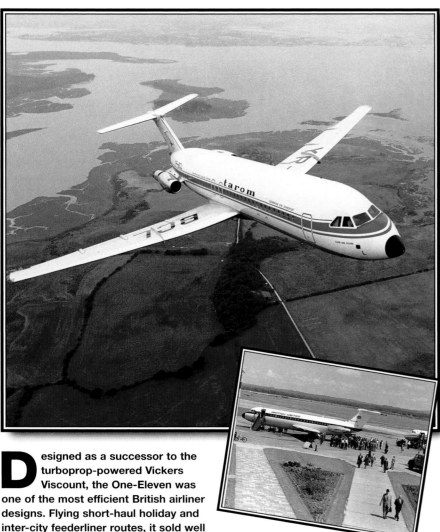

Designed as a successor to the turboprop-powered Vickers Viscount, the One-Eleven was one of the most efficient British airliner designs. Flying short-haul holiday and inter-city feederliner routes, it sold well in both America and Europe. Despite its design being over 30 years old, the One-Eleven is still a common sight, especially in Europe where the Romanian-built version still thrives.

▲ *The One-Eleven was one of the better British airline designs of the 1960s. If legal problems based on noise regulations can be avoided, it will still be a common sight for years to come.*

PHOTO FILE

BAC ONE-ELEVEN

▲ American service
American Airlines received its first One-Eleven in July 1965. It was successful despite the US Federal Aviation Authority limiting the weight of the aircraft with a two-man crew to only 36288 kg (80,015 lb).

◄ Front end
Most One-Elevens had a two-man crew, even in the United States where three-man flight decks were the norm in the 1960s.

◄ British United
The first production variant was the One-Eleven 200, of which 58 were built. British United Airlines purchased the first 10 aircraft.

High density ►
The One-Eleven avoided the mistakes of earlier British designs, and had high-density seating.

▲ Dirt runway
The ability to operate from small strips made the One-Eleven a viable operator in Africa, Asia and South America.

◄ Passengers in Peru ▲
Faucett of Peru operated One-Elevens on domestic routes, often from small, unsealed runways at high altitudes.

FACTS AND FIGURES

➤ In an ill-fated start, the BAC One-Eleven prototype first flew in August 1963, but crashed three months later.

➤ One-Eleven commercial service began with British United Airlines in April 1965.

➤ The One-Eleven was one of the few British airliners to sell well in the USA.

➤ The 220 One-Elevens sold by 1978 made it Britain's biggest aviation foreign exchange earner of its time.

➤ The Series 500, introduced in 1966, could carry up to 119 passengers.

➤ Rombac of Romania built an upgraded One-Eleven.

PROFILE

Britain's best holiday jet

The One-Eleven began as a design study by Hunting Aircraft, intended as a replacement for the successful Vickers Viscount. The H-107 was to have been a cruciform-tail rear-engined twin, with a capacity of 48 seats and a range of around 1600 km (990 mi.).

In 1960 Hunting was acquired by the British Aircraft Corporation, and the design was expanded to take 65 passengers over 1000 km (600 mi.). In April 1961, production of an initial batch of 20 aircraft was started,

and in May British United Airways became launch customer, ordering 10 Series 200 types. Vital to success was an American purchase, and Braniff International ordered six with six options in October 1961.

The One-Eleven suffered a slight setback when a test aircraft crashed in October 1963 due to a 'deep stall' arising from the T-tail design, but this was cured by control modifications. The One-Eleven then went on to have a trouble-free career, with good sales success. A new

lease of life came in 1977 when the Romanian company Interprederea Avionane took out a licence-build agreement with BAC. The first 'Rombac' One-Eleven was delivered to Tarom Romanian Airlines in 1982, and a hush-kit modification has been proposed to extend the One-Eleven's life still further.

The One-Eleven 500 series was used for inter-city routes by Bavaria Germanair.

The One-Eleven specialised in holiday flights and in servicing commuter routes between cities. American Airlines used it on the busy Boston-New York-Washington 'Jet Express', one of the world's busiest airways.

One-Eleven Series 500

Type: short-haul twin-jet airliner

Powerplant: two Rolls-Royce 55.82-kN (12,525-lb.-thrust) Spey 512-DW turbofans

Maximum speed: 871 km/h (540 m.p.h.) maximum cruise; 742 km/h (460 m.p.h.) economy cruise

Initial climb rate: 730 m/min (2,400 f.p.m.)

Range: 2380 km (3,870 mi.) with capacity payload; 3458 km (6,015 mi.) with maximum fuel

Service ceiling: 10,600 m (34,800 ft.)

Weights: basic operating weight 24,758 kg (54,468 lb.); maximum take-off weight 47,400 kg (104,498 lb.)

Payload: normal 97 passengers; maximum 119

Dimensions:
span	28.50 m (93 ft. 6 in.)
length	32.61 m (107 ft.)
height	7.47 m (24 ft. 6 in.)
wing area	95.78 m² (1,031 sq. ft.)

Fuel tanks with a capacity of 14,024 litres (3,650 gal.) were fitted, one in each wing and one in the centre section.

The wing of the 500 series had an extra 1.52-m (5-ft.) span to improve take-off performance.

ONE-ELEVEN SERIES 414EG

The BAC One-Eleven was one of the most successful European airliners before the Airbus. The 500 series was especially popular, selling well in the face of competition from Boeing and McDonnell Douglas.

BAC considered producing a stretched One-Eleven Series 700, with fuselage lengthened by 3.66 m (12 ft.) compared to the 500 series aircraft.

A 'stick-pusher' was installed as part of the flight control system. It was intended to warn pilots and prevent a recurrence of the loss of the prototype to a deep stall accident caused by the high T-tail.

A small weather radar system is fitted to the One-Eleven.

The One-Eleven was like many of its contemporaries in having five-abreast seating.

Small wing fences are located on the leading edge of the wing to control spanwise airflow.

The Spey 512-14W was capable of producing more thrust, thanks to water injection.

In an attempt to increase the life of the One-Eleven beyond new noise limits, a 'hush kit' was developed for the Spey engine, including a bypass duct lining and six-chute jet mixing exhaust silencer.

A ventral entrance was located in the rear fuselage between the engines, with a hydraulically-powered stairway. Many were sealed shut after a bizarre hijacking incident in America in which the hijacker parachuted out with a large ransom.

ACTION DATA

MAXIMUM SPEED

The new twin-jets were about 200 km/h (125 m.p.h.) faster than turboprops like the Viscount, and twice as fast as the previous decade's piston-engined aircraft. The One-Eleven did not have the speed of its long-haul rivals, but was fast enough over a short haul.

ONE-ELEVEN SERIES 500	871 km/h (540 m.p.h.)
MODEL 737-200	927 km/h (575 m.p.h.)
DC-9 SERIES 30	918 km/h (569 m.p.h.)

RANGE

Typical short-haul routes within Europe and the eastern seaboard of the United States involve flying between cities ranging from 100 km (60 mi.) to 1000 km (600 mi.) apart. The jets designed to operate such flights carry enough fuel to fly several stages without needing replenishment.

DC-9 SERIES 30 3300 km (2,050 mi.)

MODEL 737-200 4075 km (2,525 mi.)

ONE-ELEVEN SERIES 500 3458 km (2,165 mi.)

PASSENGER LOAD

In the late 1950s, when the specification for these jets was first discussed, planners were looking for aircraft with a 50-passenger capacity. However, it quickly became clear that larger planes would be needed. The One-Eleven was never stretched beyond 119 passengers, however, unlike its rivals which entered the 1990s with developed models seating between 150 and 180.

MODEL 737-200 130 passengers

DC-9 SERIES 30 115 passengers

ONE-ELEVEN SERIES 500 119 passengers

Mass-market air transporters

■ **AÉROSPATIALE CARAVELLE:** First flying in the 1950s, the elegant Caravelle was one of the earliest of the short-haul twin-jets, and set the standards by which others have been judged.

■ **MCDONNELL DOUGLAS DC-9:** A direct competitor to the One-Eleven, the DC-9 first flew in 1965. Models had a range of passenger capacities, which gave it the commercial edge.

■ **BOEING 737:** Although beaten into service by both the One-Eleven and the DC-9, Boeing's spacious twin-jet offered a wider cabin and has become the world's best-selling airliner.

BEECHCRAFT

MODEL 18

● Light passenger transport ● Long production run ● Military service

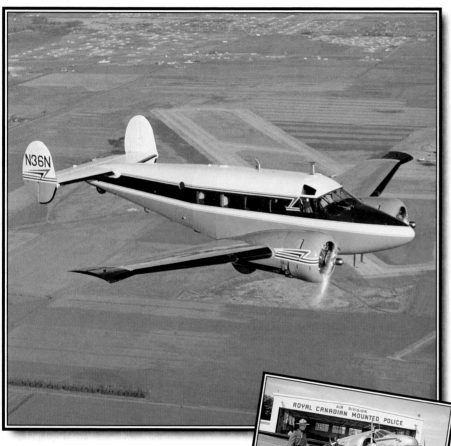

Built from the 1930s until the 1960s, the Beechcraft Model 18 was in production longer than any aircraft in the same class. This familiar handyman of the skies is a simple but effective monoplane with two engines, all-metal construction and a cabin for six occupants. The Beechcraft 18 first flew on 15 January 1937 and quickly established itself as a rugged light transport, particularly in Canada where it operated on wheels, floats and skis.

▲ Surprisingly,
the Model 18 was not an immediate bestseller. It was the greater capacity and military versions which really launched the machine into worldwide service.

BEECHCRAFT MODEL 18

◄ US Naval service
More than 1500 Model 18s were supplied to the US Navy. Carrying JRB or SNB designations they were equivalent to Army aircraft.

Personnel transport ►
Known to the US Army as the UC-45, the basic personnel transport and liaison variant was also supplied under Lend-Lease to the UK and Canada.

▼ Kansan
With its gun turret and bomb-bay the AT-11 Kansan was used as a bombing and gunnery trainer.

▼ Model 18D
Powered by Jacobs L-6 engines, the Model 18D was the only successful pre-war variant.

◄ Turbine power
Both Volpar and the Pacific Airmotive Corporation offered lengthened, turboprop-powered conversions based on the Beechcraft 18. Some could carry up to 18 passengers and most had a tricycle undercarriage.

FACTS AND FIGURES

➤ The first Model 18 test pilot, James Peyton, was chosen because of his TWA experience with multi-engine aircraft.

➤ The last of nearly 8,000 Beechcraft 18s were delivered on 26 November 1969.

➤ In the late 1940s, the Model 18 was the world's most popular business aircraft.

➤ A Beechcraft 18 owned by *Time* magazine flew more than a million kilometres on business assignments.

➤ Turboprop conversions of the Model 18 could carry 15 to 18 passengers.

➤ The first production aircraft was also the first to operate on floats.

Immortal Beechcraft design

Beechcraft created one of aviation's great success stories with its Model 18. Although it looked little different from other aircraft being developed in the 1930s, the Beechcraft 18 captured the hearts and minds of both pilots and operators, and remained in production for a record 32 years.

More recently, the Beechcraft 18 has proven a popular choice for conversion by a number of American companies, with modifications intended to provide improved performance

or greater capacity. Many of these updates involved the fitting of turboprop engines and some had major alterations to the airframe and cockpit equipment.

The US Army and the military services of a dozen countries drafted the Model 18 into service during the war years for light transport work, photoreconnaissance and pilot and navigator training. In US Army service the aircraft was designated the AT-11 Kansan. Often referred to simply as a 'twin Beech', the aircraft was given the name

Left: C-45Fs supplied to Canada became Expeditor IIIs. In the US all C-45 designations changed to UC-45 in January 1945.

Expeditor by the RAF.

Many pilots who flew this aircraft during the war later piloted it in peacetime. In post-war years, there have been many civil and military versions of this fine aircraft and many hundreds of Beechcraft 18s remain in service around the world.

Above: Designed from the outset to operate from optional floats, the Model 18 became very popular in Canada.

Super H18

Type: twin-engine light transport

Powerplant: two 336-kW (450-hp.) Pratt & Whitney R-985-AN-14B radial piston engines

Maximum speed: 375 km/h (233 m.p.h.) at 1370 m (4,495 ft.)

Maximum cruising speed: 354 km/h (220 m.p.h.) at 3050 m (10,000 ft.)

Range: 3060 km (1,900 mi.)

Service ceiling: 6525 m (21,400 ft.)

Weights: empty 2651 kg (5,8854 lb.); maximum take-off 4491 kg (9,900 lb.)

Accommodation: two pilots, plus six to nine passengers

Dimensions:
span	15.15 m	(49 ft. 8 in.)
length	10.73 m	(35 ft. 2 in.)
height	2.84 m	(9 ft. 4 in.)
wing area	33.51 m²	(361 sq. ft.)

MODEL 18

More than 9000 Model 18s have been built, and several remain in service with third-level airlines worldwide. This Eastern Caribbean Airways aircraft is typical of those still flying with radial engines.

Twin end-plate fins and rudders were planned for the Model 18 from the outset, even though some have since been converted to a single fin and rudder layout.

A crew of two is required to fly the Model 18, as the cockpit workload is higher than that of comparable modern designs.

Many surviving Model 18s have been continuously modified during their long lives. Non-standard cabin doors, similar to those of the DC-3, have been fitted to this machine.

Pratt & Whitney R-985 Wasp Junior engines have powered almost all production Model 18s, except for a few early aircraft and those converted to turboprop power. The last production aircraft, built in 1969, used the Wasp powerplant.

Beechcraft incorporated an electrically operated retractable undercarriage into the Model 18 design. This advanced feature helped to give the aircraft its high performance and sleek, modern appearance.

The normal seating capacity was for six to seven passengers. A separate compartment to the rear of the cabin accommodates a toilet and baggage compartment. Various cabin configurations have been offered, including a luxury five-seat layout with bar and folding card tables.

COMBAT DATA

MAXIMUM CRUISING SPEED

With its Pratt & Whitney radials, the AT-11 was able to reach 346 km/h even with the drag of its twin-gun dorsal turret. Therefore, the Kansan was able to provide training at speeds close to those of operational aircraft.

AT-11 KANSAN	346 km/h (215 m.p.h.)
ANSON Mk I	303 km/h (188 m.p.h.)
OXFORD Mk V	325 km/h (202 m.p.h.)

MAXIMUM RANGE

Neither of the British aircraft could match the AT-11 for range. The civilian Model 18 had good range for executive and business travel, while the Avro Anson was developed in response to a British short-range airline requirement and the Airspeed Oxford purely as a military trainer.

OXFORD Mk V 1271 km (789 mi.)

ANSON Mk I 1127 km (700 mi.)

AT-11 KANSAN 1368 km (850 mi.)

ARMAMENT

Although the Oxford Mk I could fly as a bombing and gunnery trainer, the majority of those built were multi-engined navigation trainers. The Anson saw active service with RAF Coastal Command.

AT-11 KANSAN   2 x 7.62-mm (.30 cal.) machine-guns
450-kg (990-lb.) bombload

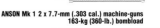

ANSON Mk 1   2 x 7.7-mm (.303 cal.) machine-guns
163-kg (360-lb.) bombload

OXFORD Mk V   none

Model 18 developments

Many military and civilian models of the Beechcraft Model 18 were built and these are still forming the basis of new conversions.

GUNNERY TRAINER: During World War II 1582 AT-11 Kansans were delivered. Some were armed with twin-gun turrets.

BOMBING TRAINER: A small bomb-bay allowed the AT-11 to carry up to ten 45-kg (100-lb.) bombs. A total of 1582 AT-11s was delivered to the USAF, and some were converted to AT-11A configuration, by the removal of the turret, for navigator training.

FLOATPLANE CONVERSION: One of the most radical and most recent Model 18s is Canada's Vancouver Island Air Seawind. The aircraft first flew in this form in 1994.

BEECHCRAFT

65 QUEEN AIR

● Twin-engined business and commuter liner ● 1960s design

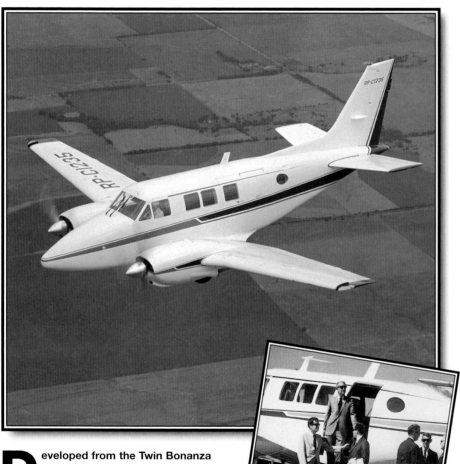

Developed from the Twin Bonanza and flown for the first time in August 1958, the Beechcraft Model 65 was the first of a series of twin-engined business aircraft to carry the name Queen Air. Despite its small size, it was equipped like an airliner, with all the systems needed for all-weather operations plus an optional weather radar. It found a ready market, and came to be used widely as an air taxi and short-haul commuter aircraft.

▲ *Beechcraft's top-selling Model 65 Queen Air was the intermediate step between the piston-engined Model 50 Twin Bonanza and the turboprop Model 90 King Air.*

BEECHCRAFT 65 QUEEN AIR

▼ **B80 with swept fin**
With the Model 65-80 in 1962, Beechcraft introduced a swept tail fin on the Queen Air. Longer-span wings were introduced in 1966 on the Model 65 Queen Air B80, seen here. In all, 242 were built.

▲ **Worldwide sales**
Queen Airs have sold around the world, including Great Britain. Many were sold to military customers who found the design ideal for communications and training duties.

▼ **Queen Airliner**
These three Model 70 Queen Airliners are of US operator Commuter Airlines. Certified in 1968, 35 were built, some with cargo pods under the fuselage.

▲ **Business liner and airliner**
Beechcraft intended the Queen Air for the roles of business and commuter airliner. In high-density configuration, the Model 70 carried nine people.

◄ **Turbine popularity**
Increasing interest in turboprop-powered commuter liners spelt the end of the piston-engined design in the 1970s. The Model 70 was one of the last models produced.

FACTS AND FIGURES

➤ French companies SFERMA and Sud Aviation designed a Queen Air with two 447-kW Turboméca Astazou turboprops.

➤ Model A65-85 was a planned pressurised version of the Model 65 Queen Air 80.

➤ The Queen Air prototype flew in August 1958, four months after design began.

➤ On 8 February 1960, a Beechcraft test pilot in a Model 65 set a world height record in that class – 10,626 m (34,853 ft.).

➤ The Model 65 Queen Air B80 was the last variant. Production ended in 1977.

➤ Fastest of the Queen Airs was the US Army's U-21A, at 426 km/h (264 m.p.h.).

PROFILE

Beech's regal prop-twins

Walter Beech's company was quick to build on the success of the Model 65. In 1962 the heavier Queen Air 80 introduced a swept tail fin and uprated Lycoming engines, while the Model A65 of the following year had increased fuel capacity. The Queen Air A80 appeared in 1964 with slightly larger wings and a cabin big enough for up to eight passengers, and the B80 introduced further minor changes in 1966. A projected pressurised variant was not built. Beechcraft marketed the Queen Air as both a business aircraft and commuter liner. The Model 70 of 1968 was available as a Queen Airliner with room for nine passenger seats in a high-density configuration.

By 1971, production was switching to a turboprop development, the eight-seat Model 90 King Air. For customers looking for a cheaper alternative to this design, the Model 65-88 was briefly available. It was effectively a piston-engined King Air.

As well as forming the basis for the King Air, the Queen Air was developed as the Swearingen Merlin business aircraft and Metro 19-seat airliner. The US Army used Queen Airs as L-23F/U-8F Seminoles and U-21A Utes.

In addition, Excalibur Aviation has rebuilt more than 160 Model 65s and 70s as Queenaire 800s and 8800s with 298-kW (400-hp.) Lycoming eight-cylinder engines, new engine nacelles and fully-enclosed wheel doors.

Left: Available from 1968, the Queen Air 70 combined the engines of the Model A65 with the wide-span wings of the Model 80. A Queen Airliner version was also available.

Below: Early production Queen Airs featured a tail assembly inherited from the Model 50 Twin Bonanza, the type it was intended to replace.

Model 65 Queen Air 80

Type: twin-engined business and commuter aircraft

Powerplant: two 283-kW (380-hp.) Lycoming IGSO-540-A1A flat-six air-cooled piston engines

Maximum speed: 406 km/h (252 m.p.h.) at 3505 m (11,500 ft.)

Maximum cruising speed: 370 km/h (229 m.p.h.)

Initial climb rate: 490 m/min (1,607 f.p.m.) at sea level

Range: 2140 km (1,330 mi.) at economic cruise speed with 45 mins reserve

Service ceiling: 10,520 m (34,500 ft.)

Weights: empty 2177 kg (4,790 lb.), maximum take-off 3629 kg (7,984 lb.)

Dimensions:
span	13.98 m	(45 ft. 10 in.)
length	10.74 m	(35 ft. 3 in.)
height	4.47 m	(14 ft. 8 in.)
wing area	25.73 m²	(277 sq. ft.)

Most Queen Airs were powered by versions of Lycoming's O-480 and O-540 flat-six, air-cooled piston engines. However, one of the last variants produced was the Model 65-A90-1 with two Pratt & Whitney PT6A turboprops. This was the only turboprop Queen Air version; the entire production run went to the US Army as the U-21A.

Initially marketed as a seven- to nine-seater, the Queen Air could accommodate up to nine passengers in airliner guise. Beech also intended that the aircraft be used as a freighter if required. To this end, passenger seating and bulkheads were easily removable.

For all-weather operation, de-icing 'boots' could be specified for the leading edges of the wings and tail.

Model A65s introduced the swept tail fin to the Queen Air. In 1968/69 Beech offered the Model A65-8200 Queen Airliner, initially known as the Model 79.

As on a number of other commuter types, the later Queen Air models featured a cargo compartment in the nose. The nose would also house navigation avionics, if fitted.

A two-spar wing of all-metal structure was standard on the Queen Air. Aluminium alloy was used in the semi-monocoque fuselage. This held the main fuel tanks; auxiliary tanks were housed in the wings.

KATS AIR TAXIS
SHOREHAM AIRPORT ☎ (0273) 464011
G-AWKX

MODEL A65 QUEEN AIR

Air taxi firms have been among the biggest users of the Queen Air. This aircraft was eventually reduced to ground instructional airframe status. Between 1967 and 1970, 96 Model A65s were built.

ACTION DATA

POWER

To increase speed and performance at altitude, more powerful turbocharged or supercharged engines were often fitted to successive models of the top-selling commuter liners. Both the Piper PA-31 and Cessna 402C used turbocharged engines.

QUEEN AIR A80 566 kW (760 hp.)	PA-31 350 CHIEFTAIN 522 kW (700 hp.)	MODEL 402C 484 kW (650 hp.)

CRUISING SPEED

While not the fastest of these three types, the Queen Air A80 had a top speed comparable to that of the Cessna 402C. Turboprop power was introduced on the King Air and pushed maximum speeds beyond 400 km/h (250 m.p.h.) and later 500 km/h (300 m.p.h.).

QUEEN AIR A80	370 km/h (229 m.p.h.)
PA-31 350 CHIEFTAIN	389 km/h (242 m.p.h.)
MODEL 402C	394 km/h (244 m.p.h.)

RANGE

Range was the Queen Air's main strength, 700-km (430-mi.) more than the Cessna 402C. The Queen Air A80 had improved fuel capacity over earlier Queen Air variants, with room for an extra 128 litres (34 gal.). Gross weight was up to just under four tons.

QUEEN AIR A80 2519 km (1,560 mi.)
PA-31 350 CHIEFTAIN 1761 km (1,090 mi.)
MODEL 402C 1822 km (1,130 mi.)

Beechcraft twins

■ **MODEL 60 DUKE:** This four- to six-seater, pressurised and turbocharged, first flew in late 1966. Production ended in 1982, with 593 built.

■ **MODEL 76 DUCHESS:** Three equipment packages (Weekender, Professional and Holiday) were available on the Duchess, launched in 1978.

■ **MODEL 90/100 KING AIR:** Developed directly from the Queen Air, the Model 90 (and 'stretched' Model 100) were turboprop-powered.

■ **MODEL 99 AIRLINER:** Beech's largest aircraft type, the 17-seat Airliner, was produced for 20 years, until 1986.

BEECHCRAFT

C99

● Feederliner family ● Widespread US service ● Reliable

▲ With the Model 99, Beechcraft established a family of sound basic design. A range of improvements and options was offered but the aircraft was never a huge sales success.

Combining 1980s technology with Beechcraft's solid experience of the earlier Model 99 and Model B99, the attractive C99 was manufactured at the Selma, Alabama, division and has performed well for about a dozen airlines, allowing small passenger loads to be flown economically. The C99 has now given way to the newer and more commercially successful Beechcraft 1900, but it continues to provide good service on many air routes.

BEECHCRAFT C99

▲ **Optional cargo door**
This demonstrator has the optional forward-hinged cargo door in front of the standard passenger door with its built-in airstair.

▲ **Queen Air heritage**
In its original form, the Model 99 showed great similarity to the Queen Air.

▲ **Extra power for the C99**
In addition to extra power, the C99 incorporated a number of other improvements, including modified undercarriage units and more modern avionics.

▲ **Excess baggage**
A large, streamlined under-fuselage pannier was offered as a customer option. This allowed the carriage of an additional 362 kg (800 lb.) of baggage or other cargo; normal stowage space is in the nose section and behind the rear seats.

▲ **Kansas research**
Having originally been delivered to Cal-State Air Lines in 1968, this Model 99 is shown flying with the University of Kansas as a research laboratory.

◄ **Big Beech**
At the time of its introduction, the Model 99 was the largest aircraft produced by the company.

FACTS AND FIGURES

➤ A total of 77 Model C99s was produced between 1982 and 1986, in addition to 163 other Model 99s previously built.

➤ Test-pilot Jim Dolbee took the Model C99 up for its first flight on 20 June 1980.

➤ The C99 is available with an optional, upward-hinged cargo door.

➤ An optional cargo pod that held 272 kg (600 lb.) of freight or baggage was available for the under-fuselage of the C99.

➤ An early Model 99 was returned to the factory and rebuilt as the C99 prototype.

➤ A movable bulkhead enables the C99 to carry a mixture of cargo and passengers.

PROFILE

Early Beechcraft feederliner

Beechcraft used major components from the highly successful Queen Air executive aircraft as the basis for the C99 airliner and its predecessors in the Model 99 family. Wing planform was very similar to that of the Queen Air, but the fuselage was longer and the Model 99 had turboprop rather than piston powerplants.

The purpose was to achieve a practical, affordable charter and feeder airliner that could efficiently carry small numbers of passengers on short flights to small airfields. Unlike the models

that came before it, the C99 had more than enough power, with 533-kW (715-hp.) engines.

Beechcraft ceased building the original Model 99 series in 1975, re-opening the lines to begin manufacture of the C99 in 1980. Deliveries began in 1981 and the aircraft remained in production for five years, before being superseded by the newer and more advanced Beechcraft 1900.

Unfortunately, although the C99 proved capable and reliable in service, it was never a great seller. It did, however, represent

a great step-up in aircraft size for Beechcraft, and allowed the company to gain valuable feeder-liner production experience.

Below: Beechcraft converted an early Model 99 into the C99 prototype during 1980. Although the production lines were re-opened, sales still remained elusive.

Above: Sunbird Airlines flew a number of C99s, losing one in a crash in August 1985. The C99 has found most favour with US airlines.

C99 Airliner

Type: commuter/cargo transport

Powerplant: two 533-kW (715-hp.), flat-rated Pratt & Whitney Canada PT6A-36 turboprops

Maximum speed: 496 km/h (308 m.p.h.) at 2440 m (8,000 ft.)

Cruising speed: 462 km/h (286 m.p.h.) at 2440 m (8,000 ft.)

Range: 1686 km (1,045 mi.) with maximum fuel

Service ceiling: 7620 m (25,000 ft.)

Weights: basic operating empty 3039 kg (6,686 lb.); maximum take-off 5125 kg (11,275 lb.)

Accommodation: two pilots, flight attendant and 14 or 15 passengers, plus provision for up to 782 kg (1,720 lb.) of cargo or baggage, or up to 1990 kg (4,378 lb.) of cargo without passengers. A movable bulkhead allows any combination of passengers and cargo

Dimensions: span 13.98 m (45 ft. 10 in.)
length 13.58 m (44 ft. 6 in.)
height 4.37 m (14 ft. 4 in.)
wing area 25.98 m² (280 sq. ft.)

MODEL B99 AIRLINER

This early aircraft was originally retained by Beechcraft and used as a demonstrator. It is fitted with the optional double cabin doors which allow large items of cargo to be loaded into the aircraft.

While single crew operation is possible, it is standard practice for the Model 99 to fly with a flight crew of two. Several avionics options were available, including weather radar.

Standard accommodation is for a maximum of 15 passengers. All passenger seats are removable to allow various combinations of commuters and freight.

All B99 Airliners were delivered with a port-side passenger door which incorporated an integral airstair. The port engine was normally shut down as passengers boarded or left the aircraft, with all systems being run from the starboard engine.

Two doors, one on either side of the nose, serve the forward baggage hold. The optional under-fuselage baggage pod increased capacity greatly, but had little effect on speed.

Unlike the Queen Air to which the Model 99 owed much of its basic design, the latter machine had a fully retracting undercarriage. Some pilots found the aircraft difficult to steer on the ground.

Two Pratt & Whitney PT6A-27 turboprops, each of 507 kW (680 hp.), powered the B99, the same engines fitted to the Model 99A Airliner.

Rubber fuel tanks in the wings give a fuel capacity of 1400 litres (370 gal.). The B99 introduced an additional 435 litres (115 gal.) of fuel capacity in the form of engine nacelle tanks.

From its introduction in 1972, the B99 did not sell well. Over four years, only 14 of the standard airliners were built, although some earlier model 99s and 99As were brought up to the B99 standard to benefit from the type's improved hot-and-high performance.

BEECH AIRCRAFT CORPORATION

N4299B

ACTION DATA

CRUISING SPEED

Cruising at a height of 2440 metres, the C99 has a marked speed advantage over the EMBRAER EMB-110P2A. It is slower than the Jetstream 31, an aircraft with significant US orders.

C99	462 km/h (286 m.p.h.)
EMB-110P2A	413 km/h (256 m.p.h.)
J31	488 km/h (303 m.p.h.)

PASSENGERS

Although it is slower than the C99, the EMB-110P2A carries more passengers. Larger loads are required for economical operations. However, on rural connections, lower capacity may be desirable.

C99 — 15 passengers

EMB-110P2A BANDEIRANTE — 21 passengers

J31 — 19 passengers

RANGE

While the J31 has achieved considerable success around the world, it cannot provide the range of the C99 or larger Bandeirante. Each of the aircraft achieves these range figures with a passenger load and reserves. It is significant that both the C99 and J31 are developments of earlier designs.

C99 1686 km (1,045 mi.)
EMB-110P2A BANDEIRANTE 2001 km (1,240 mi.)
J31 1260 km (780 mi.)

Beech turbine twins

■ **KING AIR C90B:** Basically a turboprop derivative of the Queen Air, the King Air was introduced in 1963. The C90B of 1991 introduced four-bladed propellers.

■ **SUPER KING AIR B200:** With a seating capacity in between those of the King Air and the Model 99, the B200 is highly successful. This aircraft was the 1500th built.

■ **MODEL 1900C:** Superseding the C99 in production, the Model 1900 has met with far greater success. The 1900C is the standard airliner, with seating for 19 passengers.

■ **STARSHIP 2000A:** Constructed mainly of composites, the Starship has not achieved the success it deserves. The 2000A is an improved model, based on the initial production version.

BEECHCRAFT

400

● Business jet ● Multi-engined trainer ● Air ambulance

▲ When
Beech bought the licence to build the Mitsubishi Diamond, it secured all export rights outside Japan. The aircraft has sold steadily, but has not been as popular as its competitors.

Beech was chiefly known as a maker of turboprop aircraft until the company acquired the rights to build the Mitsubishi Diamond under licence. The Beech 400 was replaced soon after by the improved Model 400A, which proved more popular with customers than the original model. Despite being known as a civil transport, more Model 400As have in fact been sold as aircrew trainers to the USAF.

BEECHCRAFT 400 EXECUTIVE TRAVEL

▼ **New avionics**
One of the few changes made to the original Mitsubishi design was the use of Collins avionics throughout and an electronic flight instrument system.

▲ **Computer designed**
The Beech 400A wing was computer designed by Mitsubishi, and is certified for unlimited life.

◀ **Executive jet**
Despite its favourable price tag, the Beech 400A is not cheap, costing about $5 million each in 1995. A Dassault Falcon 50 costs about $16 million.

Production move ▶
At first, Beech assembled components built in Japan by Mitsubishi, but in 1989 the whole assembly operation was moved to Wichita in the United States.

◀ **Long range**
Thrifty Pratt & Whitney JT15 engines give the little Beech 400A a range of more than 3500 km (2,175 mi.), and a high cruise speed.

FACTS AND FIGURES

➤ The Japanese Air Self-Defence Force operates the Beech T-400 as a crew trainer, with direction-finding systems.

➤ Production of the Model 400 totalled 58 aircraft before the 400A was introduced.

➤ The 400A has a radar system for detecting air turbulence.

➤ A Beech 400A was fitted out in air ambulance configuration for the Province of Chubut in Argentina.

➤ Increased ceiling and payload were just two of the improvements of the 400A.

➤ The Beech 400 is known to the USAF as the T-1A Jayhawk.

PROFILE

Beech builds an executive jet

Best known for its turboprop twins, the Beech company branched out into the executive jet market with the purchase of the production rights to the Mitsubishi Diamond in December 1985. The prototype had flown in 1984. Beech acquired all marketing rights outside Japan, and although production was at first carried out using sub-assemblies from Mitsubishi, the company ceased all trading outside Japan in March 1986 and Beech took on production at its base in

Wichita, Kansas. The first Beech-assembled aircraft was built in May 1986, and 25 had been delivered by January 1988.

The improved Model 400A was introduced in 1989, and at least 82 aircraft had been delivered by 1995. Designed for civil use, the 400A found success as a military crew systems trainer, winning a USAF competition for a tanker/transport trainer system. Designated T-1A Jayhawk, more than 200 were ordered by the USAF, delivery beginning in 1991. Japan followed suit,

ordering a small number of T-400 crew trainers. Civil sales continue, but the Beech aircraft faces ferocious competition from various rivals like the Hawker series, Dassault's Falcon and the evergreen Learjet range.

Below: The world market for corporate jets has been extremely crowded since the late 1980s, with a sharp downturn in world demand and a large number of competing manufacturers. Beech was lucky to secure military orders for its jet at a time of difficulty in the civil market.

Above: Costing $1 million less than a Cessna Citation VII, the 400A represents good value for the corporate client.

Model 400

Type: twin-turbofan executive jet

Powerplant: two Pratt & Whitney JT15D-5 turbofans rated at 13.19 kN (2,968 lb thrust)

Maximum speed: 899 km/h (559 m.p.h.)

Maximum Mach: 0.78

Initial climb rate: 1149 m/min (3,770 f.p.m.)

Range: 2915 km (1811 mi.) with reserves

Service ceiling: 13,230 m (43,400 ft.)

Weights: empty 4819 kg (10,624 lb.); loaded 7303 kg (16,100 lb.)

Accommodation: two crew and eight passengers in standard fit

Dimensions:
span	13.25 m (43 ft. 6 in.)
length	14.75 m (48 ft. 5 in.)
height	4.24 m (13 ft. 11 in.)
wing area	26.09 m² (281 sq. ft.)

MODEL 400A

An increase in business travel saw the demand for small executive jets explode in the late 1980s. Entering an already crowded market, Beech has achieved notable success with its design, offering a reliable and economical aircraft that is proving to be highly adaptable.

Eight passengers are seated in the 400A cabin: four in forward-facing seats and four in adjustable seats that can tilt, rotate and recline. Other seating configurations can be installed to customer requirements, including medical facilities.

The cabin has an independent pressurisation system, with an emergency system available using engine bleed air.

The 400A uses an all-moving tailplane and elevators for pitch control. The tailcone section can accommodate up to 204 kg (450 lb.) of baggage.

Standard avionics include the Collins Pro-Line 4 Electronic Flight Information System, with a three-tube display showing airspeed, altitude, vertical speed, attitude and navigation information.

The wing structure consists of machined upper and lower skins joined to two box spars, forming an integral fuel tank. A refuelling point is fitted on top of each wing. Roll control is effected by small ailerons and full semi-span narrow chord spoilers, which also act as lift dumpers.

The 400A is powered by two Pratt & Whitney JT15D-5 turbofans, fitted with Nordam thrust reversers (unlike the USAF T-1A). The rear-mounting layout reduces cabin noise. The rear fuselage fuel tank is mounted under the floor. The serial number on the tail is a United States registration.

Executive jets

■ **CHALLENGER 601:** Despite being developed as a regional business jet, many 601s have found their way into military service, such as this Canadian air force example.

■ **CITATION VII:** The main rival to the Beech 400 is the similar-looking Cessna Citation, which has been produced in various marks according to the passenger capacity required.

■ **FALCON 10:** Used as a VIP transport for government officials, Dassault's design has seen widespread service across Europe while also being exported to the United States.

■ **GULFSTREAM III:** The type has proved to be highly capable, and the Danish air force has utilised these executive-style jet airliners for SAR duties and fishery patrols.

ACTION DATA

MAXIMUM SPEED

Most business jets cruise at a high subsonic speed, usually approaching Mach 0.8. Above this speed there are penalties in airframe design and fuel consumption; it is only the latest business jets like the Gulfstream V and Citation X that can reach Mach 0.9.

BEECH JET 400	899 km/h (599 m.p.h.)
LEARJET 55B	889 km/h (552 m.p.h.)
GULFSTREAM IV	936 km/h (582 m.p.h.)

RANGE

Business jets have a ratio of fuel to empty weight that is broadly proportional. Thus, larger aircraft like the Gulfstream IV have longer range than the smaller Beech 400A. However, a 3000-km (1864-mi.) range and the ability to seat at least eight passengers in comfortable standard is the minimum most manufacturers like to produce.

BEECH JET 400	2915 km (1811 mi.)
LEARJET 55B	4168 km (2590 mi.)
GULFSTREAM IV	7960 km (4946 mi.)

CAPACITY

The exact seating arrangements aboard a business jet depend on the customer's requirements, but Beech offers the 400A in a standard eight-seat layout. More generous club class seating can be fitted to the 400A by moving the forward door.

BEECH JET 400	8
LEARJET 55B	8
GULFSTREAM IV	10

BEECHCRAFT
1900

● Best-seller ● Commuter airliner ● Corporate transport

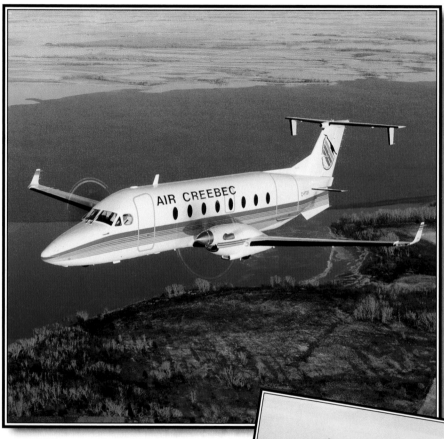

Beech re-entered the commuter and corporate airliner market in 1982, with its new 1900 airliner. Few manufacturers have more experience of building twin-engined, prop-driven transports than the company founded by Walter Beech in Wichita, Kansas, that is now part of the Raytheon Corporation. The Beech 1900 continues to be one of the best performers in the 19-seat category and a healthy order book reflects its popularity.

▲ While examples of the older Model 1900C and C-1 still soldier on, the Model 1900D has become a favourite of feeder airlines, especially in the US.

BEECHCRAFT 1900

▼ C-1 freighter
With its windows painted out, this Model 1900C-1 is flown as a freighter. A large cargo door on the port side allows cabin access.

▲ First 1900
Having performed much of the early flight testing, the prototype Model 1900 was retired in 1985.

◄ Beech 'down under'
Owned by Manerst Pty, this Model 1900D is flown by the Sydney Morning Post.

▼ Model 1900 upgrade
Having become an early operator of the Model 1900C, Continental Express later upgraded to the more capable Model 1900D.

◄ Airframe modifications
As the Model 1900C evolved into the 1900D, the aircraft acquired a profusion of additional fins, 'tailets' and horizontal surfaces.

FACTS AND FIGURES

➤ Beech flew the prototype for the Model 1900 series from the company's Wichita plant on 3 September 1982.

➤ The 'wet wing' of the Model 1900C-1 increased fuel capacity by 2593 litres (570 gal.).

➤ Mesa Airlines was the first airline to operate the improved 1900D model with a raised, 'stand-up' fuselage.

➤ Having ordered 78 Model 1900Ds by 1992, Mesa ordered a further 40 in 1994.

➤ In 1996 the Beech 1900D was available at US$4.775 million per aircraft.

Commuting around the world

Built initially as the Model 1900C Airliner, the Beech 1900 has been produced in several versions, selling well as a commuter-liner, corporate transport and military utility type. After certification by the US Federal Aviation Administration in November 1983, deliveries of the low-wing, twin-engined Model 1900 began in February 1984, with early orders including six for Resort Air of Missouri.

Changing standards within the US certification system led to production of the Model 1900C halting at 72 in 1993, by which time 173 of the improved Model 1900C-1 with additional fuel had also been sold.

In March 1989 Beech had announced its intention to launch the Model 1900D. This improved aircraft featured modified wings and ventral strakes, as well as a taller fuselage which allowed passengers to stand upright in the cabin. The new aircraft gained certification in March 1991 and was in production before the last of the Model 1900Cs had been delivered. The best selling of the Model 1900Ds is the 19-seat commuter liner, but an executive or corporate version is also available as a replacement for the Model 1900 Exec-Liner, which was derived from the earlier Model 1900C.

Below: A combination of winglets and a distinctly taller fuselage serves to differentiate the Model 1900D from all previous variants.

Above: Lifting off from the Beechcraft factory, this Model 1900D clearly shows the winglets of the type. Mesa Air is the largest 1900D operator.

Model 1900D

Type: twin-turboprop commuter airliner

Powerplant: two 954-kW (1,280-hp.) Pratt & Whitney Canada PT6A-67D turboprop engines

Maximum cruising speed: 533 km/h (331 m.p.h.) at 4875 m (16,000 ft.) and 6804 kg (15,000 lb.)

Range: 2778 km (1,726 mi.) at 1525 m (5,000 ft.), at long-range cruise power with reserves and 10 passengers

Service ceiling: 10,058 m (33,000 ft.)

Weights: empty 4815 kg (10,615 lb.); maximum take-off 7688 kg (16,949 lb.)

Accommodation: two pilots on flight deck, maximum of 19 passengers and 939 kg (2070 lb.) of baggage

Dimensions:
span	17.67 m (58 ft.)
length	17.63 m (57 ft. 10 in.)
height	4.72 m (15 ft. 6 in.)
wing area	28.80 m² (310 sq. ft.)

MODEL 1900D

USAir Express is one of many feeder lines which have found the capabilities of the Model 1900 well suited to their operations. Many of these airlines are affiliated to large international carriers.

Passenger seating is arranged in two single rows, to either side of a central aisle. Many airlines fly without a cabin attendant and customers may opt for a range of equipment levels, some of which gain extra space and save weight by omitting the toilet.

A small horizontal surface is mounted on both sides of the fuselage just ahead of the wing leading edge. This acts as a vortex generator, energising air at the leading edge to increase wing efficiency at high angles of attack and low air speeds.

Combined fuel capacity of the wing fuel tanks is 2528 litres (556 gal.). Refuelling is accomplished via a filler point in each wing leading edge, inboard of the engine nacelles. The PT6A-67D engines drive four-bladed Hartzell propellers which are fully reversible.

All Model 1900s have featured small fins known as 'tailets' beneath the tailplanes, but the 1900D introduced the ventral strakes, which improve directional stability and allow the aircraft to operate more comfortably in turbulent conditions.

Fixed auxiliary horizontal tail surfaces attached to the rear fuselage of all Model 1900s increase the aircraft's tolerance to centre of gravity changes. This allows greater flexibility of loading and layout.

USAir EXPRESS

N163YV

ACTION DATA

MAXIMUM CRUISING SPEED

Both of the American-built types have higher cruising speeds than the British Aerospace Jetstream 31. The Jetstream has proved very successful, nonetheless, but does not usually fly longer sectors where high speed is more important.

MODEL 1900D	533 km/h (331 m.p.h.)
METRO 23	542 km/h (337 m.p.h.)
JETSTREAM 31 489 km/h (304 m.p.h.)	

MAXIMUM PASSENGERS

With a potential load of up to 19 passengers, the Model 1900D and Jetstream allow airlines the option of offering a good number of seats during busy times or flying economically with fewer passengers. The Fairchild Metro 23 rarely flies with 20 seats.

MODEL 1900D 19

METRO 23 20

JETSTREAM 31 19

RANGE

With a full load of 19 passengers and fuel reserves, the Jetstream 31 falls far short of the range offered by the Metro 23. With a typical load of ten passengers the Model 1900D achieves 2778 km (1,726 mi.), but with full load range decreases to 1278 km (794 mi.).

MODEL 1900D 2778 km (1,726 mi.)

JETSTREAM 31 1191 km (740 mi.)

METRO 23 2065 km (1,283 mi.)

Raytheon's modern product range

PC-9 Mk II: Having won the US Joint Primary Aircraft Training System, the Beech/Pilatus PC-9 will be known as the Texan II.

KING AIR 350: First flown in 1988, the King Air 350 is a worthy successor to the highly successful King Air 300.

BEECHJET 400A: Based on the Mitsubishi Diamond, the Beechjet has won huge military orders as the T-1A Jayhawk.

HAWKER 1000: In 1993 Raytheon bought the 125 design from British Aerospace, producing the type under the Hawker name.

BEECHCRAFT

STARSHIP 1

● 21st-century executive transport ● Advanced canard design

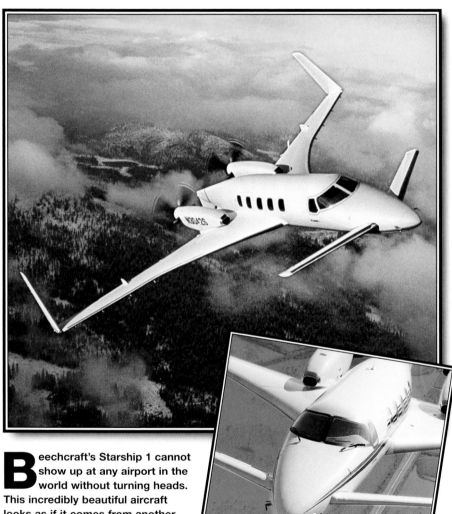

B eechcraft's Starship 1 cannot show up at any airport in the world without turning heads. This incredibly beautiful aircraft looks as if it comes from another planet, but it has the worldly duty of whisking business executives on important, long-distance trips. The Starship is a bold design, using the latest in lightweight materials to achieve speed and efficiency.

▲ The shape of things to come, or a blind avenue? Beechcraft's Starship is futuristic and a great performer, but it has not sold as well as predicted.

BEECHCRAFT STARSHIP 1

▲ Turning heads
Nothing in the skies looks remotely like the aptly-named Starship 1. The design came from America's futuristic aircraft guru, Burt Rutan.

▲ Tipsails
Lacking a conventional tail, the Starship 1 has rudders on the upturned fins at the end of each wing which enhance flight stability. Beechcraft calls these winglets 'tipsails'.

◀ Creature comforts
For the high-flying executive it's the interior that matters, and the Starship 1 is as plush as any business jet. Leather chairs, drinks bar and washroom facilities are all provided.

▲ Glass cockpit
For the pilots, the Starship 1 cockpit is as modern as the configuration. All data is presented on TV-style screens.

Canard cruiser ▶
Starship 1 has very competitive performance figures thanks to its state-of-the-art aerodynamics and fuel-efficient turboprops.

FACTS AND FIGURES

➤ Beechcraft are now offering their remaining Starships to military customers for use as special missions aircraft.

➤ Beech was known for conservative design until it created the trend-setting Starship 1.

➤ Most Starships are in the USA, but there is one based in Britain and one in Denmark.

➤ The Starship 2000Z model has improved performance and can cross the Atlantic non-stop.

➤ An 85-per-cent-sized prototype Starship was flown by Burt Rutan in August 1983.

➤ The first production Starship 1 was flown by Beechcraft in 1989.

PROFILE

A voyage into tomorrow

In 1983, a bold new aircraft for executive travel was launched when a small prototype of the Beech Starship 1 took to the air. No aircraft like it had been seen before. With its sword-like wing, pusher engines, and canard wings up front, the Starship looks and acts like a rocket ship.

On the inside, the Starship 1 is all space-age technology. Instead of standard metal construction techniques, the Starship 1 uses ultra-light composite and honeycomb materials. These are deceptively strong, but their light weight plays a major part in this

futuristic craft's amazing performance.

The first Starship 1 went into service in 1992, giving business users the ultimate power trip with its 21st-century performance. Beech fabricated 53 of these wonderful aircraft, but found the Starship 1 ahead of its time. Seen as too daring and too impertinent by stuffed

shirts in the traditional world of business, the Starship 1 is serving valiantly in the hands of a few forward-thinking users, but has now gone out of production.

Putting the engines at the back of the Starship 1 increases their effectiveness, and also makes the cabin very quiet.

The 'pusher' configuration with engines mounted well to the rear means that the passenger compartment is far enough forward to significantly reduce noise in the cabin.

The Starship is powered by two Pratt & Whitney Canada PT6 turboprops. These are mounted close together to reduce yaw in the event that one engine should fail.

STARSHIP 1

Designed to be the shape of private commercial aviation for the 21st century, the Beech Starship 1 is a bold step into the forefront of aviation technology.

In keeping with its futuristic design, the Starship has an 'all-glass' cockpit with 12 full colour and two monochrome display screens taking the place of conventional instruments.

The Starship's cabin is 5 m (16 ft. 5 in.) long, 1.68 m (5 ft. 6 in.) wide and 1.61 m (5 ft. 3 in.) high. Luxuriously equipped with reclining seats, it can accommodate eight passengers.

Since the Starship has no conventional tailfin, directional control is provided by fins called 'tipsails' mounted on the wingtips. These are both fitted with rudders.

All Starships are equipped with a weather avoidance radar in the nose.

The Starship's foreplanes are of variable geometry, sweeping forward 4° at low speeds and back 30° in high-speed cruise.

The single door at the forward end of the passenger compartment incorporates a built-in air stair.

The wing is composed of a sandwich of Nomex honeycomb, graphite epoxy and glass-reinforced plastic, with main spars of similar material bonded to the upper and lower skins. Aluminium is only used to mount the landing gear and the tipsails.

The swinging 'moustache'

Part of the highly advanced aerodynamics of the Starship is the canard foreplane, which moves to compensate for aerodynamic changes during different phases of the flight. Made from advanced composite materials, the foreplane is very strong and unlike metal will not corrode.

◄ **CRUISE CONFIGURATION**
In normal cruising flight the Starship has its canard foreplanes swept back at 30°. The sweepback is highly efficient for high-speed flight, and the amount of lift provided by the foreplanes balances that provided by the main wings. When in cruise mode vortex generators increase airflow over the elevators on the foreplane giving more positive control.

◄ **LOW-SPEED CONFIGURATION**
At low speed, the Starship uses flaps on the main wings to increase the amount of lift. These also increase the overall wing area by extending out from the wing. This upsets the delicate balance of the aircraft, so the canard foreplanes swing to 4° of forward sweep to provide extra lift themselves, thereby restoring the balance.

Starship 1

Type: eight-passenger fast business aircraft

Powerplant: two 895-kW (1200-hp.) Pratt & Whitney PT6-67A turboprop pusher engines driving McCauley five-bladed propellers

Maximum cruising speed: 621 km/h (386 m.p.h.) at 6700 m (21,982 ft.); economical cruise 546 km/h (339 m.p.h.) at 10,000 m (32,800 ft.)

Range: 2657 km (1,651 mi.) at economy cruise power; 2570 km (1,597 mi.) at maximum cruise

Service ceiling: 10,605 m (34,793 ft.)

Weights: empty 4574 kg (10,084 lb.); max take-off 6577 kg (14,500 ft.)

Accommodation: two crew (but operable by a single pilot) and seven/eight passengers

Dimensions:
span	16.58 m (54 ft. 5 in.)
length	14.05 m (46 ft. 1 in.)
height	3.96 m (13 ft.)
wing area	26.09 m² (281 sq. ft.)

ACTION DATA

ACCOMMODATION

LEARJET 36
Two crew and six passengers

STARSHIP 1
Two crew and eight passengers

P.180 AVANTI
Two crew and nine passengers

Executive aircraft have varying capacities. Most can be flown by one pilot, but almost invariably have a two-crew cockpit. Passenger capacity varies, but eight to 10 is about average.

RANGE

Most modern executive jets are designed to make long transcontinental flights, allowing busy executives to fly from New York to Chicago or from London to Rome non-stop. Perhaps the Starship's lack of range affected the sales figures, which were disappointing.

P.180 AVANTI 3187 km (1,980 mi.)
LEARJET 36 4600 km (2,858 mi.)
STARSHIP 1 2657 km (1,651 mi.)

MAXIMUM SPEED

LEARJET 36 **870 km/h (541 m.p.h.)**
STARSHIP 1 **621 km/h (386 m.p.h.)**
P.180 **500 km/h (311 m.p.h.)**

The Starship's advanced design enables it to perform as well as a jet but with all the economy of a propeller-driven machine. True jets like the Learjet are faster, but cost much more to run.

BOEING

247

● Faster than contemporary fighters ● First air-conditioned airliner

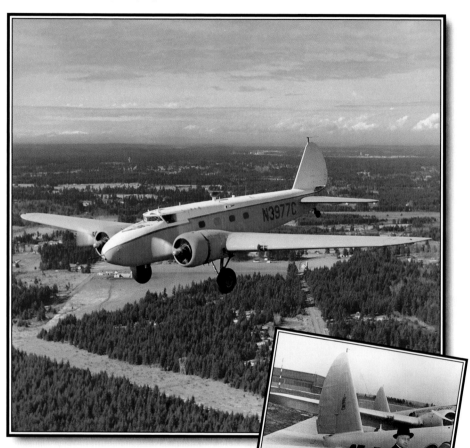

merica's first low-wing, multi-engined transport, the Boeing 247 was ahead of its time. However, several factors conspired to limit its commercial success, including the rapid rate of change in aeronautical design and aircraft performance in the 1930s. Less than six months after the 247's first flight, the Douglas DC-1 appeared, an aircraft that owed much to the Boeing and paved the way for the famous DC-3.

▲ Little more
than a month after the first
Boeing 247 was flown on 8 February 1933, it
had been handed over for airline use. By the
end of April, 14 more had been delivered.

PHOTO FILE

BOEING 247

▼ 100 million hours
Despite the loss of its mail contracts in 1934, United Air Lines became the first airline in the world to reach a total of 100 million flying hours (mainly on its Boeing 247s) on 17 June 1936.

▲ United Air Lines
United Air Lines (UAL), formed on 1 July 1931, established a fleet of 247s that helped it to reach new highs in passenger and freight revenues.

◀ Miltary service
During World War II the USAAF used 27 Boeing 247Ds for training.

Race success ▶
This United Airlines Boeing 247D achieved third place in the 1934 London to Melbourne air race.

◀ Lufthansa
Two model 247s were supplied to Lufthansa in 1934. They had the new 247D cockpit but kept the old sloping windshield.

FACTS AND FIGURES

➤ In 1934 a militarised version, the 247Y, with two nose-mounted 12.7-mm machine-guns, was delivered to China.

➤ When it first appeared, the 247 was nearly 80 km/h (50 m.p.h.) faster than other airliners.

➤ During World War II the RAF used a 247 for automatic landing system research.

➤ The sole Model 247A was specially modified as an executive transport and research machine for Pratt & Whitney.

➤ In Mexico a number of 247s remained in commercial use in the 1950s.

PROFILE

Boeing's fast airliner twin

When the 247 first entered service in March 1933 it was, above all, fast and comfortable. With United Air Lines it brought coast-to-coast schedules down from 28 hours to 20 hours 30 minutes. The aircraft cruised at 260 km/h (160 m.p.h.), rather than the 180–190 km/h (110–120 m.p.h.) of its Ford, Fokker and Boeing tri-motor predecessors. Its 10-seat cabin featured temperature control and noise insulation.

Almost the entire production run of 75 aircraft was delivered to the various airlines that made up United Air Lines. However, it was the close commercial tie-ups between UAL and Boeing that hampered attempts to sell more. When one competing airline attempted to purchase 247s and was turned down, it approached Douglas to build the DC-1, the prototype for the larger, faster DC-2.

Another handicap was the aircraft's low all-up weight. Boeing had wanted to build a 7257-kg (15,965-lb.) aircraft, but Boeing Air Transport pilots (one of the UAL companies) insisted that the aircraft would be too heavy for the Hornet engines specified. The design was therefore scaled down to 5443

kg (11,975 lb.), which limited its usefulness.

The last 13 247s were built to a faster 247D standard and most surviving early-build aircraft were eventually rebuilt as such. Some 27 saw wartime service with the USAAF as C-73s.

In 1942 the RAF received this Boeing 247 from Canada. It was used until 1948 in the development of the first automatic landing system.

In planform the tapered wing of the 247 resembled the wing of the later B-17 bomber. The balanced ailerons were constructed from aluminium alloy and a trim tab was fitted to the port aileron only.

Full cowlings were fitted to the engines of the 247D, replacing the cowling rings of earlier models. These, along with improved propellers and new gearing for the Wasp engines, made this variant of the 247 much faster.

Fixed tail surfaces had an aluminium alloy truss structure, with the rudder and elevators fabric-covered. The 247 was the first airliner with trim tabs on the elevators and rudder.

247D

United Air Line's *City of San Diego* is seen as it looked in 1941. First flown in May 1933, it was converted to 247D configuration with the new windscreen after an accident a month later.

The twin-engined Boeing 247 was the first airliner to use supercharged engines, and the first to be able to climb on one engine with a full passenger load. It was a trendsetter for the next generation of transports.

NC13326
U.S. MAIL-AM 1-11-1917
AIR EXPRESS

Retracting into the engine cowling, the 247's main landing gear was very robust. In an emergency the aircraft could land with the interconnected gear in any position from full up to full down.

The all-metal cantilever wing had interchangeable outer wings and wingtips. The wing stub was integral with the fuselage and the engine nacelle supports.

Ten passengers could be carried in the cabin, on five seats either side of a central aisle, with a jump seat for the stewardess at the rear. Baggage was carried in the nose and aft end.

247D

Type: civil transport aircraft

Powerplant: two 410-kW (550-hp.) Pratt & Whitney R-1340S-S1H-1G Wasp radials

Maximum speed: 322 km/h (200 m.p.h.)

Initial climb rate: 350 m/min (217 f.p.m.)

Range: 1199 km (745 mi.)

Service ceiling: 7740 m (25,400 ft.)

Weights: empty 4148 kg (9,125 lb.); maximum take-off 6192 kg (13,625 lb.)

Dimensions:
span 22.56 m (74 ft.)
length 15.72 m (51 ft. 7 in.)
height 3.60 m (11 ft. 10 in.)
wing area 77.68 m² (836 sq. ft.)

ACTION DATA

CRUISING SPEED

Boeing's 247 and Douglas's DC-2 offered a massive increase in speed (around 55 per cent) over previous airliners like the Tri-Motor. Each had powerful engines, an efficient wing and low-drag fuselage. Although speed was one of the most important criteria, each offered improved performance in all flight regimes.

MODEL 247D	304 km/h (188 m.p.h.)
DC-2	306 km/h (190 m.p.h.)
5-AT-D TRI-MOTOR	196 km/h (122 m.p.h.)

PASSENGERS

One area where the Model 247 was woefully inadequate was in passenger accommodation. The restriction was imposed by United Air Lines' insistence on a low all-up weight, a decision which was to have disastrous consequences for later commercial sales.

MODEL 247D	10 passengers
DC-2	14 passengers
5-AT-D TRI-MOTOR	13 passengers

RANGE

The Model 247 offered a huge improvement in range over the Tri-Motor, but was out-ranged itself by its rival, the DC-2, which almost doubled the Tri-Motor's reach. In an era of rapidly expanding air travel, speed and range became the driving factors and any successful design reaped the rewards.

MODEL 247D
1199 km (745 mi.)

DC-2
1609 km (1,000 mi.)

5-AT-D TRI-MOTOR
885 km (550 mi.)

1930s airliners

DE HAVILLAND DH.91 ALBATROSS: The DH.91 was a four-engined, fast and luxurious airliner with distinctive twin fins and rudders.

DOUGLAS DC-2: Successful rival to the Boeing 247, the DC-2 was developed for TWA and first flown in 1933. It led to the DC-3.

FORD TRI-MOTOR: In 1926 Ford flew the first prototype of its highly successful Tri-Motor. Some aircraft survived into the 1990s.

JUNKERS Ju 52/3M: Europe's most successful airliner of the 1930s, the Ju 52/3m also served with the wartime Luftwaffe.

BOEING

307 STRATOLINER

● Long-range airliner ● Military transport ● Only 10 built

From some angles, especially from above, the Boeing 307 had a familiar look. The reason for this is that the Stratoliner had a large number of features in common with Boeing's bomber of the same era, the B-17 Flying Fortress. As originally built and flown, this civil airliner was simply a B-17 with a new fuselage and built-in pressurisation system. The Stratoliner was not a commercial success, but some of the 10 aircraft built were used for decades.

▲ **In military**
service the Stratoliner was known as the C-75. Modifications to the airliner included the removal of the pressurisation system and the installation of a large fuel tank.

PHOTO FILE

BOEING 307 STRATOLINER

▼ **Ecuadorian airline**
Between 1951 and 1954 this ex-Pan Am Stratoliner was operated by Aerovias Ecuatoriana on routes between Ecuador and Miami. The aircraft later served with Quaker City Airways.

▲ **Fortress roots**
Many of the Stratoliner's features, including the wings, nacelles, powerplant and original tail surfaces, were based on the B-17C Flying Fortress bomber.

◀ **Test flight**
A pilot warms up the engines of the prototype before a test flight from Boeing Field, Seattle. This aircraft was later lost during a test flight for a foreign airline.

▼ **Stratoliner at war**
In 1942 TWA's five SA-307Bs were requisitioned by the Army Air Transport Command. In two years of service they flew more than 12 million kilometres (7 million miles) and made 3000 ocean crossings.

▲ **Control panel**
The cockpit layout of the Pan Am S-307s was fairly advanced for the time. It included duplicate sets of flight instruments and a Sperry autopilot.

FACTS AND FIGURES

➤ The first 307 Stratoliner was lost during a test flight before it could be delivered to Pan American.

➤ Pan American's three 307s were named *Comet*, *Flying Cloud* and *Rainbow*.

➤ The advertised price of a brand-new Stratoliner in 1938 was $315,000.

➤ Three French-registered Stratoliners were the only civil aircraft allowed to fly into Hanoi during the Vietnam War.

➤ Howard Hughes' personal 307 was fitted with a luxurious interior costing $250,000.

➤ The only surviving complete 307 is on display at the Pima County Air Museum.

PROFILE

Boeing's pre-war long-range liner

Engineering work by Boeing aimed at producing a civil transport based on the Flying Fortress bomber resulted in the 307 Stratoliner. The aircraft was built with a circular-section fuselage which was pressurised to provide a cabin altitude of 2440 m (8,000 ft.) when the aircraft was actually flying at 4480 m (14,700 ft.). This enabled the Stratoliner to operate with passengers at about 6000 m (20,000 ft.), an altitude well above most turbulence.

Three Stratoliners were delivered to Pan American World Airways, five to

Transcontinental & Western Airlines (TWA), and one to millionaire industrialist Howard Hughes. In fact, when Hughes' initial attempt to purchase a Stratoliner was thwarted by Boeing's commitment to two airlines, the millionaire bought control of one of the airlines, TWA, and diverted the first of its aircraft for his use. Hughes was a brilliant, eccentric figure but his plans to use the Stratoliner for a round-the-world record flight were cut short by the advent of World War II, and the aircraft ended up being his personal luxury taxi. The other

This SB-307B was acquired by Howard Hughes and was converted into an ultra-deluxe aircraft. It was later damaged in a hurricane and was converted into a houseboat.

Boeing 307s enjoyed a brief but successful stint in commercial aviation before being impressed into duties supporting the US armed forces during the war.

After the war, Boeing 307s were used by operators in Ecuador, Honduras, Saudi Arabia and Vietnam.

After the loss of the prototype it was decided to change the B-17C's vertical tail surfaces and install a new rudder and fin. These became a Boeing trademark on later aircraft.

The entirely new fuselage had a completely circular cross-section which gave sufficient room to accommodate cargo and passengers comfortably.

SA-307B Stratoliner

Type: high-altitude long-range transport

Powerplant: four 670-kW (900-hp.) Wright GR-1820 Cyclone radial piston engines

Maximum speed: 396 km/h (245 m.p.h.)

Cruising speed: 354 km/h (222 m.p.h.)

Initial climb rate: 366 m/min (6,527 f.p.m.)

Range: 3846 km (2,390 mi.)

Service ceiling: 7985 m (26,200 ft.)

Weights: empty 13,068 kg (42,000 lb.); maximum take-off 19,050 kg (28,750 lb.)

Accommodation: flight crew of five, plus up to 33 passengers in VIP configuration

Dimensions:
span 32.61 m (107 ft. 3 in.)
length 22.66 m (74 ft. 4 in.)
height 6.34 m (20 ft. 9 in.)
wing area 138.05 m² (1,485 sq. ft.)

SA-307B STRATOLINER

TWA had the largest fleet of Stratoliners and was the best-known operator. This aircraft received the spurious serial NX1940 for a sales trip. Its true identity was NX19906.

The flightdeck accommodated captain and co-pilot side-by-side, with a flight engineer and wireless operator situated behind. The navigator sat in a separate cabin behind the flightdeck.

Transcontinental & Western Airlines Stratoliners could carry up to 33 passengers in the pressurised cabin, with a galley situated at the rear. In some configurations, four convertible travel compartments were situated along the starboard side.

Standard Stratoliners were powered by four Wright Cyclone GR-1820-G102 engines of 670 kW (900 hp.). Howard Hughes had his aircraft fitted with more powerful 857-kW (1,150-hp.) Wright R-2600 Twin Cyclones.

The Stratoliner's wing was based on that of the B-17C. Extra leading-edge slots were built into the wingtips and the span was increased by 99 cm (36 in.).

ACTION DATA

PASSENGERS

Of these three pre-war airliners the Stratoliner could carry the most passengers in high-density configuration. However, on longer flights the aircraft would often be fitted with travel compartments, which reduced the capacity but increased passenger comfort.

SA-307B STRATOLINER 33
DH.91 ALBATROSS 22
Fw 200B 26

CRUISING SPEED

With its more streamlined shape the Fw 200 was easily the fastest of this trio. The Fw 200's speed and range were invaluable when it became a maritime patrol aircraft during World War II.

SA-307B STRATOLINER 354 km/h (222 m.p.h.)
DH.91 ALBATROSS 338 km/h (210 m.p.h.)
Fw 200B 390 km/h (242 m.p.h.)

RANGE

The Stratoliner's range allowed it to cover vast distances without the inconvenience of having to land and refuel. Its long range was put to good use when flying trans-oceanic routes with the US armed forces during World War II. The Albatross was let down by its lack of range and just seven were built.

Fw 200B 3219 km (2,000 mi.)
SA-307B STRATOLINER 3846 km (2,390 mi.)
DH.91 ALBATROSS 1674 km (1,040 mi.)

From bomber to airliner

■ **AVRO 691 LANCASTRIAN:** This was a high-speed, long-range transport conversion of the famous Lancaster bomber. Operators included the Canadian government and BOAC.

■ **BOEING 377 STRATOCRUISER:** Based on the B-29 Superfortress wartime bomber, the Stratocruiser served with the USAF, major US airlines and the British airline BOAC.

■ **TUPOLEV Tu-104 'CAMEL':** This airliner derivative of the Tu-16 'Badger' bomber could accommodate up to 100 passengers. About 200 were built and the aircraft served until 1981.

■ **TUPOLEV Tu-114 'CLEAT':** Derived from the mighty Tu-95 'Bear', the Tu-114 could carry up to 220 passengers and was the world's largest airliner prior to the Boeing 747.

BOEING

377 STRATOCRUISER

● Derived from the B-29 ● Luxury airliner ● Cargo lifter

The Boeing 377 set a majestic standard of air travel for the post-war world. Able to handle the New York to London route in just a little over 10 hours, the Stratocruiser pampered its clients. Those who savoured the food, drink and fine service – including sleeping berths for many – remember nostalgically that it was better than anything offered today. Ironically, this legendary servant of the skies owed its origins to the B-29 bomber.

▲ The combination of a pressurised fuselage and the ability to cruise at high speed above the turbulent lower atmosphere meant that the Boeing 377 offered new standards of comfort.

BOEING 377 STRATOCRUISER

▼ USAF transport
The USAF's C-97 Stratofreighter was in fact the forerunner to the civil Stratocruiser, and prototype trials of the airliner were conducted using an XC-97, of which three were built.

Mass ▶ production
Such was the demand for military Stratofreighters in the 1950s that the aircraft was produced at the rate of one every working day. The 500th was completed in February 1954.

▲ Bomber ancestry
The Stratocruiser's B-29 ancestry was obvious. The Stratofreighter surpassed all previous USAF transports in performance, showing just how advanced the B-29 airframe had been in 1944.

Freight loader ▶
Stratofreighters were still in service long after the passenger versions had all but disappeared from commercial routes.

◀ Crew cabin
The roomy cockpit seated two pilots with full dual controls, a navigator, flight engineer and usually a radio operator.

◀ Cold comfort
Automatic air-conditioning meant that passengers could travel in perfect comfort, even in freezing weather.

FACTS AND FIGURES

➤ When Pan American paid $24.5 million for 20 Stratocruisers, it was the biggest purchase of civil airliners up to that time.

➤ The first aircraft in the series was a military XC-97, which first flew in 1944.

➤ The KC-97 tanker version saw active service with Israel in the 1967 war.

➤ Boeing president Bill Allen decided to build 50 aircraft at the company's risk before airlines invested in the Model 377.

➤ The first Stratocruiser flew from Seattle to Washington DC in 6 hours 4 minutes.

➤ About 15 Stratocruisers were operated by Israel as military freighters.

Sky cruising in comfort

In 1942, Boeing won an Army contract for three XC-97 military transport prototypes based on the B-29 Superfortress but with a pressurised 'double-deck' fuselage optimised for freight and passengers. The C-97 became successful and the KC-97 tanker served the US Air Force and Air National Guard service to the end of the 1970s. But Boeing always saw the design as an airliner superior to the contemporary Lockheed Constellation and

Douglas DC-4, and after the war 55 examples of the civil Stratocruiser entered service with airlines like American, BOAC, Northwest, Pan American and United.

In an age when air travel was only for the rich, the Stratocruiser gave its passengers sheer opulence: well-dressed passengers lounged around the stairway between decks sipping cocktails from the lower deck bar. Later, the Stratocruiser became an unglamorous workhorse – a Red Cross flying ambulance in the 1969/70 Biafra War and a freighter hauling heavy tools for a petroleum

company in Central America. A few examples continued to fly in out-of-the-way parts of the world into the 1990s.

Right: The combination of a large, sleek airframe and features like cocktail bars were very glamorous, but were destined to die out as the age of mass air travel began.

Above: America's urgent demand for a long-range civil transport resulted in the Stratocruiser being built alongside military B-50s at the Seattle plant.

Above: Boeing began 40 years of dominance of the world airline market with the futuristic Stratocruiser.

377 Stratocruiser

Type: long-range commercial transport

Powerplant: four 2610-kW (3,500-hp.) Pratt & Whitney R-4360-TSB-6 Wasp Major 28-cylinder radial piston engines with General Electric superchargers

Maximum speed: 604 km/h (375 m.p.h.)

Cruising speed: 547 km/h (340 m.p.h.)

Range: 6759 km (4,588 mi.)

Weights: empty 38,071 kg (83,756 lb.); loaded 67,133 kg (147,693 lb.)

Accommodation: flight crew of four; typically 50 first-class or up to 117 tourist-class passengers; others with 40 first-class sleeping facilities; some with a mix of 23 first-class plus 40 tourist-class passengers

Dimensions: span 43.05 m (141 ft.)
length 33.63 m (110 ft.)
height 11.68 m (38 ft.)
wing area 164.25 m² (1,767 sq. ft.)

MODEL 377 STRATOCRUISER

This Boeing Stratocruiser entered BOAC service in 1950, and was named RMA Cabot. The aircraft served for eight years, and was then returned to Boeing who sold the machine to Transocean Air Lines.

The tall tail was an almost direct copy of the B-50 unit. The rear portion of the fin and rudder could fold sideways to allow hangar storage or maintenance.

A galley with electric ovens and refrigerators was installed in the rear of the aircraft. A water tank was located at the base of the fin.

The tailplane featured thermal anti-icing. Surprisingly for such a large aircraft, the control surfaces were still fabric covered; they were also mass-balanced to ease control.

The principal modification to the Stratofreighter involved fitting large loading doors and an internal ramp. An electrical cargo hoist ran along the entire length of the fuselage.

The main fuselage consisted of an inverted 'figure of eight' section, sometimes referred to as the 'double bubble', designed specifically for the requirements of pressurisation.

A stairway linked the upper and lower decks, with the cocktail bar at the foot of the stairs.

Power was provided by the same engines as those fitted to the B-50 Superfortress, namely the massive Pratt & Whitney R-4360 Wasp Major, a 28-cylinder four-row radial.

Sleeping berths were fitted in the forward upper fuselage, with a ladies' dressing room located ahead of it. Baggage was stored in the hold below. The forward seats in the main cabin could also be converted to berths.

ACTION DATA

SERVICE CEILING
The B-29's wing was optimised for high-altitude flight, and the Stratocruiser inherited its excellent performance at altitude. It could cruise above bad weather, and most of the competition too.

MODEL 377 STRATOCRUISER 9800 m (32,000 ft.)
DC-7 7620 m (25,000 ft.)
B-29 CONSTELLATION 7500 m (24,500 ft.)

PASSENGERS
The unusual 'figure of eight' fuselage gave the Stratocruiser a high capacity. The DC-7 and B-29 Constellation carried almost as many passengers, but the accommodation was less luxurious.

MODEL 377 STRATOCRUISER 117
DC-7 102
B-29 CONSTELLATION 107

RANGE
The broad fuselage meant that the Stratocruiser suffered more aerodynamic drag than the narrow-bodied DC-7 and Constellation, and therefore had slightly less range.

DC-7 7596 km (4,710 mi.)
B-29 CONSTELLATION 7710 km (4,780 mi.)
MODEL 377 STRATOCRUISER 6759 km (4,588 mi.)

BOEING

707

● First US jet airliner ● Private venture gamble ● Four decades of production

▲ Built as a private venture by Boeing, the Model 707 airliner revolutionised air transport after PanAm introduced it on scheduled services from New York to Europe on 26 October 1958. Over the next decade major airlines around the world moved into jet power.

The Boeing 707 was the first successful American jet airliner. Moreover, it was a genuine trailblazer, opening a new era of speed and comfort to travellers around the globe. With its four, low-slung jet engines and graceful lines, this aircraft was built for transcontinental service. However, during the decade after it first entered service in 1958, the 707 ended up spanning the world's oceans and became a familiar sight at airports worldwide.

PHOTO FILE

BOEING 707

First of a long line ▶
The very first Boeing 707, appropriately registered N70700, was in fact a Boeing Model 367-80. It was flown for the first time on 15 July 1954 and remained in use as a test aircraft for the next 30 years.

▲ Advanced 320C
This World Airways Model 707-373C is representative of the more advanced 320C versions that did not have the underfin.

▼ American Airlines big order
When American Airlines ordered 30 Boeing 707-123s on 8 November 1955 it enabled the manufacturer to start full-scale production.

▲ Braniff's sprightly 707-220
The US airline Braniff bought the shorter fuselage Model 707-220 that was fitted with the more powerful Pratt & Whitney JT4A engines. These gave it a sprightly take-off performance particularly at hot-and-high airports in South America.

◀ Lufthansa's improved 330B
A fleet of 12 of these bigger, long-range JT3D-3 turbofan-powered 707-330Bs was operated by Lufthansa on intercontinental routes from 1964. This version had new leading- and trailing-edge wing flaps, greater span and modified wingtips.

FACTS AND FIGURES

➤ The first Boeing 707 was actually rolled upside-down on one test flight.

➤ The same prototype flew from Seattle to Baltimore non-stop on 11 March 1957 at an average speed of 985 km/h (611 m.p.h.).

➤ Pan American's first 707-120 flew on 20 December 1957.

➤ Boeing engineers calculated that the 707 used 1710 km (1,060 mi.) of wiring.

➤ Dwight D. Eisenhower was the first US president to have a jet aircraft, a 707-320B.

➤ The purchase of 820 KC-135/Model 717 tankers for the USAF helped to cut the cost of the 707 to the world's airlines.

PROFILE

Boeing's famous family

Boeing entered the commercial jet age in 1954 with the 367-80, its prototype for the incredible 707. Pan American World Airways made history when it purchased jet airliners a year later, investing heavily in the Boeing 707 and contemporary Douglas DC-8.

The 707 became one of the most successful civilian transports ever built, with production exceeding 800 aircraft. A beautiful but practical design, which brought both glamour and common sense to air travel, the 707 was flown by virtually all of the West's major airlines and appeared with several powerplants. A few 707s found military roles as VIP transports, AWACS and communications aircraft.

When the 707 entered service passengers could not believe how smooth flying could be compared to propeller-driven aircraft. Now these wonderful jetliners of the 1960s are referred to as 'narrow body' ships because they gave way, beginning in the 1970s, to 'wide cabin' types like the 747 and DC-10. But every jetliner that ever flew, regardless of its size

or shape, owes a debt to the Boeing 707 which came along just when it was needed.

Above: BOAC operated the longer range Model 707-320. This had a new, more efficient wing, a longer fuselage to seat 189 passengers and greater fuel capacity. The 707-320 was fitted with powerful Rolls-Royce Conway turbofans.

Below: The Boeing 707 became the standard long-distance airliner for almost all of the world's major airlines. It is a testament to the superb initial design that a large number of 707s remain in civilian use 40 years after the type entered service.

707-320C

Type: four-engine long-range commercial transport

Powerplant: four 84.52-kN (18,900-lb.-thrust) Pratt & Whitney JT3D-7 turbofan engines

Maximum speed: 1009 km/h (625 m.p.h.)

Cruising speed: 885 km/h (549 m.p.h.)

Service ceiling: 11,890 m (39,000 ft.)

Range: 9262 km (5,742 mi.)

Weights: operating empty 66,406 kg (146,093 lb.); empty weight cargo version 64,002 kg (140,804 lb.); maximum take-off 151,318 kg (332,900 lb.)

Accommodation: two pilots, flight engineer, flight attendants; seating for 147 (14 first-class, 133 coach) to 219 (high density) passengers, plus 48.14 m³ (1,700 cu. ft.) of luggage; plus 2800 kg (6,160 lb.) of cargo

Dimensions:
span	44.42 m (145 ft. 8 in.)
length	46.61 m (152 ft. 10 in.)
height	12.93 m (42 ft. 5 in.)
wing area	283.35 m² (3,049 sq. ft.)

MODEL 720

The Boeing 720 was an intermediate-range development of the 707. It had a shorter fuselage and more efficient wings and engine.

The flight crew comprised a captain and first officer, with room for a navigator seated behind the captain and the flight engineer on the right.

The external outline, dimensions and controls of the Model 720 were almost exactly the same as the older Model 120. This meant that similar flight decks, passenger cabins and facilities could be fitted and were interchangeable.

The main external feature of the Model 720 was a modified wing leading edge giving increased sweepback and decreased thickness. This new wing gave greater fuel efficiency and a higher cruise speed.

Power was provided by four Pratt & Whitney JT3C-7 turbojets mounted in pods beneath the wings.

The 720 had an all-metal tail structure with an electrically and manually operated variable incidence tailplane. A ventral fin was fitted as standard.

The dual nose-wheel undercarriage unit retracts forwards into the fuselage.

Four-wheel main undercarriage bogies retract inwards into wingroot fairings.

IRISH INTERNATIONAL AIRLINES — EI-ALA

ACTION DATA

MAXIMUM CRUISING SPEED

Four-jet airliners could cruise at high subsonic speeds, and a DC-8 was even dived past the sound barrier. Despite claims over speed advantage, all these aircraft were about equal.

MODEL 707-120B 1000 km/h (620 m.p.h.)
DC-8-30 952 km/h (590 m.p.h.)
CV 990 982 km/h (609 m.p.h.)

MAXIMUM PASSENGERS

Of prime importance for these airliners was their ability to carry greater numbers of passengers. The Boeing and DC-8 had a big advantage over Convair.

MODEL 707-120B 189 PASSENGERS
DC-8-30 173 PASSENGERS
CV 990 121 PASSENGERS

RANGE

Another advantage of the 707 was its range, especially over the early DC-8s which had less economical engines. These big, four-engined airliners were already flying routes far beyond the capability of smaller airliners like the Comet, and it was not until the advent of the Boeing 747 that airliners had greater range.

MODEL 707-120B 11,120 km (6,894 mi.)
DC-8-30 9605 km (5,955 mi.)
CV 990 6920 km (4,290 mi.)

Early four-jet airliners

■ DE HAVILLAND DH.106 COMET: First of the jet airliners, the Comet 1 took to the air in 1949 and initial tests were very positive. However, in 1953 the first of a number of structural failures occurred, causing the Comet to miss out on commercial success.

■ CONVAIR CV 880: With a narrow-body five-seat abreast design, the Convair was actually much smaller than the Boeing, and was not a great commercial success, with only 65 built. The CV 990 was a modified version, but just 37 were produced.

■ DOUGLAS DC-8: Fiercest rival of the Boeing 707, the DC-8 did not have quite the same success but nevertheless was a capable design. When re-engined with efficient turbofans, it made a final comeback as a cargo aircraft in the late 1980s.

BOEING

727

● Three-engined ● Best-selling airliner ● Freight carrier

Boeing gambled with the 727. One of the first commercial tri-jets, the 727 redeemed the wager and became the world's best-selling jetliner. Put into service in February 1964, the 727 was an instant sensation with flight crews and passengers. Three decades later, after 101 customers purchased 727s from Boeing and dozens more picked them up second-hand, the Boeing 727 has now carried 3.9 billion passengers – more than any other jet.

▲ The 727's great strength was its fine 'hot and high' performance, easily capable of operations out of high-elevation airports like La Paz in Bolivia.

BOEING 727

◄ **Into the sunset**
Although the 727 is now facing limitations because of new noise regulations, 'hush kits' have been developed to ensure that the aircraft will be around in numbers for many years to come.

▼ **Cargo-dropping**
Boeing carried out experiments with dropping freight at low speeds, in an attempt to sell a military airlift version.

▲ **Tail checks**
Routine maintenance on modern commercial jets usually takes place at night, to allow maximum aircraft usage in peak daylight hours.

▲ **Interior**
The 727 used the Boeing 707's fuselage cross-section, with room for overhead lockers and five- or six-abreast seats.

▲ **Going up**
Working on the 727 needs a large amount of scaffolding and a 'cherry picker' to reach the high-mounted engines and tail.

▲ **Test programme**
A test pilot prepares to take the 727 prototype on its next flight. A refuelling hose is plugged into the rear fuselage.

FACTS AND FIGURES

➤ The Boeing 727 first flew at Renton Field near Seattle on 9 February 1963.

➤ In November 1963, a 727 completed a 121,000-km (75,000-mi.) world tour.

➤ Federal Express received the final new-build Boeing 727 (a 727-200F freighter) on 3 September 1984.

➤ The first 727 used by United Air Lines was donated in 1991 to the Museum of Flight in Seattle.

➤ The 727 was the first jetliner with built-in airstairs and single-point refuelling.

➤ The 727 was the first jetliner to operate at the airport in La Paz, Bolivia.

PROFILE

Tri-jet success from Boeing

The jet age began in 1952 with the entry into service of the British Comet and matured in 1958 with the arrival of the Boeing 707, but no jetliner of that era approached the sales record of the versatile, reliable Boeing 727.

Designed specifically for short- and medium-haul operations, the 727's high-lift wing and rear-mounted engines meant that it was the first aircraft capable of bringing regular scheduled jet travel to small city airfields with runways as short as 1550 m (5085 ft.).

Boeing hoped to sell 250 aircraft. The actual number of 727s delivered was nearly eight times that figure – 1,831, in a production run which lasted from 1962 to 1984. The 727 flies today in 17 passenger and freight versions.

There are some military users of the 727, but this classic airliner has made its mark as a hard-working servant of civil air commerce.

The 727 entered service in 1964, and by 1967 it was the most widely used airliner in the world. Air Canada operated the type on domestic and American routes.

Airlines like Texas-based Braniff embraced the 727 as a highly effective, fuel-efficient and reliable workhorse. It could fly several route sectors each day, maximising passenger carriage and increasing profit.

727-200

Type: medium-range passenger or cargo airliner

Powerplant: three Pratt & Whitney 64.50-kN JT8D-9A or 77.38-kN (25,889-lb.-thrust) JT8D-15 turbofans

Maximum cruise speed: 964 km/h (598 m.p.h.)

Range: 4400 km (2,728 mi.)

Service ceiling: 10,000 m (33,000 ft.)

Weights: empty 45,168 kg (99,370 lb.); loaded 86,405 kg (190,090 lb.)

Accommodation: three crew plus flight attendants; maximum 189 single-class passengers; typical load of 14 first class and 131 tourist class

Dimensions: span 32.92 m (108 ft.)
length 46.69 m (153 ft.)
height 10.36 m (34 ft.)
wing area 157.90 m² (1,699 sq. ft.)

MODEL 727-200

CS-TBW was the 13th Boeing 727 delivered to Transportes Aereos Portugueses, or TAP. The 727's old engines mean that it does not compare favourably with the latest generation of jets, although it remains a useful performer thanks to its trouble-free reliability.

The rear-mounted three-engine layout was chosen so that the wings were free of engine mountings and could be designed with new features.

With a fuselage width the same as the 707 (and the later 737 and 757), the 727 can seat economy-class passengers six abreast.

The wing fuel tank in the outboard wing contains 31,000 litres (8,000 gal.) of fuel.

The central air intake feeds air to the third engine via a long duct.

The central engine is located on the centreline in the rear of the fuselage.

Most 727s soldier on with the reliable but noisy and uneconomical Pratt & Whitney JT8D turbofan. Rolls-Royce has proposed re-engining Delta Airlines' 727s with its advanced Tay engine.

The 727 has the three-man cockpit, including a flight engineer, which was standard in the 1960s.

Boeing stretched the 727-100's fuselage by 6 metres to produce the 727-200 series, with maximum passenger capacity increased from 131 to 189.

The 727 wing features ailerons and spoilers for roll control, and Krüger flaps for high efficiency at low speed. The high-lift devices fitted were the most advanced of their day.

Many airlines are fitting 'hush-kit' noise suppression systems to their 727 engines to enable the aircraft to continue operating after 'Stage Three' noise abatement regulations come into force worldwide in the late 1990s.

ACTION DATA

MAXIMUM CRUISE SPEED

The first generation of tri-jets were as fast as their four-jet contemporaries, even though they had 25 per cent less power. They were also far more economical; fitting the engines at the back cuts drag and leaves the wing clear and uncluttered for efficient lift.

MODEL 727-200	964 km/h (598 m.p.h.)
TRIDENT	960 km/h (595 m.p.h.)
Tu-154 'CARELESS'	950 km/h (590 m.p.h.)

RANGE

The tri-jets were not designed for intercontinental flying; they were intended to service routes ranging from 200 km (125 mi.) to 3000 km (1,860 mi.) in length. The ability to use second-line airports and make fast turnarounds was more important than a huge range.

| 727-200 4400 km (2,780 mi.) | TRIDENT 5000 km (3,105 mi.) | Tu-154 3900 km (2,418 mi.) |

The tri-jet rivals

■ **HAWKER SIDDELEY TRIDENT:** An almost exact contemporary of the 727, the Trident was at least as good a flyer, but its smaller capacity and less effective short-field ability meant that it lost out in the sales battles with the Boeing jet.

■ **TUPOLEV Tu-154:** Tupolev engineers copied Boeing's high-lift wing for their tri-jet to enable operations from rough Siberian airfields. Allied to more powerful engines, this gave the 154 the required performance, but economy was never great.

■ **DOUGLAS DC-10:** The explosion in demand for air travel in the 1960s saw the first wide-bodies appear only six years after the 727. Designed to fly similar routes to the 189-seat Boeing jet, the DC-10 could carry up to 380 passengers.

BOEING

737 SERIES 100–500

● Short-haul transport ● Twin-jet ● World's best-selling airliner

Boeing's chunky Model 737 is the world's most popular twin-engined airliner, and has been operated in greater numbers than any commercial aircraft since the classic DC-3. Passengers are seated in a fuselage based on the Boeing 707, wide enough to accommodate six abreast in comfort. The 737's wing provides good lift and handling, and permits this workhorse to use even small-town airfields.

▲ The 737's wide fuselage has enough room to carry a large number of passengers in a relatively short aircraft, without sacrificing passenger comfort.

BOEING 737 SERIES 100–500

▲ Short-haul workhorse
The Boeing 737 was designed for frequent short-haul flights. Airlines find the latest variants very cost-effective on busy domestic and European routes.

New engines ▼
To fit bigger engines on the low-slung 737 wing, it was necessary to flatten the nacelles.

▲ Twin-jet
The wing-mounted engines on the 737 went against the 1960s trend towards rear-mounted jets, but most current jets follow the 737 pattern.

Spacious cabin ▶
Because it uses the 707's hull cross-section the Model 737 comfortably seats six abreast, whereas its 1960s rivals could only seat five.

▲ Mass production
The 737 is the world's most popular airliner. More than 3100 have been built, and orders continue to flood in.

Family of jets ▶
The latest variants of the 737 are the stretched 737-400 and the smaller 737-500.

FACTS AND FIGURES

➤ The 737 has passed Boeing's 727 and the competing DC-9/MD-80 to become the world's best-selling airliner.

➤ In all, 3100 Boeing 737s have been delivered; 700 are in the air at any one time.

➤ In 55 million flights, the 737 fleet has carried 4.24 billion passengers.

➤ The Boeing 737-300, -400 and -500 now in production are powered by 97.86-kN (22,000 lb thrust) CFM56-3 engines.

➤ Nineteen Boeing 737s, called CT-43s, are used by the USAF for navigator training.

➤ Indonesia employs the 737 Surveiller for maritime patrol.

PROFILE

Short-haul stalwart

Following the popular 707 and 727, the now-familiar Boeing 737 began enriching air commerce soon after the first aircraft flew on 9 April 1967. From a business standpoint, this twin-engined jet was a stroke of genius. Almost 3000 of these great aircraft are flying, or will fly, with several dozen airlines.

Lufthansa had a strong role in inspiring and backing the 737 and was the first company to offer passenger service, beginning on 10 February 1968. Newer versions with longer fuselage and bigger engines

have enabled the Boeing 737 to serve a wider diversity of airfields and operators. Though only two countries (the USA and Indonesia) have found a military duty for this well-known civil servant, others use the 737 as a VIP transport.

To pilots, the Boeing 737 is a super ship to fly, offering excellent handling and performance. The 737 is regarded as the best aircraft in its class, and is likely to be moving passengers in comfort for many years to come.

The 737 was built with the same fuselage cross-section as the Boeing 707 and the 727. Not only did this ease the company's manufacturing requirements, but it also gave the 737 a wider body than its rivals.

The short undercarriage and low-set wings mean that the 737's cabin is not too much of a climb for passengers using airstairs.

Putting the engines on the wings meant that the fuselage could be more lightly built, the weight saved being used to carry as many as 10 extra passengers.

Very few 737s have been delivered for military use. Among the few exceptions are the 737 Surveillers developed by Boeing for the Indonesian air force. They are equipped with a Motorola side-looking radar.

737-400

Type: short-/medium-range transport

Powerplant: two 97.86-kN (22,000 lb thrust) CFM International CFM56-3C turbofan engines

Maximum speed: 935 km/h (581 m.p.h.) at 7165 m (23,500 ft.)

Cruising speed: 900 km/h (559 m.p.h.)

Range: 5000 km (3,107 mi.)

Weights: empty 33,434 kg (73,709 lb.); loaded 62,822 kg (138,499 lb.)

Accommodation: typically, 146 passengers in two classes

Dimensions:
span 28.88 m (28 ft. 7 in.)
length 36.45 m (119 ft. 7 in.)
height 11.13 m (36 ft. 6 in.)
wing area 105.40 m² (1,135 sq. ft.)

MODEL 737-200

The first major variant of the Boeing 737, the Model 200 was built in large numbers. More than 1100 examples were delivered between 1967 and 1988.

Early 737s included a flight engineer in addition to two pilots, but a two-man flight crew soon became the norm.

The 737 was initially powered by two Pratt & Whitney JT8D turbofans. More than 1000 examples of the 737-200 were sold before larger and more fuel-efficient engines became standard.

Passenger capacity aboard the 737-200 varied between 100 and 130, depending on the proportion of economy-class to business-class passengers.

Amberair **G-BOSA**

A tiny auxiliary power unit at the base of the tail allows the 737 to keep lights and air conditioning running and to start main engines without the need for ground support.

ACTION DATA

MAXIMUM CRUISING SPEED

737-400	900 km/h (559 m.p.h.)	
A320	905 km/h (562 m.p.h.)	
MD-80	885 km/h (550 m.p.h.)	

The 737 has a maximum speed of about 930 km/h (578 m.p.h.), but cruises a little more slowly. To minimise fuel consumption and hence achieve maximum range, the 737 pilot selects an economical cruise speed of about 800 km/h (500 m.p.h.).

AIRCRAFT SALES

The Boeing 737 is easily the most successful post-war airliner in terms of numbers ordered, having overtaken the Boeing 727 in the 1980s. But the short-haul twin-jet market is possibly the busiest and most profitable aircraft manufacturing sector in the world, and demand for such jets is high. By the end of 1993 more than 6150 examples of the 737 and its two main rivals had been delivered or were on order.

BOEING MODEL 737 SERIES 3100
DC-9/MD-80/MD-90 2600
A320 2400

RANGE

Although described as a short-haul airliner, the standard 737-400 could just about make a non-stop transatlantic crossing. However, where it and its competitors are most effective is in the regular, cycle-after-cycle business travel routes, making several flights daily.

MD-80 4600 km (2,858 mi.)
A320 5190 km (3,225 mi.)
MODEL 737-400 5000 km (3,107 mi.)

737s for every occasion

737-100: The original Boeing 737 first flew on 9 April 1967. Only 30 were sold before production switched to the 737-200.

737-200: Widely sold to airlines around the world, the Dash-200 was stretched by 2 metres and could seat 12 more passengers.

737-300: Launched in 1981, the Dash-300 has modern, quiet, fuel-efficient engines, and can carry up to 149 passengers.

737-400: Success with the Dash-300 led to the even longer Dash-400, which flew in 1988 and can seat up to 170 passengers.

737-500: The latest variant of the 737 trades capacity for extra range. The Dash-500 first flew in 1989, and has a range of over 5500 km (3,400 mi.).

BOEING

737 SERIES 600-800

● New generation airliner ● Latest in family ● Three versions

As the world's best-selling jet airliner, the Model 737 has been the mainstay of Boeing's short-medium haul airliner product range since the 1970s. The success of the new-generation 737s, released in the mid-1980s, proved that the design was as popular as ever and prompted Boeing to design a third generation of Model 737s. Originally called the Model 737X, the three new variants have already received orders from more than 25 airlines.

▲ *Boeing has conducted an extensive promotion and advertising campaign for the new 737s. This demonstrator appeared at the Paris Air Salon in June 1997.*

BOEING 737 SERIES 600-800

◀ High-tech assembly
For the manufacture of the aircraft a specially-built integration tool is used. It features electric-driven power cylinders that position the major parts accurately. Laser measurement tools and portable co-ordinate machines ensure alignment and precise fitting.

Reducing costs ▶
To reduce costs the fuselages are manufactured at Wichita, Kansas, and are shipped via rail in one piece to the assembly site at Renton, Washington.

▲ Largest variant
The largest of the original series this 737-800 is seen shortly after one of the initial test flights in August 1997. The first delivery was made to Hapag-Lloyd in April 1998.

◀ Test programme
Seen in formation with a T-38 Talon chase plane, the first 737-700 to fly undergoes trials. The flight test programme will involve 10 aircraft: four 737-700s, three 737-800s and three 737-600s.

◀ First of many
The first of the new series of 737s to be presented to the public was the Series 700. It was unveiled at a lavish ceremony at the company's manufacturing site at Renton, near Seattle, Washington, in December 1996.

FACTS AND FIGURES

➤ All new generation Model 737s are fully digitally defined, as are all the major manufacturing tools.

➤ The largest order so far has been from GE Capital Aviation Services for 80 aircraft.

➤ Boeing launched a fourth and even larger new model, designated 737-900, in 1997.

➤ The new models are powered by the new CFM56-7 engines produced as a joint venture by General Electric and Snecma.

➤ Prices range between US$36-40 million depending on the equipment fit.

➤ The CFM56-7B powerplant was tested on a modified Boeing 747 in January 1996.

PROFILE

Next generation airliner

In the light of the growing success of the European Airbus A320 series Boeing decided, in 1990, to produce a third-generation of its highly successful Boeing 737 airliner. To help tailor the new design to meet customers' requirements, Boeing asked more than 30 airlines to help define the Model 737X.

Results of research culminated in Boeing announcing three new versions. The Series 600 is the smallest of the trio seating 108 passengers

in standard layout accommodation. Launch customer is the Scandinavian airline SAS and the first flight was made in January 1998.

The Series 700 was the first of the new generation to fly in December 1996 and carries 128 passengers. Southwest Airlines became the first customer of the new generation, ordering 63 700s before construction of the first aircraft had even begun. Southwest received its first aircraft in October 1997.

The biggest of the family is the Series 800 able to seat 162 in

a two-class layout with the first deliveries in April 1998. With 517 of the new generation 737s ordered by 1 January 1997, the aircraft seems to have a very healthy future and with its energy-saving wings and engines it will achieve significant sales well into the 21st century.

Below: The first airline to receive the 737-700 was Southwest Airlines. They have ordered 63 examples with options on 63 more.

Above: The new 737s possess superior range and speed performance compared to the previous variants.

737-800

Type: twin-turbofan short-medium range airliner

Powerplant: two 116.5-kN (26,200-lb.-thrust) CFM International CFM56-7B turbofan engines

Maximum operating speed: Mach 0.82

Range: 5426 km (3,364 mi.) with maximum passenger load

Cruising altitude: 10,730 m (35,200 ft.)

Weights: operating empty 41,554 kg (91,419 lb.); maximum take-off 70,535 kg (155,177 lb.)

Accommodation: Alternative cabin layouts for 162 to 189 passengers; overhead baggage capacity of 9.3 m³ (329 cu. ft.)

Dimensions:
span	34.31 m	(112 ft. 6 in.)
length	39.47 m	(129 ft. 6 in.)
height	12.55 m	(41 ft. 2 in.)
wing area	125 m²	(1,345 sq. ft.)

Olympic Airways of Greece have become the one of the latest customers for the Boeing 737-800. The current deal is for four firm orders and four options. This is expected to grow to a final figure of 25.

The two crew are seated side-by-side. Cockpit instrumentation includes a systems common display screen (CDS) and a six-screen liquid crystal display.

Accommodation can vary between 162 and 189. Typical layouts include 12 four-abreast first class seats plus 150 six-abreast tourist class seats or 189 six-abreast tourist class seats. Lavatories are located forward and aft and an over-wing emergency exit is fitted on both sides of the fuselage. To reduce weight the interior uses advanced crushed core materials.

The tailplane is constructed of aluminium alloy. For strength and reduced weight the elevators and rudder contain graphite/Kevlar, carbon-fibre reinforced plastic (CFRP) and glass-fibre reinforced plastic (GFRP). The tail surfaces are larger than those fitted to second-generation Boeing 737s.

The hydraulically-operated undercarriage is of retractable tricycle type with free-fall emergency extension. The main units have no undercarriage door with the wheels forming the well seal instead. Heavy-duty brakes are fitted as standard.

Two CFM International CFM56-7B turbofan engines power the new generation aircraft. With an improved low-pressure compressor this unit is more efficient than that fitted to second-generation 737s.

Fitted at the rear of the fuselage is the aircraft's auxiliary power unit (APU). The APU provides the air supply and electric power in flight as well as power for engine starting on the ground.

ACTION DATA

CAPACITY

In standard two-class configuration, the Airbus A321 offers the highest passenger capacity which helps reduce the cost per passenger. Boeing's new 737-900 will have similar capacity to this aircraft. Boeing's take-over of McDonnell Douglas in 1997 has placed the MD-90's future in doubt because of its similarity in capacity to Boeing's third-generation 737 series.

737-800 — **162 PASSENGERS**
A321 — **185 PASSENGERS**
MD-90-30 — **153 PASSENGERS**

RANGE

The efficiency of the engines and relatively large fuel capacity for an aircraft of its size ensure that the 737-800 outperforms its competitors in range with a full load of passengers.

737-800 5426 km (3,364 mi.)
MD-90-30 4216 km (2,614 mi.)
A321 4260 km (2,640 mi.)

THRUST

As the lightest of the three types, the MD-90 requires slightly less powerful engines than the 737 or A321. The extra power and size of the A321 allow extra capacity but more power also equates to higher fuel consumption and therefore higher fuel costs.

737-800 **233 kW (52,415 lb.-thrust)**
A321 **266.8 kW (60,020 lb.-thrust)**
MD-90-30 **222.4 kW (50,030 lb.-thrust)**

Other CFM56-powered aircraft

■ **AIRBUS A340:** Four 138.8-kN CFM56-5C2 engines power Airbus' long-range A340. The type entered service with Air France and Lufthansa in March 1993.

■ **BOEING E-3D:** Purchased by the RAF, the E-3D differs from US variants of the E-3 by being powered by the 106.8-kN (24,025-lb.-thrust) CFM56-2A-3.

■ **BOEING E-6 MERCURY:** Based on the venerable Boeing 707, the E-6 is powered by the F108-CF-100 engine which is the military equivalent of the CFM56-2A-2.

■ **DOUGLAS DC-8 SUPER 70:** The CFM56-powered DC-8 established a long distance point-to-point record in March 1983. It flew 13,220 km (8,200 mi.) in 15 hours 46 minutes.

BOEING

747 SERIES 100-200

● World's largest airliner ● Ultra-long-range load carrier

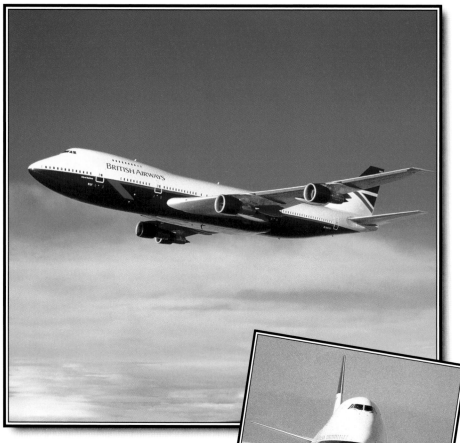

A true giant of the skies, the Boeing 747 revolutionised air travel by carrying more people further, and at lower cost, than any aircraft before it. Called the 'Jumbo Jet' because of its wide-body capacity, the 747 introduced size and economy to the world's airline routes. It is regarded today as the backbone of air transport, and provides efficiency and comfort for business travellers and tourists around the globe.

▲ *Few shapes are as distinctive as Boeing's 'Jumbo Jet', the Model 747. Over 1000 of these graceful giants are in service around the globe, and even Concorde could not replace them as the ultimate airline status symbol.*

BOEING 747 SERIES 100-200

▼ **Plane-maker to the world**
The Boeing Airplane Company built its first aircraft in 1919. Since then it has become the largest manufacturer of civil aircraft in history, and 747s will be rolling out for years to come.

◄ **Air Force One** ▲
Two specially modified 747-200s, called VC-25s, serve as the personal aircraft of the President of the United States. When the President is on board their radio callsign is 'Air Force One'.

▼ **Space Shuttle transporter**
Every NASA Space Shuttle mission begins with a Boeing 747. NASA operates two Boeing 747s which carry the Space Shuttle from its landing site at Edwards AFB in California across the country to the Shuttle launch site at Cape Canaveral in Florida.

▲ **Super freighter**
Few aircraft can rival the 747 as a cargo-carrier. Special freight versions, the 747Fs, are fitted with upward-swinging noses and special roller floors so that cargo can easily be rolled in and out. Like ordinary passenger Jumbo Jets the 747 freighter can also carry sizable loads under the floor, in its belly.

FACTS AND FIGURES

➤ With the 747-100's fuel capacity of 178,709 litres (39,310 gal.), a Cessna 150 lightplane can fly 1.8m km (1.1m mi.).

➤ The 747 was chosen for the earthly job of transporting the Space Shuttle orbiter.

➤ 747s carry more passengers each year than the population of Germany.

➤ The interior of a Boeing 747 contains 5000 km (3,100 mi.) of electrical wiring.

➤ The main undercarriage on the 747 has four 'legs' and 16 wheels with disc brakes and individual anti-skid locks.

➤ Special versions of the 747 flying in Japan can carry 566 passengers.

PROFILE

King-size ruler of the airways

The demand for Boeing 747s remains strong even today. Airlines are happier with the idea of new 747 versions rather than possible new 600-seat concepts.

The 747 was a huge gamble by Boeing, which risked $1 billion in the belief that the world was ready for a bigger, more efficient airliner able to carry 400 passengers. Made possible by dramatic progress with jet engines, so large that a man can stand in their air intakes, the Boeing 747 suddenly made airline travel accessible to millions who had never flown before. The 747 first flew in 1969, and it was several years before the number of people snapping up tickets justified such a colossal investment. But Boeing was right in predicting a Jumbo Jet revolution. The 747 has since appeared in several versions, including a long-range model which easily flies non-stop from London to Tokyo. A handful of 747s have also found freight-carrying and military uses.

Today the 747 is still impressive for its size, and looks awesome when seen close-up. And more than 60 airline companies also appreciate the Boeing 747 for its practical design and economic operating costs.

Few could have foreseen that Boeing's gamble with the original 747 would pay off with the aircraft becoming the backbone of international travel.

747-200B

Type: high-capacity commercial transport

Powerplant: four 243.55-kN (54,800 lb-thrust) Pratt & Whitney JT9D turbofans

Cruising speed: 940 km/h (584 m.p.h.) at 6096 m (20,000 ft.)

Range: 10,500 km (6,524 mi.) (normal payload)

Cruising ceiling: 13,715 m (45,000 ft.)

Weights: empty 173,272 kg (382,000 lb.); loaded 356,100 kg (785,066 lb.); maximum take-off 377,800 kg (832,906 kg.)

Passenger load: 490 seats maximum; typically 394 seats including 24 first-class, 70 business-class and 290 standard-class passengers

Dimensions:
span	59.64 m (195 ft. 8 in.)
length	70.66 m (231 ft. 10 in.)
height	19.33 m (63 ft. 5 in.)
wing area	510.95 m² (5,500 sq. ft.)

MODEL 747-200F

The Boeing 747 is a true giant of the air. Able to carry nearly 600 passengers or vast amounts of cargo, it lives up to its name – Jumbo Jet.

The upward-swinging nose on the 747F freighter means that even the largest items can be loaded with ease.

The 747 has proved exceptionally popular in Japan, where two airlines, JAL and All Nippon, fly 747s as a commuter airliner with nearly 600 seats on board.

The fuselage length of the 747 is longer than the distance covered by the Wright Brothers' first flight in 1908.

The tip of a 747's fin is more than 19 m (62 ft.) from the ground – taller than a four-storey house.

The 747's main undercarriage needs 16 wheels to spread the load of such a heavy aircraft and avoid damaging runways.

The Saudi Royal family owns several private 747s with sumptuous fittings inside – the ultimate 'bizjet'.

The 747F revolutionised the carriage of freight by air. Several airlines, such as Nippon Cargo Airlines, fly only freighter versions of the Jumbo Jet.

Nippon Cargo Airlines

ACTION DATA

MAXIMUM SPEED

The Boeing 747 is the largest airliner ever to have entered large-scale service, but it is also one of the fastest; its four powerful engines drive it to a maximum of almost nine-tenths the speed of sound.

747-200	989 km/h (615 m.p.h.)
DC-10	908 km/h (564 m.p.h.)
DC-8 SERIES 63	960 km/h (597 m.p.h.)

PAYLOAD

The 747 is designed to carry heavy loads of passengers or cargo over great distances. Earlier airliners could not carry as much fuel and could not match the big Boeing's performance.

747-200 394 mixed-class passengers or 100 tons of cargo

DC-10 270 mixed-class passengers or 46 tons of cargo

DC-8 SRS.63 200 mixed-class passengers or 30 tons of cargo

RANGE

Today any modern jet airliner designed for long-haul operations must be able to fly from London to Tokyo non-stop – an unbelievable distance only 20 years ago.

747-200	10,500 km (6,524 mi.)
DC-1	7500 km (4,660 mi.)
DC-8 SRS.63	7250 km (4,505 mi.)

Trans-Atlantic crossing

DEPARTURE: On leaving any American airport bound for Europe, a 747 will climb slowly to about 10,000 m (33,000 ft.). Initially under local control over the United States, after about an hour it will be switched to the air traffic control at Gander in Newfoundland.

OCEANIC CONTROL: Once aircraft are out of VHF radio range (about 300 km (185 mi.) from land) they rely on short-wave radio to talk to Gander Oceanic Control. The controllers there monitor the aircraft's progress, but there is no Atlantic radar coverage.

HIGH POINT: As it burns fuel the 747 gets lighter and climbs higher. Halfway across the Atlantic control is switched to Shanwick, based in Scotland but broadcast from Ireland. First sight of dry land is often the lush green landscape of Ireland.

FINAL APPROACH: At the end of its Atlantic crossing the 747 leaves Oceanic Control and returns to normal air traffic control, relayed across European national air traffic control systems, until it reaches its destination.

BOEING

747 SERIES 300/400

● Still the world's largest airliner ● Greater range ● More economical

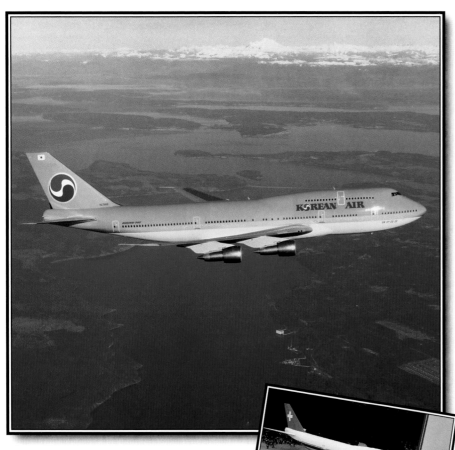

The Boeing 747-300/400 jetliner is the advanced version of the famous 'Jumbo', optimised to carry a large number of passengers at economical cost. While earlier 747s revolutionised air travel with their size, wide bodies and enormous capacity, these 'dash 300' and 'dash 400' versions increase further the number of travellers that can be whisked over intercontinental distances. These are the 'heavy haulers' of air commerce today.

▲ One of the most successful commercial aircraft of all time, the 747 looks set to continue its winning ways thanks to the introduction of the series 300 and much-improved 400.

PHOTO FILE

BOEING 747 SERIES 300/400

▼ World's largest
Just like its predecessors, the high-tech 747-400 has proved a popular choice with many airlines. In the large long-range sector of the market, it remains unrivalled in terms of passenger capacity.

▲ 'Big Top'
Singapore Airlines acquired 14 series 300 aircraft which were christened 'Big Top'. These have since been augmented by 24 747-400 'Mega Tops'.

New freighter ▶
Currently the latest variant to enter service, the 747-400F is a second-generation 747 freighter. It features the strengthened wing and glass cockpit of the passenger 400, but retains the original fuselage profile with the short upper deck.

◀ Belgian Jumbos
Sabena, the Belgian flag carrier, currently operates two 747-300s on long-haul routes. One of its aircraft is seen here on the ramp at Zaventem, near Brussels.

Standardised fleet ▶
Hong Kong's Cathay Pacific, based at Kai Tak airport, has a sizeable number of stretched 'Jumbos'. All 747s in the Cathay fleet are powered by ultra-efficient Rolls-Royce RB211 turbofans.

FACTS AND FIGURES

➤ Initial customers for the 747-300 were UTA of France and Swissair. Their first aircraft were delivered early in 1983.

➤ Today, more than 400 of the stretched upper deck 'Jumbos' have been ordered.

➤ Three different powerplants were simultaneously certified for the 747-400.

➤ A high-density model, designed for the Japanese domestic market, can accommodate up to 509 passengers.

➤ Despite the bulkier upper fuselage, the 747-300 is faster than previous versions.

➤ Unlike in previous versions, the tailplane structure of the 747-400 houses fuel.

PROFILE

Superjet from Seattle

The Boeing 747-300 of 1982 improved on the world's best-known airliner by adding an upper deck to accommodate up to 91 tourist-class passengers. The first examples of the new 'Stretched Upper Deck' (SUD) variant were delivered to Swissair and UTA, the largest independent airline in France. It has since become a popular aircraft for many carriers on long-haul routes.

Realising the potential of this latest version, Boeing went a step further and unveiled the 747-400 in 1988. This has a fully digital flight deck for two pilots (eliminating the third flight-crew position), plus wingtip extensions (including upward-pointing, 1.85-m (6-ft.) winglets for greater economy) and increased range. In common with previous variants, three different powerplants manufactured by Pratt & Whitney, General Electric and Rolls-Royce are available as options on the 747-400.

Pilots are delighted with the modern, all-glass cockpit of the 747-400 which has reduced the workload considerably, although additional complete second crews are often employed by airlines to reduce fatigue. A further version, the 747-400F has since been introduced. This is a dedicated freighter variant and incorporates the cockpit and strengthened wing of the passenger version. It first flew in May 1993 and has subsequently been delivered to 16 operators, the first being Air France.

Left: Even lesser known airlines, such as VARIG of Brazil, have acquired 747-300s which are perfectly suited to their requirements.

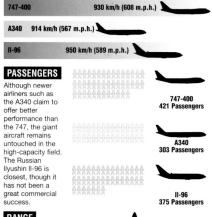

Above: Possibly one of the most famous liveries of recent times is that of Virgin Atlantic airways. In addition to a number of 747s, it also operates the rival Airbus A340.

747-400

Type: high-capacity long haul airliner

Powerplant: four high-bypass-ratio turbofans rated at 258 kN (58,040 lb.-thrust) (engines available Pratt & Whitney PW4056, General Electric CF6-80C2 or Rolls-Royce RB-211 425G)

Maximum speed: 980 km/h (608 m.p.h.)

Range: 13,398 km (8,307 mi.)

Service ceiling: 13,716 m (45,000 ft.)

Weights: empty 182,754 kg (402,059 lb.); loaded 394,625 kg (868,175 lb.)

Take-off run: 3322 m (10,900 ft.)

Accommodation: two (flight deck), 390 passengers in standard configuration

Dimensions:
span	64.44 m (211 ft. 4 in.)
length	70.66 m (231 ft. 9 in.)
height	19.41 m (63 ft. 8 in.)
wing area	511 m² (5,498 sq. ft.)

747-300

Z5-BAT is one of two series 300s currently flying with Suid Afrikaanse Lugdiens (South African Airways). The airline is based at Johannesburg and uses its 747s on major long-haul routes.

Despite its huge size, the cockpit of the 747 is surprisingly small. On the series 300 the cockpit remains essentially unchanged from earlier variants, with a multitude of conventional dial instruments.

On the upper deck, up to 91 economy-class passengers can be seated. This is more than the entire capacity of the Boeing Model 377 Stratocruiser of 1948. SUD 747s have proved so popular in service that older aircraft are being modified as such. The 747 was designed from the start to permit features introduced on new models to be retrofitted to older aircraft with considerable ease.

Capacity on the main deck remains unaltered from the earlier 747-200B with provision for up to 450 passengers. Some aircraft were delivered as, or have since been modified to 'Combi' variants and designated 747-300BCs. These aircraft can be configured for all-freight, all-passenger or both. A distinguishing feature of this variant is a large cargo door mounted on the port side of the rear fuselage.

Underneath the passenger cabin are two enormous baggage holds, one located fore and the other aft. Many airlines use the excess space for cargo in addition to luggage.

Although the 'Jumbo' was initially powered by Pratt & Whitney high-bypass-ratio JT9D turbofans, other powerplants have since become available. On the series 300, optional engines are the General Electric CF-60 and Rolls-Royce RB-211.

Each wing features two enormous sets of triple-slotted flaps. The amount of lift they generate at slow speeds is immense, considering that a fully laden 747-300 weighs 351,534 kg (773,375 lb.) on take-off. Low speed ailerons and spoilers provide braking.

Mounted in the tail unit is an APU (Auxiliary Power Unit). Whilst the aircraft is on the ground this operates the 747's major systems, such as the electrics, heating and air conditioning.

ACTION DATA

CRUISING SPEED

Modern airliners are powered by highly efficient and powerful turbofans which are also extremely quiet. As the largest airliner in the world, the 747 requires the most powerful engines. Its cruising speed is roughly comparable to that of rival airliners, however.

747-400	930 km/h (608 m.p.h.)
A340	914 km/h (567 m.p.h.)
Il-96	950 km/h (589 m.p.h.)

PASSENGERS

Although newer airliners such as the A340 claim to offer better performance than the 747, the giant aircraft remains untouched in the high-capacity field. The Russian Ilyushin Il-96 is closest, though it has not been a great commercial success.

747-400 421 Passengers

A340 303 Passengers

Il-96 375 Passengers

RANGE

With the 747-400, Boeing has felt no need to offer an improved Special Performance long-range model, thanks to the increased range of the new aircraft. On long, less popular routes, the Airbus A340 has proved successful. It can fly nearly 14,000 km (8,500 mi.) unrefuelled.

747-400 13,390 km (8,3067 mi.)

A340 13,612 km (8,440 mi.)

Il-96 11,482 km (7,120 mi.)

Other 747 variants

747-200B: Still flying with many carriers around the world, the early 747 variants were pioneers in low-cost air travel for the masses.

747-200F: Based on the 200 airliner, this version is a freighter with an upward hinging nose. It entered service in the mid-1970s.

747 SP: An extra-long-range variant, the SP featured a taller tail and short fuselage. Taiwan's China Airlines was a major user of the type.

E-4B COMMAND POST: These aircraft are equipped to become the wartime emergency base for the US President and his advisors.

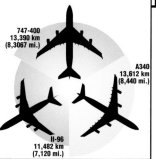

BOEING
747SP

● Long-range variant ● Shortened fuselage ● Record breaker

An almost forgotten member of the Jumbo Jet family, the 747 Special Performance, or SP, is the aircraft that most dramatically altered the 747's appearance. Designed to fly higher, faster and further than any 747 model of its time, the 747SP is easily identified by its compact look caused by its shortened fuselage. As it is lighter and can carry more fuel, the SP can fly non-stop over distances of up to 11,000 km (6,800 mi.).

▲ After exhaustive flight tests, the 747SP was certificated on 4 February 1976. Pan American airlines made the first commercial flight, between New York and Tokyo, two months later.

BOEING 747SP

▼ Long-legged Jumbo
A reduction in passenger capacity and an increase in fuel made the 747SP ideal for lower density, long-range routes.

▲ Launch customer
Pan Am was the first customer for the SP. The airline soon achieved the amazing average daily utilisation rate of 14.1 hours per aircraft.

▼ Major modifications
In addition to its shortened fuselage, the SP also featured a lighter wing structure, a taller fin and rudder, and new trailing-edge flaps.

▲ Far East service
Ideally suited to cover the vast area of Chinese interests, this SP was one of four sold to the Civil Aviation Administration of China.

The Big Orange ▶
One of the most distinctive airlines of the 1970s was Braniff International, which painted its 747 fleet bright orange. After Braniff went into receivership, this aircraft was sold to the government of Oman.

FACTS AND FIGURES

➤ Forty-five Boeing 747SPs were built; 39 with Pratt & Whitney engines and six with Rolls-Royce powerplants.

➤ On its first flight on 4 July 1975, the 747SP reached a speed of Mach 0.92.

➤ Six 747SPs have been operated as luxury VIP transports in the Middle East.

➤ An SAA 747SP broke the non-stop distance record for a civil aircraft, flying 16,560 km (10,270 mi.) from New York to Cape Town.

➤ The height of a Boeing 747SP is equivalent to that of a six-storey building.

➤ A former American Airlines 747SP is now operated by the Kazakhstan government.

PROFILE

Trans-global Jumbo

When the US Federal Aviation Administration certified the Boeing 747SP in February 1976, the world had a jetliner which was able to carry passengers unprecedented distances, at speed and in comfort.

The ability to traverse great distances has always been a challenge to the success of commercial aviation. In the 1950s the propeller-driven Douglas DC-7 could fly from San Francisco to Tokyo with stops only at Honolulu and Wake Island. In the 1960s the

jet-powered Boeing 707 still needed to stop in Honolulu. Even the wide-bodied Boeing 747, for all its qualities, was not truly a globe-girdling airliner, until the introduction of the ultra-long-range 747SP.

Although Pan American was the first customer in 1973, the 747SP proved extremely valuable to small national carriers, such as Air Mauritius, which required range but not the capacity of a standard 747.

In April 1976 a Pan Am SP broke the record for the longest

non-stop flight by a civil aircraft. This was followed, in 1988, by a special charter flight in which another Pan Am 747SP flew around the world in 46 hours and 26 minutes. Actual flying time on the three-stage flight was 39 hours and 26 minutes.

Many remaining 747SPs are reaching the end of their service lives and are being replaced by the 747-400 and Airbus A340.

Boeing's 'mini-Jumbo' retained the twin-deck forward fuselage of the 747, but three rear-fuselage sections were removed. This gave the SP model its compact shape.

747SP 21

Type: long-range commercial transport

Powerplant: four 208.8-kN (46,970-lb.-thrust) Pratt & Whitney JT9D-7A turbofans or, alternatively, four 222.8-kN (50,120-lb.-thrust) Rolls-Royce RB.211-524B turbofan engines

Cruising speed: 940 km/h at 6096 m

Range: up to 11,397 km (7,070 mi.) with 305 passengers and fuel reserves

Cruising ceiling: 13,715 m (45,000 ft.)

Weights: empty 151,454 kg (333,120 lb.); loaded 317,515 kg (698,530 lb.)

Accommodation: two pilots, flight engineer, up to 12 passenger cabin attendants and (typically) 331 to 370 passengers over distances of up to 10,900 km (6,760 mi.)

Dimensions:

span	59.64 m	(195 ft. 7 in.)
length	56.31 m	(249 ft. 6 in.)
height	19.94 m	(65 ft. 5 in.)
wing area	510.95 m² (5,498 sq. ft.)	

Constructed at Boeing's main production centre in Seattle, the 747SP had a fairly trouble-free seven-month test programme.

MODEL 747SP 21

Named *Clipper Lindbergh* after the pioneering US pilot Charles Lindbergh, this SP was delivered to Pan Am in May 1977. After nine years of service it was transferred to United Air Lines.

A normal crew of three sat on the flightdeck above the main deck. There was also provision for two observer stations. The avionics and equipment were equivalent to that fitted to the standard Boeing 747.

Several versions of different powerplants were available to SP customers. The General Electric CF645A2 or -50E2-F had a power output of 206.8 kN (46,520 lb.-thrust); the Rolls-Royce RB.211-524B had 222.8 kN (50,120 lb.-thrust); and the Pratt & Whitney JT9D-7A had 208.8 kN (46,970 lb.-thrust).

The main consideration of the 747SP design was to reduce weight while maintaining the 747's phenomenal fuel capacity. This was achieved by removing two straight and one tapered section from the fuselage, giving a total reduction in length of 14.60 m (48 ft.).

To give the necessary lateral stability, the tailfin was heightened by 1.52 m (5 ft.). The rudder was also modified into a double-hinged arrangement. To help reduce weight the landing gear had a lighter-weight structure.

To help counter possible instability in pitch, the tailplane had an increased span of 3.05 m (10 ft.), but maintained a similar form to the conventional 747.

Long-range airliner variants

■ **AIRBUS A300-600R:** First flown in 1987, the 600R featured an extra fuel tank in the tailplane and an increased maximum take-off weight. It had a maximum range of 7840 km (4,870 mi.).

■ **LOCKHEED L1011-500 TRISTAR:** With a shortened fuselage and extra fuel tanks in the centre section, the L1011-500 has a range of 9905 km (6,150 mi.).

■ **McDONNELL DOUGLAS DC-10 SERIES 40:** The Series 40 was fitted with Pratt & Whitney JT9D-59A engines and had a range of 7505 km (4660 mi.).

ACTION DATA

RANGE

Although the TriStar Series 500 and the DC-10 Series 40 were both long-range versions of their standard type, neither could match the globe-spanning range of the SP. It was not until the A340 entered service that an airliner could exceed the SP's performance.

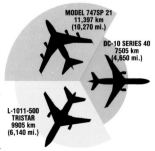

MODEL 747SP 21
11,397 km
(10,270 mi.)

DC-10 SERIES 40
7505 km
(4,650 mi.)

L-1011-500 TRISTAR
9905 km
(6,140 mi.)

BOEING

757

● Short/medium haul ● Twin-engine airliner ● Best-seller

▲ The nose of the first 757 takes shape. The 757 and 767 were designed to have a similar profile, but the nose areas are slightly different.

A familiar sight at airports, the Boeing 757 was designed to replace the long-serving 727 tri-jet as the workhorse of the world's airlines. The aircraft incorporated many advanced new features while retaining the traditional Boeing strengths of comfort, economy and reliability. And with that reliability proven, this twin-jet was cleared for trans-ocean operations, previously a preserve of three- or four-engined types. It is now one of the world's most successful airliners.

PHOTO FILE

BOEING 757

Big twin ▶
Boeing's huge four-jet 747 may be the company's most famous product, but since the 757 its airliners have all been efficient twin-engined designs.

▲ **Pilot comfort**
The 757's cockpit is very comfortable for the crew. It is fitted with a blend of old- and new-style instruments.

◀ **Taking shape**
The first two Rolls-Royce-powered production 757s, both of which were delivered to Eastern Airlines, undergo final assembly. Two non-production machines had already been built, and were used for 10 months of tests.

▲ **Flying to the sun**
Iberia is one of many users of 757s, primarily carrying people to sunshine holiday destinations.

▼ **Water testing**
A vital part of any new airliner's test programme is a water-spray ingestion run. The first 757 was checked to see whether its engines could withstand the water thrown up from the runway.

▲ **Rollout day**
The rollout of the 757 was a big event for Boeing, as it was the first new airliner the company had built since the 747 in 1969.

FACTS AND FIGURES

➤ Boeing claims that the 757 freighter can hold six million golf balls.

➤ Mexico's Fuerza Aérea Mexicana operates a 757-225 as a VIP presidential aircraft.

➤ The first aircraft, a Boeing 757-200, flew on 18 February 1982.

➤ The 757 fleet has flown almost the equivalent of 5000 round trips between the Earth and the Moon.

➤ Boeing almost built a re-engined and re-designed 727 instead of the 757.

➤ United Airlines is the biggest 757 operator, with 89 in service.

PROFILE

Boeing's ever-popular twin

The Pratt & Whitney-powered 757 got off to a firm start when Delta airlines ordered 60 of the aircraft in the mid-1980s.

The Boeing 757 narrow-body airliner is an effective aircraft for commercial carriers all over the world. It was one of the first practical turbofan-powered, short-/medium-range airliners, well known for its passenger-carrying ability but with an equal capability as a freighter.

Originally intended for short-haul duties, the 757ER has been cleared for extended-range ocean flights and now has an intercontinental range.

The fine job being carried out by hundreds of 757s around the globe is due to a number of improvements, including digital instruments in place of some clock-style gauges, advanced flight controls and fuel-efficient engines.

These features put the 757 in the class of new airliners which operate with two flight crew members instead of three. It is also far more economical than preceding jets. For airline companies, these are solid financial incentives, encouraging them to buy the 757.

With hundreds of aircraft on order the 757 promises to be a top-selling airliner, following in the footsteps of Boeing's previous models.

The narrow fuselage profile of the 757 easily distinguished it from the 767. Despite the fuselage having a common cross-section to the 707, 727 and 737, both it and the wing were entirely new designs.

The 757's highly efficient turbofans offered superb fuel efficiency when spiralling fuel costs put a number of operators of older aircraft out of business.

The elevators have a lightweight graphite epoxy honeycomb skin construction, built by Vought Aircraft.

Most tourist-class accommodation is in six-abreast configuration. First-class seating is usually four abreast.

757-200

Type: twin-engine medium-range transport

Powerplant: two 166.37-kN (37,320-lb.-thrust) Rolls-Royce RB211-535C, or 169.93-kN (38,119-lb.-thrust) Pratt & Whitney PW2037, or 178.38-kN (40,015-lb.-thrust) RB211-535E4, or 185.50-kN (41,613-lb.-thrust) Pratt & Whitney PW2040 high-bypass turbofans

Maximum speed: 981 km/h (608 m.p.h.)

Range: 5150 km (3,193 mi.) with maximum load; 7400 km (4,588 mi.) at maximum economy

Service ceiling: 13,932 m (45,700 ft.)

Weights: empty 57,180 kg (125,796 lb.); loaded 113,400 kg (249,480 lb.)

Accommodation: two pilots, six attendants; typically 194 passengers in mixed-class service; 239 passengers on charter; up to 39,690 kg (87,318 lb.) of cargo and pallets in freighter version

Dimensions:
span	38.05 m (124 ft. 9 in.)
length	47.35 m (155 ft. 9 in.)
height	13.60 m (44 ft. 7 in.)
wing area	181.25 m² (1,950 sq. ft.)

MODEL 757-2B6

Royal Air Maroc, Morocco's flag-carrier, flies an all-Boeing fleet, including two 757s. They operate throughout Europe and the Middle East as well as to a small number of American destinations.

The tail designs of Singapore Airlines, LTU and Royal Air Maroc, operators of the 757 in three continents.

Most 757s are passenger carriers with a full complement of cabin windows. There is also a pure freighter version which is windowless.

The wing control surfaces consist of flaps, slats and spoilers. The spoilers act as airbrakes and complement the ailerons in flight.

The 757's flight deck is made by Boeing's military aircraft division.

Launch customers for the 757 specified Rolls-Royce RB211 engines. Since the mid-1980s, Pratt & Whitney engines have been offered as alternatives.

The landing gear features carbon disc brake technology. The main units have four wheels each.

The lower fuselage has an under-floor cargo volume of over 50 m³ (1,766 cu. ft.).

ACTION DATA

RANGE

The 757 has greater range than both its Boeing predecessor and the McDonnell Douglas MD-80, a stretched and upgraded version of the old DC-9. Although the 757 is classified as a medium-range airliner, it has been cleared for long-range over-ocean operations.

MODEL 727	MODEL 757	MD-80
4000 km (2,480 mi.)	7400 km (4,588 mi.)	5000 km (3,100 mi.)

Boeing's narrow-body dynasty

MODEL 707: The epoch-making Boeing 707 set the future of commercial aviation after the false dawn with Britain's Comet. It introduced the six-abreast cabin now standard on narrow bodies.

MODEL 727: Boeing's best seller in the 1970s, the 727 was for two decades the dominant short- and medium-haul jet in the world, until dethroned by the 737 and the 757.

MODEL 737: Originally intended as the 727's short-haul companion, the 737 has fathered its own family of jets in the 100- to 150-seat class, and is the world's best-selling airliner.

BOEING
767

● Third-generation airliner ● Medium-/long-range wide-body

▲ The Model 767
was Boeing's first wide-bodied, twin-engined aircraft. The aircraft flies automatically, from the take-off climb until landing, with the help of 140 microprocessors and computers.

A modern, long-range jetliner, the Boeing Model 767 is a based on design work which was started in the 1970s. One of several twin-engined airliners intended for operation by two flightdeck crew, the 767 entered service in 1982 and has become a familiar sight at airports worldwide. With the same high-tech cockpit as the 757, the 767 offers airlines a profitable aircraft mid-way in size between the narrow-bodied 757 and the 'jumbo' 747 and 777.

BOEING 767

▲ 767-300 cockpit
Six cathode-ray tube displays have replaced many of the traditional dials fitted in earlier airliners. These display both navigation and systems data.

▲ Prototype N767BA in flight
The 767 first flew in September 1981. United Air Lines flew the first passenger services in August 1982.

▼ On the line at Everett
Brand-new 767s await final checks and delivery outside Boeing's Everett Field plant.

▲ The world's favourite airline
In mid-1997 British Airways had 25 Model 767-300ERs, all powered by Rolls-Royce RB211 turbofan engines.

'Star Wars' laboratory ▶
The 767-200 prototype was configured with a 26.2-m (35-ft.) long dorsal cupola to test a long-wavelength infra-red sensor, which was intended to detect ballistic missiles as part of the Strategic Defense Initiative.

FACTS AND FIGURES

➤ The first Model 767 was rolled out on 4 August 1981 and made its maiden flight on 26 September 1981.

➤ A typical Boeing 767, straight out of the factory, has 3,140,000 separate parts.

➤ The production rate in early 1997 was four aircraft a month.

➤ Since 8 September 1982, Model 767s have carried more than 820 million passengers.

➤ Boeing claims that a 767 is 54 per cent more fuel-efficient than a Boeing 727.

➤ By mid-1997, 663 of 764 Boeing 767s ordered had been delivered.

PROFILE

Transoceanic wide-bodied twin

Numerous improvements over previous Boeing jetliners made their first appearance on the Model 767. Its wing is thicker, longer and less swept than those of earlier Boeings, and the shape is said to contribute to its excellent take-off performance and fuel economy. The 767's cabin is more than one metre (three feet) wider than the single-aisle, narrow-bodied Boeing jetliners.

The 767 has been ordered by a dozen of the world's major airlines needing an aircraft with new-generation technology and twin-aisle passenger cabin convenience. Ever since making

its first revenue flight with United Air Lines in August 1982, the 767 has established an excellent record for reliability and efficiency. Its extended-range twin-engine operations, or ETOPS, qualification also made the type attractive to airlines flying transoceanic routes.

The 767 has been produced in standard -200 form and as the stretched -300, both of which have an extended-range 'ER' variant. There is also a freighter version. The longer 767-400ER, which will have 303 seats, was announced in 1997 and entered service in 2000.

ZK-NBA Aotearoa was Air New Zealand's first 767-200 and was built in 1985. The airline later operated -200ER and -300ER variants.

An important feature of the 767 family is its ETOPS qualification. This permits the twin-engined aircraft to fly transoceanic routes provided that it remains within two or three hours of an alternative airfield. Such a capability is possible with its modern ultra-reliable engines.

Sub-contractors producing different parts of the 767's structure include Boeing Helicopters (wing leading edges), Northrop Grumman (wing centre section), Canadair (rear fuselage) and Mitsubishi (cargo doors).

The -200ER and -300ER 'extended-range' variants of the basic aircraft have extra fuel tanks, giving a total tankage of 91,379 litres (24,142 gal.). The refuelling point is on the port outer wing.

767-300ER

Type: twin-engined long-range wide-bodied airliner

Powerplant: two 252.4-kN (80,925-lb.-thrust) Pratt & Whitney PW4056 or 266.9-kN (60,042-lb.-thrust) General Electric CF6-80C2B4 or Rolls-Royce RB211-542H turbofans

Cruising speed: Mach 0.80

Range: (with reserves) 11,230 km (6,965 mi.)

Service ceiling: 12,192 m (40,000 ft.)

Weights: empty 81,374 kg (179,023 lb.); maximum take-off 181,437 kg (399,161 lb.)

Accommodation: basic 269 passengers (24 first-class and 245 tourist-class); maximum capacity 350 passengers

Cargo hold volume: 147.0 m³ (5,191 cu. ft.)

Dimensions:
span	47.57 m (156 ft.)
length	54.94 m (180 ft. 3 in.)
height	15.85 m (52 ft.)
wing area	283.30 m² (3,048 sq. ft.)

MODEL 767-2Q8ER

S7-AAS Aldabra first flew in July 1989 and was delivered to the International Lease Finance Corporation for lease to Air Seychelles.

One of the innovations of the 767 was its two-person flightdeck, in which the functions of the former flight engineer were performed by the two pilots.

The basic 767-200 accommodates 224 passengers in standard configuration, including 18 in first-class seating. Single-class layouts are possible for between 247 and 290 passengers, although the latter requires eight-abreast seating and extra emergency exits over the wings. The 'stretched' 767-300 can seat between 269 and 350 passengers.

One of three engine types may be specified by the 767 customer. This 767-200ER is powered by General Electric CF6 turbofans. Rolls-Royce RB211s or Pratt & Whitney PW4000s are the other options.

In response to interest from the US company United Parcel Service, Boeing launched a freight version of the -300ER called the -300F. This is distinguished by its lack of passenger windows and a new cargo door on the port side of the forward fuselage.

ACTION DATA

PASSENGERS

The basic 767-200 competes directly with the Airbus A310, the -200 version of which carries a similar number of passengers. The DC-10-30 and -40 also sought sales in the small wide-body market.

MODEL 767-200	224
A310-200	220
DC-10-40	255

CARGO HOLD VOLUME

Underfloor capacity for freight is an important feature of modern airliners as passenger flights often carry small freight items at lucrative rates. The larger DC-10 is the leader in this respect.

MODEL 767-200	111.3 m³ (3,930 cu. ft.)
A310-200	102.1 m³ (3,605 cu. ft.)
DC-10-40	155.4 m³ (5,487 cu. ft.)

MAXIMUM RANGE

The A310 has a better range performance than the 767-200, and this was addressed by Boeing in the extended-range version, the -200ER. DC-10s also had a reputation for long range.

767-200	5963 km (3,700 mi.)
A310-200	6759 km (4,190 mi.)
DC-10-40	6485 km (4,020 mi.)

Model 767 development

TRI-JET 7X7: Both the 767 and the narrow-bodied 757 can trace their roots back to the 7X7 and 7N7 proposals of the mid-1970s. The 767 was initially a tri-jet design of similar configuration to the DC-10 and TriStar.

NEW DESIGN: During the design process different tail configurations were proposed, including this T-tail which was similar to that of the 727. The tri-jet was to be produced in co-operation with Italian and Japanese partners.

E-767 AWACS: Once the twin-jet configuration had been chosen and was in production, Boeing worked on military versions, like the Airborne Warning and Control System 'E-767' for Japan's armed forces.

BREGUET

763 PROVENCE

● Twin deck ● Passenger and freight transport ● Long service

A fter building the twin-engined Breguet 500 airliner during the German occupation, in 1944 Breguet started looking at larger aircraft. To provide a worthwhile passenger and cargo load, the firm decided to develop a twin-deck airliner named the Deux-Ponts, or two decks. The prototype flew in 1949, and 18, called the Sahara, were used as military transports. Air France operated 12 Deux-Ponts under the name Provence.

▲ The 763 Provence airliner and the 765 Sahara military transport were the principal variants which stemmed from the Breguet 761 design. Both types served extensively in Algiers.

BREGUET 763 PROVENCE

Parachute drop ▶
All three of the 761S were used in the mid-1950s for military trials. Here the rear doors have been removed to drop supplies.

▲ Pre-production aircraft
The 761S aircraft had a new central fin and Pratt & Whitney R-2800-B31 engines.

▲ Prototype Breguet 761
Unlike the production models, the prototype was powered by SNECMA-built 1178-kW Gnome-Rhône 14R engines. It also lacked a central fin.

◀ Into Africa
One of the pre-production machines was leased to Air Algerie for a short time early in the 1950s.

◀ Commercial freighter
Air France used its 763s in passenger, combined passenger/freight and all-cargo configurations. The Provence ended its days with the airline as a large-capacity airlifter and served until 1971.

▲ Military lifter
The rear door of the 765 Sahara lowered to form a ramp for loading vehicles.

FACTS AND FIGURES

➤ Air France gave its 12 763s the class name Provence, but they were more popularly known as Deux-Ponts.

➤ Provences were the first post-war French production aircraft to fly with Air France.

➤ Air France was ordered to buy the 763s by the French Minister of Transport.

➤ Military Saharas could hold 146 fully-equipped troops, 85 stretchers with attendants or large military vehicles.

➤ Saharas were powered by R-2800-CB17s with an output of 1417 kW (1,900 hp.).

➤ The last of the Saharas belonging to the Armée de l'Air was retired in 1972.

PROFILE

Twin-deck French design

In their original configuration, the Air France Provences had 59 tourist-class seats on the upper deck and 48 second-class seats on the lower. They were used on routes to North Africa and between Paris and London.

The original Deux-Ponts prototype had twin fins and rudders, but a central fin was added on later aircraft. The Provence had a distinctive central rounded fin, and some modifications to the wing camber were required to meet Air France's payload requirements.

The seats on the lower deck, and the rear staircase connecting the two levels, could be stowed to make room for cargo. The rear fuselage sides consisted of doors which opened sideways for loading.

After being replaced by newer airliners, six Provences were sold to the French air force. The other six were modified as freighters, with winches and lifts to the upper deck, under the name Universal. They were used to transport Olympus engines for Concorde from Bristol to

Below: The sheer size of the 763 dominated airfield parking areas. The Hamilton Standard propellers were 4.22 m (13 ft. 10 in.) in diameter and could provide reverse thrust on landing.

Above: An Air Algerie 761S performs a low-level flypast, showing the tall, double-deck fuselage to advantage.

Toulouse and could also ferry up to 12 cars and their passengers. Maximum payload of the freighter version was increased to 13,150 kg (28,930 lb.), and up to 29 seats could be installed on the upper deck.

763 Provence

Type: twin-deck airliner

Powerplant: four 1566-kW (2,100-hp.) Pratt & Whitney R-2800-CA18 18-cylinder two-row air-cooled radial engines

Maximum cruising speed: 390 km/h (242 m.p.h.) at 3050 m (10,000 ft.)

Range: 2290 km (1,420 mi.) with full load; 4100 km (2,542 mi.) with maximum fuel

Weights: empty 32,241 kg (70,930 lb.); maximum take-off 51,600 kg (23,857 lb.)

Payload: 107 passengers or 10,844 kg (23,857 lb.)

Dimensions:
span	42.99 m (141 ft.)
length	28.94 m (94 ft. 11 in.)
height	9.91 m (32 ft. 6 in.)
wing area	185.40 m² (1,995 sq. ft.)

763 PROVENCE

This Air France aircraft was used exclusively on the airline's North African routes to Algeria and Tunisia.

Before it accepted the Provence, Air France insisted that the cockpit was modified for three-man operation rather than the four crew of the 761S.

Pratt & Whitney engines replaced the French powerplants early on. The R-2800-CA18 radial had its 14 cylinders arranged in two rows and boosted take-off power with water injection.

Passengers sat on two decks: the upper, tourist-class, deck seated 59, while the second-class deck accommodated 48. In the combi role a moveable bulkhead separated the cargo and passengers.

Only the series prototype, the 761, flew without the additional centre fin. This was rounded at its trailing edge to blend into the rear-fuselage contours and was not fitted with any control surfaces.

A high-set position was chosen for the tailplanes, which kept them clear of the considerable propeller wash. Tall fins and rudders, of narrow chord, were mounted inboard of each tailplane tip. A French flag was painted on both sides.

Large clamshell doors allowed easy access to the cabin for loading cargo. An inset door acted as the main passenger entrance, with a staircase to the upper deck.

F-BASY

AIR FRANCE

Breguet legacy

■ **273:** First flown in 1934, 15 of these reconnaissance bombers were sold to Venezuela and six to China.

■ **470 FULGAR:** This sleek, 14-seat airliner was based on the 462 Vultur and built only in prototype form.

■ **482:** A post-war design for research into bomber development, only one of these elegant aircraft was built.

■ **941:** One prototype and four production examples of this STOL transport were built, but no market was found.

ACTION DATA

MAXIMUM CRUISE SPEED

A development of the B-29 Superfortress, the Boeing Stratocruiser was a highly advanced and powerful aircraft, which benefited from wartime development in a non-occupied country. The Avro Tudor was faster than the Provence, but was plagued by accidents.

763 PROVENCE	**390 km/h (242 m.p.h.)**
377 STRATOCRUISER	**547 km/h (339 m.p.h.)**
G89 TUDOR 2	**460 km/h (270 m.p.h.)**

PASSENGERS

The Provence could accommodate 107 passengers in comfort, but 135 could be seated in a high-density layout. The Stratocruiser also used a double-deck layout; the lower deck, where the B-29's bomb-bay used to be, was used for baggage and cargo.

763 PROVENCE 107

377 STRATOCRUISER 112

G89 TUDOR 2 80

RANGE

Long range was a key feature of the Stratocruiser, allowing intercontinental flights. Breguet designed the Provence for short-to medium-range services, especially for French colonial states in North Africa for which its 4100-km range was more than adequate.

763 PROVENCE	**4100 km (2,542 mi.)**
377 STRATOCRUISER	**6759 km (4,190 mi.)**
G89 TUDOR 2	**3750 km (2,330 mi.)**

BRISTOL
170 FREIGHTER

● World War II RAF design ● Worldwide service ● Car ferry

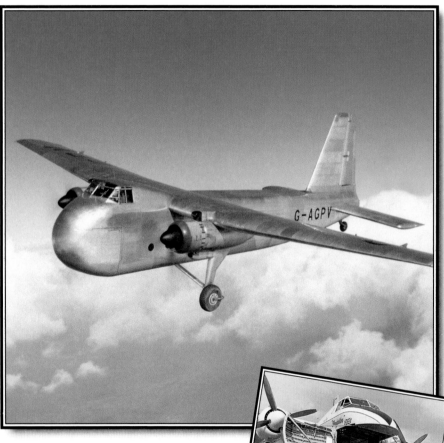

Bristol started to design the Type 170 as a military transport in 1944. Then, with the end of World War II in sight, it was changed to a commercial freight and passenger carrier. The original versions were the Mk I Freighter, with nose doors, and the Mk II Wayfarer, which had seats for up to 36 passengers. The first prototype flew in December 1945, and the sole survivor of the 214 that were built was still operating in Canada nearly 50 years later.

▲ *Bristol's*
Freighter made its name as a car ferry across the English Channel, but Type 170s saw extensive service around the world hauling a multitude of loads.

PHOTO FILE
BRISTOL 170 FREIGHTER

◄ **Enlarged Freighter Mk 32**
Perhaps the best known version was the Mk 32, which was developed for Silver City Airways for car ferry operations. The fuselage was lengthened by 1.52 m (5 ft.) to accommodate three cars and 23 passengers, and the tail area was increased.

▲ **In its twilight years**
This ex-RNZAF B.170 was briefly flown by the appropriately named Hercules Airways.

◄ **The last airworthy Freighter**
This aircraft was written-off in an accident over Enstone, Oxfordshire, in July 1996.

▲ **Supplying Canada's Eskimos**
Freighters have served around the world, often hauling heavy loads in harsh weather conditions. This Mk 31 spent its short life in Canada with two air freight companies, and crashed in Alberta in 1955.

▲ **Mk 31 modifications**
After two accidents caused by structural failure of the tail fin, a dorsal fin was added. In addition, the Mk 31 had more powerful engines and a higher gross weight. G-AINK was the first production example.

FACTS AND FIGURES

➤ One Silver City Freighter carried 117 refugees on one flight after the break up of India and Pakistan in 1947.

➤ Safe Air of New Zealand flew Freighters for 35 years and, at one time, operated 11.

➤ In all, 214 aircraft, including both civil and military variants, were produced.

➤ Versions of the B.170 with tricycle undercarriage and tail loading ramps were proposed but not built.

➤ Type 170s were built between December 1945 and March 1958.

➤ In 1963 there were 112 still in service; by 1970, 40 civil examples remained.

PROFILE

Jungle freighter turned car ferry

The Type 170 was designed with a fixed undercarriage. Lighter than a retractable type, it was also cheaper, and meant that there was no need for a hydraulic system.

The last 170s were delivered in 1958, but passenger and cargo airlines used them well into the 1980s. Safe Air of New Zealand operated the type for 35 years until 1986. Successive models introduced new wings, more powerful Hercules 734 engines and

bigger fuel tanks (Mk 21), a dorsal fin and an increased gross weight (Mk 31).

Silver City Air Freight Services started a car ferry service between Lympe in England and Le Touquet in France in July 1948. The service continued for many years and in the early 1950s the Mk 32, with its longer fuselage, was developed specifically for car transport. By 1962 Silver City had a total of 24 Freighters in service.

Other Type 170s were built as Mk 31M military transports for the air forces of Australia, Burma, Canada, Iraq, New Zealand and Pakistan. They could carry up to 30 fully equipped troops or 28 stretcher cases plus attendants.

Safe Air (formerly Straits Air Freight Express) in New Zealand was the last major operator of the Freighter. The aircraft were withdrawn from service in 1986.

FREIGHTER MK 31M

Delivered to the Royal New Zealand Air Force (RNZAF) in March 1955, this aircraft was retired in 1978. Sold in 1981, it was used for freight operations in the UK and Canada and, as C-FDFC, was the last airworthy B.170.

The fixed undercarriage was less prone to mechanical failure. As the 170 had a short range and low top speed, the benefits of retractable gear would have been negligible.

The nose cargo door meant that the cockpit had to be positioned above the forward fuselage. Except for this, the general layout of the 170 was based on that of the RAF's Bombay transport, with which it shared a number of features.

Two of Bristol's own Hercules radial engines powered the Freighter. Those fitted to the earliest versions produced 1249 kW (1,675-hp.), while the Mk 31 was propelled by 1476-kW (1,980-hp.) engines. Renowned for its reliability, Safe Air in New Zealand claimed, in March 1985, to be using an aircraft powered by a Hercules which had accumulated 20,987 hours.

Windows were fitted in the nose doors of a Freighter Mk I employed to survey Persian oilfields in 1947. Later, a number of military Freighters, including those for the RNZAF, were built with nose windows.

The original RAF specification required that the aircraft was able to carry a 3-tonne (3-ton) Army truck. Loading was made easy by the nose 'clam shell' doors. These were omitted in the Wayfarer all-passenger version.

Most B.170s were built with cabin windows regardless of their intended role. The Wayfarer airliner version could seat up to 32 passengers.

INSTONE G-BISU
ATLANTIC AIR TRANSPORT

Freighter Mk 32

Type: commercial freight and/or passenger transport

Powerplant: two 1476-kW (1,980-hp.) Bristol Hercules 734 radial engines

Maximum speed: 362 km/h (224 m.p.h.)

Initial climb rate: 420 m/min (1,380 f.p.m.) at sea level

Range: 1320 km (820 mi.)

Service ceiling: 7470 m (24,500 ft.)

Weights: empty 13,400 kg (29,480 ft.); maximum take-off 19,960 kg (43,912 lb.)

Payload: three cars plus 23 passengers, or 60 passengers

Dimensions:
span	32.92 m (108 ft.)
length	22.35 m (73 ft. 4 in.)
height	7.62 m (25 ft.)
wing area	138.14 m² (1,486 sq. ft.)

ACTION DATA

RANGE

Range was not a major consideration in the Freighter's design. Because it had to compete for orders with the large numbers of cheap, surplus wartime aircraft like the DC-3 (C-47), its price and load-carrying capacity were its main selling points.

FREIGHTER	1320 km (819 mi.)
DC-3	2400 km/h (1,490 mi.)
ATL.98 CARVAIR	3700 km/h (2,300 mi.)

ACCOMMODATION

The Mk 32 could carry as many as 60 passengers in an all-passenger configuration. As a car ferry it was far more versatile than the DC-3, but its capacity was soon found to be insufficient and led to the development of the Carvair.

FREIGHTER Mk 32 — 3 cars and 23 passengers
DC-3 — 24 passengers
ATL.98 CARVAIR — 5 cars and 25 passengers

Freighter versatility

■ **SMALL CONSIGNMENTS:** Here a Silver City Air Freight Services Freighter is loaded with ice cream, sometime in the 1960s. The 'clam shell' nose doors, a legacy of the aircraft's military origins, allowed straightforward loading of a variety of cargoes, from the smallest boxes to bulky containers and medium-sized cars.

■ **CUSTOM-BUILT LOADER:** In New Zealand Safe Air, in conjunction with the operators of the country's railway system, operated a 'rail-air' service across Cook Strait. A specially designed, wheeled deck was built for the loading of containers or, in this case, horse boxes. Note the rail tracks under the deck's wheels.

■ **CAR FERRY:** Another of Silver City's Freighters, this time a Mk 32, demonstrates the type's capacity as a car ferry. These Minis were part of a priority consignment en route to France. The Mk 32 was, perhaps, the best known version of the Freighter and ferrying cars across the Channel was its main role. The aircraft was well suited to the task.

BRISTOL

BRITANNIA

● Long-haul airliner ● Early turboprop ● RAF transport

With its advanced turboprop engines and long range, the Bristol Type 175 Britannia should have made a great impact in the airliner market of the early 1950s. However, protracted development meant that by the time it entered service in 1957 jet airliners like the Boeing 707 were only a year away. Nevertheless, the Britannia did see valuable service as a passenger- and cargo-carrying aircraft for civil and military operators.

▲ *Although the first prototype Britannia flew in 1952, the production aircraft did not enter service until 1957. Only 60 airliners were built, the remaining aircraft being military transports.*

BRISTOL BRITANNIA

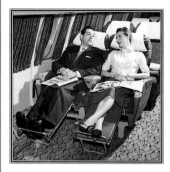

1950s airliner ▶
Representing the pinnacle of propeller-driven airliners, the Britannia was soon overtaken by the introduction of the first generation of jet airliners.

◀ Luxury accommodation
The original Series 100 aircraft built for BOAC could be configured for either 60 first-class or 93 tourist-class passengers.

▼ Five-man crew
The Britannia carried a flight deck crew of between three and five, including a flight engineer, navigator and two pilots.

Overseas production ▶
Most Britannias were built at Bristol's Filton factory, although a small number were constructed by Short Brothers, Belfast, and by Canadair as the CL-44 with different engines.

▼ Military service
The Britannia was the Royal Air Force Transport Command's first turboprop transport aircraft. Twenty-three were delivered in all.

FACTS AND FIGURES

➤ Israeli airline El Al began a record 9817-km (6,096 mi.) non-stop service between New York and Tel Aviv on 19 December 1957.

➤ The second Britannia built crashed during a test flight in February 1954.

➤ The CL-28 Argus maritime patrol aircraft was another Canadian derivative.

➤ The Britannia's size and relatively quiet engines earned it the nickname 'Whispering Giant'.

➤ Other Britannia airliner users included Cubana and Canadian Pacific.

➤ The Canadair CL-44 was a Britannia derivative with Rolls-Royce Tyne engines.

PROFILE

The 'Whispering Giant'

The Bristol Aircraft Company submitted its Type 175 design in 1947 to meet a British Overseas Airways Corporation requirement for a high-capacity civil transport.

Originally intended to be powered by Bristol Centaurus piston engines, the advanced but troublesome Proteus was substituted early on. At a time when the de Havilland Comet jet airliner appeared risky and untried, the Britannia was

expected to sell well. However, teething problems, mainly involving the engines, delayed service entry until early 1957 – the prototype's maiden flight had taken place on 16 August 1952. Potential sales were badly hit when a prototype Britannia force-landed while being evaluated by the chairman of the Dutch airline KLM.

Until the early 1960s the Britannia was progressively developed in different versions

with a stretched fuselage, greater range and floor strengthening for freight haulage.

Although produced in relatively small numbers, the type served and operated with great success for airlines all around the world and a few remained in service until the late 1980s, having been converted into cargo freighters.

Early engine problems caused a BOAC Britannia to suffer a complete engine failure in cloud over Uganda in 1956.

BOAC operated both the Series 100 and the stretched, long-range Series 300 versions, numbering 26 in all.

Britannia Series 310

Type: four-engined turboprop airliner

Powerplant: four 3072-kW (4,120-hp.) Rolls-Royce Proteus turboprop engines

Maximum speed: 639 km/h (396 m.p.h.)

Range: 6869 km (4,260 mi.) with maximum payload

Service ceiling: 7315 m (24,000 ft.)

Maximum passengers: 133

Weights: empty 37,438 kg (82,364 lb.); maximum take-off 83,915 kg (184,613 lb.)

Dimensions:
span	43.36 m (142 ft. 3 in.)
length	37.87 m (124 ft. 3 in.)
height	11.43 m (37 ft. 6 in.)
wing area	192.77 m² (2,074 sq. ft.)

BRITANNIA C.MK 1

The Britannia 253 entered service with the Royal Air Force as the Britannia C.Mk 1. The second Britannia delivered, XL636, entered service in 1959 with No. 99 Squadron.

The Bristol Proteus turboprop engines were originally designed for the ill-fated Bristol Brabazon II and Saunders-Roe Princess airliners.

The fuselage was a pressurised, aluminium-alloy structure with a maximum diameter of 3.66 m (12 ft.).

When equipped as a troop carrier, the Britannia carried 115 rearward-facing seats.

ROYAL AIR FORCE TRANSPORT COMMAND

XL636

636

While allocated to No. 99 Squadron, XL636 was named 'Argo'.

The 20 Britannia Mk 1s were long-range, all-purpose transports with a strengthened floor and large freight door.

The positioning of the aircraft's engine jet pipes meant that the Messier bogie main landing gear had to retract backwards.

Defence cuts in 1975 spelled the end for the bulk of the RAF Britannia fleet. XL636 was sold and flew briefly as a civilian freighter from 1976.

ACTION DATA

ACCOMMODATION

The Canadair CL-44D was a stretched version of the Britannia and consequently carried more passengers. The Soviet Ilyushin Il-18 had a slightly narrower and shorter fuselage.

BRITANNIA SERIES 310
133 PASSENGERS

CL-44D
178 PASSENGERS

Il-18V
100 PASSENGERS

Turboprop airliners of the 1950s

CANADAIR CL-44: This licence-built version of the Britannia was more than 3 m (10 ft.) longer than the largest British-built Britannias. The CL-44D-4 had a hinged aft fuselage section to simplify freight handling.

TUPOLEV Tu-116: The largest and heaviest commercial airliner before the advent of the Boeing 747, the Tu-116 was a development of the Tu-95 swept-wing turboprop bomber and first flew in 1957.

VICKERS VISCOUNT: The first civil airliner powered by turboprop engines, the first Viscount flew in 1948 and entered service in 1953. In all, 444 were built for service worldwide, with later versions seating up to 71 passengers.

BRITISH AEROSPACE

JETSTREAM 31/41

● 19-/29-seat commuterliner ● Handley Page design ● In production

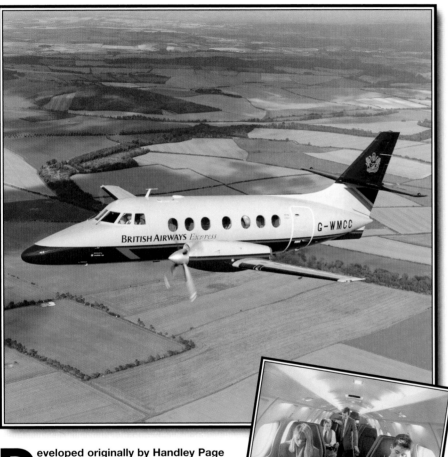

Developed originally by Handley Page and flown for the first time in August 1967, the Jetstream has been in production for 30 years. It was taken over by Scottish Aviation, which built 26 as navigation trainers for the RAF, and then relaunched as the Jetstream 31 by British Aerospace (BAe) in 1978. In its latest incarnation as the 29-seater Jetstream 41, the design is the sole product of Jetstream Aircraft Limited, a BAe subsidiary.

▲ *Jetstreams*
are available in various configurations: airliner, corporate, executive shuttle and special role, and can accommodate between eight and 19 passengers or special equipment.

BRITISH AEROSPACE JETSTREAM 31/41

◄ 31s and Super 31s
Airlines operating under the American Eagle name have taken delivery of several 31s and Super 31s.

▼ In service in the Low Countries
Netherlines, later part of the KLM Cityhopper group, started operating Jetstream 31s in 1985.

▼ Over the Firth of Forth
Loganair's Jetstream 41s have joined the British Regional Airlines fleet, which includes 13 examples of the 29-seat type. G-LOGJ is now G-MAJC.

▲ Birmingham Executive Airways
This company operated Jetstream 31s, with high-quality executive interiors, between the West Midlands and Copenhagen, Milan and Zurich.

◄ Canadian commuterliners
Ontario Express, a Canadian Partner airline, took delivery of the first of 14 Jetstream 31s in 1987. Ontario Express operates services across the province.

FACTS AND FIGURES

➤ The Jetstream started life as the Handley Page H.P.137 with an envisaged capacity of 12 to 20 passengers.

➤ After Handley Page's failure, American backers attempted to restart production.

➤ By June 1996, 101 J41s had been ordered, more than half by North American airlines.

➤ Introduced in 1987, the Jetstream Super 31 has more powerful engines and improved cabin comfort.

➤ Saudi Arabia uses two J31s, fitted with Tornado IDS avionics, to train aircrew.

➤ Field Aircraft finished the interiors of Jetstream 31s.

PROFILE

Handley Page's commuterliner reborn

Flown for the first time in March 1980, the Jetstream 31 was based on the Garrett-engined Mk 3 which the USAF had ordered, but later cancelled, as the C-10A.

In 1987 British Aerospace announced the Jetstream Super 31, which offered a 400-kg (880-lb.) increase in maximum take-off weight (a result of more powerful engines), plus many detail improvements. Both models have found customers as 19-seat regional airliners, although they have also been sold as eight- to 12-seat corporate transports, air

ambulance and special missions military aircraft.

Growth in commuter traffic has seen regional aircraft become larger, and in 1989 BAe started the development of the 29-seat Jetstream 41. Again, US-based feeder airlines have been the main customers, but the type is in service worldwide.

The 41 has more powerful TPE331 engines than the 31, enabling it to cruise at 540 km/h (335 m.p.h.) compared to the Super 31's speed of 435 km/h (270 m.p.h.). Payloads have increased steadily since the model's launch, and in 1995

water-methanol injection was introduced to improve performance in 'hot and high' conditions. Since 1996 Jetstreams have been marketed by Aero International (Regional), a consortium of Jetstream, Avro International and ATR.

Below: Delivered in 1993, G-WAWR (now G-MAJD) was the sixth J41 off the production line. Manx Airlines is now part of British Regional Airlines.

Above: Seen prior to delivery, this Jetstream 31 is finished in the livery of Sun-Air of Scandinavia.

Jetstream 41

Type: regional airliner

Powerplant: two 1230-kW (1,650-hp.) Garrett TPE331-14GR/HR turboprops

Maximum speed: 547 km/h (339 m.p.h.) at 6100 m (20,000 ft.)

Initial climb rate: 670 m/min (2,200 f.p.m.)

Range: 1433 km (890 mi.) with 29 passengers and in-flight refuelling reserves

Service ceiling: 7925 m (26,000 ft.)

Weights: empty 6416 kg (14,115 lb.); maximum take-off 10,886 kg (23,949 lb.)

Accommodation: flight crew of two, one attendant plus up to 29 passengers

Dimensions:
span	18.29 m	(60 ft.)
length	19.25 m	(63 ft. 2 in.)
height	5.74 m	(17 ft. 11 in.)
wing area	32.59 m²	(351 sq. ft.)

JETSTREAM 31

Flown in June 1985, N409AE was delivered to Metro Express, which operated the aircraft under the American Eagle feederliner banner. After less than two years of service, the aircraft was leased to Chapparal Airlines.

In its original form, the Handley Page design was powered by two Turboméca Astazou turboprops. Scottish Aviation took over the programme after Handley Page went bankrupt, only to be taken over itself by British Aerospace shortly afterwards. At this stage, the Jetstream 31 was developed with more powerful Garrett AiResearch TPE331s.

The main passenger cabin holds up to 19 passengers in a high-density commuter configuration. With an executive interior the aircraft is spacious and fitted with eight to 10 seats. The cabin is pressurised, heated, ventilated and air-conditioned.

Depending upon the regulations of a given country, Jetstream 31s may be fitted with dual controls for operation by one or two pilots.

N409AE

American Eagle

A commonly fitted extra on Jetstreams in feederliner service is a distinctive underfuselage baggage pod. This allows a maximum number of passengers to be carried.

Aluminium alloy is used in the construction of the semi-monocoque fuselage. In February 1994, the manufacturer increased airframe life from 30,000 to 40,000 hours.

ACTION DATA

PASSENGERS

BAe's Jetstream 31 is one of a number of aircraft competing for the lucrative 19-seater market. It has the advantage of being pressurised, unlike the EMB-110 and Do 228, allowing flight at higher altitudes to avoid bad weather.

31	19 passengers
EMB-110P2A BANDEIRANTE	21 passengers
Do 228-200	19 passengers

MAXIMUM CRUISING SPEED

In terms of its maximum cruising speed, the Jetstream 31 has an edge over the EMBRAER EMB-110 and Dornier Do 228. This allows faster journey times and therefore higher aircraft utilisation, which, in turn, give economical operations.

31	489 km/h (303 m.p.h.)
EMB-110P2A	413 km/h (256 m.p.h.)
Do 228-200	428 km/h (265 m.p.h.)

TAKE-OFF RUN

Jetstreams have an appreciably longer take-off run than both the Bandeirante and Do 228. The Dornier's short take-off and landing (STOL) performance is a result of its wing design. Both the Do 228 and EMB-110 have a useful rough-field capability.

Do 228-200	EMB-110P2A BANDEIRANTE	31
411 m (1,350 ft.)	675 m (2,215 ft.)	1569 m (5,150 ft.)

Jetstream 31s worldwide feederliner service

AUSTRALIA: VH-TQK was originally delivered to Queensland Air in September 1986. By 1988 it was serving with Eastern Australia Airlines, operating under the Australian banner.

GERMANY: Contactair was an early Jetstream 31 customer, and received this aircraft in 1983. After a period in Sweden, in 1992 it was leased to Sun-Air in Denmark.

UNITED KINGDOM: The fourth 31 off the production line, G-BKHI operated with Peregrine Air Services for three and a half years. By 1992 it was registered in Denmark.

UNITED STATES: Express Airlines took delivery of this pallet-equipped Jetstream 31 in 1986. It operated in Northwest Airlink colours, and provided feeder services for Northwest Airlines.

BRITISH AEROSPACE

125

● Best seller ● Civilian and military customers ● Luxury interior

Now manufactured by Raytheon and known as the Hawker 800, the 125 was built successively by de Havilland, Hawker Siddeley and British Aerospace and was in production for more than 30 years. It became established as the world's best-selling mid-size biz-jet and was one of Europe's most successful civil aircraft programmes. With continuous development, performance has increased and the most recent model can fly across the Atlantic.

▲ *When customers* *select a 125 or Hawker jet, they receive an aircraft that is equipped to their specification and is backed up by a global servicing network with 30 years of experience.*

BRITISH AEROSPACE 125

▲ Corporate comfort
Although the exact layout of the cabin is designed to customer requirements, this view represents a typical Hawker 800 interior.

▲ Intercontinental business
British Aerospace launched the BAe 1000 in October 1989 and Raytheon adopted the design as the Hawker 1000. An 84-cm (3-ft.) fuselage extension allows extra fuel to be carried, giving a maximum range of 6204 km (3,850 mi.).

▲ International sales success
BAe 125 and Hawker business jets are in the service of large companies, air forces and individuals worldwide. This is a Yemeni-registered machine.

▼ Australian interest
Carlton and United Breweries use this BAe 125-800 to transport staff across Australia.

▲ British Aerospace biz-jet
British Aerospace first flew the 125-800 in May 1983. This is the company aircraft, which also served as a demonstrator. By January 1995, 273 aircraft had been built and orders continued to be placed. Raytheon bought BAe Corporate Jets, including the 125, for $372 million in August 1993.

FACTS AND FIGURES

➤ Although the 125-800 first flew in 1983 it was not awarded Russian certification until 1993.

➤ Maximum operating altitude was reached on the 125-800's first flight.

➤ On-board entertainments include a CD player and video LCD screen.

➤ Having first flown on 16 June 1990, the BAe 1000 was certified on 26 November 1990 after an 800-hour test programme.

➤ The Hawker 1000 has higher powered engines with thrust reversers.

➤ Maximum passenger capacity of the Hawker 1000 has been increased to 15.

Dominating the luxury market

A primary reason for the 125's popularity is its cabin. The original designers insisted on 1.75 m (5 ft 9 in.) of headroom, which makes long journeys much more comfortable. It is big enough to carry 14 passengers, although eight seats is the norm and three passengers is a typical load.

Another reason the 125 is popular is that the process of continuous development has seen range increase steadily to reach 5318 km (3302 mi.) with maximum payload for the Hawker 800 (formerly the 125-800) and even more for the latest Hawker 1000. For journeys of that length comfort is a necessity, and cabin furnishings usually reflect the highest standards of luxury.

Even before the sale to Raytheon, most 125 interiors were designed by Arkansas Aerospace at Little Rock. Expense is rarely the main consideration in designing the interior, and the experts who furnish the cabin boast that they can literally design the seats to fit the chairman. The finest materials are used to achieve the feel of opulence while minimising weight. Business aircraft have to earn their living, however, and now computers and communications links are likely to be as important as a well stocked drinks cabinet.

Above: Famous excavator manufacturer J.C. Bamford has been a long-standing customer of British Aerospace business jets.

Above: Several earlier aircraft continue in service, a prime example being this BAe 125-700.

125-800

Type: business jet

Powerplant: two 19.13-kN (4,300-lb.-thrust) AlliedSignal TFE731-5R-1H turbofans

Maximum speed: 845 km/h (524 mi.) at 8840 m (29,000 ft.)

Climb rate: 945 m/min (4,000 f.p.m.) at sea level

Range: 5232 km (3,245 mi.) with maximum fuel

Service ceiling: 13,100 m (43,000 ft.)

Weights: empty 7076 kg (15,567 lb.); maximum take-off 12,428 kg (27,342 lb.)

Accommodation: two crew and up to 14 passengers

Dimensions:
span	15.66 m (51 ft. 4 in.)
length	15.60 m (51 ft. 2 in.)
height	5.36 m (17 ft. 7 in.)
wing area	34.75 m² (374 sq. ft.)

125 CC.Mk 3

No. 32 (The Royal) Squadron of the RAF flies six 125 CC.Mk 3 aircraft on Royal and VIP passenger transport duties. The machines are based on the civilian 125-700 airframe.

Individual operators choose their own cabin layout. RAF machines typically fly in an eight-seat configuration for the VIP transport of high-ranking officers.

There are a generous number of large cabin windows, giving passengers a good outside view. In addition, comfort is increased by the provision of individual tables and galley facilities.

AlliedSignal (Garrett) TFE731 turbofans of 16.46 kN (3,700 lb.-thrust) power the CC.Mk 3. To provide fleet commonality and to improve performance, earlier turbojet-powered RAF 125s were re-engined with these turbofans.

Placing the engines at the rear of the cabin minimises internal noise, but requires the tailplanes to be positioned high up on the fin, clear of jet blast.

ZE395

While the CC.Mk 3 can safely be operated by a crew of two, a third crewmember is sometimes carried. The 125 has served the RAF for many years.

A neat fairing covers the wing carry-through structure which runs beneath the cabin floor, allowing maximum internal volume.

A distinctive feature of the Series 700/CC.Mk 3 aircraft is this large ventral fin. Series 800 aircraft dispensed with it, but have an extended fin leading edge.

Other roles of the 125

■ **AIR AMBULANCE:** Typical of a number of 125s fitted with a hospital interior, this BAe 125-800 is flown by the Swiss air-ambulance service.

■ **NAVIGATION TRAINER:** Based on the early Hawker Siddeley 125 Series 1A/B, the Dominie T.Mk 1 has been the standard navigation trainer of the RAF since 1966.

■ **SEARCH AND RESCUE:** Japan's Air Self-Defence Force is currently receiving the U-125A SAR and maritime patrol variant of the Hawker 800.

ACTION DATA

PASSENGERS

In a typical executive layout these aircraft carry similar passenger loads, although all could accommodate more people at the expense of comfort. Typically, passenger loads would be lower than those shown, but the Astra SP lacks the versatility of its competitors.

HAWKER 800	8 passengers
LEARJET 60	9 passengers
ASTRA SP	6 passengers

CABIN HEIGHT

To achieve the ultimate in luxury travel, cabin height is an important factor since company executives prefer not to stoop as they move about the aircraft. The Hawker 800 has a distinct advantage.

HAWKER 800	1.75 m (5 ft. 9 in.)
LEARJET 60	1.71 m (5 ft. 7 in.)
ASTRA SP	1.70 m (5 ft. 6 in.)

RANGE

Although the Astra SP has a greater range than the Hawker 800, it cannot match its versatility or pedigree. The Learjet 60 trails in terms of range, but offers greater seating capacity. The similarity of design means that manufacturers must compete fiercely and closely match customer needs to win orders.

HAWKER 800	5232 km (3,245 mi.)
LEARJET 60	5074 km (3,150 mi.)
ASTRA SP	5215 km (3,475 mi.)

BRITISH AEROSPACE/AVRO
146/RJ

● 'WhisperJet' ● STOL performance ● VIP transport

T he graceful, efficient British Aerospace 146 (now known by its new name Avro Regional Jet) was designed to provide economical service to small airfields where runway length and noise constraints prohibit most airliners from operating. The Regional Jet lives up to its billing as one of the quietest planes in the sky. It remains popular and successful, although its manufacturer has undergone several corporate changes since 1983.

▲ The 146 had some success in penetrating the American feederliner market during the 1980s. Air Wisconsin was the initial US operator of the type, flying its first passengers in June 1983.

PHOTO FILE

BRITISH AEROSPACE/AVRO 146/RJ

◀ Hot and high
Excellent performance makes the 146 ideal for operations from the high plains of Africa. Good utilisation rates are another major plus.

▼ All-new cockpit
The new RJ series features an updated, user-friendly cockpit layout and new flight systems, helping to reduce pilot workload.

◀ Cabin comfort
The interior of the 146 is very passenger-friendly. The manufacturer claims that it is the world's most comfortable 100-seat aircraft.

▼ First off the line
The first operator of the 146 was Dan-Air who received this aircraft in May 1983.

Environmentally friendly ▶
The quiet, efficient and smokeless engines are a far cry from early turbojets.

FACTS AND FIGURES

➤ The 146-200 can accommodate up to 18.3 m³ (24 cu. yd.) of freight.

➤ Textron Inc., manufacturer of the Regional Jet's engines, has built 31,000 turbine engines in 37 years.

➤ Extensive ground tests were equivalent to 168,000 individual 45-minute flights.

➤ The landing gear of the Avro Regional Jet is wider than that of a C-130 Hercules.

➤ The 146 can make 200,000 landings without repairs to its undercarriage.

➤ Standard fuel capacity of the Regional Jet is 11,729 litres (3,100 gal.), and a 12,901-litre (3,400-gal.) option is also offered.

PROFILE

Quiet STOL short-hauler

The Avro Regional Jet whisks passengers aloft at a standard of comfort and convenience that was never before possible in a short-distance transport.

The Regional Jet has survived difficult times since it was first announced on 29 August 1973. It has had three names since then: the Hawker-Siddeley HS 146, followed by British Aerospace 146 and eventually the Avro Regional Jet (RJ). Despite the RJ being very

popular, efforts to sell a military version failed, and commercial sales have not attained their full potential. Passengers like being able to stand in the aisle and pilots enjoy the easy handling qualities of this aircraft.

The first carrier to operate the Regional Jet was Dan-Air, on 27 May 1983, and the BAe 146-200 and 146-300 'stretched' models entered service with Air Wisconsin in 1983 and 1987, respectively.

Because it is quiet and does

not disturb the neighbourhoods around airfields, this is the only jetliner allowed into several city airports, including John Wayne Airport in Orange County, California.

Thanks to its impressive low-noise performance the 146-300QT (Quiet Trader) is widely used on nocturnal courier and freight operations.

The key to the 146's quiet performance are the four Textron Lycoming turbofan engines. The aircraft is so quiet in flight that it is nicknamed the 'WhisperJet'.

The large T-tail provides good longitudinal stability. The manually operated elevators are responsive and the rudder is power assisted.

The highly efficient wings give outstanding field performance and help to reduce fuel consumption. To increase lift for take-off and landing, large Fowler flaps are fitted along 78 per cent of the trailing edge of the wing.

The undercarriage is fairly robust and is suitable for rough-field operations. Anti-skid units are fitted to the braking system.

RJ 100

Type: short-range commercial transport

Powerplant: four 31.14-kN (6,985-hp.) Textron Lycoming LF 507 turbofan engines

Cruising speed: 670 km/h (415 m.p.h.) at 8800 m (29,000 ft.)

Range: 2909 km (1,800 mi.)

Weights: operating empty 22,453 kg (49,397 lb.) (146-100), 23,269 kg (51,192 lb.) (146-200); maximum take-off 38,102 kg (83,824 lb.) (146-100), 42,184 kg (92,805 lb.) (146-200)

Accommodation: two pilots plus 100 passengers in a standard airline layout; maximum of 128 passengers in high-density layout

Dimensions:
span	26.21 m	(86 ft.)
length	30.99 m	(101 ft. 8 in.)
height	8.59 m	(28 ft. 2 in.)
wing area	77.29 m²	(832 sq. ft.)

146-200

Continental Express operates the 146-200 on busy business routes in the USA. When production of the 146 ended in 1993 the fleet had flown more than 1.6 million hours.

Almost all the essential flying instruments are duplicated so that either pilot can comfortably fly the 146. From 1990 the RJ series incorporated 'glass cockpit' features.

The 146 has a relatively wide fuselage for an aircraft of its size, allowing six-abreast seating. Stretching the fuselage has produced the varying capacity of the RJ series from the short RJ 70 to the fully stretched RJ 100.

CONTINENTAL EXPRESS

N406XV

A pair of large petal airbrakes are fitted at the base of the fin. These are spread to increase drag when landing and form the tailcone when closed.

ACTION DATA

PASSENGER LOAD

The RJ100 currently competes with Airbus Industrie's twin-engined A319, a shortened version of the A320. These airliners fill the gap left by the retirement of the earlier leader in this class, the Boeing 737-200.

RJ100	A319	737-200
128 passengers	130 passengers	130 passengers

NOISE LEVEL

Noise is becoming a problem for turbo-jet powered airliners of the 1960s and 1970s. Some operators are fitting 'hush kits' to their aircraft to avoid having to replace them altogether.

84-85 db take-off	97-98 db approach	85-86 db take-off	96-97 db approach	95-96 db take-off	101-102 db approach
RJ100		A319		737-200	

TAKE-OFF RUN

STOL (Short Take-Off and Landing) ability is a major selling point of the 146/RJ, allowing it to operate from airports with shorter landing strips. They are ideal for small inner-city airports.

737-200 2073 m (6,800 ft.)
A319 1829 m (6,000 ft.)
RJ100 1692 m (5,550 ft.)

Multi-roles for the 146/RJ

■ **QUIET TRADER:** With a large side-mounted cargo door, which allows quick loading of bulky freight, the QT is an ideal cargo aircraft especially at night when noise regulations are stringent.

■ **MILITARY ROLE:** A 'proof of concept' demonstrator, the 146STA was designed as a military transport. Here a long-wheelbase Land Rover is loaded using a ramp.

■ **MOUNTAIN OPERATIONS:** The 146 is ideal for operations in hot or high conditions. Druk Air operates the 146 flying tourists in the Himalaya Mountains of Nepal.

■ **ROYAL APPOINTMENT:** No. 32 (The Royal) Squadron operates three 146CC.Mk 2s. Fitted out with high-specification interiors, they are used by the Royal Family for official engagements.

BRITTEN-NORMAN

ISLANDER

● Light utility ● Dirt-strip transport ● Coastal patrol

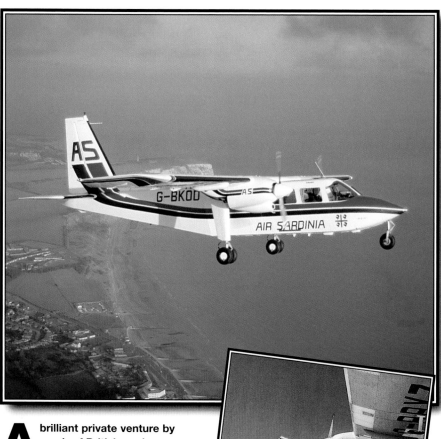

A brilliant private venture by a pair of British engineers, the Britten-Norman Islander began as a short-haul transport for the African nation of Cameroon and has gone on to become one of the most successful small airliners of all time. The high-wing, twin-engine Islander is testimony to common sense. It is a practical and pragmatic machine which has triumphed in service with 350 operators in 120 countries.

▲ *Reliability and a very adaptable airframe allow the Islander to operate in scorching deserts in Africa and the frozen wastes of Alaska. The aircraft thrives on difficult conditions, and at one time was considered for use in rural China.*

BRITTEN-NORMAN ISLANDER

▼ **Police patrol**
Malawi's police received this Islander. The aircraft has sold very widely to military and police forces in Africa and Asia.

◀ **Target tug**
This Islander, towing a bright target drogue, was the 1000th BN-2 to be built at the factory on the Isle of Wight.

▲ **Jungle warrior**
The military Defender is operated by the Belize Defence Force. It is armed with rocket and gun pods, and carries out patrols against drug-runners.

▼ **Survey plane**
Equipped for photographic survey and mapping work, this Islander contains a large camera in the rear cabin.

▲ **Dutch patrol**
The Netherlands police operates two Turbine Islanders fitted with special communications equipment, weather radar and infra-red sensors.

FACTS AND FIGURES

➤ Since 1969, the Islander has been produced in Romania by the manufacturer known today as Romaero.

➤ A three-engine version called the Trislander first flew in 1970.

➤ The Islander made its maiden flight on 13 June 1965.

➤ As late as 1994, Shenzhen Aircraft of China considered building Trislanders.

➤ The Defender 4000 armed version of the Islander made its public debut at the 1994 Farnborough air show.

➤ A turboprop version of the Islander was first tested in 1977.

PROFILE

Flying pick-up for everyone

In 1963, John Britten and Desmond Norman designed an aircraft to operate from crude airfields with low acquisition and operating costs, initially for an air taxi operator flying between Cameroon's cities of Doula and Tiko. The Britten-Norman Islander emerged as a short-haul airliner, mid-way in size between the Piper Apache, which holds

fewer passengers, and the DC-3, which is larger than many users need. By 1967, when Scotland's Loganair became the first airline to put the private-venture Islander into service, it was clear that the Britten-Norman aircraft would be a success with small airlines around the world.

Less obvious were other purposes for which the Islander

was ideal. The aircraft has succeeded with law enforcement, coast guard and drug interdiction agencies. A multi-sensor version carries the APG-66 radar of the F-16 fighter in its enlarged nose. The Defender 4000 is a potent military variant capable of handling Sea Skua missiles and Sting Ray torpedoes, and an AEW version was also projected.

Utility aircraft have a difficult life, often operating in remote areas where maintenance and safety are not a priority. Islanders have a safety record that is second to none.

BN-2B Islander

Type: nine-seat regional transport

Powerplant: two 194-kW (260-hp.) Lycoming O-540-E4C5 piston engines

Maximum speed: 257 km/h (159 m.p.h.)

Range: 2032 km (1,260 mi.)

Service ceiling: 4938 m (16,200 ft.)

Weights: empty 5900 kg (12,890 lb.); maximum take-off 6600 kg (14,520 lb.)

Accommodation: single pilot, nine bench-type passenger seats, provision for 880 kg (1,936 lb.) of personal baggage and cargo

Dimensions:
span	14.93 m	(49 ft.)
length	10.87 m	(35 ft. 7 in.)
height	4.18 m	(13 ft. 8 in.)
wing area	30.19 m²	(325 sq. ft.)

BN-2 ISLANDER

A single Islander was operated by Transkei Airways, flying in the former South African 'homeland'. Transkei Airways acquired the aircraft from a Kenyan operator.

The Islander is powered by simple, reliable Lycoming air-cooled flat six engines. The BN-2T Turbine Islander uses Allison 250 B-17 turboprops, giving increased performance at altitude.

The Islander's span was increased after trials of the prototype to increase the rate of climb.

The Lycoming engine drives a two-bladed constant-speed metal propeller.

Fuel is stored in wing tanks, including a wingtip tank.

There is no central aisle in the cabin, so front and rear doors are needed for entry.

The Islander has two seats for a pilot and co-pilot. The nose contains a small baggage compartment.

ZS-XGF

TRANSKEI AIRWAYS

Some Islanders and Defenders have a special rear cabin door that can be opened in flight for use by parachutists.

A specially strengthened undercarriage with low-pressure tyres allows operation from rough strips.

Islanders around the world

CIVILIAN USERS: The Islander's rugged dependability, short-field performance and ease of use make it popular with small airlines like Northern of Australia, which flies regular routes into small unprepared airstrips in the outback.

MILITARY USERS: The same qualities which make the Islander such a fine bush aircraft make it an ideal light military transport and liaison aircraft. This example of the Mauritanian air force is armed with air-to-surface rockets.

TRISLANDER: The Trislander is a stretched version of the original design with a uniquely positioned third engine. It has been operated by a number of civil and military users, including the Botswana Defence Force.

ACTION DATA

PASSENGER LOAD

The Islander is ideal for short-run flights to and from remote communities, being rugged and dependable yet simple and more economical to operate than the larger Twin Otter or the more complex PC-6. It can also be used to drop parachutists, for which role the bench seats are generally removed.

BN-2B ISLANDER — 9 passengers
DHC-6 TWIN OTTER — 20 passengers
PC-6 TURBO-PORTER — 10 passengers

RANGE

Most Islanders have the extended wing which was developed after trials with the prototype, and can carry enough fuel to make fairly long flights. Maximum range is achieved by flying at 59 per cent power at an optimum cruising altitude of 3660 metres.

DHC-6 TWIN OTTER 1700 km (1,050 mi.)
BN-2B ISLANDER 2032 km (1,260 mi.)
PC-6 TURBO-PORTER 1600 km (990 mi.)

TAKE-OFF RUN

The Islander has excellent STOL (short take-off and landing) characteristics. It matches the performance of the Twin Otter, also in worldwide back-country use, but it cannot equal the Turbo-Porter, which has a high-lift wing with double-slotted flaps and single-slotted ailerons.

PC-6 TURBO-PORTER 110 m (360 ft.)
BN-2B ISLANDER 203 m (665 ft.)
DHC-6 TWIN OTTER 213 m (700 ft.)

BRITTEN-NORMAN

TRISLANDER

● Tri-motor feederliner ● Based on Islander design ● More than 70 built

Built on the Isle of Wight, the nine-seat Islander has been one of Britain's most successful commercial aircraft. More than 1200 have been sold to operators in more than 120 countries. In 1970, six years after the Islander's first flight, Britten-Norman converted the second prototype to 18-seat configuration by adding a 2.3-m (7-ft. 6-in.) fuselage section and installing a third engine in the tail fin. The result was the Trislander.

▲ *The Trislander could carry nearly twice as many passengers as the earlier aircraft. The total number produced, however, was far less than the successful Islander.*

PHOTO FILE

BRITTEN-NORMAN TRISLANDER

▼ First Trislander
In prototype form the Trislander's third engine was mounted on a shortened tailfin. This was soon altered with a fin extension above the engine nacelle.

▲ Jamaican feederliner
Like the Islander before it, the Trislander was widely exported and aircraft served on all five continents.

▲ STOL performance
Trislanders had the same short take-off and landing (STOL) capability as the Islander, utilising the lengthened version of the latter's high-lift wing.

▲ Flared wingtips
The Trislander has flared wingtips like the Islander. These were a Britten-Norman trademark.

Launch customer ▶
Aurigny Air Services took delivery of its first Trislander in 1971 and in 1994 had the largest fleet.

FACTS AND FIGURES

➤ First flown on 11 September 1970, the Trislander prototype appeared at the Farnborough air show later that day.

➤ The last factory-built Trislander went to the Botswana defence force in 1984.

➤ In the early-1970s Trislander production was moved to Fairey's Belgian factory.

➤ The Trislander 4 was available with a standby rocket engine in case of engine failure on take-off.

➤ The Trislander 3 was a standard Trislander 2 certified for US operation.

➤ Sixty Trislanders were built for export to Africa, Asia, Australia and South America.

Loganair used Trislanders to provide a service to the Scottish highlands and islands.

Tri-motor from the Isle of Wight

In addition to the stretched fuselage, modified tail and extra engine, the Trislander had a longer wing than the Islander plus new main landing gear with bigger wheels and tyres. Later aircraft also had a baggage compartment in an extended nose assembly.

The Trislander took to the air in September 1970. The first customer was Aurigny Air Services, in the Channel Islands, which remains the biggest operator. Like the original Islander, the three-engined

model has very low operating costs, and additional flights can be scheduled without incurring prohibitive expense. Its seats can be removed quickly so that cargo can be carried when the aircraft does not have a full load of passengers.

In all, 72 Trislanders had been completed by the time production ended in 1984. There have been attempts to return the aircraft to production, but none of these has yet to come to fruition. The rights to the Trislander were sold in 1982

to the International Aviation Corporation of Florida, which planned to build the type as the Tri-Commutair. None was built, however, and the last 10 kits were subsequently sold in Australia. In 1994 Pilatus Britten-Norman (as the company has been known since 1979) had abortive discussions with a Chinese company in an attempt to restart production. Two of these uncompleted airframes were finished and delivered to Aurigny Air Services in 1996.

The Trislander prototype flies alongside a standard Islander, and clearly shows the differences between the two designs.

BN-2A MK III TRISLANDER 2

Aurigny Air Services' distinctive yellow-liveried Trislanders continue to provide a service between the Channel Islands and mainland Britain. G-OTSB was later re-registered G-RBSI and was among nine Trislanders operated by the company in 1997.

Originally, a 60-cm (23-in.) fuselage stretch was planned for the Islander (a prototype of which was flown in 1986), but this was abandoned in favour of the 2.3-m (7-ft. 6-in.) extension and extra engine of the Trislander.

The second Islander prototype was rebuilt with a fin-mounted engine to serve as the Trislander prototype. Initially, the tailfin did not extend above the engine nacelle, but later, in an effort to improve handling, the fin area was increased.

An optional feature found on many Trislanders is the extended nose which has 0.62 m³ (22 cu. ft.) of luggage capacity. This is supported by a steerable nosewheel.

Three Lycoming O-540 flat-six cylinder engines, as fitted to most Islanders, power the Trislander. Each is rated at 194 kW (260 hp.) and drives a Hartzell two-bladed propeller. Unlike the Islander, all Trislanders are piston-engined.

To support the extra weight at the rear of the aircraft, new landing gear was fitted with larger wheels and tyres than those of the Islander. The wing is 1.21 m (4 ft.) longer than that of the Islander.

An unusual option on Trislander 4s was a 1.56-kN (350-lb.-thrust) rocket engine which provided 12 seconds of thrust in case of engine failure. This was mounted below the rear engine nacelle.

Post-war tri-motor transports

■ **DE HAVILLAND AUSTRALIA DHA-3 DROVER:** This utility transport, with eight seats, initially flew in 1948. The first aircraft entered airline service, and others were used by flying doctors.

■ **NORTHROP N.23 PIONEER:** Built as a 40-passenger STOL commercial transport and first flown in 1946, the Pioneer was later developed as the C-125 Raider transport for the USAF.

■ **SPECIALISED AIRCRAFT TRI TURBO-3:** An attempt to breathe new life into the faithful DC-3/C-47, this 1970s conversion involved replacing two radial engines with three PT6 turboprops.

CANADAIR

C-4 ARGONAUT

● Canadian DC-4 ● Merlin engined ● No survivors

During World War II it became obvious that Trans Canada Airlines would need a suitable aircraft for use on both North Atlantic and domestic routes after hostilities ended. The Canadian government selected the Douglas DC-4 and a licence was granted for its manufacture in Canada. This 'north of the border' variant differed from the standard DC-4 in being powered by Rolls-Royce Merlin engines and having a pressurised fuselage.

▲ Compared to previous airliners, the Canadair DC-4M was a considerable improvement. One problem with the aircraft was the exceptionally high level of cabin noise in most variants.

PHOTO FILE

CANADAIR C-4 ARGONAUT

▼ **Star performer**
Here freight is loaded aboard a North Star, somewhere in Canada. These aircraft proved ideal for high-altitude operations.

▲ **First off the line**
Serialed CF-TEN-X, the prototype DC-4M first flew in July 1946. It was used on a number of proving flights before being converted into a military C-54GM and delivered to the RCAF in late 1952.

▼ **Virtual redesign**
Following on from the DC-4M-1 was a pressurised version, the DC-4M-2. Although dimensionally the same, this variant was essentially a new aircraft, featuring many components from the larger DC-6.

▲ **Pacific tragedy**
Canadian Pacific Airlines operated four North Stars briefly during the early 1950s. This one was lost in a crash in Tokyo.

British Argonauts ▶
Purchased as an interim type, BOAC's C-4s were given the class name Argonaut and primarily employed on services between London, Africa and the Far East. Their service record was so good that the airline operated them for more than 10 years.

FACTS AND FIGURES

➤ Trans Canada Airways began operating DC-4Ms on its transatlantic routes in early 1947, domestic services following.

➤ Royal Canadian Air Force (RCAF) C-54Ms were used extensively in the Korean War.

➤ A Trans Canada machine, CF-TFD, flew into a mountain, killing all on board.

➤ Mrs Howe, wife of the Minister of Reconstruction and Supply, christened the Canadian-built DC-4 the 'North Star'.

➤ By 1975 only a single example of the North Star was still in commercial use.

➤ One RCAF machine was unique in being powered by air-cooled radial engines.

PROFILE

Forgotten cousin of the DC-4

Trans Canada Airways purchased the first of 20 DC-4Ms in October 1947, after having borrowed six unpressurised RCAF aircraft. The British Overseas Airways Corporation (BOAC) ordered 22 aircraft, christened Argonauts, the following November, and all had been delivered by early 1949. Soon after its introduction the type was earning 30 per cent of the airline's revenue.

In service the DC-4M-2s (as the pressurised aircraft were known) were well received.

The Rolls-Royce Merlin engines gave the aircraft much better performance at altitude than standard US-built DC-4s, though the North Stars gained a reputation for excessive cabin noise caused by the engine exhaust systems. This problem was never really solved, so Canadair went ahead with the development of the radial-engined C-5, one of which was built and delivered to the RCAF.

With only 71 airframes built, and a sizeable number lost in flying accidents, a C-4 North

Star was a rare sight by the early 1970s. A handful were passed on to small operators, who used them primarily as freighters. In addition, a single example was retained by the RCAF for scientific exploration purposes. This, and the last flying commercial example, another ex-RCAF machine, were finally scrapped in 1976.

Left: RCAF North Stars were all delivered as unpressurised aircraft and featured nose radomes. Most were broken up in the 1960s, but one continued to serve until 1976 on survey duties.

Above: One of the BOAC Argonauts, Atalanta, has a special place in British history; it was the aircraft which carried the newly-crowned Queen Elizabeth II to South Africa in 1952.

C-4 North Star

Type: long-range transport

Powerplant: four 1312-kW (1,760-hp.) Rolls-Royce Merlin 622 liquid-cooled in-line piston engines

Maximum speed: 523 km/h (324 m.p.h.) at 7680 m (25,000 ft.)

Cruising speed: 466 km/h (289 m.p.h.) at 3720 m (12,000 ft.)

Range: 5150 km (3,193 mi.)

Service ceiling: 8990 m (29,500 ft.)

Weights: empty 21,243 kg (46,735 lb.); maximum take-off 37,331 kg (82,128 lb.)

Accommodation: crew of four, plus up to 62 passengers (typically) plus approx. 2600 kg (5,720 lb.) of freight

Dimensions:
span	35.81 m (117 ft. 5 in.)
length	28.54 m (93 ft. 7 in.)
height	8.39 m (27 ft. 6 in.)
wing area	135.63 m² (1,459 sq. ft.)

C-4

Delivered to the British Overseas Airways Corporation in August 1949, this example served with BOAC for 11 years. In February 1960 it was purchased by Aden Airways which operated the aircraft until it was retired in 1963.

When originally delivered to BOAC the C-4 aircraft were configured to carry 40 passengers. This seating plan was very flexible, however, and was altered by Aden Airways to permit carriage of more passengers on high-density routes.

Aden Airways acquired this C-4 from BOAC and it retained a very similar colour scheme to that used by its previous owner. Many fledgling African airlines bought second-hand aircraft from major European airlines.

G-ALHR

ADEN AIRWAYS

The cockpit was fitted out for a maximum crew of four, comprising the pilot, co-pilot, navigator and flight engineer. Later the crew was often reduced to three.

The C-4, unlike its DC-4 brother, was powered by four Rolls-Royce Merlin 622 or 724 in-line piston engines. Passengers did find the noise level from the engines to be high.

To carry a mixed load of passengers and freight the forward fuselage could be converted into a cargo hold. The rear fuselage could carry 16 passengers or accommodate a VIP area.

The C-4 had a conventional fin and rudder design identical to the DC-4 on which it was based. The controls were said to be light and responsive. A supporting pole could be attached to the bulge beneath the fuselage to prevent the aircraft tipping onto its tail during loading.

ACTION DATA

MAXIMUM SPEED

Fitting Rolls-Royce Merlins to the DC-4 airframe considerably improved performance and the North Star was much faster than its radial-engined American cousin. The Avro Tudor II was also fitted with Merlins but was larger and slightly slower.

C-4	523 km/h (324 m.p.h.)
DC-4-1009	451 km/h (280 m.p.h.)
689 TUDOR II	475 km/h (295 m.p.h.)

SERVICE CEILING

Trans Canada Airlines purchased North Stars with the intention of operating them on North Atlantic routes and at high altitudes. The Merlins were chosen as a powerplant primarily because they offered better performance for this role than the radial engines fitted to the DC-4.

C-4	DC-4-1009	689 TUDOR II
8990 m (29,500 ft.)	6800 m (22,300 ft.)	7790 m (25,550 ft.)

RANGE

In addition to giving the aircraft greater speed and better performance at altitude, the Merlins also increased endurance over that of the American DC-4s. The C-4 was still not as capable in this respect as the Tudor, which was used on long routes to Africa.

C-4: 5150 km (3,193 mi.)
689 TUDOR II: 5750 km (3,565 mi.)
DC-4-1009: 4023 km (2,495 mi.)

Propeller-driven aircraft from Canadair

■ **CANADAIR CL-44:** Essentially a copy of the Bristol Britannia, the CL-44 differed in being fitted with more powerful Rolls-Royce Tyne turboprops and featuring a strengthened airframe.

■ **CANADAIR CL-28 (CP-107) ARGUS:** Also based on the Britannia, this was a dedicated maritime patrol aircraft and featured a completely new unpressurised fuselage.

■ **CANADAIR CL-215:** Developed in the early 1960s, this amphibian has proved very useful as a water bomber and sizeable numbers have been exported around the world.

CANADAIR

REGIONAL JET

● Extended range ● Pioneering design ● Jet airliner

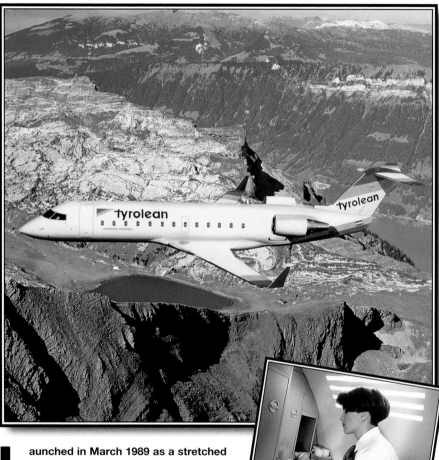

L aunched in March 1989 as a stretched development of the Challenger 601, Canadair's 50-seat Regional Jet flew for the first time in May 1991 and entered service in November 1992. The idea was to provide an aircraft able to operate on routes that would be uneconomical with bigger jets. It has been highly successful as a regional airliner, and has been used as the basis for the Canadair Special Edition business jet, and the Corporate JetLiner.

▲ In the competitive world of small jet airliners the Canadair Regional Jet offers the client an extremely high level of comfort, not often found in the smaller civil airliners.

CANADAIR REGIONAL JET

◄ Regional racer
Owned and operated by the former racing driver Niki Lauda, Lauda Air began operations with the Regional Jet in April 1994. Operating from Austria and using Vienna as a hub, the aircraft flew to Berlin and Manchester.

Advanced airliner ▶
A major milestone was reached on 16 October 1990, when the first Regional Jet reached the closing stages of construction.

▼ Corporate operations
Used by the Xerox Corporation for ferrying employees across the United States, the aircraft is able to accommodate 30 passengers.

▼ High flyer
Slicing through a city skyline, the Regional Jet takes advantage of all the latest aviation technology for its design. The sleek design and large winglets are a feature of the aircraft.

▲ Future flights
Canadair's first Regional Jet wore an extremely smart and complex colour scheme. The aircraft was exhibited at numerous aviation events in a bid to increase sales.

FACTS AND FIGURES

➤ The Regional Jet is the first modern airliner to be designed for the short-to-medium stage length market.

➤ Canadair has produced more than 4000 aircraft in its history.

➤ Flights can be made from Rome to Hamburg non-stop.

➤ With an increase in the demand for small airliners the Regional Jet was designed to replace the Challenger.

➤ The second Regional Jet made its first flight on 2 August 1991.

➤ Several European airlines have adopted the airliner in service.

Flying into the future

Compared with the Canadair Challenger 601, the Regional Jet has a bigger wing for improved lift at low airspeeds, and winglets to reduce drag. The fuselage has been extended by a total of 6.1 m (20 ft.) and there are two additional emergency exits.

As the world's first 50-seat jet airliner, the RJ has opened up a new market for small, high-performance airliners offering the sort of amenities found on traditional airliners, such as galleys for hot meals and ample headroom. It has proved even more economical than expected, burning some 10 per cent less fuel than originally predicted.

Lufthansa CityLine was the first airline operator, and by September 1997 a total of 16 airlines in 10 countries, mainly in Europe and North America, had ordered 286 examples.

The Corporate JetLiner is intended for use by industrial companies and government agencies as an alternative to airlines. It can be configured to carry from 18 to 35 passengers over ranges of up to 4167 km (2,600 mi.). The Special Edition version is a wide-body business jet with luxurious accommodation for up to 19 passengers and a range of 5778 km (3,528 mi.).

Above: In passing a succession of commercial aviation tests the prototype Regional Jet accomplished the amazing feat of completing five flights within the first week of testing, a civil record that stands to this day.
Right: Used for internal flights, Air Canada's Regional Jets wear a large maple leaf on their tail.

Though not installed on current aircraft a head-up display has been tested on the Regional Jet. This has proved to be extremely effective during limited visibility landings. As yet no operator has requested this modification.

RJ Series 200

Type: long-range regional jet airliner

Powerplant: two 41-kN (9,225-lb.-thrust) General Electric CF34-3A1 single-stage turbofan engines

Cruising speed: 859 km/h (533 m.p.h.); long-range cruise 786 km/h (487 m.p.h.)

Initial climb rate: 463 m/min (1,518 f.p.m.)

Range: 1787 km (1,108 mi.)

Service ceiling: 11,278 m (37,000 ft.)

Weights: empty 13,236 kg (29,119 lb.); maximum take-off 21,523 kg (47,350 lb.)

Accommodation: two pilots, plus flight attendants and up to 50 passengers

Dimensions: span 21.44 m (70 ft. 4 in.)
length 26.95 m (88 ft. 5 in.)
height 6.30 m (20 ft. 8 in.)
wing area 48.31 m² (520 sq. ft.)

REGIONAL JET

This example operates with Ansett Aviation Services of Australia. Ansett has chosen to have its aircraft wear a rather muted colour scheme compared to some that are in service.

Various options are available for the Regional Jet. If required the aircraft can be fitted with a flight management system to reduce the pilots' workload.

General Electric worked closely with Canadair to incorporate the changes that were necessary to the engine and engine nacelle. This reduced costs enormously.

During early developmental test flights an instrument boom was attached to the nose of the aircraft to allow data to be recorded and analysed after each flight. This was eventually removed.

A range of seating options is available for the aircraft depending on the operator. For high-density routes the aircraft can accommodate as many as 50 passengers.

A common feature on many modern airliners is the addition of winglets. This provides additional lift, by reducing wing-tip turbulence, and improves the handling of the aircraft.

Power is provided by two General Electric turbofan engines. These were installed on the aircraft after negotiations with GE for an engine that was readily accessible to the market and was easy for airlines to maintain.

ACTION DATA

MAXIMUM CRUISING SPEED
Canadair has incorporated many of the latest advances in aviation technology in its Regional Jet which has resulted in an impressive service speed. By operating at a high cruise speed the aircraft is able to cover huge distances at relatively little cost to the operator.

REGIONAL JET 200 — 859 km/h (533 m.p.h.)
F 70 — 856 km/h (530 m.p.h.)
RJ 85 — 763 km/h (473 m.p.h.)

RANGE
Having become one of the leaders in the manufacture of small commercial airliners, Canadair sought to improve their aircraft range with the Regional Jet. Though it does not offer the greatest range in its class, the RJ 200 is still very cost effective.

F 70 1981 km (1,228 mi.)
RJ 85 2129 km (1,320 mi.)
REGIONAL JET 200 1787 km (1,108 mi.)

CAPACITY
Designed to operate on domestic routes where the ability to carry a large number of passengers is not essential, the Regional Jet 200 still offers one of the largest passenger loads for its class. Although larger aircraft are able to carry more passengers this has not affected sales of the Regional Jet 200.

REGIONAL JET 200 50 passengers
F 70 79 passengers
RJ 85 85 passengers

Competitive Canadair

CHALLENGER 601: Developed for domestic civil flights, the Challenger is also operated by the RCAF. The aircraft is currently being replaced in civilian service by the Regional Jet.

DASH-8: The turbo-prop-powered Dash-8 is seen as a cost-effective alternative to some jet airliners. An all-purpose cargo version has also been produced.

LEARJET 60: Having established itself as a leader in the civil jet market, the Learjet has been constantly improved. This example is one of the latest variants.

CESSNA

MODEL A SERIES

● Air racer ● One-piece cantilever wing ● Commercial aircraft

▲ *Slender looking and with the performance of a racing aircraft, Cessna's Model A series took the American civil aircraft market by storm, achieving huge sales success.*

Clyde V. Cessna's first aircraft was a Blériot-type monoplane built in 1911 and powered by a 45-kW Elbridge engine. By the end of 1927 he had his own company and had constructed the prototype of his first production aircraft, the Model A. It offered high performance, without sacrificing comfort and utility, and served as the basis for the Cessna business for the next 25 years. It was also notable as the first of many light aircraft built by Cessna.

PHOTO FILE

CESSNA MODEL A SERIES

◀ Firm favourite
A long-time favourite with civilian operators, the Cessna Model AW used a Warner powerplant which overcame some of the problems encountered with the earlier troublesome Anzani engine.

Pioneering design ▶
Cessna was one of the first companies to make practical use of an internally braced wing design, on its Model A.

Surprise performance ▶
The little air-cooled Warner 'Scarab' engine gave the Model A a performance level that was comparable to that of larger aircraft. This allowed the aircraft to compete successfully in numerous air races and exhibitions across America in an effort to increase sales.

◀ Classic design
The design of the Cessna Model A series was so outstanding that it remained relatively unchanged for 25 years, apart from the adoption of different engines.

Engine choice ▶
Cessna sold the aircraft with a range of optional powerplants. This particular aircraft is the Model AC, the suffix 'C' denoting the Comet engine. However, the Warner engine was found to give the best performance.

FACTS AND FIGURES

➤ In 1929 a Model AW became the first civil aircraft to be flown to Siberia, flying more than 16,000 km (9,900 mi.) from the U.S.

➤ Cessna Model As were among the first aircraft used as corporate transports.

➤ Clyde Cessna's aviation activities date back to 1911.

➤ The fuselage was built up of welded chrome-moly steel tubing, lightly faired to shape and fabric covered.

➤ Wheel brakes were available on later models of the aircraft.

➤ Positioned on the rear fuselage was a rubber cord-supported tail-skid.

PROFILE

Wichita's light plane pioneer

Internally braced wings made their debut on a light commercial aircraft in the Cessna Model A. In 1928 a slightly modified Model AA became the first certificated version of the 'Cessna Cantilever Monoplane' series which was to prove so popular with flyers between the wars.

Able to accommodate three or four people, the Model AA was powered by a French 89-kW (120-hp.) Anzani radial engine, as there was no suitable American design in the required power range. A number of variants followed, each powered by a different engine type, as Cessna experimented with alternatives.

The most promising was the Model AW's Warner Scarab; this version was produced during 1929. In all, Model A production totalled 70, including 48 AWs. The Model BW followed, this being a 'sportsman's' version of the Model AW, which was powered by a 164-kW (220-hp.) Wright J5. Thirteen were built.

Chrome-moly steel tube was used in the Model A's fuselage structure, its wings had wooden framing and the entire aircraft was fabric covered. This gave a strong, but lightweight airframe and contributed to its lively performance. In fact, Model As were victorious as racing aircraft during the 1928 US season.

Below: Thanks to their excellent construction numerous Model A Series aircraft survive to this day. They are often seen at air shows in the United States.

Above: American businesses were quick to adopt the aircraft as executive transports.

Model AW

Type: single engine light passenger aircraft

Powerplant: one 82-kW (110-hp.) Warner Scarab seven-cylinder radial engine

Maximum speed: 201 km/h (125 m.p.h.); cruising speed 168 km/h (104 m.p.h.)

Initial climb rate: 188 m/min (617 f.p.m.)

Range: 1013 km (628 mi.)

Service ceiling: 3657 m (12,000 ft.)

Weights: empty 555 kg (1,220 lb.); maximum take-off 1025 kg (2,255 lb.)

Accommodation: one pilot and three passengers

Dimensions:
span	12.19 m (40 ft.)
length	7.58 m (24 ft. 10 in.)
height	1.86 m (6 ft. 2 in.)
wing area	20.80 m² (224 sq. ft.)

After problems with the early Anzani engine, Cessna installed a Warner Scarab engine on later aircraft, resulting in a marked increase in the performance of the aircraft.

Despite its small dimensions the Model A was capable of carrying three passengers. Two were seated on a bench-type seat in the rear cockpit, with the other seated alongside the pilot.

The fuselage was built up of welded chrome-moly steel tubing faired to shape and then covered with fabric, resulting in a finished fuselage that was light but extremely strong.

A large rudder gave the aircraft excellent handling, which was well appreciated by pilots competing in air races.

NC6448

To meet the requirement of operating from grass runways and unprepared strips, Cessna equipped the Model A with exceptionally large wheels.

The tail section of the undercarriage was a sprung-cord rubber tail-skid. This was lighter than an equivalent tailwheel arrangement which helped to reduced the overall weight of the aircraft.

MODEL AW

With performance equal to the racing aircraft of the period, the Cessna Model AW was able to offer the American public a small high-speed passenger aircraft which was purchased readily.

ACTION DATA

POWER

The lightweight design of the Model A required only a small powerplant to be used on the aircraft. Later models like the AW were fitted with improved engines, ensuring that their performance remained outstanding in comparison to other larger types such as de Havilland's Puss Moth and the Beech Model 10.

MODEL AW 82 kW (110 hp.)	MODEL 10-D 168 kW (225 hp.)	D.H. 80A PUSS MOTH 97 kW (130 hp.)

MAXIMUM SPEED

Although the Model AW was developed as a passenger aircraft, the high speed of the aircraft saw it competing in numerous air races across America during the twenties, often beating specially constructed designs. Despite this, larger passenger aircraft still just outstripped the Model AW for speed.

MODEL AW	201 km/h (125 m.p.h.)
MODEL 10-D	203 km/h (126 m.p.h.)
D.H. 80A PUSS MOTH	206 km/h (128 m.p.h.)

SERVICE CEILING

Despite its lightweight design, the Model AW was unable to achieve the high altitudes of the larger types such as the Beech Model 10 and de Havilland Puss Moth. For its class, though, the service ceiling of the Model AW was more than adequate.

MODEL AW	MODEL 10-D	D.H. 80A PUSS MOTH
3657 m (12,000 ft.)	3960 m (13,000 ft.)	5334 m (17,500 ft.)

Successful Cessnas

■ **THE COMET:** The first aircraft constructed by Cessna with an enclosed cockpit, the aircraft was displayed at air shows throughout the United States.

■ **DC-6:** Developed in 1928, the DC-6 was produced in two variants. Although it was a capable design, the economic recession in the thirties hindered sales of the aircraft.

■ **MODEL C-34:** Flying for the first time in June 1935, the C-34 displayed all the hallmarks of Cessna's light aircraft. Later models were pressed into limited military service.

CESSNA

401-441

● Air taxi ● Military communications ● Executive transport

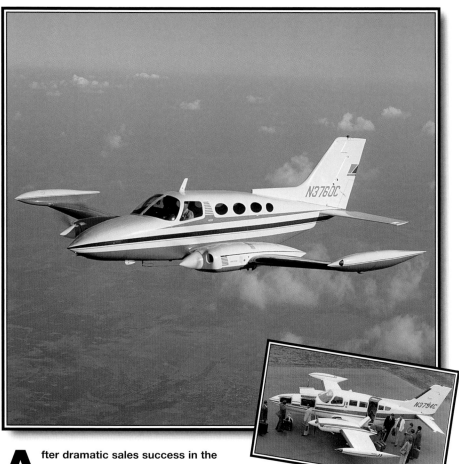

▲ Not only is the Cessna 400 Series in widespread operation as a passenger carrier, the Cessna 402 Utiliner also has a secondary light freight-carrying ability. This aircraft can have its seats removed and has double doors to facilitate access. Permanent tip tanks are fitted to the wings of the Utiliner to increase the aircraft's endurance.

After dramatic sales success in the 1950s and 1960s with their light, single- and twin-engined private aircraft, in 1962 Cessna made the move into the business aircraft market with the Model 411. This aircraft was an immediate success and it spawned numerous variants, with the latest remaining in production until 1987. The Cessna 400 family is still a common sight around the world today, whether operated as business aircraft or commuter liners.

CESSNA 401-441

Golden Eagle ▶
Pressurised for passenger comfort, the Cessna 421 was developed into the turboprop Model 425 Corsair.

▲ Worldwide service
Cessna 402s were sold to commuter airlines in every continent. This 402B, of Brazilian airline Transportes Aéreos Regionais (TAM), is fitted with turbocharged engines for high-altitude performance.

▲ Avoiding the storms
The Conquest executive version was available with a Bendix colour weather radar to help avoid storms.

◀ Sales success
The basic form of the 411 was kept throughout the series, including the 10-seat Golden Eagle.

Turbo power ▶
Cessna stepped into the turboprop market with the Model 441 Conquest pressurised executive transport, which has accommodation for up to 11 passengers. Some 360 were sold.

FACTS AND FIGURES

➤ Cessna use the 400 Series designation to distinguish medium twin-engined aircraft with a power output of more than 447 kW.

➤ The Cessna 411 gained certification on 17 August 1964.

➤ Cessna 400 Series aircraft are used for communications by more than 20 air arms.

➤ In February 1960, Cessna acquired a 49 per cent stake in French company, Avions Max Holste, which became Reims Aviation.

➤ The basic price for a new Cessna 402C in 1981 was $282,000.

➤ From 1980, Cessna offered a 35-month warranty on all 400 Series aircraft.

PROFILE

Successful twin-engined family

Entering service in 1964, the Cessna 401 introduced the new six-seat 'cabin class' business aircraft to the world. In the following 20 years, this initial design produced a whole family of best-selling twin-engined aircraft, enhancing Cessna's reputation as one of the world's biggest general aviation manufacturers.

The most successful version was the 10-seat Model 402 convertible passenger/freight aircraft also known as the Utiliner or Businessliner. Other versions, such as the pressurised Model 414 Chancellor and 421 Golden Eagle, quickly followed as sales increased around the world. Showing the versatility of the 400 Series airframe, Cessna decided in the mid-1970s to expand into the twin-turboprop market – previously dominated by the Beech King Air – with the Model 441 Conquest. After early tailplane problems (resulting in a fatal crash), the turboprop Conquest and the smaller Model 425 Corsair became popular with the executive market. In 1975, Cessna launched a stretched version of the Model 402B, called the 404 Titan, which sold well to small commuter airlines. An even larger 14-seat version, called the Caravan II, was produced by Reims in France. However, by 1986, liability problems had forced Cessna to halt its light/medium piston aircraft production.

Above: Liability problems in the United States have been resolved and it is hoped that 400 Series production may resume.

Right: To provide a smaller pressurised twin, Cessna developed the six-seat Model 414 Chancellor.

Model 441 Conquest

Type: twin-engined pressurised executive transport

Powerplant: two 474-kW (636-hp.) Garrett TPE331-8 turboprop engines

Maximum speed: 547 km/h (340 m.p.h.) at 4875 m (16,000 ft.)

Maximum cruising speed: 542 km/h (337 m.p.h.) at 7315 m (24,000 ft.)

Range: 4096 km (2,545 mi.)

Service ceiling: 11,275 m (37,000 ft.)

Weights: empty 2670 kg (5,886 lb.); maximum take-off 4468 kg (9,850 lb.)

Accommodation: 11 passengers

Dimensions:
span	15.04 m	(49 ft. 4 in.)
length	11.89 m	(39 ft.)
height	4.01 m	(13 ft. 2 in.)
wing area	23.56 m²	(236 sq. ft.)

MODEL 404 TITAN

Cessna's versatile Titan was available in three versions: the Titan Ambassador passenger carrier, the Titan Courier convertible passenger/freight transport, and the Titan Freighter cargo aircraft.

As well as dual controls, the Titan was usually equipped with factory-installed avionics systems and equipment packages.

Power was provided by two 280-kW (375-hp.) Continental GTSIO-520-M turbocharged engines, giving an increase of more than 30 per cent in kg/km per litre over the Model 402.

The Titan's tail unit differed from the Model 402B in having an extended fin and a tailplane with 12° of dihedral. These measures gave the larger Titan sufficient directional control.

A number of different cabin interiors were offered with the Titan. The Ambassador version was available with an executive interior, whereas the Courier could be fitted with removable seats for up to 10 passengers. The final variant, the Freighter, featured impact-resistant interiors to protect the fuselage from damage by cargo.

The Titan is basically a stretched Model 402B and its nose shares this aircraft's profile. Space in the nose is taken up by a luggage compartment.

The wings and landing gear were similar to those fitted to the Model 441 Conquest, which was developed at the same time.

ACTION DATA

CRUISING SPEED

Although the Mojave does not benefit from turboprop power, its sleek lines give it a higher cruising speed than the similarly piston-engined Model 414A. The C90A is turboprop-powered.

MODEL 414A	357 km/h (222 m.p.h.)
KING AIR C90A	448 km/h (278 m.p.h.)
PA-31P-350 MOJAVE	435 km/h (270 m.p.h.)

TAKE-OFF RUN

Again, the added power of turboprop engines gives the King Air a decisive advantage over piston-engined rivals. The Mojave and Model 414 use a similar amount of runway. All the aircraft are able to operate from smaller airfields with short strips.

MODEL 414A 791 m (2,595 ft.)

KING AIR C90A 689 m (2,260 ft.)

PA-31P-350 MOJAVE 753 m (2,470 ft.)

RANGE

Early versions of the King Air do not have the range of later models. Both the Mojave and the Model 414 have sufficient range to carry out commuterliner or internal executive flights. The maximum range of the 414A increases to 2459 km (1,528 mi.) if the aircraft is empty, allowing positioning flights over long distances.

MODEL 414A 1823 km (1,133 mi.)

KING AIR C90A 1612 km (1,000 mi.)

PA-31P-350 MOJAVE 2061 km (1,281 mi.)

Cessna 400 Series family

■ **MODEL 402B:** The 10-seat Model 402 was the most numerous variant of the 400 Series, with more than 1000 produced. The prototype first flew in August 1965.

■ **MODEL 404 TITAN:** First flying on 26 February 1975, the Titan was initially delivered at a rate of about 80 per year. In 1981 the basic price for a new Titan was $415,000.

■ **MODEL 441 CONQUEST:** After early structural problems, the Conquest achieved a fair market share of the twin-turboprop executive market. The production run totalled 362 aircraft.

CESSNA

CITATION

● Luxury jet family ● Straight and swept wings ● High performance

On 15 September 1969 the first Cessna Fanjet 500 made its initial flight. Immediately renamed Model 500 Citation, it launched Cessna into the highly competitive business jet market. Competitors doubted the new aircraft, but Cessna persevered and has produced a range of jets which fulfil the needs of business travellers in the USA and around the world. The aircraft have increasingly become a symbol of corporate power.

▲ *Business jets have become a useful transport and status symbol for companies and individuals across America. Sports personalities such as Jack Nicklaus are among the Citation customers and serve to give the aircraft an even more glamorous image.*

PHOTO FILE

CESSNA **CITATION**

▼ Rough business
A Citation 501 prototype demonstrates the aircraft's ability to operate from grass air strips.

▲ Comfort and Citation II
Seating 6 to 10, the 689 Model 550s delivered by January 1995 have luxurious interiors.

Sweeping new Citation ▶
NASA helped Cessna to design the wing for the advanced Model 650 Citation III. Compared to the previous model, the Citation III had only the name in common.

▼ Cessna's 'Nearjet'
Competitors referred to the Citation I as the 'Nearjet' because of its conventional appearance. When production ceased in 1976, 350 had been built.

▲ Simpler and cheaper
Having abandoned the more expensive Citation IV, Cessna developed the lower-cost Citation VI. From the outside this model is identical to the III.

FACTS AND FIGURES

➤ A single-pilot version of the Citation I was certified on 7 January 1977 as the Model 501 Citation I/SP.

➤ During flight tests the Citation III has been taken to Mach 0.90 in a dive.

➤ Golfer Arnold Palmer has also ordered a Model 750 Citation X after his Citation III.

➤ The Citation Excel combines a short version of the Citation X's cabin with Citation V Ultra wings and tail.

➤ Cessna designed the Citation V as a successor to the Citation I and II.

➤ The hi-tech Citation X features a glass cockpit and transatlantic range.

PROFILE

Cessna's winning business jet

Cessna ensured the long-term success of its Citation family by producing a stylish design which offered the utmost in modern jet performance at an affordable price.

Even the original straight-winged models, with their narrow, sleek fuselages and rear-mounted engines, were extremely elegant aircraft. Companies and celebrities were quick to recognise the image-enhancing properties of owning a Citation. Any doubts about the ability of a manufacturer of light piston-engined aircraft to produce a jet were dispelled by Cessna's experience with the USAF's T-37/A-37 programme.

During 1976 Cessna began work on the Citation III. Intended as a development of the straight-winged I and II, the aircraft emerged as a radically new design with swept wings and a higher cabin ceiling. The increase in height made the aircraft even more desirable, and orders from the US and abroad flooded in. The first

In August 1987 Cessna announced the Citation V. This model brought the straight-winged Citations up to modern standards.

delivery was made to golfer Arnold Palmer in 1983. Subsequent Citations have offered improved performance and comfort, and culminated in the Mach 0.92-capable Citation X.

A gravity refuelling point is located on the upper surface of each wing, with the primary high-pressure point on the starboard rear fuselage.

Most of the airframe is of light-alloy construction. The fuselage is of circular section and of fail-safe structure in pressurised areas.

The wing leading-edge is de-iced by engine bleed air, while the tailplane is de-iced electrically. No provision is made for fin de-icing, although the engine intakes are protected from ice build-up.

The high-mounted T-tail has a variable incidence tailplane and elevators. All tail surfaces are of light alloy.

Citation VI

Type: 6- to 10-seat passenger business jet

Powerplant: two 16.24-kN (3,650-lb.-thrust) AlliedSignal TFE731-3B-100S turbofans

Maximum cruising speed: 885 km/h (350 m.p.h.) at 2440 m (8,000 ft.)

Initial climb rate: 1127 m/min (3,700 f.p.m.) at sea level

Range: 4345 km (2,694 mi.) with two crew and four passengers and 45-minute reserves

Service ceiling: 15,545 m (51,000 ft.)

Weights: empty 5851 kg (12,872 lb.); maximum take-off 9979 kg (21,954 lb.)

Accommodation: maximum of 10 passengers according to cabin layout; standard seating for six passengers with toilet at rear

Dimensions:
span	16.31 m (53 ft. 6 in.)
length	16.90 m (55 ft. 5 in.)
height	5.12 m (16 ft. 9 in.)
wing area	28.99 m² (312 sq. ft.)

MODEL 650 CITATION VI

Although it is a smart aircraft with good performance, the Citation VI was launched at a time of general recession. Sales of the $8,200,000 jet have been slow.

A radome at the extreme nose covers a high-resolution Honeywell Primus 300SL colour weather radar. A hold for crew baggage is also incorporated into the nose section.

In order to make the Citation VI more affordable, Cessna limited the avionics options and offered only standard layouts for the cabin. The cabin is heated, pressurised and air-conditioned and is usually configured in a six-seat layout. Passenger seats are fully adjustable and have full harnesses.

The AlliedSignal TFE731 turbofans are pod-mounted high on the rear fuselage and are positioned to provide optimum maintenance convenience with minimum cabin noise. Hydraulically-operated thrust reversers are standard.

N652CC

Two crew members fly the Citation VI. An electronic flight instrumentation system is optional on this lower-specified model.

Emergency back-up systems are provided for both the nosewheel steering and anti-skid braking system.

This small door on the fuselage side serves the electrically heated 1.56 m³ (55-cu. ft.) passenger baggage compartment. At the forward end of the fuselage the main entrance door incorporates an airstair, while an emergency exit is situated on the starboard side above the wing.

ACTION DATA

COSTS
Initial purchase price is an important factor for business jet operators, especially if they require a fleet of aircraft. Customers wanting to seat 10 passengers in absolute comfort must pay a large amount for the performance and high prestige of the Citation X.

MODEL 750 CITATION X $12.95m
HAWKER 800 $9.90m
LEARJET 45 $6.10m

ACCOMMODATION
Executive jets rarely fly with a full complement of passengers. Each of these aircraft is therefore able to transport a typical load of six to 10 passengers over long ranges. The customer can specify cabin layout and many aircraft do not carry the maximum number of seats.

MODEL 750 CITATION X 12 passengers
HAWKER 800 14 passengers
LEARJET 45 10 passengers

RANGE

The Citation X truly excels with its long range. Most business jets offering such extreme range are much larger and may therefore prove to be less economical to operate. These aircraft are also more expensive to buy and require longer runways.

MODEL 750 CITATION X 6117 km (3,792 mi.)
HAWKER 800 5232 km (3,244 mi.)
LEARJET 45 4074 km (2,525 mi.)

Special mission Citation

■ **FLIGHT CHECKING:** The US Federal Aviation Administration has used this early-model Citation for checking and calibrating airport navigation and approach systems.

■ **VIP AND PRIORITY TRANSPORT:** A few Citations are used by the military in the VIP and courier roles. This Model 500 belongs to the Venezuelan air force.

■ **RADAR TRAINING:** Fifteen Model 552 Citations replaced T-39 Sabreliners in US Navy service. They operated as T-47As and were used as flying classrooms for student radar operators.

CONVAIR

CV 240-CV 440

● Best-selling airliners ● Turboprop conversions ● Long-serving freighters

▲ The secret
of the 240's success was its
ability to be constantly upgraded, at a time
when rapid advances in technology could
make an aircraft obsolete in only a few years.

American Airlines' search for a
DC-3 replacement in 1945 was
the spur to the development of
the long-serving series of twin-engined
airliners from Convair. Originating with
the Convair 240, it was to evolve into
the 440, one of the top-performing
piston airliners of all time. They were
a real success in the new age of
post-war air commerce, particularly
when converted to turboprop power.

PHOTO FILE

CONVAIR CV 240-CV 440

◀ **Immaculate**
This beautifully cared-for
Convair 440 was operated
by Prinair. The Allison-
powered version was later
known as the 580, and was
the most powerful variant.

Napier turboprop ▶
Convair tested the 340 series with the
latest-technology Napier Eland turboprops.
The modified aircraft were known as 'Eland
Convairs' and were designated Convair 540.

USAF models ▶
The USAF used
the CV 240 (as
the C-131) for
cargo, medevac
and electronics
testing. It was
also used for
navigation
training,
designated T-29.

▲ **Lufthansa**
The Convair 340 was the first type ordered
by the new Lufthansa after the war. The
aircraft began operations in 1955, and
Convair 440s appeared in 1957.

No more flying ▶
Although Convair twins still serve in South
America, their numbers are dwindling and
many are being cannibalised for spares.

FACTS AND FIGURES

➤ The 'Convairliner' first flew in July 1946,
six months ahead of the Martin 2-0-2.

➤ The Convair 340 introduced in 1951 had a
fuselage 'stretch' of 1.37 m (4 ft. 6 in.)
and typically hauled 44 passengers.

➤ The final new model, the piston Convair
440, was the heaviest and most powerful.

➤ Military versions of the Convair included
the US Air Force T-29 trainer and C-131
transport.

➤ At least 200 Convair twins were
converted to turboprop propulsion.

➤ More than 500 Convairliners were built
between 1947 and 1958.

PROFILE

Convair's long-lasting twins

Consolidated Vultee, or Convair, was a key player in the post-war race with Boeing, Douglas and Martin to build short- and medium-haul airliners for the blossoming aircraft market. No one achieved the impossible dream of replacing the DC-3, but the 'Convairliner' series came close. The Convair 240 first flew a year after the war and was of great interest to potential users. When it entered service with American Airlines in 1948, it was immediately hailed as one of the finest aircraft in its class.

The piston-engined 240 was improved over time with more powerful engines and greater strength. It was succeeded by the 340 and 440, and the turboprop 540, 580, 600 and 640. Convairliners served with airlines large and small in 33 countries, and their economy and reliability meant that they remained in use well into the jet age.

For many years Convair twins were put to use hauling skiers and package tourists into remote mountain townships, while others were used as VIP transports. John F. Kennedy used a Convair to travel around the USA on his successful 1960 Presidential campaign.

Dozens of Convairs can still be seen in service today, many having been converted to serve as freighters.

Below: Still going strong. This Aerochacos 240 receives the careful attention of a marshal with a fire extinguisher while starting engines. Many 240s remain in service, especially as freight carriers.

Above: One of the earliest customers for Convair twins was KLM, who used them from 1948 to 1964.

CV 440

Type: medium-range transport

Powerplant: two 1864-kW (2,500-hp.) Pratt & Whitney R-2800-CB16 or -CB17 piston engines

Maximum cruising speed: 493 km/h (306 m.p.h.) at 3960 m (13,000 ft.)

Range: 2100 km (1,300 mi.) with max. payload

Service ceiling: 7590 m (25,000 ft.)

Weights: empty 15,111 kg (33,244 lb.); loaded 22,226 kg (48,897 lb.)

Accommodation: two pilots, flight engineer, two stewardesses; 52 passengers

Dimensions:
span	27.97 m (91 ft. 9 in.)
length	22.76 m (74 ft. 8 in.)
height	8.20 m (26 ft. 11 in.)
wing area	75.90 m² (817 sq. ft.)

CV 240

Braniff International Airlines used both the Convair 240, acquired when it merged with Mid-Continent Airlines, and Convair 340s, which it purchased directly.

The cockpit accommodated two pilots. Some airlines also flew with a radio operator.

The original Twin Wasp radial piston engines fitted to the 240 model were almost identical to the engines that powered the Hellcat fighters of the wartime US Navy.

Even though pressurisation and higher cruising altitudes enhanced the ride for the passengers, cabin noise was an ever-present problem with the early Convair twins, as it was with all piston-powered airliners. The problem was greatly reduced in the turboprop versions.

Freight versions of the Convair twins featured a large cargo door on the rear of the fuselage.

The distinctive tall tail design remained almost unchanged throughout the production run of the Convair twins.

Weather-mapping radar was optional in the Convair 340 and standard in the 440.

Curtiss and Hamilton Standard propellers were fitted to the Convair 240.

Engine cowling changes were frequent in the Convair twins. The original 240s had an efficient design that maximised cooling with low drag.

The wing of the 240 was enlarged for the 340 version, to give better high-altitude performance.

BRANIFF International AIRWAYS

N3427

BRANIFF

ACTION DATA

MAXIMUM SPEED

The Convair's powerful Wasp engines and clean lines gave it a far superior speed to earlier aircraft. However, the days of the piston engine were numbered, as turboprop-powered airliners like the Viscount were already in service.

CV 240	430 km/h (267 m.p.h.)
DC-3	350 km/h (217 m.p.h.)
VISCOUNT	560 km/h (347 m.p.h.)

PASSENGER LOAD

When the DC-3 was designed, civil air travel was still in its infancy. Both the Convair and the Viscount were designed from the outset with much greater capacity, reflecting the growing size of post-war passenger air travel.

CV 240	DC-3	VISCOUNT
40 PASSENGERS	21 PASSENGERS	47 PASSENGERS

RANGE

Bigger overall size and a large fuel load gave the Convair a good range with a typical passenger load. This was much reduced when flying at maximum all-up weight.

CV 240	DC-3	VISCOUNT
3200 km (1,985 mi.)	2575 km (1,600 mi.)	2775 km (1,720 mi.)

Successors to the DC-3

■ MARTIN 4-0-4: Built for the same market as the Convair, and similar in appearance and performance, the Martin did not sell as well.

■ VICKERS VIKING: Britain's Viking was contemporary with the Convair, but its tubby, tail-dragging design was the product of an earlier generation.

■ ILYUSHIN Il-14: Built in huge numbers, the Il-14 was smaller than the Convair. It can still be found flying in many former Communist states.

■ FOKKER F27: The turboprop revolutionised airliner design. Flying a decade after the Convair, the F27 was faster and more economical.

■ HAWKER SIDDELEY HS.748: Dating from the early 1960s, the turboprop HS.748 has been sold to more than 70 operators worldwide.

CONVAIR

880/990

● Long-range airliner ● Rival of the Boeing 707 ● Freighter

▲ Raquel Tejada christened the 990 over its distinctive wing bulges with champagne. Despite its high speed, the Convair was not as commercially viable as its rivals and had little success.

C onvair's 880 and 990 were less successful than first-generation jetliners produced by Boeing (707) and Douglas (DC-8), but during their moment of glory they made an impact. Aerodynamically the aircraft was quite impressive, and an 880 was even dived through the sound barrier. Unfortunately, it was also troublesome and costly to operate. Despite their grace and beauty, these aircraft eventually brought ruin to the manufacturer.

CONVAIR 880/990

▲ Asia Pacific
Garuda of Indonesia operated the 990 on Pacific routes. The 990 was modified with Krueger flaps and new engine nozzle fairings.

NASA Convair ▶
NASA operated three Convair 990s, including this one named Galileo II based at Dryden Air Force Base. Among the aircraft's many tasks was testing the undercarriage for the Space Shuttle.

▲ Interior
Convair made much of the 880's interior, but it was the five-abreast seating that airlines did not find attractive.

◀ Spantax takes off
Charter airline Spantax was a major customer. It operated 14 Convair 990s, with a maximum of 12 in service at any one time.

▲ Japanese 880
Japan Air Lines took delivery of seven 880s, two of which were destroyed in service.

FACTS AND FIGURES

➤ Convair cancelled plans to finish the 880 airliner in gold metal and to nickname it the Golden Arrow.

➤ The Convair 880 first flew on 27 January 1959; the 990 on 24 January 1961.

➤ Total production of these jetliners was 65 Convair 880s and 37 Convair 990s.

➤ When Convair first built the 880 it offered the aircraft at only $4.7 million, compared to $130 million for today's Boeing 777.

➤ Initial customers for the 990 included American, Swissair and Garuda airlines.

➤ A single Convair 880, known as the UC-880, was flown by the US Navy.

PROFILE

Convair's last gamble

It should have been a great success, offering high performance and stylish interior fittings, but the Convair 880 eventually bankrupted its manufacturer. The 880 came on to the market just before the Boeing 707 and Douglas DC-8, but it was flawed by having five-abreast seating unlike the six-abreast arrangement of its rivals. The reduced passenger capacity meant potential customers did not favour the 880 despite its slightly higher speed. The aircraft's numerical designation, 880, was in fact

its maximum speed in feet per second.

Sadly, the Convair jetliners were followed by a great deal of financial difficulty, with aircraft being sold in unprofitable deals. While the 880 developed normally, the 990 was impaired by aerodynamic shortcomings that took time and investment to fix. The distinct bulges on the wings, known as 'Küchemann's Carrots' reduced transonic drag. One Convair 880 was even dived through the sound barrier.

Research improved the entire fleet, but in the end money was the ruin of the 880 and 990, and

Above: Peru was one of the last customers for new-build 990s, together with Garuda of Indonesia. The 990 had a brief life with its original operators, and often went on to serve with charter lines.

the financial aftermath shortened Convair's life. By 1981 only Spantax was operating the 990 commercially, the remnants of just 37 built. In 1987, one aircraft was taken out of storage and delivered to South Africa, and one is also used by NASA for testing new equipment.

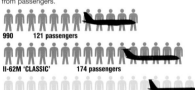

Above: It was lack of orders from domestic users which brought about the end of the 880. Deals with airlines it did attract were often badly negotiated, like the one with American Airlines that involved buying back DC-7s at twice their value.

990

Type: medium-range transport

Powerplant: four 68.57-kN (15,425-lb.-thrust) General Electric CJ805-23B turbofan engines

Maximum speed: 990 km/h (615 m.p.h.) at 6095 m (20,000 ft.)

Cruising speed: 895 km/h (555 m.p.h.) at 10,670 m (35,000 ft.)

Range: 8770 km (5,440 mi.)

Service ceiling: 12,495 m (41,000 ft.)

Weights: empty 54,839 kg (120,645 lb.); maximum take-off 114,759 kg (252,469 lb.)

Accommodation: two pilots, flight engineer, flight attendants and 121 passengers, 12 in first-class seating and 108 in economy seating, plus up to 8000 kg (17,600 lb.) of cargo

Dimensions:
span	36.58 m (120 ft.)
length	42.43 m (139 ft.)
height	12.04 m (39 ft 6 in.)
wing area	209.03 m² (2,249 sq. ft.)

990

Despite offering higher performance and better capacity than its predecessor, the 990 was no more successful. Scandinavian Airways System is one of a very few airlines to have operated Convair's last production airliner.

The cockpit accommodated a pilot and co-pilot side by side and a navigator and flight engineer behind.

Power for the early 880s was supplied by four J79 turbojets, the same engine that powered the McDonnell Douglas Phantom. The 990 used the modified General Electric CJ-805 turbofan.

The 990 had increased capacity over the 880, being about 3 m (10 ft.) longer and accommodating 96–121 passengers in five-abreast seating.

At the rear of the fuselage there was a plug-type door and toilets behind the passenger cabin. A Hamilton Standard air-conditioning system was fitted in the cabin.

Scandinavian Airways System ordered two 990s and also leased two aircraft purchased by Swissair.

Passengers entered through a door on the port side. The four-abreast first class section was immediately behind.

The four engines were fitted with thrust reversers and noise suppressors. Four of the so-called 'Küchemann's Carrots' mounted in the trailing edge were filled with fuel.

The highly swept wing was an all-metal, twin-spar structure mounted at 7° dihedral. The wing had an additional auxiliary spar at the root. The leading edge was double-skinned, with the space between used as a duct for thermal de-icing.

ACTION DATA

PASSENGERS

Lack of passenger capacity was the downfall of the 990. The jet used almost as much fuel as other airliners but earned less money from passengers.

990	121 passengers
Il-62M 'CLASSIC'	174 passengers
MODEL 707	189 passengers

MAXIMUM SPEED

Thanks to its sleek lines and powerful engines, the 990 was as fast as any other large airliner, although most airlines would gladly have traded some of the speed for extra capacity.

990	990 km/h (614 m.p.h.)
Il-62M 'CLASSIC'	920 km/h (570 m.p.h.)
MODEL 707	1000 km/h (620 m.p.h.)

RANGE

Another fault of the 990 was its lack of range. This was not a great problem for those sold to the American market, but it limited international sales.

990	8770 km (5,440 mi.)
Il-62M 'CLASSIC'	7800 km (4,836 mi.)
MODEL 707	11,120 km (6,894 mi.)

Convair 880 and 990 operators

CATHAY PACIFIC: Flying routes from Hong Kong, Cathay Pacific were among the last non-charter operators of the Convair jets.

DELTA: Flying international and domestic services, Delta also operated the rival Boeing 707 and DC-8 in large numbers.

NORTHEASTERN: One of the American customers that made more use of the 880 than most, Northeastern used it on domestic routes.

TRANSWORLD AIRLINES: TWA first flew 880s in 1961, but three years later it supplemented them with Boeing 707s and 727s.

CURTISS

CW-20

● Pre-war passenger design ● Wartime transport ● Post-war freighter

I nspired by the Boeing 247 and Douglas DC-2, the CW-20 airliner had a promising future when it first flew in 1940. However, World War II intervened and the Commando, as it was named, became the largest and heaviest twin-engined aircraft to serve with American forces. By the end of the war, technology had by-passed the Curtiss aircraft. Although it was too late for first-line passenger duty, the CW-20 remained in use as a cargo carrier in the civilian world.

▲ Curtiss
planned to put the CW-20 back into production as an airliner after the war. The availability of surplus military CW-20s and other aircraft, however, meant that no more were built.

CURTISS CW-20

◀ **Large twin-engined design**
Although similar in configuration to its great rival, the DC-3/C-47, the C-46 had 66 per cent more power. It was also a larger aircraft with a load capacity closer to that of the DC-4/C-54.

▼ **Veteran in the frozen north**
The small number of C-46s that have survived into the 1990s have had many owners. This Canadian aircraft carries the remnants of a US registration.

▼ **Wartime transport**
This CW-20T was fitted with a single tail and entered USAAC service as a C-55. Named St. Louis, it was sold to British Overseas Airways in 1941.

▼ **CW-20T with twin fins**
Completed in 1940, the prototype CW-20T featured twin tail fins on a dihedral tailplane. Two Wright R-2600 Twin Cyclones powered the aircraft.

◀ **Feederliner Commando**
A smaller number of C-46s entered service as feederliners with small US airlines.

FACTS AND FIGURES

➤ In recent years the CW-20 was operated in Latin America, especially in Bolivia, hauling a variety of cargoes.

➤ Of the 3182 Commandos built, 300 were still in service in 1985.

➤ The US Navy took delivery of 160 C-46As, designated R5C-1s.

➤ About a dozen Commandos have been preserved around the world, including a C-46D in the USAF Museum in Ohio.

➤ During the mid-1960s, C-46s supported covert US operations in Laos and Vietnam.

➤ In 1996 Everts Air Fuel used three C-46s to deliver fuel to remote Alaskan towns.

'Demobbed' Commandos

When it first appeared Curtiss-Wright called the CW-20 the Substratosphere Transport. It was a giant – the largest twin-engined airline transport ever built in the US. The company planned several versions, including one which would have been able to accommodate 20 passengers in sleeping berths.

Curtiss' chief designer, George A. Page, had intended to give passenger carriers an airliner with a profit-making capability that was superior

to that of existing models, including the new and unproven Douglas DC-3. It was only World War II which prevented the CW-20 from realising its potential as a civil airliner.

After 1945 war-weary C-46s (as CW-20s were known to the USAAF) found work around the world. Until the 1960s many remained in USAF ownership but were leased to airlines. Some of these were small feederlines, but most were freight-hauling companies. A number of C-46s

went to Europe, but the majority remained on the American continent, especially in South America. Although most have now been retired, a few C-46s are still flying.

Below: Alaskan airline Reeve Aleutian used C-46s to provide a service from Anchorage to remote towns, including oil-producing areas.

Above: A stepped cockpit windscreen, which was first used on the XC-26B, was incorporated in the 17 C-46Es. This C-46E belongs to Air America.

C-46 COMMANDO

N74171 was among 10 ex-USAAF C-46s leased by Pan Am in 1948 and used as freighters in the Caribbean and Central America. They were returned to the Army in 1953.

Having evaluated the first CW-20 as the C-55, the USAAC ordered the type into quantity production as the C-46. It filled an urgent requirement for an air transport aircraft. The CW-20 was an all-metal design, although the control surfaces were fabric-covered.

Most post-war US-registered CW-20s were employed as freighters. Those used as feederliners often had windows installed in the fuselage, as on the original CW-20, and a stair-door was sometimes installed in place of the cargo doors.

De-icing 'boots' on the leading edges of the wings and tailplane were pneumatically operated.

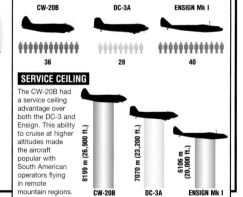

Production C-46s were equipped with two of the widely-used Pratt & Whitney R-2800 Double Wasp 18-cylinder two-row radials.

Although intended as a passenger design, with the onset of war the Commando entered production as a freighter. Consequently, it had only four cabin windows on the port side and five on the starboard side.

The 'double-bubble' semi-monocoque fuselage had a huge main cabin with a capacity of 65.13 m³ (2,300 cu. ft.). There was also a rear underfloor cargo compartment and a third compartment under the forward fuselage.

ACTION DATA

PASSENGERS

If World War II had not intervened the greater passenger capacity of the CW-20 would have made it popular with US airlines. The Ensign was a British design which was built in only limited numbers.

CW-20B	DC-3A	ENSIGN Mk I
36	28	40

SERVICE CEILING

The CW-20B had a service ceiling advantage over both the DC-3 and Ensign. This ability to cruise at higher altitudes made the aircraft popular with South American operators flying in remote mountain regions.

CW-20B 8199 m (26,900 ft.) / DC-3A 7070 m (23,200 ft.) / ENSIGN Mk I 6106 m (20,000 ft.)

RANGE

Although it had a load-carrying advantage over the DC-3, the CW-20B had a shorter range. The Ensign was intended for short-haul routes and was limited to journeys of about 1350 km (805 mi.) when carrying a payload.

CW-20B 2414 km (1,500 mi.) / DC-3A 3420 km (2,120 mi.) / ENSIGN Mk I 1384 km (860 mi.)

Multi-coloured civilian Commandos

■ **LUFTHANSA:** Lufthansa began freight operations in 1958, using aircraft like the C-46. In conjunction with British European Airways, it offered a service linking London and several German cities.

■ **AEROPESCA COLOMBIA:** The third operator of HK 812, a war-surplus C-46, was Aeropesca Colombia. This company was one of a number of lesser-known Latin American operators.

■ **TRANSPORTES AEREOS BOLIVAR:** This C-46F returned to the US in the 1960s, after been flown by two Chinese operators post-war. Before entering service in Bolivia it flew in the Caribbean.

DASSAULT

FALCON

● Long-range business transport ● Dassault's executive jet family

Designed in the late 1950s, the Falcon opened up new horizons in business transportation. This is an exciting executive jet intended for easy adaptation to other duties. Combining luxury with long range and superb flying characteristics, the Falcon has evolved into a family of aircraft. In varying sizes and configurations, these are among the world's best executive transports. Falcons are also used for coastal patrol and other duties.

▲ Most Falcons are in civilian use, but the French Aéronavale uses the aircraft for radar training and transport and to act as an intercept target.

DASSAULT FALCON

◄ Family formation
The secret of the Falcon's success has been in having an aircraft for every customer's requirements. Shown here are (front to rear) the Falcon 100, 200, 50 and 900.

▲ Bizjet office
Like most business jets, the Falcon has a pleasant, spacious cockpit. The latest versions have multi-function displays and state-of-the-art navigation systems.

▼ Company flagship
The largest of the Falcon family is the 900. Its vast range and high capacity make it the king of corporate jets.

▲ Falcon factory
The Falcon 50 is assembled at the Dassault factory at Bordeaux-Mérignac. After 30 years the Falcon is still in production, with the 2000 variant.

Corporate limousine ►
A Falcon 200 is the stylish way for an executive to arrive in town. Many Falcons have luxurious cabin interiors with every facility, as well as high performance and very long range.

FACTS AND FIGURES

➤ Nearly 1000 examples of the Falcon family are now flying around the world.

➤ The first prototype in the Falcon family made its initial flight on 4 May 1963.

➤ Nine engine types have been offered to customers or considered for use with different versions of the Falcon.

➤ The US Coast Guard's 41 HU-25 Guardians include nine HU-25C Night Stalkers, which use AN/APG-66 radar to detect smugglers.

➤ Falcon jets have flown over 1400 million km (930 million mi.), equal to 10 trips to Mars.

➤ The latest Falcon 2000 (Falcon X) has twin CFE738 engines.

PROFILE

France's flying limousine

Dassault, together with Sud-Aviation, developed the beautiful, twin-jet Falcon 20 (originally known in France as the Mystère 20) as the first in a successful line of attractive, sensible aircraft for business transport and other uses in 1963. This great flying-machine acquired intercontinental range as new Falcons took to the air, including the Falcon 50 and Falcon 900 tri-jets and the powerful twin-jet Falcon 2000, each larger and further-reaching.

Together, this family of aircraft has revolutionised executive travel and brought distant cities in the world closer together.

It was inevitable that this quality jet would be used for VIP transport by dignitaries ranging from the French president to the King of Morocco. The Falcon 20 freighter has proven a reliable hauler in the hands of users like Federal Express. Members of the Falcon family are also doing a fine job in maritime patrol for operators which include the US

Coast Guard and the Japanese Air Self-Defence Force. The Royal Navy uses the Falcon 20 for simulating attacks on shipping and for electronic warfare training.

The Falcon 50 is a rarity among bizjets in having three engines, though the larger Russian-designed Yak-42 also has three.

The advanced technology wing sweeps back at 29° inboard and 24.5° outboard. The structural boxes within the wing also serve as fuel tanks.

The sharply waisted rear fuselage and engine pods were computer-designed for maximum smoothness of airflow.

Falcon 50

Type: long-range executive jet

Powerplant: three 16.46-kN (3,700 lb-thrust) Garrett TFE731-3-1C turbofans

Maximum cruising speed: 870 km/h (541 m.p.h.)

Range: 6500 km (4,039 mi.) at Mach 0.75 with eight passengers

Weights: empty 9000 kg (19,842 lb.); loaded 17,600 kg (38,801 lb.)

Accommodation: two pilots and eight to 10 passengers; up to 14 passengers in a maximum-density layout

Dimensions:
span 18.86 m (61 ft. 11 in.)
length 18.52 m (60 ft. 9 in.)
height 6.97 m (22 ft. 10 in.)
wing area 46.83 m² (504 sq. ft.)

FALCON 900

The Falcon 900 has vast intercontinental range carrying a highly impressive load of 19 passengers. This capability, along with its relatively low operating costs, has helped to establish good sales figures in the all-important corporate jet market.

Falcons have a crew of two pilots, and usually a cabin attendant. Military Falcons often have navigation students or electronic warfare operators as well.

The capacious wide-body fuselage of the Falcon 900 gives the cabin almost twice the volume of the Falcon 50. It also has a greater fuel capacity than the twin-jet Falcons, giving much greater range.

The interior of the Falcon can incorporate a wide range of layouts. Typically the cabin is divided into three sections containing swivel 'sleeping' chairs, a dining area, fold-away beds and a conference table.

Falcons are powered by Garrett TFE731 turbofans. These efficient and reliable engines are also used in Learjets, Cessna Citations and BAe 125s.

N327K

The Falcon 50/900 wing is a more modern design than that of the 20/200. It is optimised to provide maximum comfort and economy at Mach 0.82 cruise.

Falcons have a 2.55-m³ (90-cu. ft.) baggage compartment at the rear of the fuselage. It is located within the pressurised section of the fuselage, so that delicate or pressure-sensitive items can be carried in safety.

ACTION DATA

RANGE

Modern multinational companies do business all over the world. The corporate jets they use reflect that trend, those at the top of the scale having intercontinental range. The Falcon is one of the best performers on the market, with capabilities beaten only by the very sophisticated and very expensive American-built Gulfstream IV.

BAe 125-800 — 5500 km (3,418 mi.)
FALCON 50 — 6500 km (4,039 mi.)
GULFSTREAM IV — 7820 km (4,859 mi.)

MAXIMUM CRUISING SPEED

BAe 125-800	845 km/h (525 m.p.h.)
GULFSTREAM IV	936 km/h (582 m.p.h.)
FALCON 50	870 km/h (541 m.p.h.)

The first generation of business jets were often slower than commercial jets. Modern executive jets have grown in speed, range and capability, and an aircraft like the Falcon has airliner-like performance but with considerably greater comfort for the passengers.

PAYLOAD

The Falcon 50 is a little smaller than other high-end corporate jets. To provide more competition for the likes of Gulfstream and British Aerospace, Dassault introduced the Falcon 900 in the mid-1980s. This has a wide range of seating options to a maximum of 19 passengers, doubling the capacity of the Falcon 50.

GULFSTREAM IV — 3 crew, 19 passengers
BAe 125-800 — 2 crew, 14 passengers
FALCON 50 — 2 crew, 8/10 passengers

Dassault's bizjet family

■ **FALCON 10/100:** First flown in 1970, the 100 was originally called the Minifalcon, as it was essentially a scaled-down Falcon 20.

■ **FALCON 20/200:** This features General Electric CF700 turbofans. Later Falcon 20s had enlarged fuel capacity and engine power.

■ **FALCON 50:** The first Falcon with three engines, the 50 was a larger aircraft with much greater range than earlier twin-jets.

■ **FALCON 900:** The top-of-the-range Falcon 900 is designed to carry up to 19 passengers over intercontinental ranges.

DASSAULT-BREGUET

MERCURE

● Short-range airliner ● One operator ● Financial disaster

▲ When the
Dassault company placed the
Mercure into production they were anticipating
sales of 300 examples by 1980. The total sale
of only 10 aircraft led to a large loss.

Despite its similarity to the successful Boeing 737 the Mercure never gained the success of its US counterpart. When Dassault developed the Mercure at the start of the 1970s it seemed ideal for short-haul air routes, but it was rushed into production prematurely, when orders for only 10 had been received. With inferior fuel capacity, the Mercure could not compete with the 737 and the aircraft gained no further orders.

PHOTO FILE

DASSAULT-BREGUET MERCURE

◀ First to fly
The first Mercure prototype was registered F-WTCC. 'TCC' stood for Transport Court-Courier (short-range transport).

▼ Production centre
Final assembly of the Mercure took place at the Dassault factory in Istres, southeast France.

▼ Unveiling the Mercure
The first Mercure was rolled out at Bordeaux-Mérignac airport on 4 April 1971, just 23 months after work began.

Sole customer ▶
Air Inter was the only airline to operate the Mercure. The airline received an annual subsidy of £850,000 during the 1980s to offset the high cost of spares.

Destined to fail ▶
Unable to compete with the American Boeing 737 and Douglas DC-9 in terms of range or operating economy, the Mercure never received the orders anticipated as airlines opted for the US-built aircraft.

FACTS AND FIGURES

➤ An annual subsidy from the French government helped to underwrite operating costs for the Mercure fleet.

➤ The prototype Dassault Mercure first took to the air on 28 May 1971.

➤ Air Inter placed its initial order for 10 Mercures on 29 January 1972.

➤ The first Mercure equipped for airline operations was delivered to Air Inter on 16 May 1974.

➤ The prototype was at first equipped with less powerful JT8D-11 turbofan engines.

➤ For the Mercure to break even it needed to achieve sales of 125 to 150 aircraft.

PROFILE

France's failed twin-jet

Dassault produced the Mercure airliner following the success of the manufacturer's Mystère/Falcon business jets. The Mercure was similar to (but had shorter range than) the Boeing 737, which brilliantly took advantage of the need for a short- to medium-haul passenger craft. However, Dassault made a major financial mistake by giving the 'go ahead' to the Mercure after only 10 had been ordered by Air Inter.

This low-wing, twin-jet aircraft was very pleasing in its general configuration and was equipped to provide travellers with speed and comfort. Pilots found the Mercure to be friendly and relatively easy to master.

With hindsight, however, it is easy to see that the Mercure was a miscalculation: faced with strong competition, especially from the Boeing 737 and the Douglas DC-9, Dassault's designers erred badly in providing so small a fuel capacity that the Mercure could not complete most services without time-consuming refuelling. Even though much of the design and development of this plane was subsidised by the French government, the Mercure never proved economical for Air Inter, the domestic carrier which

ordered all 10 machines.

Orders for the improved Mercure 200 never materialised and the project was abandoned at a huge loss.

The Mercure has now been retired from service, although several examples have been saved for museums.

Above: The Air Inter Mercures appeared in a number of colour schemes. This scheme was the last, applied in the mid-1980s.

Left: The second prototype, F-WTMD, was fitted with the production JT8D-15 engine.

MERCURE 100

In the mid-1980s Air Inter operated Mercure 100s on short-haul routes, mainly within France. This aircraft served with Air Inter throughout its service life before being retired in the early 1990s.

Mercure 100

Type: twin-engined short-range transport

Powerplant: two 68.95-kN (15,510-lb.-thrust) Pratt & Whitney JT8D-15 turbofan engines

Maximum speed: 941 km/h (583 m.p.h.) at 6096 m (20,000 ft.)

Maximum cruising speed: 925 km/h (574 m.p.h.) at 6096 m (20,000 ft.)

Range: 756 km (470 mi.)

Service ceiling: est. 12,000 m (39,300 ft.)

Weights: empty operating 31,800 kg (69,960 lb.); maximum take-off 56,500 kg (124,300 lb.)

Accommodation: two pilots, flight engineer, two cabin crew, passenger load of (typically) 120 to 150, maximum 162, plus up to 4400 kg (9,680 lb.) of baggage

Dimensions:
span 30.56 m (100 ft. 3 in.)
length 34.84 m (114 ft. 3 in.)
height 11.37 m (37 ft. 4 in.)
wing area 116 m² (1,248 sq. ft.)

The crew of two were seated side-by-side in the cockpit with two extra optional seats. The basic Mercure 100 was designed for all-weather (Cat III) operation and a Garrett AiResearch auxiliary power unit provided emergency electrical power and power for engine starting.

The typical mixed-class layout for the interior of the cabin comprised 12 four-abreast seats at 96.5-cm (38-in.) pitch and 120 six-abreast seats at 81.5-cm (32-in.) pitch. Galleys were included at the front and rear and the cabin windows were polarised to reduce glare.

Of cantilever low-wing monoplane form, the Mercure's wings were of two-spar fail-safe structure. Two triple-slotted flaps and a single aileron were fitted on the trailing edge of each wing. Spoilers were fitted to the upper surface to reduce lift when necessary.

For lateral control the rudder was divided into two independent parts, negating the need for trim tabs. The tailplane was of variable incidence type, to be used for emergency pitch control in the event of elevator failure.

The Mercure contained three baggage holds beneath the cabin floor. One was situated forward of the wings and two aft. The two cargo service doors were fitted to the starboard side of the fuselage.

The retractable tricycle-type undercarriage had twin wheels with shock absorbers on each unit. The nosewheel was steerable through 70° left or right.

Fitted in underwing pods were two Pratt & Whitney JT8D-15 turbofan engines with thrust reversers and Dassault-developed noise absorbers.

ACTION DATA

PASSENGERS

Although the Mercure 100 was capable of carrying more passengers than contemporary twin-jets, it could not operate as economically. However, if the Model 737 had not been such an exceptional airliner, the Mercure, with its good capacity, would have been more successful.

MERCURE 100	162
ONE-ELEVEN SERIES 500	119
ADVANCED 737-200	130

SPEED

One area where the Mercure excelled was cruising speed, reducing travel time for passengers. Unfortunately, the Mercure was only suitable for short-range routes, making the extra speed irrelevant.

MERCURE 100	925 km/h (574 m.p.h.)
ONE-ELEVEN	871 km/h (540 m.p.h.)
737-200	856 km/h (530 m.p.h.)

RANGE

The major disadvantage of the Mercure was its poor range. Its main competitor, the 737, could fly more than five times as far. The BAC 1-11 was also only suitable for routes of modest length.

ADVANCED 737-200 4179 km (2,590 mi.)
ONE-ELEVEN SERIES 500 2744 km (1,705 mi.)
MERCURE 100 756 km (470 mi.)

French airliner projects

AÉROSPATIALE SE 210 CARAVELLE: As the first French turbojet-powered airliner, the Caravelle had a then-unique engine layout of twin engines attached to the rear fuselage. A small number are still in service more than 40 years after the first flight.

AÉROSPATIALE/BAC CONCORDE: The world's only supersonic jet airliner in regular service was an Anglo-French product which became the flagship of Air France and British Airways. It remained in service for over a quarter of a century.

AIRBUS INDUSTRIE A300: The first in the line of successful Airbus products, the A300 first flew in 1972. It sold well and there is a successful freighter version. The European Airbus concern is based at Toulouse, France.

DE HAVILLAND

DH.104 DOVE

● Light transport ● Executive versions ● Military communications

Designed immediately after the end of World War II, the DH.104 Dove was an excellent transport aircraft which was produced to carry passengers over short distances. It was meant to fill the short-haul transport role that had been performed by the elegant pre-war DH.89 Dragon Rapide biplane. The Dove was a pleasing and practical airliner and a general-purpose aerial servant. It was also developed for military communications duties as the Devon.

▲ As well as having a long and successful career as a short-haul airliner, the Dove was also used extensively by large commercial companies such as Imperial Oil Limited.

PHOTO FILE

DE HAVILLAND DH.104 DOVE

◄ Devon down under
With the RAF and the Royal Navy, New Zealand also operated the Devon military variant.

▼ Riley conversion
Sky Tours Hawaii operated five modernised Doves featuring a swept tail and Lycoming engines.

▼ Float equipped
The sole Dove to be fitted with floats was converted by de Havilland Canada and is seen flying over Toronto in 1947. It was quickly realised that the Dove was more suited to land operations.

**Indian ►
service**
Three Devon C.Mk 1s, from an initial batch of four, are seen in formation prior to delivery to the Indian air force.

◄ Company transport
Painted in British Aerospace colours, this Dove 8 served as a company transport from Brough in Yorkshire until the late 1980s.

FACTS AND FIGURES

➤ The Dove was the first British transport to use reversible-pitch propellers for assisted braking.

➤ Versions of the Dove were used for pest control and as air ambulances.

➤ More than 500 Doves were manufactured before production ended in 1968.

➤ Apache Airlines of Arizona used much-modified Doves for passenger flights over the Grand Canyon.

➤ About 100 aircraft were built for military use as the Devon.

➤ More than 30 Doves have been preserved in museums around the world.

First of the executive transports

The Dove was an attractive, low-wing, twin-engined aircraft with tricycle gear, which was developed to take advantage of the prosperous market for short-haul airliners that was expected at the end of World War II.

From 1945, the Dove proved that it was one aircraft that had been designed correctly from the start. Production Doves had a dorsal fin (not found on the prototype) and a domed roof to provide more headroom for the pilots, but the first Dove was very much like the last. Owners, pilots and passengers always had high confidence in this very satisfying aircraft.

Several engines were used on the Dove. It was a flexible and versatile machine, and performed well in most climates. The pilot was not provided with any luxury in terms of leg room or moving space, but he held a commanding view from his perch located about one metre behind and above the nosewheel. Pilots admired the Dove's responsiveness and gentle handling qualities.

Although the Dove has now retired from the commercial airline scene, a small number of these fine aircraft still perform charter work and business flying.

Above: The Dove prototype, G-AGPJ, took to the air on 25 September 1945, coinciding with de Havilland's 25th anniversary.

Below: Development of the Dove involved only a minor tail redesign thanks to the excellence of the initial design.

DH.104 Dove 7

Type: twin-engined light transport

Powerplant: two 246-kW (330-hp.) de Havilland Gipsy Moth Queen 70 or 298-kW (400-hp.) Gipsy Queen 70 Mk 3 in-line piston engines

Maximum speed: 378 km/h (234 m.p.h.)

Cruising speed: 261 km/h (178 m.p.h.)

Range: 1891 km (1,175 mi.)

Service ceiling: 6615 m (21,700 ft.)

Weights: empty 2985 kg (6,567 lb.); maximum take-off 4060 kg (8,932 lb.)

Accommodation: two pilots, flight attendant, eight to 11 passengers or up to 9300 kg (20,503 lb.) of freight or cargo

Dimensions:

span	17.37 m (57 ft.)
length	11.99 m (39 ft 4 in.)
height	4.06 m (13 ft. 4 in.)
wing area	31.12 m² (335 sq. ft.)

DH.104 Dove 1

In 1947 Belgian airline SABENA ordered six Dove 1s. Three were used for regional operations in the Belgian Congo, and three for services between Brussels and Deauville.

The de Havilland Gipsy Queen engines were developed throughout the Dove's 14-year production life. The Gipsy Queen 70-3 fitted to this model could produce 246 kW (330 hp.).

The domed roof above the cockpit gave the aircrew sufficient headroom for comfortable operation. Many of the early Doves had a full glass cabin roof to increase the field of vision.

Developed to replace the Dragon Rapide, the Dove was a low-wing monoplane of semi-monocoque, entirely metal construction except for the fabric-covered elevators and rudder.

The Dove was initially offered to airlines with accommodation for eight passengers, or 11 with reduced baggage space and no toilet. The successful executive Dove 2 had luxury seating for six.

The only significant design change during development was a remodelling of the dorsal fin into the now familiar curve. This change gave improved control when flying on one engine.

One company which offered modernised Doves was the Riley Aeronautics Corporation, which fitted Lycoming engines and totally redesigned the tail, fitting an angular swept fin.

SABENA

OO-AWD

ACTION DATA

CRUISING SPEED

Of the three designs, only the Dove was a new aircraft. The Avro 19 was a civilian variant of the wartime Anson, and the Consul was developed from the Oxford. The more modern Dove had a higher cruising speed than its two rivals.

DH.104 DOVE 6	288 km/h (178 m.p.h.)
19 SERIES 1	280 km/h (174 m.p.h.)
AS.65 CONSUL	233 km/h (144 m.p.h.)

PASSENGERS

All three aircraft were intended for the feederliner market and therefore had a fairly low passenger capacity. The Consul was the weakest of the three, being able to carry only six passengers.

DH.104 DOVE 6	8
19 SERIES 1	9
AS.65 CONSUL	6

RANGE

Intended for the executive market as well as being a feederliner aircraft, the Dove had by far the best range performance, giving it greater flexibility. The Avro 19 and Consul could only operate on short-haul routes and were not suitable for executive use.

DH.104 DOVE 6
1722 km
(1,175 mi.)

AS.65 CONSUL
1022 km
(633 mi.)

19 SERIES 1
982 km
(609 mi.)

Post-war de Havilland airliners

■ **DH.106 COMET:** The world's first jet-engined airliner took to the air in July 1949. Early versions were plagued by a number of crashes.

■ **DH.114 HERON:** The Heron was basically a scaled-up Dove with four engines. Able to carry up to 17 passengers, it first flew in May 1950.

■ **DH.121 TRIDENT:** Designed as a short-haul jet transport, the Trident was eventually produced by the Hawker Siddeley company.

■ **DH.125:** Another design started before the absorption into Hawker Siddeley, the 125 replaced the Dove in the executive market.

DE HAVILLAND

DH.106 COMET

● World's first jet airliner ● Long service history ● Military transport

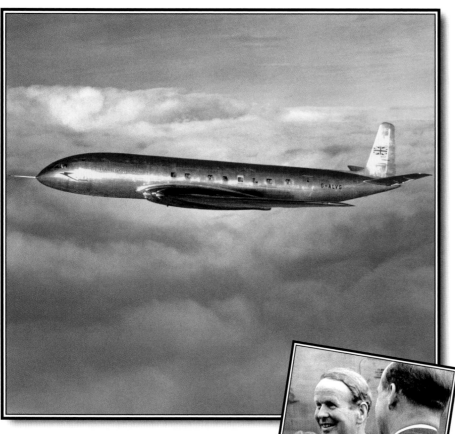

Triumph and tragedy stalked the de Havilland Comet. The world's first jet airliner was so advanced that it had no rival after inaugurating civil jet services in 1952. But when Comets mysteriously started plunging from the sky, detective work on the wreckage revealed a structural fault. Comets were grounded, and headlines called the plane a tragic failure. Although the improved Comet 4 was the first transatlantic jet airliner and flew successfully for many years, the plane was never to live down its early problems.

▲ *World War II*
night-fighter ace John Cunningham flew the prototype Comet in 1949, revolutionising passenger air transport and ushering in the jet age.

DE HAVILLAND DH.106 COMET

▼ Veteran workhorse
The last UK operator was Dan-Air who used the Comet 4B for charter flights to Mediterranean holiday destinations. After its initial design and safety problems the Comet gave its customers great service for 30 years.

▲ Sleek design
Fitting four engines in the wingroots reduced drag, and gave the Comet pleasing lines. But engineers did not much like this layout, as it gave poor access during maintenance.

▲ Flying the world
A reception committee greets the first Comet to arrive in New Zealand. The aircraft slashed flight times dramatically, establishing jet routes all over the world.

▲ Comet becomes Nimrod
The Nimrod maritime aircraft was derived from the Comet 4 airframe. Entering service in October 1969, Nimrods will be patrolling Britain's coasts for some time.

Airborne radar testbed ▶
The Comet airframe was used as a testbed for an airborne early-warning radar aircraft. The aircraft did not prove successful in this role.

FACTS AND FIGURES

➤ The first production Comet made its maiden flight on 9 January 1951.

➤ The first commercial flights by the Comet were freight-only trips between Britain and South Africa.

➤ Britain and Canada were the only users of military transport Comets.

➤ The Comet 2 used Rolls-Royce Avon engines, as used in the Lightning fighter.

➤ Two Comet 4C airframes were converted as prototypes for the Nimrod maritime patrol aircraft.

➤ The sole Comet 3 introduced the long fuselage used on production Comet 4s.

PROFILE

The world's first jet airliner

When the Comet began commercial jet service in May 1952, it was the flagship of Britain's aviation industry. Apart from its grace and elegance, the Comet was an engineering marvel, almost unmatched in its aerodynamics, structure and propulsion.

The Comet 1 and 2 were the envy of the world until tragedy struck and they began falling from the sky. The inflight destruction of a Comet near Calcutta on 2 May 1953, the first anniversary of BOAC's commercial service, captured attention everywhere.

Two more disasters followed. Eventually, investigators found fatigue cracks on wreckage recovered from the Mediterranean, the evidence of a structural fault. Planes were grounded and production halted. The Comet seemed doomed. But de Havilland made 'fixes' and regained public confidence with the Comet 4 in the 1960s.

Unfortunately, by this time, the de Havilland jet was flying in a world dominated by bigger and faster airliners from Boeing and Douglas, and although it proved reliable and effective, the Comet never achieved the

The extended-range Comet 4C introduced jet operations to a number of airlines in South America and the Middle East. Sudan Airways operated the type until the mid-1970s.

success that had seemed certain in the heady days of a decade before. Nevertheless, the Comet 4 continued giving excellent service until the end of the 1970s, a remarkable achievement for an aircraft designed in the 1940s.

The short-span Comet 4B was designed for short-haul operations, and could carry 100 passengers. It was initially purchased by British European Airways and Olympic Airways of Greece.

DH.106 Comet 4B

Type: medium-range passenger transport

Powerplant: four 46.71-kN (10,500-lb.-thrust) Rolls-Royce Mk 542 Avon turbojets; later Mk 525B

Maximum cruising speed: 856 km/h (532 m.p.h.) at sea level

Range: 3700 km (2,300 mi.) with maximum load, later increased to 5400 km (3,360 mi.)

Service ceiling: 12,500 m (41,000 ft.)

Weights: empty 33,483 kg (73,800 lb.); loaded 70,762 kg (156,000 lb.), later increased to 73,483 kg (162,000 lb.)

Accommodation: two pilots, one or two flight engineers, stewardesses, and 101 to 119 passengers in one or two classes

Dimensions: span 32.87 m (107 ft. 9 in.)
length 35.97 m (118 ft.)
height 8.69 m (28 ft. 6 in.)
wing area 191.28 m² (2,060 sq. ft.)

DH.106 COMET 4C

The Comet 4C was the most successful of the series, and featured a long fuselage and new wing. Middle East Airways was one of many customers from the region to purchase this aircraft.

The Comet was one of the first pressurised commercial aircraft, and once the catastrophic metal fatigue problem was solved it offered passengers a very comfortable flight.

The Comet 4 series was nearly 8 m (26 ft.) longer than the Comet 1. Originally designed to house a maximum of 101 passengers, as a charter airliner in its later life it had a capacity of 119.

The wing was very efficient and gave the Comet a lower stall speed than many contemporary propeller-driven aircraft. Most of it was taken up by a huge sealed fuel tank.

The fuselage was pressurised to give a 2000-m (6,500 ft) cabin pressure when flying at 12,000 m (40,000 ft). Four-abreast one- or two-class seating was the norm.

The Comet originated long before swept-wing data became general knowledge, and the tail was of conventional straight design.

MIDDLE EAST AIRLINES **M·E·A** OD-ADT

The flight deck accommodated two pilots, a flight engineer and a navigator.

The Comet's engines were buried in the wingroots. More efficient aerodynamically than 'podded' engines as on the Boeing 707, they were less easy to maintain and upgrade.

The external fuel tank mounted on the lower leading edge of the wing was the main identification feature of the Comet 4C.

Half a century of service

■ **COMET 2:** Serving as a military transport until the late-1960s, the Comet 2 was redesigned following the tragic accidents involving the original civil aircraft. It had thicker skin, and the square-cut windows which had generated the metal fatigue causing the crashes were replaced by oval cut-outs.

■ **COMET 4:** The first jet into regular transatlantic service, the Comet 4 proved itself a safe and reliable airliner. The most successful of the Comets, it was manufactured in three versions and could seat up to 119 passengers. The 67 aircraft built served with airlines all over the world.

■ **NIMROD:** Based on the Comet airframe, the heavily modified Nimrod maritime patrol aircraft has equipped the RAF since the 1970s. One of the most effective anti-submarine patrollers in the world, the Nimrod is still in front-line use. The Comet family has completed more than half a century of service.

ACTION DATA

SERVICE CEILING

The big advantage of the jet over piston-engined airliners is its ability to fly far above the weather. It also creates far less vibration in the airframe than propellers. Passengers on early Comet flights could not believe the smoothness of the ride, compared to the bumping and bouncing of even the best prop-driven machines. It also made good business sense: jet fuel economy improves at high altitude, giving early jet airliners such as the Comet and Boeing 707 transatlantic range.

12,500 m (41,000 ft.)		11,500 m (36,000 ft.)
	6500 m (21,300 ft.)	
DH.106 COMET	DC-7	MODEL 707

DE HAVILLAND

DH.114 HERON

● Based on the Dove ● VIP variants ● Re-engined versions

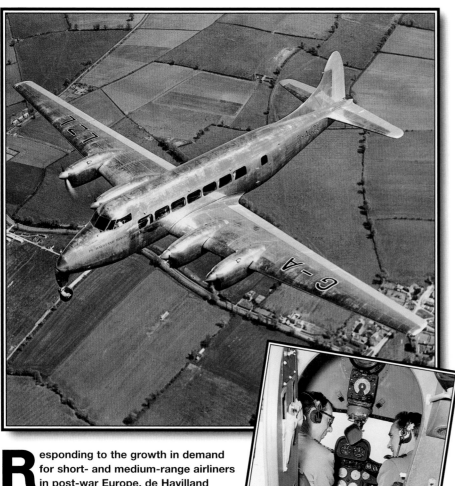

Responding to the growth in demand for short- and medium-range airliners in post-war Europe, de Havilland designed a larger, four-engined version of the Dove. Named Heron, it was built in smaller numbers than its predecessor but went on to serve with distinction with both civil and military operators. In the 1970s a number of Herons were fitted with Lycoming turboprops and many of these remained in service until the late 1980s.

▲ *The well laid-out cockpit accommodated two pilots with dual controls side-by-side. Passengers were seated two abreast. The cabin had a central aisle and a toilet at the rear.*

DE HAVILLAND DH.114 HERON

◄ **In the outback**
Butler Air Transport operated the Heron Mk I on mail and air-bus services in New South Wales.

▼ **Heron commuterliner**
Heron Mk Is of the Belgian airline SABENA established one of the first commuterline routes in Europe.

▼ **By Royal Command**
Delivered to the Queen's Flight in 1955, XH375 was flown extensively by HRH Prince Philip.

▼ **Turbine power**
In May 1969 Saunders Aircraft Corp. of Canada flew its first Heron fitted with two PT-6A turboprop engines. Renamed ST-27, 13 aircraft were converted, including this ex-Queen's Flight example which was delivered to Skywest Canada in 1972.

◄ **Riley conversions**
Named Riley Turbo Skyliners, these Herons were fitted with turbocharged Lycoming engines, which gave improved payload and performance.

FACTS AND FIGURES

➤ The Heron prototype, registered G-ALZL, was first flown by G.H. Pike at Hatfield on 10 May 1950.

➤ With retractable landing gear the Mk 2 was 32 km/h (20 m.p.h.) faster.

➤ A Heron Mk 2B was the personal aircraft of Prince Talal al Saud of Saudi Arabia.

➤ A custom-built version, the Mk 2E, with 12 seats (including four VIP seats) and a galley was flown by Ferranti Ltd.

➤ VIP Herons were used by King Feisal of Iraq and King Hussein of Jordan.

➤ Total Heron production reached 148, of which 52 were fixed-undercarriage Mk Is.

PROFILE

Big brother of the Dove

Designed in 1949 under the direction of W.A. Tamblin, the Heron was intended to be a simple and rugged machine, economical enough for short- and medium-range services in areas without properly prepared airfields. Based largely on the Dove, the Heron had four Gipsy Queen engines, which gave the aircraft exceptional short-field performance. After 180 hours of development flying, the only major alteration was the fitting of a sharply dihedral tailplane.

After tropical trials had been completed at Khartoum and Nairobi, production was established at Hatfield. The first example was flown 21000 km to be delivered to New Zealand National Airways.

After only seven aircraft had been built, production was moved to Chester and the improved Mk 2, with retractable landing gear, was introduced. By the mid-1960s the type had seen service in more than 30 countries and many examples had been fitted with luxury interiors for VIP and executive transport duties.

Herons were also operated as air ambulances by British European Airways and as mailplanes in Australia, as well as serving with the RAF's Queen's Flight and the Royal Navy.

Two fixed undercarriage Mk IBs were operated by the Scottish division of BEA. Often operating from beach airstrips, they flew ambulance and scheduled services between Scottish islands.

The prototype Heron was fitted with a straight tailplane, but testing revealed that one with dihedral provided greater stability and this was therefore adopted on subsequent marks.

The wing was basically a scaled-up version of that fitted to the Dove. It was set at a lower dihedral than the tailplane.

DH.114 Heron Mk 2B

Type: four-engined short- to medium-range airliner or executive aircraft

Powerplant: four 186.4-kW (250-hp.) de Havilland Gipsy Queen 30 Mk 2 piston engines

Cruising speed: 266 km/h (165 m.p.h.)

Initial climb rate: 323 m/min (1,060 f.p.m.)

Range: 1296 km (805 mi.)

Service ceiling: 5639 m (18,500 ft.)

Weights: empty 3622 kg (7,698 lb.); maximum take-off 5897 kg (12,975 lb.)

Accommodation: two pilots and 14 passengers (17 passengers if fitted without toilet)

Dimensions:
span	21.79 m	(71 ft. 6 in.)
length	14.78 m	(48 ft. 6 in.)
height	4.75 m	(15 ft. 7 in.)
wing area	46.36 m²	(499 sq. ft.)

TURBO SKYLINER

When Riley re-engined a number of Herons the resulting Turbo Skyliner gave the aircraft a new lease of life. This example was operated by Sunflower Airlines of Fiji on tourist flights.

Very similar to the Dove, the Heron's cockpit was well-equipped for the 1950s but did not feature modern equipment such as weather radar.

With two-abreast seating, most airliner Herons were configured to carry 14 passengers. A central aisle allowed access for a flight attendant.

The tail unit was similar to that of the Dove. The rounded form of the fin and rudder was typical of de Havilland designs.

sunflower airlines

DQ-FDY

Re-engined Turbo Skyliners replaced the original Gipsy Queen units with turbo-charged Lycoming IO-540 piston engines.

The original Mk I Herons had fixed landing gear, but this was replaced by a retractable unit from the Mk 2 onwards. The Riley conversions had the retractable gear.

The upwardly-swept rear fuselage prevented the tail hitting the ground during rotation. A baggage hold and a toilet was situated in the rear fuselage.

ACTION DATA

CRUISING SPEED
Designed 15 years after the ubiquitous DC-3, the Heron had an edge in speed, although in short-range operations the difference was negligible. The smaller, more streamlined Beech Model 18 was faster, making it an ideal executive aircraft.

DH.114 HERON Mk 2D	295 km/h (183 m.p.h.)
DC-3C	274 km/h (170 m.p.h.)
MODEL H18	339 km/h (210 m.p.h.)

PASSENGERS
The DC-3 was a much larger design and was intended to carry more passengers over longer distances than the Heron. The Heron could carry 17 passengers but 14 was a normal load. The smaller Model 18 carried fewer passengers, making it less economic.

DH.114 HERON Mk 2D	17
DC-3C	32
MODEL H18	10

RANGE
All three types could operate short- or medium-range services. Good range was significant for sales in Africa and North America, where towns and cities are separated by long distances. Range was also very important in the executive role to reduce travelling time for businessmen.

DH.114 HERON Mk 2D 1473 km (805 mi.)

DC-3C 1650 km (1,025 mi.)

MODEL H18 1200 km (745 mi.)

De Havilland short-haul propliners

■ **DH.84 DRAGON:** First flown in 1932, the Dragon was the result of a Hillman Airways requirement for a six-seat passenger aircraft.

■ **DH.89 DRAGON RAPIDE:** A direct development of the Dragon, more than 700 DH.89s were built for civil and military customers.

■ **DH.95 FLAMINGO:** Able to carry up to 18 passengers, only one DH.95 entered civilian service before World War II halted production.

■ **DH.104 DOVE:** The Dove was Great Britain's first post-war airliner to enter service, and could carry up to 11 passengers.

DE HAVILLAND CANADA

DHC-2 BEAVER

● Rugged dependability ● Short take-off and landing

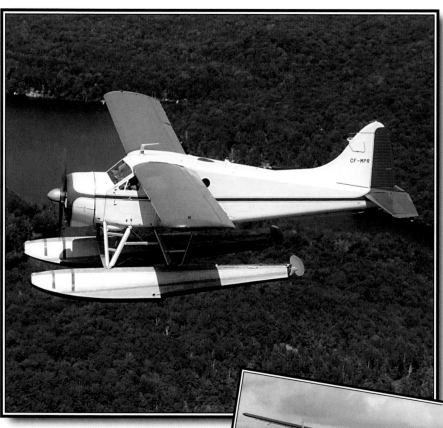

Flying in the frozen north presents a real challenge. It takes a very special aircraft to slip into narrow fjords on floats, or to take off from a glacier using skis. Whether you are a cargo hauler delivering people and supplies to remote communities or a policeman enforcing the law over thousands of square kilometres of trackless wilderness, you need an aircraft like the remarkable Canadian de Havilland Beaver to do the job.

▲ The Beaver is a classic wild-country floatplane. It has an immensely tough high-wing airframe with a capacious cabin, and is powered by a rugged and dependable radial engine.

DE HAVILLAND CANADA DHC-2 BEAVER

Fishing trip ▶
The annual salmon season brings thousands of well-heeled anglers to the rivers and lakes of Canada. Very often, the only way to the best waters is by Beaver.

▼ On the water
New rules apply when you fly from water. Apart from the obvious like avoiding floating debris on take-off, pilots have to learn tricks such as using the propeller thrust and water rudder to prevent the aircraft 'weather cocking' into wind.

▲ Flying in the wilderness
The Beaver has been plying its trade over the lakes, forests and mountains of Canada's northern wilderness and other countries for nearly 50 years.

◀ Forest fire
The basic concept of the Beaver as a high-wing, STOL-capable transport has been expanded to produce the larger DHC-3 Otter. Both designs have been adapted as fire-bombers, using specially modified floats to scoop up water from lakes.

▲ Amphibian
Deploying wheels within its floats, the versatile Beaver can land on runways. Landing on lakes is actually easier than using a normal runway.

FACTS AND FIGURES

➤ The prototype Beaver made its first flight on 16 August 1947.

➤ Its five-hour endurance makes the slow-flying Beaver ideal for wilderness search-and-rescue missions.

➤ Sixty enlarged, 10-passenger turboprop-powered Beaver IIIs were produced.

➤ The Beaver inspired a larger cousin, the 14-passenger DHC-3 Otter, also widely used for bush flying in the Arctic.

➤ Civil and military DHC-2s have been operated by 65 countries.

➤ More than 1700 Beavers were produced between 1947 and 1965.

PROFILE

Flying in grizzly bear country

The Royal Canadian Mounted Police set an example for all when they carry out bush flying missions with the sturdy DHC-2 Beaver. Designed in 1946-47, the Beaver was tailor-made for adventurous flying under harsh conditions.

With its ability to use wheels, skis, floats or amphibious pontoons, the Beaver can go just about everywhere. Bush pilots use the DHC-2 to haul provisions to remote locations, both in summer and in winter, when temperatures in northern Canada can be as low as minus 40°C (-40°F).

At the height of its career, the Beaver could be found hard at work in every continent, including Antarctica. Superb short take-off ability means that it can operate in remote locations that other aircraft would find impossible.

It is that quality which even now, half a century after its first flight, makes the DHC-2 Beaver a highly effective bush transport.

The Beaver's long, straight wing configuration gives it a good short take-off capability. This design feature was retained for its larger brother, the DHC-3 Otter.

In plan view, the huge area of the twin floats is immediately apparent. While essential for water operations, they cause a lot of drag in flight. This is why floatplanes are never as fast or as economical as planes with conventional landing gear.

DHC-2 BEAVER

Still in service all over the world, the DHC-2 Beaver remains the classic bush float aircraft, its name being almost synonymous with the role.

The Beaver has an extremely austere cockpit, but it has everything required for its role, including a good view down to the water from the large side windows.

Almost all floatplanes are high-winged, since this gives the pilot the best view of the water. It also keeps the wing free of any high waves during take-off and landing.

The prominent wires leading to the tail are aerials; good radio communications are essential to bush pilots. Beavers frequently carry long-range HF sets as well as air-band radios.

Most Beavers are powered by the tried-and-tested Pratt & Whitney Wasp Junior engine, but other engines have been fitted. The turboprop Garrett TPE 331 gives a useful increase in performance.

Designed to house a pilot and seven passengers, the cabin can alternatively hold up to 680 kg (1,500 lb.) of cargo.

The Beaver's fuselage is of all-metal monocoque construction. The door is wider than usual, specifically to allow standard American 45-gallon (205 litres) oil drums to be rolled directly into the cabin, and hatches in the rear cabin bulkhead allow long cargo such as drilling rods to be carried.

Compartmentalised to maintain buoyancy even when holed, the floats are built to withstand the severe pounding they get on take-off and landing. They have small retractable rudders, and are fitted with bilge pumps to flush out the water that inevitably finds its way through joints and seams.

DHC-2 Beaver

Type: light utility transport

Powerplant: one 936-kW (1.255-hp.) Pratt & Whitney R-985 Wasp Junior radial piston engine

Maximum speed: 262 km/h (163 m.p.h.) at 1524 m (5000 ft.)

Range: 1180 km (733 mi.)

Service ceiling: 5485 m (18,000 ft.)

Weights: empty 1923 kg (4,240 lb.); loaded 2313 kg (5,100 lb.)

Accommodation: pilot and up to seven passengers, or 680 kg (1,500 lb.) of freight on strengthened cabin floor

Dimensions:
span 14.63 m (48 ft.)
length 9.22 m (30 ft. 3 in.)
height 2.74 m (9 ft.)
wing area 23.22 m² (250 sq. ft.)

The Royal New Zealand Air Force, one of more than 20 air arms to use the type, used ski-fitted Beavers to patrol the snow-covered peaks and fjords of the country's South Island.

ACTION DATA

PAYLOAD

Light aircraft are a key to communications in wilderness areas, and the most successful aircraft are those that can be modified to carry cargo as well as passengers. The popular aircraft of the Cessna 180 series are, like the Beaver, landplanes which can be fitted with floats. The Buccaneer is by contrast a flying-boat, whose hull provides the buoyancy in water.

DHC-2 BEAVER 7 passengers or 680 kg (1,500 lb.) of cargo

CESSNA 185 5 passengers or 360 kg (794 lb.) of cargo

LA-4 BUCCANEER 5 passengers plus baggage

Water manoeuvres

PLOUGH TURN:
Floatplanes, like sailboats, will turn into the wind if left to themselves. To turn across the wind, you need to use a lot of engine power. This pulls the nose high, digging the rudders deep into the water. A small turn to the right allows the rudders to have more effect.

SAILING FLOATPLANES:
In strong wind, you can use two methods to manoeuvre from A to B:

1 Use engine power to taxi across the wind, then trim and cut power and sail backwards.

2 Drift backwards and then use power in combination with the wind to travel sideways.

Use power and wind to travel sideways

METHOD 1

Sail backwards

Sail backwards

METHOD 2

Use power and wind to travel sideways

STRONG WIND

DE HAVILLAND CANADA
DHC-6 TWIN OTTER

● Short take-off ● Regional airliner ● Utility floatplane

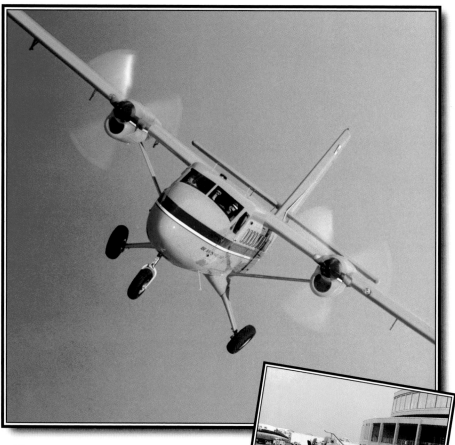

A dmired for its versatility and flexibility, the DHC-6 Twin Otter is a great commuter airliner and utility transport. It was developed in the mid-1960s to provide passenger services to remote airstrips, like those in the hinterlands of Canada where short take-off and landing capability is a 'must'. The Twin Otter also excels at air ambulance and maritime surveillance duties, and is used as a military light transport.

▲ The smallest of de Havilland of Canada's fleet of short take-off aircraft, the Twin Otter has set the standard by which light utility aircraft are judged.

DE HAVILLAND CANADA DHC-6 TWIN OTTER

▼ **Float liner**
In British Columbia's lake district, the DHC-6 offers the only way to reach remote areas. All floatplane versions have the early-series style short nose.

▲ **Surveillance Otter**
Demonstrated at the Paris Air Show, this Twin Otter was fitted with a chin-mounted radar for surveillance and search-and-rescue missions.

◀ **Water bomber**
Firefighting is another important role of the DHC-6. Water is carried in the floats.

Brymon Airways ▶
One of the many small operators using Twin Otters was Brymon Airways, based in the UK.

Ice skater ▶
The British Antarctic Survey uses a ski-equipped Twin Otter for resupply missions in the frozen South Pole.

FACTS AND FIGURES

➤ Engine power of the Twin Otter was increased by changing from PT6A-6 to PT6A-20 to PT6A-27 powerplants.

➤ The US Air Force Academy uses three Twin Otters for parachute training.

➤ When production ended in 1988 more than 830 Twin Otters had been built.

➤ Twin Otters with large 'Vistaliner' windows are used for aerial tours of the Grand Canyon.

➤ The prototype, with PT6A-6 engines, made its initial flight on 20 May 1965.

➤ Twin Otters at Sondrestrom, Greenland, routinely fly in temperatures of -10°C (14°F).

PROFILE

Canada's pocket turboprop

A Twin Otter can handle just about any job. It is the champion of small airlines eager to provide comfort and economy while carrying passengers into remote locations. As a landplane the Twin Otter operates successfully from semi-paved runways as short as 200 m (700 ft.). In its pontoon-equipped seaplane version the DHC-6 is a lifeline for the remote areas of Canada where lakes are more numerous than airfields. Twin Otters also fly routinely on skis in Greenland and on the polar ice cap.

This aircraft was improved constantly during manufacture. As three major versions rolled out of the factory, speed, take-off and landing characteristics, and load-carrying capacity were upgraded. Later series 200 and 300 Twin Otters are distinguished by a longer nose.

Intended for service with commuter airlines, Twin Otters have also seen widespread use with air forces and government agencies. In 1982, DHC offered the DHC-6-300M COIN counter-insurgency aircraft, with a cabin-mounted machine-gun and armour, and the -300MR maritime patrol version, with a search radar under the nose.

Left: Twin Otters are seen all over the world, but especially in hilly countries, such as Chile, Nepal and Switzerland, where short take-off performance is essential.

Above: DHC-6s are vital to many small Third World countries, often making up the majority of some airline fleets.

DHC-6-300 Twin Otter

Type: utility STOL (short take-off and landing) transport

Powerplant: two 486-kW (650-hp.) Pratt & Whitney Canada PT6A-27 turboprop engines

Maximum speed: 338 km/h (210 m.p.h.) at 3050 m (10,000 ft.)

Range: 1297 km (804 mi.)

Service ceiling: 8140 m (26,700 ft.)

Weights: operating empty 3363 kg (7,400 lb.); maximum take-off 5670 kg (12,474 lb.)

Accommodation: two pilots, 13 to 18 passengers (early aircraft), 20 passengers (later aircraft)

Dimensions:
span	19.81 m (65 ft.)
seaplane length	15.09 m (49 ft. 5 in.)
landplane length	15.77 m (51 ft. 9 in.)
height	6.05 m (19 ft. 10 in.)
wing area	39.02 m² (420 sq. ft.)

DHC-6-300 TWIN OTTER

Produced between 1964 and 1988, the Twin Otter sold widely to regional airlines around the world, as well as to Canadian operators like norOntair.

This Twin Otter is one of the longer nosed aircraft. The cockpit seats two pilots.

Reliability is a great feature of the Twin Otter, thanks to its PT6 turboprops.

The Twin Otter's short take-off performance is aided by full-span, double-slotted trailing-edge flaps. The outer sections operate differentially as ailerons.

The Twin Otter design used basically the same fuselage section as de Havilland's Otter.

CF-TVP

norOntair

The military versions with nose radar often have extra vertical tailfins outboard to provide greater stability.

The fixed undercarriage is stressed for operation from rough airstrips. Skis or floats are optional.

A special ventral baggage pod can be fitted to the Twin Otter for carrying up to 272 kg (600 lb.) of baggage or freight.

ACTION DATA

TAKE-OFF RUN

The Twin Otter has good take-off performance. The An-28 is almost as capable and often flies from desolate airstrips deep in the Russian taiga, like the Twin Otter in Canada's interior.

DHC-6-300 TWIN OTTER 213 m (700 ft.)
An-28 'CASH' 260 m (850 ft.)
Do 28 347 m (1,138 ft.)

RANGE

Twin Otters generally fly short-range missions from one city to another, typically around 800 km. The range figure given for the Twin Otter is with a 1134-kg payload. The Twin Otter offers a useful range and payload capability for a small aircraft.

DHC-6-300 TWIN OTTER 1297 km (804 mi.)
Do 28 1810 km (1,122 mi.)
An-28 'CASH' 1365 km (846 mi.)

PAYLOAD

Larger than the Do 28, the Twin Otter can lift greater loads. However, the small An 28 can also carry two tons. The Twin Otter and the Antonov both carry 17 passengers.

DHC-6-300 TWIN OTTER 1941 kg (4,270 lb.)
An-28 'CASH' 2000 kg (4,400 lb.)
Do 28 700 kg (1,540 lb.)

Twin Otters at work

COASTAL PATROL: This series 300M has a radar nose and twin rocket pods under the port wing for offensive maritime patrol work.

SKI OTTER: This Canadian-registered Twin Otter takes off from a frozen lake on a passenger flight using skis. In summer the same aircraft can take off from lakes with the simple addition of a float undercarriage.

SPRAY MISSION: With a large ventral hopper fitted, the Twin Otter can carry out missions like crop spraying or locust spraying.

FIRE BOMBER: Another vital mission for Canadian Twin Otters is fire-bombing. Using nearby lakes for a refill of its float tanks, the Twin Otter can respond to a fire in minutes and make many flights a day.

DE HAVILLAND CANADA
DHC-7 DASH 7

● Four engines ● STOL performance ● Low noise output

Possessing an impressive STOL (Short Take Off and Land) capability, the Dash 7 offers the medium level airline operator an economical aircraft that is large enough to carry up to 50 passengers in four-engine safety. Turboprops not only use less fuel than jets, they can also be considerably quieter and the Dash 7 has been particularly welcomed by managers of urban airports where low aircraft noise levels are of paramount importance.

▲ *The first British airline operator of the Dash 7 was Brymon Airways. Like many smaller airlines they found the aircraft highly efficient on short haul commuter routes to regional airports.*

▲ **In control**
The cockpit layout is fairly conventional. The dual controls allow either pilot to fly the aircraft, with the major instruments also duplicated.

▲ **Four-prop power**
The four Pratt & Whitney turboprops that power the Dash 7 give the aircraft unrivaled STOL performance for airliners in the 50-seat class.

◀ **Island-hopping**
Danish airline Grønlandsfly operated their Dash 7 on flights connecting provincial airports and to islands such as the Faroes.

▼ **Regional airliner**
Dash 7s have been a common sight at regional hub airports all over the United States. Quick turnaround times and a useful passenger load are major assets.

▲ **Best seller**
In the mid 1980s the Dash 7 was probably the world's most popular STOL airliner. This example flew with Norwegian airline Widerøe.

FACTS AND FIGURES

➤ The DHC-7 was announced in October 1968 as the first QSTOL (Quiet Short Take Off and Land) airliner.

➤ The total production run of Dash 7s was 1110.

➤ Customers for the Dash 7 totalled 35, located in 22 different countries.

➤ The Canadian Armed Forces ordered two military Dash 7s designated CC-132.

➤ The Dash 7 is one of the few airliners currently allowed to operate into London City Airport.

➤ The U.S. Army use 'Grizzly Hunter' Dash 7s for drug interdiction duties.

PROFILE

Dashing STOL performer

The first of two prototype Dash 7s made its maiden flight on 27 March 1975, and in basic Series 100 configuration the aircraft's launch customer was Rocky Mountain Airways, which inaugurated services on 3 February 1978. Further development produced the Series 150 and the similar 151 Freighter of 1986 with an increased maximum take-off weight of 21,275 kg (46,900 lb.) compared to the standard 19,913 kg (43,900 lb.). The extra weight was partially taken up by a greater fuel capacity.

The Dash 7's outstanding STOL capability and low engine noise levels made it popular with regional airlines serving some of the more demanding airports in the world, and those like London City Airport, which were obliged to impose strict aircraft noise levels as a condition of the operating license. Among the world's airlines that fly the Dash 7 are Brymon Airways, Hawaiian Airlines, Greenlandair and Air Niugin.

The Dash 7 production lines closed some two years after the takeover of de Havilland Canada by the US giant Boeing in 1986, the decision being taken to concentrate on a twin-engine successor, the Dash 8. The last Dash 7 was delivered to Tyrolean Airways of Austria in 1988.

Amazing short take-off and landing performance allows the Dash 7 to operate from small airfields where other airliners of this size cannot. A long wing fitted with large flaps combined with four powerful engines are the key to its performance.

The tail unit is of cantilever all-metal construction in a T-tail form. The horn balance elevators are cable operated and are fitted with a de-icing boot.

The slightly dihedral wings have double-slotted flaps extending over approximately 80 percent of the trailing edge.

Dash 7

Type: STOL regional airliner

Powerplant: four 835-kW (1,120-hp.) Pratt & Whitney Canada PT6A-50 turboprops.

Maximum cruising speed: 426 km/h (265 m.p.h.)

Service ceiling: 7315 m (24,000 ft.)

Initial climb rate: 372 m/min (1,220 f.p.m.)

Accommodation: 50 passengers (standard).

Range: 1270 km (790 mi.)

Weights: empty 12,534 kg (27,633 lb.); max take-off 21,274 kg (46,902 lb.)

Dimensions:
span	28.35 m (93 ft.)
length	24.54 m (80 ft. 6 in.)
height	7.98 m (26 ft. 2 in.)
wing area	82.31 m² (886 sq. ft.)

DASH 7 SERIES 100

England's Brymon Airways initially ordered three Dash 7s, of which G-BRYA was the first delivered. They primarily served connecting Heathrow to Plymouth, Newquay and the Channel Islands.

The flight crew of two have dual controls fitted as standard. Other pilot aids include an RCA Primus 40 weather radar and a Sperry SPZ-700 autopilot.

Dash 7s are powered by four Pratt & Whitney Canada PT6A-50 turboprops rated at 835 kW (1,120 hp.). Each engine drives a Hamilton Standard constant-speed fully-feathering reversible-pitch four-blade propeller of slow-turning type to reduce noise level.

The cabin can hold up to 50 passengers seated in pairs on each side of the central aisle. Emergency exits are provided on each side at the front of the cabin and on the starboard side at the rear.

The landing gear is of Menasco retractable type, with twin wheels on all units. The wheels are fitted with an anti-skid braking system.

The baggage compartment at the rear of the aircraft can carry up to 1000 kg (2,200 lb.) of luggage or cargo.

Under the rear fuselage is a small retractable tailskid. This prevents the rear fuselage touching the runway on takeoff or landing.

Operating from a STOLport

The Dash 7's ability to operate from short runways at small regional or inner city airports with very low noise output is almost unique in the 50-seat class airliners.

STEEP APPROACH: To operate into a city STOLport the Dash 7 adopts a very steep approach path to clear obstacles such as large buildings.

TAKE-OFF: City STOLports have a limited length of runway for operations. The Dash 7 can get airborne with a short take-off run even with a full load.

DEPARTURE: Not only does the Dash 7 have to climb steeply to avoid tall buildings within a city, but it also has to do so within strict noise regulations. The Dash 7 achieves this by using powerful but very quiet engines.

ACTION DATA

SPEED

The high-lift wing which gives the Dash 7 its tremendous STOL performance causes more drag than the wings of its competitors. This drag makes the Dash 7 about 30 m.p.h. slower at maximum cruising speed.

DASH 7	426 km/h (265 m.p.h.)
F27	480 km/h (298 m.p.h.)
748	451 km/h (280 m.p.h.)

TAKE-OFF RUN

The Dash 7's STOL performance is emphasized by comparing its take-off run to that of its competitors. It can become airborne in less than half the distance of the 748 and just over one-third of the distance of the F27.

DASH 7	748	F27
366 m (1,200 ft.)	823 m (2,700 ft.)	991 m (3,250 ft.)

ACCOMMODATION

All three types carry a similar passenger load. However, only the Dash 7 can offer passenger services from smaller regional or city airports. Despite having four engines to its competitors' two, the Dash 7 has similar fuel economy with a full passenger load.

DASH 7	F27	748
50 passengers	60 passengers	58 passengers

117

DE HAVILLAND CANADA

DHC-8 DASH 8

● Short-range transport ● Stretched variants ● USAF applications

Since the first Dash 8 made its maiden flight in June 1983, the type has become a regional airline workhorse. The original 37-seat fuselage has been stretched to accommodate 50 passengers in the Series 300, and the Dash 8-400 will have capacity for 70 seats. In the meantime, ownership of de Havilland Canada has passed from the Canadian government via Boeing to its current owner, Bombardier Aerospace.

▲ *Launched in 1980, the Dash 8 had attracted 519 orders by early 1997, with a total of 447 delivered. Each costs approximately US $10 million. The type appears to have a rosy future.*

DE HAVILLAND CANADA **DHC-8 DASH 8**

◀ Indigenous powerplant
All Dash 8s are powered by Pratt & Whitney Canada turboprops. Reversible-pitch propellers are standard.

▼ Stretched version
Featuring a 6.83-m fuselage stretch, the Dash 8 Series 400 first flew in early 1998. It has been developed with Mitsubishi of Japan.

▼ Regional airliner routes
British Airways Express, based at Gatwick Airport, flies the Dash 8 alongside other regional rivals, the ATR 42, ATR 72 and the RJ 100. In the summer additional routes are flown to Bremen and Luxembourg.

▼ American sales
A subsidiary of one of the largest airlines, United, United Express operates 10 Dash 8s, flying feeder services from over 60 US cities.

◀ Dash family
Canada's City Express airline not only operates the Dash 8 Series 100, but also its four-engined predecessor, the Dash 7. Here both types overfly the city of Toronto.

FACTS AND FIGURES

➤ With its increased speed and payload the Series 200 is operated by, among others, National Jet Systems for maritime patrol.

➤ Introduced in 1990, the Series 100A features increased passenger headroom.

➤ Canada's military Dash 8s are known as the CC-142, and the CT-142 trainer.

➤ A single Dash 8 Series 100 is used by the Norwegian Civil Aviation Administration for navaid calibration.

➤ The original prototype Dash 8, registered C-GDNK, first flew on 20 June 1983.

➤ The Dash 8 received its FAA certification for civil operations in September 1984.

PROFILE

Canada's capable commuter

The sales potential of the Dash 8 range has been increased by the stretched 300 and new 400 Series aircraft.

Although they may be small in comparison with the big jets operated by the major airlines, modern turboprops lack little in sophistication. The Dash 8-400 will have 3602-kW (4,830-hp.) PW150 engines and an integrated avionics suite featuring large liquid-crystal display screens. Earlier versions of the twin-turboprop were equipped more conventionally. They have found customers around the world, operating as feeders for major airlines, often flying from smaller airports on short-haul, low-density routes whose traffic would not support operations by bigger types, and as corporate

transports fitted with fewer, but larger, seats.

The original Series 100 was available with either 1603-kW (2,150-hp.) PW121 engines as the higher-performance Model 103, or with 1491-kW (2,380-hp.) PW120As as the Model 102. Considerably larger, the Series 300 seats a maximum of 56 passengers and is powered by 1775-kW (3,000-hp.) PW123s. Otherwise, the 300's main change is a fuselage stretch of 3.43 m

(11 ft. 3 in.). Along with the regional airliners, there have been special-purpose military versions of the Dash 8. Canada uses the CC-142 transport and CT-142 navigation trainer, while the US Air Force has two E-9s equipped with a comprehensive avionics suite for range support operations.

DASH 8 SERIES 100

C-GGTO was the fifth Dash 8 to be built and was delivered to City Express in September 1985. Subsequently withdrawn from service and stored at Toronto, it is owned by Canopus.

In typical configuration, the Dash 8 Series 100 carries a payload of 37 passengers in four-abreast seating, plus buffet, toilet and luggage section.

A crew of two flies the Dash 8, with accommodation also provided on the flight deck for a cabin attendant. Avionics include a Primus 800 colour weather radar. The fuselage is fully pressurised and air-conditioned, and the Dash 8Q version features reduced cabin noise.

Each of the twin wheel main undercarriage units retracts into an engine nacelle. The nose wheels are steerable, and have Goodrich brakes.

The Pratt & Whitney Canada PW120A turboprop mounted in each nacelle powers a Hamilton Standard four-bladed constant-speed propeller. A pressure refuelling point is mounted above each engine.

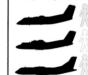

As well as emergency exits on each side of the aircraft, the port fuselage side contains a large airstair door for passenger access, and an inward-opening cargo door aft.

The structure of the DHC Dash 8 is primarily of conventional adhesive bonded aluminium, but trailing edges and wheel doors are made of strong yet light Kevlar/Nomex composites.

C-GGTO

Dash 8 Series 300A

Type: twin-turboprop regional transport

Powerplant: two 1775-kW (2,380-hp.) Pratt & Whitney Canada PW123A turboprops

Maximum cruising speed: 532 km/h (330 m.p.h.)

Take-off field length: 1085 m (3,360 ft.)

Maximum climb rate: 549 m/min (1,800 f.p.m.) at sea level

Range: 1527 km (950 mi.) with 50 passengers

Service ceiling: 7620 m (25,000 ft.)

Weights: operating empty 11,666 kg (25,665 lb.), maximum take-off 18,642 kg (41,012 lb.)

Accommodation: maximum 56 passengers

Dimensions: span 27.43 m (90 ft.)
length 25.68 m (84 ft 3 in.)
height 7.49 m (24 ft. 7 in.)
wing area 56.21 m² (605 sq. ft.)

ACTION DATA

MAXIMUM PASSENGERS

Standard seating for up to 50 passengers is offered by the Dash 8 Series 300, but accommodation for 56 is possible in a high-density configuration. The ATR 42-300 is a main competitor.

DASH 8-300 56 passengers
DASH 7-100 54 passengers
ATR 42-300 50 passengers

TAKE-OFF FIELD LENGTH

De Havilland Canada aimed the Dash 7 at specialist operators, with Short Take-Off and Landing (STOL) requirements as a priority. This capability was less important for the Dash 8, which was built to offer a take-off field length of about 1000 m (3,300 ft.), and has similar take-off performance to the ATR 42-300.

DASH 8-300 1085 m (3,360 ft.)
DASH 7-100 689 m (2,260 ft.)
ATR 42-300 1090 m (3,575 ft.)

RANGE

With a maximum passenger load, the Dash 8 Series 300A is able to fly a 1527-km (955-mi.) sector on standard fuel. The ATR 42-300 offers better range, but only with a smaller passenger load, while the more specialised Dash 7 Series 100 offers least range but has a far superior short-field performance.

DASH 8-300 1527 km (955 mi.)
DASH 7-100 1362 km (845 mi.)
ATR 42-300 1946 km (1,210 mi.)

Dash 8 civil operators

TALAIR (PAPUA NEW GUINEA): Four Dash 8s are currently flown in New Guinea; all carry native P2 codes. The Talair aircraft shown here, the 102nd built, was delivered in 1986.

BRYMON EUROPEAN (UK): Based in Plymouth, Brymon's mid-1997 fleet included seven Series 300 Dash 8s, and two Dash 7s, flying from throughout the UK to Paris and Jersey.

EASTERN METRO EXPRESS (US): This, the seventh Dash 8 to be delivered, flew with Westinghouse's Metro Airlines before being transferred to Allegheny Commuter Airlines in early 1993.

DORNIER

KOMET/DELPHIN/MERKUR

● All-metal airliners ● Flying-boats and landplanes ● In service until 1934

Although it might fairly be considered one of the ugliest aircraft ever built, the Do Cs II Delphin (Dolphin), or L 1, led to a long line of German airliners which served faithfully from water and land between 1920 and 1934. Serving mainly in Germany, the Delphin/Komet/Merkur series also sold in modest numbers to operators around the world. A float-equipped Merkur (Mercury) was used on a daring flight from Zürich to Cape Town in 1926–27.

▲ *Unusual for their all-metal construction, the Delphin, Komet and Merkur airliners gave good performance and were well equipped for their era. Services were flown by Lufthansa across Germany and Europe.*

DORNIER KOMET/DELPHIN/MERKUR

First of the Komets ▶
Seated in an open cockpit mounted at the wing leading edge and directly behind the engine, the pilot of the Komet I had a very uncomfortable workplace. The four passengers were accommodated in more comfort.

▼ Dolphin gets airborne
Less angular than previous models, the Delphin III seated the pilot at the front of the cabin.

▲ Foreign evaluation
During the late 1920s a single Delphin III was evaluated by Britain's Air Ministry. No more examples were acquired.

◀ South American floatplane
Syndicato Condor used this float-equipped Merkur on airline services in Brazil. A similar aircraft, CH 171, flew with two passengers from Zürich to Cape Town in 100 hours of flying during 1926–27.

Route extensions ▶
From 2 May 1927, the Moscow-Königsberg route flown by Deruluft was extended to Berlin. The airline was a German-Russian organisation and employed up to nine Merkurs on the service.

FACTS AND FIGURES

➤ Early Komets were powered by 138-kW (185-hp.) BMW IIIa engines, but they exceeded Allied-imposed ceiling limits.

➤ Two designations were applied to the Delphin III: Do L 3 and Do L Bas.

➤ One example of the Komet was flown with the cockpit behind the wing.

➤ Delphin III customers could specify either round or square windows for the rear part of the cabin.

➤ All Lufthansa Komet Is were converted to Komet IIs with 186-kW (250-hp.) engines.

➤ Komet IIIs in Japan were given several Merkur features.

PROFILE

All-metal Dolphin, Comet and Mercury

Even by the standards of 1920, the Delphin was an odd-looking aircraft which paid no attention to the concept of streamlining. Constructed from duralumin and steel, the aircraft seated four or five passengers in the cabin, with the pilot sitting in an exposed position immediately behind the high-mounted engine.

A lengthened version known as the Do L 1a appeared in 1922, with an engine cowling which extended back over the cockpit to form a roof. Further lengthening produced the six- or seven-seat Do L 2 Delphin II,

which placed the pilot in the forward section of the passenger cabin. Like all of the early Delphins, the Do L 2 did not sell well. Dornier's Swiss factory produced a 13-seat Delphin III during 1927 which sold in some numbers.

Both the Komet I and II were basically landplane variants of the L 1 Delphin. The first Do CIII Komet flew in 1921 and both types served faithfully until the last was retired in 1930. Following the trend of Delphin development, Dornier produced the Komet III as a derivation of

Above: Two aircraft were used by Ad Astra Aero, the second registered as CH 171. Both were later passed to Swissair, CH 171 gaining floats.

Below: This Do L 1a Delphin wears Japanese markings. Several countries were keen to gain experience of the Delphin's all-metal construction, which employed a combination of steel and light alloys.

the Delphin III. A more powerful engine and minor airframe modifications produced the well-used Merkur, examples of which were built new and by conversion.

Merkur II

Type: passenger transport

Powerplant: one 373-kW (500-hp.) BMW VI V-12 piston engine

Maximum speed: 192 km/h (119 m.p.h.)

Cruising speed: 180 km/h (111 m.p.h.)

Range: 750 km (465 mi.)

Service ceiling: 4000 m (13,120 ft.)

Weights: empty 2780 kg (6,129 lb.), maximum take-off 4100 kg (9,039 lb.)

Accommodation: two crew and six to eight passengers

Dimensions:
span	19.60 m	(64 ft. 2 in.)
length	12.85 m	(42 ft. 1 in.)
height	3.56 m	(11 ft. 6 in.)
wing area	62 m²	(618 sq. ft.)

Komet and Merkur pilots enjoyed few comforts and must have suffered particularly on flights into the Soviet Union. The wing of the Komet III and Merkur did at least provide some protection, the cockpits of earlier Komets being mounted above the wing.

Aerodynamic balancing surfaces were applied to the ailerons and elevators of the Merkur. They were also a feature of the Delphin and Komet.

MERKUR I

Lufthansa appears to have operated at least 36 Merkurs, seven of which were converted from Komet IIIs. The last was withdrawn in 1934.

LUFT HANSA
D-1102

BMW VI engines of 335 kW (450 hp.) powered the Merkur and some modified Komet IIIs. The radiator was strut-mounted beneath the engine cowling.

Up to eight passengers could be accommodated in the Merkur, with large cabin windows providing an excellent view of the ground.

Like the Komet and earlier Delphin, the Merkur featured all-metal construction. This was an advanced feature for the period and provoked a great deal of evaluative testing by other manufacturers.

There were few obvious differences between the Komet III and Merkur. The latter, however, had no external bracing of the tailplane. It did have a more powerful engine, and featured a cut-out in the trailing edge of the wing centre-section.

ACTION DATA

CRUISING SPEED

With its faster cruising speed, the Westland Limousine II offered shorter journey times, but represented less advanced technology since it retained the biplane layout and was therefore of limited appeal to passengers. Most of the Komet's principal rivals were employing high-set monoplane wings.

KOMET I	130 km/h (81 m.p.h.)
LIMOUSINE II	145 km/h (90 m.p.h.)
F.II	120 km/h (74 m.p.h.)

PASSENGERS

Although the Fokker F.II accommodated one more passenger than the Komet I, this extra person was seated in an open cockpit alongside the pilot! The Limousine II was limited to three passengers, which made it less useful.

KOMET I 4 passengers

LIMOUSINE II 3 passengers

F.II 5 passengers

RANGE

Excellent range was a key feature of the F.II, but its slower cruising speed would make flights uncomfortably long, especially for the fifth passenger. The Komet II had considerably greater range than the Komet I. The Limousine II had greater range than the Komet I, but did not make a great impact on European airline routes.

KOMET I 600 km (372 mi.)

LIMOUSINE II 644 km (399 mi.)

F.II 1200 km (744 mi.)

Inter-war civilian Dorniers

■ **LIBELLE:** In answer to an anticipated enthusiasm for seaplanes in post-World War I Germany, Dornier produced the Libelle (Dragonfly) training flying-boat.

■ **Do J WAL:** Built in large numbers and in a confusing array of variants, the Wal was one of the most successful inter-war flying-boats. Early aircraft were completed in Italy.

■ **Do X:** Only three examples of this remarkable flying-boat were built, one for Germany and two for Italy. In 1929 a record 169 people were carried on a single flight.

■ **Do 11:** Few examples of the Do 11 commercial freighter were built. Although a few appeared on the German civil register, it is likely that they saw only limited use.

DORNIER

Do X

● Pioneering flying-boat ● Largest aircraft of its time

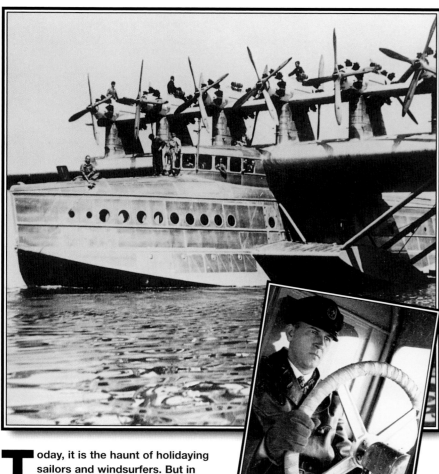

▲ *The appropriately-named Richard Wagner, Dornier's chief test pilot, was behind the huge control wheel of the titanic flying-boat for its first flight.*

Today, it is the haunt of holidaying sailors and windsurfers. But in 1929 Lake Constance was the home of the world's largest aeroplane. Created by the legendary designer Dr Claudius Dornier as a trans-Atlantic passenger carrier, the huge 12-engined Dornier Do X was a marginal performer which was never to be a commercial proposition. But it pushed back the boundaries of aviation.

PHOTO FILE

DORNIER Do X

The main attraction ▶
The Do X drew great crowds wherever and whenever it appeared.

▲ Innovation
Claudius Dornier was one of aviation's great pioneers. He had many successful flying-boats in the early 1920s, refining the design features that would eventually appear on the Do X.

▲ Luxury accommodation
Flying in the 1920s and 1930s was only for the rich, and the sumptuous interior of the Do X reflects the luxury which they would have expected.

▲ Power
Twelve radial engines made the Do X the most powerful aircraft of its day.

At home on water ▶
The Do X was a boat that could fly, rather than an aeroplane that could float.

FACTS AND FIGURES

➤ The Do X's record passenger load stood at a crew of 10, 150 invited passengers, and nine stowaways.

➤ In its initial form, the Do X took a snail-like 20 minutes to reach a height of 600 metres (2,000 ft.).

➤ The wings were thick enough to allow an engineer access to the engines.

➤ On one attempted flight, the Do X ran for 13 km (8 miles) without being able to lift off.

➤ Even with more powerful engines, the Do X cruised at a leisurely 175 km/h (110 m.p.h.).

➤ The Do X was in the air for a total of 211 hours on its maiden transatlantic voyage – spread over a period of 19 months!

PROFILE

Transatlantic Titan

The only revolutionary thing about the massive Dornier Do X was its size. But this alone represented a huge leap into the unknown.

At 56 tons all-up weight, it was by far the largest aircraft in the world. But in spite of having more power than any aircraft of its time, the Do X was never more than a marginal performer. The huge flying-boat was painfully slow, and took an age to reach its meagre operating height of less than 1250 metres (3,300 ft.).

But the Do X represented Germany's reappearance on the world aviation stage, only a decade after its industry had been dismantled at the end of World War I. And that rebirth was celebrated by an epoch-making maiden voyage, from Europe to Africa, across the Atlantic to South America, and on to New York and back.

The Do X lifts majestically from the surface of Lake Constance on the morning of 12 July 1929.

The huge machine was eventually handed over to Lufthansa, but the airliner was not commercially viable, and never took any fare-paying passengers. It was to end its days in a Berlin museum and was destroyed in an air raid in 1945.

The Do X's successful, if delayed, flight to New York gave a great boost to the German aircraft industry, which was recovering from the crippling blow of World War I.

Do X

Type: experimental passenger flying-boat

Powerplant: 12 450-kW (660-hp.) Curtiss Conqueror nine-cylinder radial engines

Maximum speed: 210 km/h (130 m.p.h.); cruising speed 175 km/h (110 m.p.h.)

Time to height: 14 minutes to 1000 m (3,280 ft.)

Maximum range: 2200 km (1,370 mi.)

Service ceiling: 1250 m (4,100 ft.)

Weights: empty 32,675 kg (72,040 lb.); loaded 56,000 kg (123,406 lb.)

Payload: 15,325 kg (33,790 lb.), comprising 14 crew, 66 passengers; record flight from Lake Constance, 10 crew, 150 passengers and nine stowaways – a total of 169 people

Dimensions:	span	48.00 m (157 ft. 5 in.)
	length	40.05 m (131 ft. 2 in.)
	height	10.10 m (33 ft. 1 in.)
	wing area	250 m² (2,690 sq. ft.)

DO X 'MONSTER OF THE SEA'

Dornier's huge flying-boat was an attempt to revolutionise air transport. Unfortunately ambition outstripped available technology, and it was not a success.

The pilot of the Do X sat at the front of the upper deck, behind a large steering-wheel. Smaller wheels controlled trim in flight and the rudder in the water.

The Do X had 12 engines in six nacelles above the wing. The wing was thick enough for a crawlspace, which led to ladders up to each nacelle, allowing engineers free access to the engines, even in flight.

The upper deck was occupied by the flight engineer, navigators, maintenance technicians and radio operators.

The Do X was originally powered by 12 British-designed Bristol Jupiter radial engines, but for the Atlantic crossing they were replaced by 12 slightly more powerful Curtiss Conquerors.

Passengers were carried in two cabins fore and aft of the wing leading edge. The bar and smoking room were in the bow, and the galley was at the rear. Baggage was stowed aft of the galley.

The Do X was fitted with a rudder at the rear of the keel to enable the aircraft to be steered while on the water.

The hull and wing of the Do X was of all-metal construction, but the heavy weight and lack of power meant that it could never reach its designed operating altitude.

Large tail surfaces gave the Do X fair stability. For added control, an extra horizontal tailplane was attached to the fuselage.

D-1929

DORN

With the Do X across the Atlantic

■ **DEPARTURE:** The trip was made in easy stages, with calls at seaplane bases at Amsterdam (left) and Calshott in the south of England. Wherever the Do X went, it drew sightseeing crowds.

■ **WEST AFRICA:** In spite of its huge fuel load the Do X had limited range, so the Atlantic crossing had to be made at its narrowest point. On 3 June 1931 the Do X set off from Portuguese Guinea.

■ **FLYING DOWN TO RIO:** Seventeen days later, the Do X reached Rio de Janeiro. The widest part of the crossing, from the Cape Verde Islands to Fernando Noronha, took 13 hours.

■ **WELCOME TO NEW YORK:** Over the next eight weeks, the Do X worked its way up South and North America via the Caribbean. The huge plane caused a sensation on reaching New York.

■ **HOME AGAIN:** After wintering in America, the Do X crossed the North Atlantic via Newfoundland and the Azores. On 24 May 1932 it landed on Berlin's Müggelsee to a tumultuous welcome.

DORNIER

Do 228

● Twin-engined commuter ● Advanced wing ● Military versions

▲ The Do 228 has sold well, especially in smaller aviation markets like the Kingdom of Bhutan. Its rugged yet advanced design has made it a prime candidate for overseas construction and a number have been assembled in India.

With its advanced wing design, which contributes to an excellent range and load capability, the Dornier Do 228 has become a top seller around the world. In production since the mid-1980s, it has been the economical choice of small airlines and air forces in both hemispheres. Because of its versatility the Do 228 has been adapted to perform a variety of roles from transport to pollution surveillance.

DORNIER Do 228

◄ **Analogue panel**
The Do 228 contains relatively old-fashioned instrumentation, rather than a modern 'glass cockpit'.

▲ **Maritime reconnaissance**
The Royal Thai Navy has three Do 228s equipped to carry out maritime reconnaissance. The radome under the fuselage contains a Bendix 1500 radar scanner. Indian coast guard aircraft also carry radar, plus additional equipment.

▲ **Family likeness**
The Do 228 uses the same fuselage cross-section as the earlier Dornier 128 – a turboprop version of the Do 28D Skyservant of the 1960s.

▼ **Military users**
Although the German armed forces make little use of the Do 228, India has become the largest military customer with examples flying with the air force, navy and coast guard.

▲ **Advanced wing**
Known as the Tragflügel Neuer Technologie, or TNT, the advanced technology wing fitted to the Do 228 was trialled on a modified Do 28 in June 1979. A similar wing is also used on the new Do 328.

FACTS AND FIGURES

➤ Work on the Do 228's wing was partly financed by the German Federal Ministry of Research and Technology.

➤ The air ambulance version can carry six stretchers with nine patients sitting.

➤ By early 1996 227 Do 228s had been delivered to 80 customers.

➤ Over a million kilometres of flying time in the Do 228 helped with the design of the new Do 328 airliner.

➤ Used Do 228 airliners are now being converted into cargo aircraft.

➤ The Royal Omani police air wing operates two Do 228-100s.

PROFILE

Dornier's turboprop twin

With its drooping nose and bulging main undercarriage fairing, the Do 228 was developed by Dornier (now part of Deutsche Aerospace AG) and was the first post-war aircraft from this famous company to reflect advanced engineering skills.

In fact, the Do 228 was an amalgamation of the basic fuselage design of earlier post-war Dorniers and a new advanced composite wing. From the outset two airframe sizes were offered: the 15-seater Do 228-100, which first flew on 28 March 1981, and the larger -200 series, which took to the air just six weeks later.

By 1986 orders from 40 customers had been received, many from small airlines in Third World states. The Dornier has also been produced under licence by India's Hindustan Aeronautics, while China's Harbin company considered plans to manufacture the aircraft. Sales in the United States and other developed nations have been limited, however, partly due to the aircraft's lack of cabin pressurisation.

An American analysis of the Do 228 concluded that no other airliner can carry the same passenger load over the same distances. Production of the improved Do 228-212 is winding down, although manufacture of the Do 228-201 continues in India.

Left: A number of special versions of the Do 228 are available, including maritime patrol and pollution surveillance models.

Below: Being a high-wing design, the Do 228 has an undercarriage which retracts into the fuselage.

Do 228-200

Type: twin-engine commuter airliner

Powerplant: two 533-kW (715-hp.) Allied Signal (Garrett AiResearch) TPE331-5-252D turboprop engines

Maximum speed: 440 km/h (273 m.p.h.)

Range: 2704 km (1,676 mi.)

Service ceiling: 8535 m (28,000 ft.)

Weights: empty 3547 kg (7,800 lb.); maximum take-off 5700 kg (12,640 lb.)

Accommodation: two pilots, flight attendant and up to 19 passengers, or up to six stretchers (air ambulance role) or 2200 kg (4,480 lb.) of freight

Dimensions:
span	16.97 m	(55 ft. 8 in.)
length	16.56 m	(54 ft. 4 in.)
height	4.86 m	(15 ft. 11 in.)
wing area	32 m²	(344 sq. ft.)

Do 228-200

F-OGOF is a Do 228-200 working in the colours of Air Guadeloupe. The majority of Dorniers have been equipped as commuter aircraft.

A Hartzell four-blade, constant-speed, fully feathering, reversible-pitch metal propeller is fitted to each engine.

The leading-edge, wingtips, Fowler single-slotted trailing-edge flaps and ailerons are all of composite construction.

The widely used Allied Signal (formerly Garrett) TPE331 turboprop powers the Do 228.

A flight deck crew of two occupy the cockpit, and the cabin is able to accommodate up to 19 passengers.

The main undercarriage retracts into a large fairing beneath the fuselage, which saves internal space. Landing lights are incorporated ahead of the undercarriage doors.

The main passenger entry and exit point is the large double door at the rear of the aircraft. This also functions as a cargo door on freight versions.

The fuselage of the Do 228-200 is 1.52 m (5 ft.) longer than the earlier Do 228-100. It is able to carry four more passengers and additional baggage.

AIR GUADELOUPE

F-OGOF

ACTION DATA

MAXIMUM CRUISING SPEED

The Do 228 was designed some time after the L-410 and DHC-6 and benefits from better aerodynamics and more powerful engines. It therefore has a higher top speed.

Do 228-200	428 km/h (273 m.p.h.)
DHC-6-300	338 km/h (210 m.p.h.)
L-410UVP-E	380 km/h (339 m.p.h.)

RANGE

The Dornier's fuel efficiency and therefore range have benefited from the design of its wing. The DHC-6's wing is optimised for short take-off and landing (STOL) performance rather than range.

Do 228-200 2704 km (1,676 mi.)

DHC-6-300 1297 km (804 mi.)

L-410UVP-E 546 km (339 mi.)

SERVICE CEILING

The Dornier has a slightly higher service ceiling than is typical of modern commuter aircraft of its type and size. This is largely a result of the good lifting properties of the wing and the efficiency of the Allied Signal engines at high altitude.

Do 228-200	DHC-6-300	L-410UVP-E
8535 m (28,000 ft.)	8140 m (27,000 ft.)	7050 m (23,100 ft.)

Twin-engined light commuters

■ **DE HAVILLAND CANADA DHC-6 TWIN OTTER:** Building on their single-engined STOL aircraft experience, de Havilland of Canada came up with the DHC-6 which first flew in 1965. Over 800 were built before production ceased in 1988.

■ **LET L-410:** Still in production in the Czech Republic, the L-410 19-seater dates from 1969 and has seen wide use in the former Eastern Bloc, in particular the former Soviet Union. A larger L-610 is under development for the Western market.

■ **BRITISH AEROSPACE JETSTREAM:** A Handley Page design until the company went bankrupt, the Jetstream became a Scottish Aviation product in the 1970s. Early versions used Astazou engines; more recent models have Garrett powerplants.

DOUGLAS

DC-3

● Twin-prop airliner ● Most important transport in history

▲ The DC-3 was a dramatic improvement over passenger aircraft that had gone before. It is a stunning testament to the excellence of the design that hundreds are still in operational service after 60 years.

The DC-3 changed the world. No other aircraft has done as much. First flown in the 1930s, this classic Douglas airliner has operated in every country across the face of the globe. It has succeeded at just about every job it has been given, from crop-spraying via executive transport to cargo-hauling. But the DC-3 achieved immortality because it created commercial passenger travel as we know it today.

PHOTO FILE

DOUGLAS DC-3

Commercial pioneer ▶
A Swissair DC-3 heads out over the English Channel on its way to Zurich. The DC-3 was standard equipment with most European airlines in the early post-war years.

▼ Comfortable travel
The DC-3 revolutionised air travel in the USA, offering its pre-war passengers speedy flights and unrivalled comfort.

▲ Still working after all these years
More than 300 civil DC-3s still fly in the 21st century, doing everything from hauling cargo around South America to giving pleasure trips and making air show appearances as examples of flying history.

Military survivor ▶
Variants of the DC-3 continue to serve in large numbers with more than 30 air forces. This is a South African Defence Force Dakota.

▼ Mercy mission
DC-3s have been used all over the world for flying aid missions, including United Nations work. The DC-3 is suited to such work because of its low operational costs.

▲ Heyday of the DC-3
Howard Hughes was the second customer for the DC-3, ordering a dozen examples for Trans-continental and Western (which became TWA).

FACTS AND FIGURES

➤ The 17 December 1935 maiden flight of the DC-3 was the 32nd anniversary of the Wright Brothers' first powered flight.

➤ 10,636 DC-3s were manufactured in the USA, 4878 being built in 1944 alone.

➤ The Super DC-3, first flown on 23 June 1949, offered many improvements but was not purchased by airlines.

➤ Air Atlantique, based in Coventry in the UK, use a fleet of DC-3's as pollution control aircraft.

➤ In continuous service for more than 60 years, the DC-3 is the most important civil aircraft in history.

➤ At least 300 civil DC-3s remain in service in more than 30 countries.

PROFILE

Workhorse for the world

The DC-3 first entered service with American Airlines in 1936, and before World War II conscripted the great Douglas transport for military duty a dozen airlines seized the chance to provide travellers with its unprecedented comfort and convenience. Five distinct series were built for civil customers before the war. Since then, over 100 airlines have flown DC-3s, often using ex-military aircraft from the 10,000

built during World War II.

Originally, the DC-3 was a sleeper transport with 14 double seats which became upper and lower berths. Over time, the interior has carried people and things in every combination imaginable. Sixty years after its first flight, the DC-3 is still flying and working around the world.

Military DC-3s acquired many new names, including Dakota, C-47 and R4D. General Dwight Eisenhower called the C-47 one

of the four most important weapons of World War II.

The military DC-3 has tackled just about every job, from electronic spying to Antarctic exploration. It has even fought: decades after first donning camouflage, the AC-47 gunship was one of the most potent warplanes used in Vietnam.

Many hundreds of commercial DC-3s are still plying their trade all around the world.

The DC-3 was flown by two pilots, with one or two cabin crew to take care of the paying passengers.

The immensely strong cantilever wing was skinned with aluminium. The sweepback of the outer leading edge made the DC-3 easy to recognise.

The DC-3's smooth lines gave it an economic edge. It cost about the same to fly a given route as a Ford Trimotor, but carried three times the payload and did it in half the time.

DC-3

Type: short-/medium-range transport

Powerplant: two 895-kW (1,100-hp.) Pratt & Whitney R-1830-S1C3G Twin Wasp radial piston engines

Maximum speed: 370 km/h (230 m.p.h.) at 2590 m (8,500 ft.)

Range: 2400 km (1,500 mi.)

Service ceiling: 7070 m (24,000 ft.)

Weights: empty 7650 kg (16,800 lb.); loaded 11,430 kg (25,000 lb.)

Accommodation: two pilots, two stewardesses, and 21 to 28 passengers; (or 14 with sleeping provisions) or up to 2750 kg (6,000 lb.) of cargo

Dimensions: span   28.96 m (95 ft. 6 in.)
length   19.65 m (63 ft. 9 in.)
height   5.17 m (16 ft. 11 in.)
wing area 91.69 m² (987 sq. ft.)

DC-3 SLEEPER TRANSPORT

American Airlines were the launch customers for the DC-3. They wanted an aircraft which could outclass the Boeing 247s and DC-2s used by their rivals, and the new airliner provided everything they wanted.

American Airlines, today one of the world's largest carriers, was founded in 1934 as a successor to American Airways. The company has a long history of sponsoring major aircraft designs.

The cabin of the DC-3 was originally designed to house 14 passengers in sleeping berths. This was soon changed to an all-seater arrangement, however, with 21 passengers being carried in seven rows of three seats.

The retractable main undercarriage was driven by a hydraulic pump, and took 15 seconds to raise or be lowered.

The DC-3 could be powered either by nine-cylinder Wright Cyclone or 14-cylinder Twin Wasp radial engines. Each could deliver about 750 kW (975 hp.).

ACTION DATA

RANGE

The DC-3's excellent range made it one of the first aircraft suitable for one-stop coast-to-coast flights across the USA. Although the Boeing 247 was the first of the truly modern airliners, it could not compete with the later DC-3 since it was much smaller and carried less fuel.

1000 km (620 mi.)	1200 km (745 mi.)	2400 km (1,500 mi.)
Ju 52	MODEL 247	DC-3

MAXIMUM SPEED

247	322 km/h (206 m.p.h.)
DC-3	370 km/h (230 m.p.h.)
Ju 52	290 km/h (180 m.p.h.)

Less than three years separate the first flights of the three-motored Ju 52 and the DC-3, but it was a whole generation in terms of technology and passenger comfort. The Junkers design was the culmination in a series which had started in 1919, while the Douglas was the start of a new era in passenger transport.

PAYLOAD

When the Boeing 247 was designed in the early 1930s, 10 passengers seemed like a good load. Few could have foreseen the rise in popularity of air travel, which the much greater carrying capacity of the DC-3 did so much to foster. The success of the DC-3 in carrying larger loads opened up air travel to much of the population.

DC-3 — 21 passengers and 3 crew

Ju 52 — 17 passengers and 3 crew

247 — 10 passengers and 3 crew

From biplanes to monoplanes: the early American airliners

CURTISS CONDOR: This large biplane was pretty much the state-of-the-art in airliner design in the 1920s, and it was used extensively on mail and passenger routes in the USA well into the 1930s. It could not compete in speed or comfort with the new monoplanes, however.

FORD TRIMOTOR: As revolutionary in its way as the DC-3, the Trimotor was the impetus behind the first great expansion in airline travel. Although uncomfortable and noisy for modern tastes, by the standards of the time it offered its passengers a lot.

BOEING MODEL 247: Flying in 1933, the Model 247 was the first twin-engined, all-metal, low-wing monoplane airliner with retractable landing gear to enter service.

DOUGLAS

DC-4 SKYMASTER

● Four-engined airliner ● Many surplus C-54s converted

▲ During World War II the C-54 gained an impressive reputation as a transoceanic aircraft. USAAF machines made 79,642 such flights with only three ditchings, one of which was a deliberate test crash.

A generation of skilled pilots, who had learned their trade in wartime, took the DC-4 on its global expeditions, allowing aviation to truly touch the entire world for the first time. The Douglas DC-4 had the ability to span oceans and allowed intercontinental travel. Although the development of this four-engined airliner was placed in limbo by World War II, in the immediate post-war years the DC-4 was a trailblazer.

PHOTO FILE

DOUGLAS DC-4 SKYMASTER

▲ Reliable workhorse
Many USAAF and RAF pilots who had flown C-54s during World War II became airline pilots after the war.

▲ Dutch Skymaster
Dutch airlines KLM and KNILM took delivery of both converted C-54s and new-build DC-4-1009s. These were used on routes to the Dutch East Indies after a proving flight in November 1945.

▲ North Atlantic service
Air France began its North Atlantic service with new and war-surplus DC-4s.

▲ Down-under freighter
The DC-4 was used worldwide during the post-war years. This Australian example was flown by Ansett, and Australian National Airways operated DC-4s on Pacific routes from 1946.

▲ Pan Am pioneer
Pan American used the DC-4 to pioneer trans-pacific routes and also for cargo services.

◀ Preserved in Holland
This South African-registered aircraft is operated by the Dutch Dakota Association.

FACTS AND FIGURES

➤ Some US airlines painted square black frames around their DC-4s' round windows to make them look like DC-6s.

➤ The DC-4 could fly from New York to Los Angeles in 14 hours 30 minutes.

➤ American, Eastern and United Airlines ordered the first commercial DC-4s.

➤ US airline Braniff used JATO (jet-assisted take-off) for high-altitude DC-4 take-offs from La Paz, Bolivia.

➤ The DC-4 prototype was actually a C-54 and first flew on 14 February 1942.

➤ Canadair built one DC-4 with R-2800 radial engines as the C-5.

PROFILE

Skymaster service

Designed as a civil airliner but first taking to the air as the C-54 wearing military colours, the DC-4 initially flew in 1942. The dream of new standards in US domestic air travel had to be put aside while the war was in progress, but when military needs receded after 1945 Douglas built 79 civil DC-4s.

These, along with large numbers of ex-military versions, gave valuable service in the United States on long-range passenger and cargo flights and went on to pioneer many transoceanic routes. DC-4s served as the backbone of many airlines until more advanced, pressurised types became available.

DC-4s and converted C-54s soldiered on with some of the world's smaller airlines for a number of decades.

Several versions of the DC-4 were built, including those produced in Canada by Canadair as the C-4, powered by Rolls-Royce engines. Both civil and military models are remembered for their contribution to the 1948 Berlin Airlift.

Operators found the DC-4 extremely reliable, which was important on long flights, especially over transoceanic routes when fatigue, bad weather and communications made flying difficult. Although not a match for the DC-6s and Constellations which replaced the DC-4, the type was to see extensive service with smaller airlines for many years.

As a cost-cutting measure BOAC specified as much British equipment as possible to be fitted to its C-4s. This produced a saving of $200,000 per aircraft.

The main wing had a constant taper to the leading and trailing edges and a cross-section typical of Douglas aircraft with three spars.

Although Douglas sold 79 new DC-4s after World War II, most of the machines that entered service were converted ex-USAAF aircraft. These often retained the port-side cargo door that was not fitted to aircraft built before and after the war.

C-4 'ARGONAUT'

Astraea was one of 22 C-4s delivered to the British Overseas Airways Corporation in 1949. As BOAC's 'Argonaut' class they were used on Far Eastern, Middle Eastern and South American routes until 1960.

The original cabin layout of the DC-4 allowed for 40 passengers, or 28 sleeping births for overnight services. After World War II some converted C-54s could carry as many as 86 passengers in a high-density seating arrangement. Canadair C-4s were distinguished by their square windows, which indicated that the cabin was pressurised, unlike most DC-4s.

All three DC-4 undercarriage units retracted forwards; the nose gear into the forward fuselage, the main gear into the engine nacelle.

Four Rolls-Royce Merlin 626s replaced the Pratt & Whitney R-2000s installed in DC-4s. Merlins were fitted with superchargers and had better high-altitude performance. They were also cheaper, as they could be purchased duty-free unlike the American engines.

When loading the aircraft without the engines running, a pole could be fitted between the special tail bracket and the ground to prevent the aircraft from overbalancing.

DC-4-1009

Type: long-range transport

Powerplant: four 1081-kW (1,450-hp.) Pratt & Whitney R-2000-2SD13G Twin Wasp radial piston engines

Maximum speed: 451 km/h (280 m.p.h.) at 4265 m (14,000 ft.)

Cruising speed: 365 km/h (226 m.p.h.) at 3050 m (10,000 ft.)

Range: 4023 km (2,500 mi.)

Service ceiling: 6800 m (22,300 ft.)

Weights: empty 19640 kg; maximum take-off 33,112 kg (72,846 lb.)

Accommodation: crew of five, plus up to 44 passengers, baggage and freight for day use, or 22 passengers, baggage and freight as a sleeper transport

Dimensions:
span	35.81 m (117 ft. 6 in.)
length	28.60 m (93 ft. 10 in.)
height	8.38 m (29 ft. 2 in.)
wing area	135.63 m² (1,459 sq. ft.)

ACTION DATA

CRUISING SPEED

Here, the cruising speeds of the DC-4 and its predecessor and successor are compared. Intended for domestic use, the DC-4 delivered major improvements in coast-to-coast travel times.

DC-4-1009	365 km/h (226 m.p.h.)
DC-3C	274 km/h (170 m.p.h.)
DC-6A	507 km/h (314 m.p.h.)

PASSENGER LOAD

The larger capacity of the DC-4 and DC-6 allowed greater economies for operators, who in turn were able pass this on to the passenger in the form of cheaper fares. This increased the popularity of air travel.

DC-4-1009	44
DC-3C	32
DC-6A	52

RANGE

One of the greatest improvements of four-engined types was their range performance. Although originally designed for domestic use, the DC-4 pioneered transoceanic routes. Its use was short-lived, however, as new pressurised types like the DC-6 began to enter service.

DC-3C 1650 km (1,025 mi.)
DC-6A 4710 km (2,920 mi.)
DC-4-1009 4023 km (2,500 mi.)

War surplus aircraft for the airlines

■ **AVRO YORK:** The York was designed to an RAF specification for a long-range transport. A number were sold to airlines after the war.

■ **CURTISS C-46 COMMANDO:** The CW-20 was another pre-war design that was pressed into military service and was used mainly as a freighter.

■ **DOUGLAS C-47 SKYTRAIN:** Like the DC-4, the war-surplus military versions of the DC-3 were converted into airliners in large numbers.

■ **LOCKHEED C-69 CONSTELLATION:** Ordered by TWA and flown from 1943, the first 20 'Connies' were impressed into USAAF service.

DOUGLAS

DC-6

● Long-range airliner ● Freighter ● Military transport

A beautiful and functional airliner of the post-World War II years, the Douglas DC-6 was a fine aircraft that advanced the contribution made to aerial commerce by the successful Douglas family of transports. When it entered service in 1947, the DC-6 combined a high standard of comfort with long range. Primarily a passenger carrier, the DC-6 also performed well as a civil freighter and, in small numbers, as a military transport.

▲ Based on the successful wartime Douglas DC-4, which had made more than 80,000 transatlantic crossings, the pressurised DC-6 offered greater range and increased passenger comfort.

DOUGLAS DC-6

◀ Atlantic Clipper
Pan American used the improved DC-6 on transatlantic routes throughout the 1950s, until propeller-driven airliners were replaced by vastly more efficient jets like the Boeing 707.

▲ Long service
Even when it was overtaken by turboprops and jets, the DC-6 continued to be an economic proposition for cargo charters well into the 1990s. Although expensive to run, they were very cheap to buy.

▲ Airline stalwart
The DC-6B was the main passenger variant, with 288 being completed and delivered to airlines all over the world. Some were used on scheduled services into the 1970s.

Tourist special ▶
Pan American ordered 45 88-seat DC-6Bs for use on the airline's tourist-class services. Previous airliners had catered almost exclusively to the luxury trade, and 54 passengers was a more normal first-class load.

FACTS AND FIGURES

➤ The DC-6 made its maiden flight in Santa Monica, California, on 15 February 1946.

➤ The first DC-6s were delivered to American Airlines and United Air Lines on 20 November 1946.

➤ Two DC-6Bs were modified with a swinging tail to ease cargo loading.

➤ The US Air Transport Association estimates that first-line DC-6s carried over 100 million passengers.

➤ Total production of DC-6s, including military variants, numbered 704 aircraft.

➤ The final DC-6 was delivered to Yugoslavia on 17 November 1958.

PROFILE

Piston power across the oceans

In the 1950s, when air travel was still an experience available to only a small, well-heeled segment of the population, the Douglas DC-6 offered style and elegance. Seating space was generous, and travellers were pampered with gourmet meals and fine wines.

The DC-6, with its clean lines and straightforward shape, was a development of the earlier DC-4. It offered improved performance and the lowest operating costs of any airliner in its class, making it the most sought-after long-range commercial transport of its time.

It was the first Douglas transport to have cabin pressurisation. Later versions, the DC-6A, DC-6B and DC-6C, introduced improvements in the R-2800 piston engines, passenger accommodation and cargo capacity.

The introduction of jet-powered airliners such as the Boeing 707 in the late-1950s rapidly relegated the DC-6 to second-level routes, but the aircraft remained popular because of its low purchase price, operating costs and reputation for reliability.

US Air Force C-118 and US Navy R6D transports were successful military versions of this fine aircraft, serving troops throughout the world.

DC-6B

Type: long-range transport

Powerplant: four 1864-kW (2,500-hp.) Pratt & Whitney R-2800-CB17 Double Wasp radial piston engines

Maximum speed: 645 km/h (400 m.p.h.)

Cruising speed: 507 km/h (314 m.p.h.)

Range with maximum payload: 4836 km (3,000 mi.)

Range with maximum fuel: 7596 km (4,700 mi.)

Service ceiling: 7620 m (25,000 ft.)

Weights: empty 25,110 kg (55,357 lb.); maximum take-off 48,534 kg (106,775 lb.)

Accommodation: two pilots, flight engineer and stewardesses; 48 to 52 passengers in standard seating; up to 88 passengers in high-density configuration

Dimensions: span   35.81 m (117 ft. 6 in.)
length   32.18 m (105 ft. 6 in.)
height   8.74 m (28 ft. 8 in.)
wing area 135.91 m² (1,462 sq. ft.)

Half a century on, the DC-6 is still going strong. In recent years it has worked for cargo airlines like Instone (below) and Air Atlantique (above), which still uses the type from its base in Coventry.

DC-6B

KLM operated the DC-6 throughout the 1950s, using the type on the company's extensive route network to Africa and South America.

Early piston-engined airliners like the DC-6 usually had a five-man flight crew on long-haul flights, including two pilots, two flight engineers and a navigator.

Developed from the DC-4, the DC-6 had a new pressurised fuselage of larger dimensions. It was able to carry more passengers in greater comfort than its predecessor.

Passenger capacity of the DC-6B varied considerably. As a luxury transport it could carry 54 people, but this increased to 88 passengers in tourist configuration, or 92 for short-haul high-density routes.

The square cabin windows were a feature of the DC-6 and the succeeding DC-7, replacing the round windows of the DC-4 from which they were developed. They offered a larger glazed area and gave passengers a better view.

After their passenger-carrying days were over, two DC-6Bs were converted to freighters, with swinging tails to allow for the loading of bulky cargo.

PH-DFK

THE FLYING DUTCHMAN

KLM

JAN HUYGHEN VAN LINSCHOTEN

The DC-6 had no radar, although the stretched DC-7 was one of the first commercial aircraft to be fitted with weather radar as standard.

Power was provided by four Pratt & Whitney Double Wasp radial piston engines, initially delivering 1790 kW (2,400 hp.) of power, but later upgraded to 1864 kW (2,500 hp.) with water injection.

The DC-6 used the same 35.81-m (117-ft. 6-in.) span wings as the DC-4, the only difference being a more rugged undercarriage to cope with heavier take-off weights.

The DC-6B was designed as a passenger carrier, and lacked the large upward-hinging cargo doors fitted to most freighter variants.

ACTION DATA

PASSENGER LOAD

The explosive growth in commercial aviation is reflected in the increase in passenger loads of Douglas airliners. Capacity more than doubled in the 15 years between the DC-3 and DC-6, and a decade later the DC-8 was carrying over seven times as many people.

DC-3   24 passengers
DC-6   58 passengers
DC-8   173 passengers

Variations on the DC-6

■ **MILITARY TRANSPORT:** Designed to a military specification, the DC-6 was ordered by the US Air Force as the C-118A. It could carry 74 fully-equipped troops or more than 12 tons of cargo.

■ **GOOD SAMARITAN:** The C-118 could hold 60 stretchers and was often used as a flying ambulance. It was the main USAF aeromedical evacuation aircraft in the early Vietnam years.

■ **FIRE BOMBER:** Several DC-6s have been modified as fire-fighters, with a ventral pannier tank which is normally loaded with fire retardant chemicals.

■ **FREIGHT MASTER:** Starting out as a freighter design, the DC-6 has returned to the role in the twilight of its career. It is used to carry a wide variety of cargo – even light aircraft.

DOUGLAS

DC-7

● **Piston-engined airliner** ● **Improved DC-6** ● **Trans-oceanic flights**

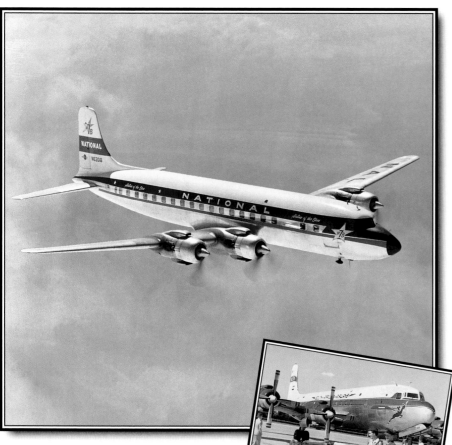

Last of the Douglas propeller-driven airliners, the DC-7 was developed for head-to-head competition with the Lockheed Super Constellation. The DC-7 became a classic in its own right, spanning the world's oceans in an age when air commerce was slower than today, but provided luxurious service. The ultimate version, the DC-7C 'Seven Seas', was slightly enlarged and had very long range, allowing it to cover marathon distances.

▲ *In a scene from a bygone era of luxury travel, passengers drive out to the tarmac to be greeted by the crew of their DC-7 before boarding for a flight to South Africa.*

DOUGLAS DC-7

◀ **Douglas airliners**
Lined up with other Douglas products, the DC-7 brought major improvements to operators.

▼ **British operations**
Passengers disembark from a BOAC-operated DC-7 after returning to one of London's airports.

▲ **All American operations**
DC-7s were supplied to American airline operators in the process of establishing themselves in what was a growing market. Pan American operated the type as the 'Super 7'; orders also came from overseas.

▲ **Graceful lines**
Displaying the beauty that only piston airliners possessed, a DC-7 sets out on a long flight.

◀ **Second hand**
After serving as airliners many aircraft were sold to be used as cargo carriers in the Third World.

FACTS AND FIGURES

➤ The initial DC-7 was a direct development of the DC-6B with the fuselage lengthened for extra seats.

➤ Total production of DC-7s amounted to 337 of all variants.

➤ A non-stop route between London and New York began on 13 June 1955.

➤ In the late 1990s fewer than 10 DC-7's remained in service, as cargo aircraft in South America and Africa.

➤ Some aircraft had an under-fuselage tank fitted and were used for fire-fighting.

➤ The DC-7 was eventually replaced by the jet-powered Douglas DC-8.

PROFILE

Transatlantic pioneer

Entering service in 1953, the Douglas DC-7 was the jewel in the crown of a dynasty of Douglas passenger aircraft. It was created to compete with Lockheed's Super Constellation, but as it turned out, the two aircraft represented the pinnacle of the development of piston-engined airliners.

American Airlines was the first purchaser of the DC-7, a direct development of the successful DC-6B. Its Wright Turbo-Compound engines added exhaust 'push' to the thrust provided by propellers. Many

users bought DC-7s with greater fuel capacity, among them Pan American which inaugurated a non-stop London-New York service on 13 June 1955. Even then, more fuel capacity was needed. To improve the reach of this airliner, Douglas created the DC-7C 'Seven Seas' version with longer 'legs'.

Although the DC-7 series was popular, its operating costs were comparatively high, largely because of its complicated engines. DC-7s were soon replaced by the first turboprop- and turbojet-powered machines.

Above: With its cargo doors open, a DC-7 is loaded with supplies for a flight to South America. Many small airlines operated the aircraft in the transport role.

Right: Resplendent in a blue and white airliner finish, an early production DC-7B climbs high into the sky for a transatlantic flight.

DC-7C

Type: passenger transport

Powerplant: four 2535-kW (3,400-hp.) Wright R-3350-18EA-1 Turbo-Compound radial piston engines

Maximum speed: 653 km/h (405 m.p.h.) at 6615 m (21,700 ft.)

Accommodation: 189 passengers plus crew

Initial climb rate: 536 m/min (21,700 ft.)

Range: 7410 km (4,600 mi.) with maximum payload; 9075 km (5,626 mi.) with maximum fuel

Service ceiling: 6615 m (21,700 ft.)

Weights: empty 33,005 kg (72,611 lb.); maximum take-off 64,864 kg (142,700 lb.)

Dimensions: span   38.86 m (127 ft. 5 in.)
length 34.21 m (112 ft. 3 in.)
height 9.70 m (31 ft. 10 in.)
wing area 152.08 m² (1,636 sq.ft.)

DC-7C

The flight deck of the aircraft remained similar throughout the DC-7 series and allowed pilots to convert from earlier Douglas aircraft with ease.

With a stretched fuselage, the passenger cabin of the DC-7 was spacious compared to that of the DC-6. This was an advantage on long transatlantic flights. Passenger comfort was an important feature.

Delivered to Pan American World Airways in 1956 this DC-7 was known as the *Clipper Blue Jacket*. After sterling service it was sold to an operator in Bermuda, where the aircraft was written-off in an accident.

To allow the aircraft to operate at higher weights, various structural modifications were made to the DC-7. One of these was an increase in the height of the tail.

Many airline operators name their aircraft to increase publicity for their expanding fleets. Pan American World Airways was a leader in this field, painting names on the noses of all its aircraft.

The four Wright engines proved to be unreliable on early versions of the aircraft, but after modifications requested by operators a satisfactory level of performance was achieved. Compared to later jet engines, maintenance turned out to be costly, however.

After being retired as commercial airliners many DC-7s found themselves serving as cargo aircraft on shorter domestic routes in South America. This often necessitated the installation of two large cargo doors on the left side of the fuselage.

Douglas airliner family

■ DC-3: After achieving legendary status during World War II, the civilian DC-3 variant continues to serve with various airlines.

■ DC-4: Developed from the DC-3 to offer improved range and a larger load capability the DC-4 operated with many non-US airlines.

■ DC-6: Having served its time as an airliner this example now operates as a 'fire-bomber', fighting forest fires in France.

■ DC-8: The first Douglas jet airliner brought an end to its propeller-driven airliners. Reduced operating costs were a vital feature.

ACTION DATA

MAXIMUM SPEED

Steady advances in piston engine design saw a gradual increase in the speeds of post-war airliners. The DC-7 offered a vast improvement compared to the wartime DC-3, but both were eventually superseded by the new jet powered DC-8.

DC-7C	653 km/h (405 m.p.h.)
DC-3C	274 km/h (170 m.p.h.)
DC-8-50	932 km/h (578 m.p.h.)

MAXIMUM RANGE

An increase in range offered airliner operators a wider choice of destinations. The DC-7 brought with it the ability routinely to fly non-stop across the Atlantic and over many Pacific routes. Gradual development of the aircraft saw the fuel load increased allowing further destinations to be reached. The DC-3 was not able to compete.

DC-7C 7410 km (4,600 mi.)
DC-3C 1650 km (1,023 mi.)
DC-8-50 6700 km (4,150 mi.)

PASSENGERS

As the power of the engines increased, so airliners became larger, allowing an increase in passenger loads. The small size of the DC-3 is obvious when compared to the later Douglas products such as the DC-7.

DC-7C 105 passengers
DC-3C 32 passengers
DC-8-50 189 passengers

DOUGLAS

DC-8

● Four-jet airliner ● Long-serving cargo carrier ● Rival of the 707

▲ Technically just as good as its rivals, the DC-8 had a mixed history. Airline economics meant that it was often worth more second-hand in the late 1960s than when it was first built.

Airlines converted from propellers to jets with two aircraft, the Douglas DC-8 and the Boeing Model 707. Douglas leaped into the jet transport field with great success, even though it had no indirect subsidy from the US military, which Boeing received for its jet tankers. It seemed as though the DC-8 had lost the edge to the Boeing 707, but with modifications it has had a longer career, especially as a freighter.

DOUGLAS DC-8

▲ **Ground school**
Learning to fly a DC-8 with United Airlines meant starting on the ground. With 30 aircraft refitted, United was the biggest customer for the re-engined DC-8 Super 71.

▲ **Swissair into the jet age**
Having used Douglas turboprops, Swissair chose the DC-8 to go into the jet age, with the first aircraft entering service in 1960. The airline also ordered the rival Convair 880, which was less cost effective.

▼ **San Francisco**
American operators acquired many second-hand DC-8s in the 1960s. This group is at San Francisco airport in 1967.

▲ **Ageing flight deck**
The technology of flight decks in the 1950s was a long way from modern aircraft, with simple dials and switches and no screens.

▲ **Freight hauler**
Cargolux was one of many airlines that bought up DC-8s for freight operations. These aircraft, which were not re-engined, were replaced by Boeing 747s in the late 1980s.

Big and noisy ▶
Built with Rolls-Royce Conway or Pratt & Whitney JT4 engines, DC-8s were thirsty and noisy, but many have been fitted with the quiet and efficient CFM-56.

FACTS AND FIGURES

➤ The DC-8 prototype first flew on 30 May 1958 at Edwards air base in California.

➤ The DC-8 entered service in September 1959, but at first lacked range.

➤ In August 1961 a DC-8 became the first jetliner to fly faster than sound by diving steeply from 15,877 m (52,000 ft.).

➤ The DC-8 Super 61 flew in March 1966, the first of many stretched models.

➤ The stretched DC-8 had the longest range of any jetliner when United used it on Baltimore – Honolulu flights.

➤ A single DC-8 is operated by the US Navy as an electronic research aircraft.

PROFILE

Douglas flies into the jet age

Douglas' long experience with passenger travel was epitomised by the great DC-8 family of successful jetliners, from the elegant prototype of 1958 to the 'stretched' Super 60/70 series, many of which still fly today with secondary users.

The DC-8 was a more conservative design than the rival Boeing 707, with a less swept wing and no leading-edge lift devices and, unusually for the time, no wing fences or vortex generators. It was slightly cheaper, and the later-series aircraft introduced in the mid-1960s had very long range.

With the oil crisis of 1973, the DC-8 gained new popularity because it was the biggest narrow-body aircraft available. Though production ended in 1972, second-hand aircraft with low airframe hours were trading at high prices.

New noise regulations drafted in the 1970s threatened to put many DC-8s out of business before their time, so many were re-engined in the early 1980s with CFM-56 engines. Once again the DC-8 made a come-back, with 'scrap value' examples suddenly in demand as freighters. Many still fly today, some with modernised cockpits and engine 'hush kits'.

The DC-8 was never as successful as the rival Boeing 707, but it has gained a niche of its own, especially with new engines. The development of wide bodies meant that it was obsolete by the 1970s.

DC-8 Super 63
Type: long-range transport

Powerplant: four 84.52-kN (19,000-lb.-thrust) Pratt & Whitney JT3D-7 turbofans

Maximum cruising speed: 966 km/h (599 m.p.h.) at 9145 m (30,000 ft.)

Range: with max. payload 7242 km (4,490 mi.)

Service ceiling: about 12,690 m (42,000 ft.)

Weights: empty 69,739 kg (153,426 lb.); loaded 158,760 kg (502,698 lb.)

Accommodation: as a freighter, maximum payload over short distances up to 52,000 kg (114,400 lb.); as an airliner, up to 259 passengers depending on configuration

Dimensions: span 45.24 m (148 ft. 5 in.); length 57.12 m (187 ft. 4 in.); height 12.93 m (42 ft. 5 in.); wing area 271.92 m² (2,926 sq.ft.)

DC-8 SERIES 30

KLM Royal Dutch Airlines began using the DC-8 in 1960, and subsequently used Series 30, 53 and Super 63 variants on services to New York, Sydney and Tokyo. They were replaced by Airbus A310s in 1983.

Many early DC-8s had a navigator as well as a pilot, co-pilot and flight engineer. United Parcels Service has upgraded its DC-8s with advanced EFIS cockpits.

Five small spoilers were mounted ahead of the flap sections. These automatically activated when the nosewheel hit the ground, to destroy any remaining wing lift on landing.

The DC-8 had an unusual aileron arrangement. The aileron consisted of two parts, the outer being used only at low speeds. Tabs were mounted on the inner sections.

The tail was a three-spar unit with a full-span one-piece rudder. It housed the aerials for the HF and VHF radios and the VOR navigation system.

Small cheek inlets admitted air for the air-conditioning system. A weather radar dish was housed in the nose behind a black dielectric radome.

Large baggage holds were provided forward and aft of the wing, with a combined capacity of 36 m³ (1,272 cu. ft.). The doors were on the starboard side.

The DC-8 was most commonly powered by Pratt & Whitney engines. The JT3D had distinct half cowls that ejected bypass air from the compressor.

The wing was virtually one enormous fuel tank between the spars, containing 87,360 litres (23,000 gal.) of fuel.

The fuselage was of double circular section, with the upper lobe being of greater diameter than the lower lobe, giving the characteristic 'pinched' look to the airframe.

ACTION DATA

PASSENGER CAPACITY

Airliners designed in the late 1950s were intended to have a passenger capacity of around 120. The unprecedented rise in demand for air transport saw larger, longer versions quickly put into production, with much more densely packed seating. None of the big four-jets were stretched as far as the DC-8, however, which could carry more passengers than any other airliner until the arrival of the wide-body jets in the 1970s.

707-320B 189 passengers
DC-8 SUPER 63 259 passengers
SUPER VC10 187 passengers

Stretching the DC-8

DC-8 SERIES 10: The first models of the DC-8 were all of the same size, variations being largely confined to powerplant, fuel capacity and range. Pan American were the first users of the type, flying 20 Series 10 aircraft on domestic routes.

DC-8 SERIES 61 and SERIES 63: Douglas offered a stretched version of the DC-8 in the mid-1960s, to compete with Boeing. The Series 61 and 63 models were 11.18 m (36 ft. 8 in.) longer than the original and could carry 259 passengers.

DC-8 SERIES 62: Stretched only by 2.03 m (6 ft. 8 in.), the Series 62 had extra fuel and aerodynamic refinements to give a very long range. The Series 63 incorporated the same improvements with the long fuselage of the Series 61.

EMBRAER

EMB-110 BANDEIRANTE

● Twin-engined commuter ● Up to 21 seats ● Brazilian success

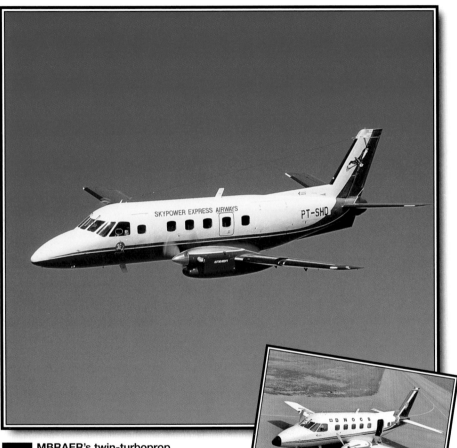

E MBRAER's twin-turboprop Bandeirante (Pioneer) was created for the Brazilian air force, but became a respected civil transport which played a key role in the foundation of Brazil's aerospace industry and development of vast country's internal air network. The Bandeirante proved to be a fine short-haul airliner, providing good service to passengers and paving the way for the Brasilia airliner which is used worldwide.

▲ An important market for the Bandeirante was the United States. It sold well there and around the world, with examples entering service as far apart as France and New Zealand.

EMBRAER EMB-110 BANDEIRANTE

▼ **Foundation for Brazilian industry**
As well as helping to establish the country's internal air transport network, EMB-110 production was a cornerstone of Brazil's fledgling aviation industry.

▲ **Brazilian air force C-95**
The first customer for the Bandeirante was the Brazilian air force, which designated the aircraft C-95 and has become a major operator of the type.

Dolphin's dozen ▶
Dolphin Airways of Tampa, Florida, operated 12 Bandeirantes in the early 1980s, serving 22 cities in five US states. This is the EMB-110P1 version.

▼ **Two variants**
The EMB-110P1 and -110P2 were the two main commuter variants: the former had a 'quick-change' interior and cargo door, and the latter an 85-cm longer fuselage.

Conventional ▶ cockpit
The cockpit accommodated two pilots and its layout was fairly typical of similar aircraft in the 1970s.

FACTS AND FIGURES

➤ In all, 490 Bandeirantes were built by EMBRAER between August 1969 and September 1990.

➤ Currently being replaced by newer craft, EMB-110s still serve with several nations.

➤ The military prototype for this series of aircraft first flew on 26 October 1968.

➤ The first flight of a production EMB-110 Bandeirante was made successfully on 9 August 1972.

➤ French engineer Max Holste was mainly responsible for the Bandeirante's design.

➤ The EMB-110 was the basis for the short-fuselage EMB-121 Xingu business aircraft.

Brazilian pioneer twin

The hinterlands of Brazil, including vast stretches of Amazon jungle, have been opened up by the EMBRAER EMB-110 Bandeirante, a sensible and practical small airliner that is bringing civilisation to the wilderness. The 1968 decision to build this aircraft as the C-95 for the Brazilian air force led to the creation of EMBRAER the following year and to hundreds of Bandeirantes for small- and medium-sized air carriers.

The smooth-handling EMB-110 allows pilots to fly in and out of small airfields confident of having sufficient power to avoid take-off and landing mishaps. Both pilots and mechanics praise the simplicity and practicality of the Bandeirante, although its range and passenger-carrying capacity are limited.

The EMB-110 is used primarily as a feederliner and has seen service worldwide. There is also a seven-seat executive transport version, as well as a geophysical survey variant with additional wing tanks. Plans for a pressurised version were abandoned, but the experience gained was used in producing the subsequent EMB-120 Brasilia airliner. Production of the Bandeirante ceased in 1990 after 490 had been delivered.

YC-95 (EMB-100) serial number 2131 was the second Bandeirante prototype. The first production model, the EMB-110, had a longer fuselage and redesigned nose and cabin windows.

The EMB-110's cabin was enlarged while the aircraft was in production. The initial commercial variant, the EMB-110C, held 15 passengers; the largest version was the EMB-110P2 which could accommodate 21.

A 450-W landing light was fitted to each wing so that the aircraft could both see and be seen.

EMB-110P1 Bandeirante

Type: 18-seat commuter airliner and general utility aircraft

Powerplant: two 559-kW (750-hp.) Pratt & Whitney Canada PT-6A-34 turboprop engines

Maximum cruising speed: 411 km/h (255 m.p.h.) at sea level

Range: 2010 km (1,246 mi.) with maximum fuel and reserves

Service ceiling: 6550 m (21,500 ft.)

Weights: empty 3590 kg (7,900 lb.); maximum take-off 5900 kg (12,980 lb.)

Accommodation: two crew and up to 18 passengers

Dimensions:
span	15.32 m	(50 ft. 3 in.)
length	15.10 m	(49 ft. 6 in.)
height	4.91 m	(16 ft. 1 in.)
wing area	29.10 m²	(313 sq. ft.)

EMB-110P1 BANDEIRANTE

This EMB-110P1 was operated by Florida commuter airline Dolphin Airways from 1981. Under the strict certification rules in the USA the EMB-110P1 was modified to allow a higher gross take-off weight.

Many American carriers operate large fleets of Bandeirantes and use it to bridge the gap between 8- and 10-seat light aircraft and the larger 30- and 40-seat turboprops.

The standard Bandeirante crew consists of a pilot and co-pilot. The stressed acrylic centre windscreen panels are 13 mm (½-in.) thick.

Both the main and nose undercarriages retract forward, each leg being supported by a single wheel.

Two top-selling Pratt & Whitney Canada PT-6A turboprops supply the power to drive a three-blade Hartzell propeller.

The nose of the EMB-110 contains a Bendix- or RCA-built radar array.

The EMB-110P series introduces a forward passenger door, which was not fitted to the earlier, shorter models.

Internal wing fuel tanks have a total capacity of 1690 litres (440 gal.), giving a range of over 2000 km (1,250 mi.).

As the EMB-110P1 is able to be quickly converted to a cargo aircraft it is fitted with a large cargo door on the port side.

The EMB-110P2 version differs from the -110P1 not only in having a longer fuselage, but it also has provision for a toilet.

DOLPHIN **N61DA** JET POWER

ACTION DATA

RANGE

In the vast Brazilian wilderness, where the Bandeirante is used, good range is important as airstrips tend to be some distance apart. The Metro on the other hand is intended for the relatively short distances between US airports.

EMB-110P1 BANDEIRANTE 2010 km (1,246 mi.)
METRO 23 1450 km (900 mi.)
Do 328-200 2704 km (1,676 mi.)

PASSENGER LOAD

All three types are designed to carry around 18/19 passengers and larger versions have also been produced to transport bigger loads. Cargo doors can be specified so that the aircraft can be used for freight.

EMB-110P1 BANDEIRANTE 18 passengers
METRO 23 19 passengers
Do 328-200 19 passengers

MAXIMUM CRUISING SPEED

Fairchild's Metro is a relatively fast aircraft compared to others in the same class. The Do 328, although not as quick, has a good climb rate and cruising altitude.

EMB-110P1	411 km/h (255 m.p.h.)
METRO 23	534 km/h (331 m.p.h.)
Do 328-200	428 km/h (265 m.p.h.)

Small commuter propliners

■ BEECHCRAFT MODEL 99: The Model 99 Airliner was essentially an enlarged Queen Air executive twin with room for up to 15 passengers. Production ceased in 1986.

■ BRITTEN-NORMAN TRISLANDER: The Trislander of 1970 grew out of the successful twin-engined Islander. The last were built in 1984; plans to restart production have stalled.

■ DE HAVILLAND CANADA DHC-6: The Twin Otter STOL transport was built between 1965 and 1988 and considerable numbers remain in service worldwide, including floatplane variants.

■ FAIRCHILD METRO IIIA: Metros date from the 1960s and follow a Swearingen Aircraft design. Stretched and updated versions are still produced.

EMBRAER

EMB-120 BRASILIA

● Brazilian design ● Pressurised twin turboprop ● Military versions

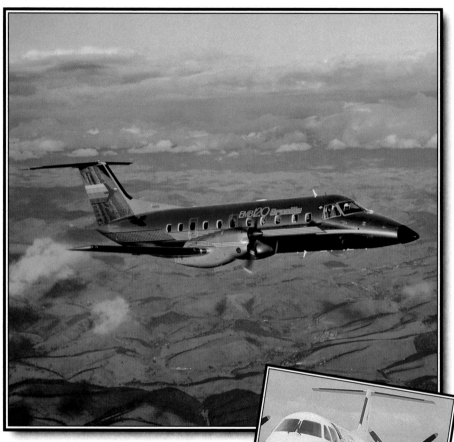

A number of projects aimed at producing a pressurised, higher capacity derivative of the successful EMBRAER Bandeirante 19-seater culminated in the 1979 launch of an entirely new design – the Brasilia. Seating up to 30 passengers and powered by two Pratt & Whitney Canada PW100 turbines, the EMB-120 has secured more than 300 orders from around the world and has been in service for more than a decade.

▲ *Since the launch of the highly successful Bandeirante, EMBRAER of Brazil has developed into a respected aircraft manufacturer producing a range of commercial and military designs.*

EMBRAER EMB-120 BRASILIA

▼ **Conventional cockpit**
Brasilia cockpits mainly have analogue instruments and feature a conventional array of avionics systems, including weather radar.

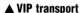

▲ **VIP transport**
The Brazilian air force's 6° Esquadrao de Transporte Aérea and Grupo de Transporte Especial operates 10 VC-97s.

▼ **Third prototype**
PT-ZBC was the third EMB-120 off the production line. Here it is seen in a factory finish with the EMBRAER logo on the fin.

▲ **Launch customer**
Atlantic Southeast of Atlanta, Georgia, was the first customer and put the EMB-120 into service in October 1985. Early aircraft were powered by smaller 1119-kW (1,500-hp.) PW115 engines.

Regional sales success ▶
Comair is one of the largest US regional airlines and in 1997 operated a fleet of 40 Brasilias, providing feeder services for Delta Airlines.

FACTS AND FIGURES

➤ In June 1995, US airline SkyWest purchased 10 EMB-120ERs for $75 million; the cost included spare parts and training.

➤ Composite materials make up 10 per cent of the Brasilia's empty weight.

➤ The 300th Brasilia was delivered in September 1995.

➤ Brazil's air force has ordered five EMB-120SA early warning aircraft, equipped with fuselage-mounted radar.

➤ By January 1996, Brasilias had carried nearly 86 million passengers.

➤ EMBRAER's EMB-145 regional jet airliner uses EMB-120 parts, including the cockpit.

PROFILE

Improved successor to the Bandeirante

Left: Air Midwest, at the time providing feeder services for American Eagle, was an early customer. It has since re-equipped with larger Beech 1900Ds.

Although the Brasilia shared the Bandeirante's basic layout, it differed in some important respects. The fuselage was of circular section with a T-tail, but the low-mounted, unswept wings were retained.

After the prototype's first flight on 27 July 1983, the Paris Air Salon of 1985 was chosen to mark the first delivery to the launch customer – the US airline Atlantic Southeast.

From 1993 more powerful PW118 engines replaced the original PW115s (both members of the PW100 family), although a version with PW118A engines, had been produced in 1987. This model was designed for 'hot-and-high' operations in warmer climates.

In 1994 the EMB-120ER Brasilia Advanced became the standard production version. Improvements included a higher maximum take-off weight, to allow for greater fuel capacity and better range, and decreased cabin noise levels. Earlier aircraft can also be retrofitted to the -120ER standard. All-cargo and mixed configuration versions are also offered by EMBRAER, but have not yet been bought.

However, the EMB-120QC 'quick-change' variant (able to carry either 30 passengers or 3500 kg (7,700 lb.) of freight) entered service with Total Linheas Aereas of Brazil in 1993. A corporate version was ordered by United Technologies in 1986, while Brazil's air force has bought 10 VC-97 VIP transports.

Above: The United States is an important market and one in which the EMBRAER Brasilia has performed well. This aircraft belongs to United Express.

EMB-120ER Brasilia Advanced

Type: pressurised twin-turboprop transport

Powerplant: two 1342-kW (1,800-hp.) Pratt & Whitney PW118 or PW118A turboprops

Maximum level speed: 606 km/h (376 m.p.h.) at 6100 m (20,000 ft.)

Initial climb rate: 762 m/min (2,500 f.p.m.) at sea level

Range: 1575 km (975 mi.) at 9150 m (30,000 ft.) with maximum fuel, payload and reserves

Service ceiling: 9755 m (32,000 ft.)

Weights: empty equipped 7150 kg (15,730 lb.); maximum take-off 11,990 kg (23,353 lb.)

Accommodation: three crew and up to 30 passengers or 3500 kg (7,700 lb.) of cargo

Dimensions: span 19.78 m (64 ft. 11 in.)
length 20.07 m (65 ft. 10 in.)
height 6.35 m (20 ft. 10 in.)
wing area 39.43 m² (424 sq. ft.)

EMB-120 BRASILIA

N180YV is one of a fleet of 20 EMB-120s operated by five airlines under the United Express banner, providing feeder services for United Airlines. Sixty cities are served from five main hubs.

Standard EMB-120 passenger configuration allows for 30 seats in one of two possible configurations, each with three seats abreast. Other features include an attendant's seat, galley and toilet. As well as pressurisation, air-conditioning is a standard feature.

Among the changes made to the EMB-120ER was the deletion of the de-icing 'boot' on the leading edge of the tailfin.

Baggage is stowed in a compartment behind the main cabin. 'Quick-change' freight variants use the cargo bay door to load the main cabin.

A crew of two flies the Brasilia from a modern cockpit. A small nose radome houses a weather radar scanner.

Passengers board via an airstair incorporated into the cabin door at the front of the port side of the aircraft. This allows the machine to operate from airfields with minimal ground facilities.

Pratt & Whitney's PW100 turbine family powers the Brasilia. The first examples used two PW115s, with later aircraft having more powerful PW118s or PW118As.

EMBRAER has marketed an all-freight version of the Brasilia with a 4000-kg capacity and the 'quick-change' EMB120QC variant with a maximum load of 3500 kg.

ACTION DATA

CRUISING SPEED

The Brasilia has a comparable cruising speed to other types in the 30-seater category, like the Jetstream J41 and Dornier 328, although the latter is marginally quicker. The oldest of these three designs, the Jetstream, is also the slowest.

EMB-120ER BRASILIA	580 km/h (360 m.p.h.)
J41	547 km/h (340 m.p.h.)
Do 328-110	620 km/h (384 m.p.h.)

PASSENGERS

All three designs are aimed at the 30-seat regional market. Both the J41 and Brasilia have sold well in the United States, although sales of the Dornier have been slow to materialise. Stretched versions of the Jetstream and Dornier have also been built or projected.

EMB-120ER BRASILIA ADVANCED 30 passengers
J41 29 passengers
Do 328-110 33 passengers

RANGE

Once again the most modern of these designs has the best performance. The Dornier, first flown in the 1990s, has a better range than the Brasilia, whereas the older J41's range is over 250 km (165 mi.) less than that of the Do 328. Long range is often a good selling point to airlines.

Do 328-110 1666 km (1,035 mi.)
EMB-120ER BRASILIA ADVANCED 1575 km (975 mi.)
J41 1403 km (870 mi.)

T-tailed pressurised turbine twins

■ **BEECHCRAFT MODEL 1900:** This 21-seat regional aircraft, derived from the Model 200, first flew in September 1982. The Model 1900D followed with a 35.6-cm (14-in.) deeper fuselage.

■ **DE HAVILLAND CANADA DHC-8 DASH 8:** Demand for 30- to 40-seat regional airliners in the late 1970s led DHC to design the Dash 8. This first flew in mid-1983 and worldwide sales followed.

■ **DORNIER Do 328:** Another 30-seater, the Do 328 has not been successful in what is a crowded market. First flown in 1991, the aircraft entered service in Switzerland in 1993.

■ **PIPER PA-42 CHEYENNE III:** Cheyenne III can trace its design origins back to the piston-engined PA-31 Navajo of the mid-1960s. The main cabin holds 11 passengers.

FAIRCHILD

MERLIN/METRO

● Executive airliner ● Turboprop engines ● Streamlined design

FAIRCHILD MERLIN/METRO

▼ **Magnificent Merlin**
Fairchild undertook modifications to the Merlin series, allowing the aircraft to remain at the cutting edge of the highly competitive regional airliner market.

▲ **Clean lines**
The exceptionally streamlined design of the Merlin has enabled the aircraft to become one of the most eye-catching airliners around. This is highlighted by this example's attractive colour scheme.

European service ▶
Flying the demanding route over the Alps, Austrian airline Trans Adria utilises a Merlin IVA. The Merlin is proving to be a great success, able to provide a regular service in some of the most harsh weather conditions.

◀ **Flying the flag**
Operating within the United States as a commuter airliner, the Merlin is used to provide feeder connection flights to a host of major airlines. They operate from most of America's major city airports.

Multipurpose Merlin ▶
Often referred to as the 'sewer tube', because of its long circular fuselage design, the Merlin is equipped with a large rear-mounted cargo hatch and a forward passenger door.

One of the more distinctive turboprop commuter and business aircraft design families, the Merlin and Metro can trace their origins back to the 1960s. Swearingen Aircraft was founded in San Antonio, Texas, in 1959 by Edward J. Swearingen. His company began by offering turboprop conversions for existing aircraft, but in 1964 launched an all-new design – the Merlin. From this was developed a pressurised commuter aircraft – the Metro.

▲ *With its long range and spacious internal design, the Fairchild Merlin and Metro series has found a ready market with both commercial and corporate users.*

FACTS AND FIGURES

➤ Swearingen's financial difficulties in 1971 led to early merger talks with Piper, though these came to naught.

➤ PT6A engines were offered again on the Metro IIIA after requests from US airlines.

➤ One UC-26C was fitted with radar for use by the US ANG as a drug interdictor.

➤ The Metro II, introduced in 1974, offered an optional rocket unit for assisted take-offs from 'hot and high' airfields.

➤ An all-freight version of the Metro 23 is known as the Expediter.

➤ In 1997 Merlins and Metros share the same fuselage, but have different interiors.

Cutting edge commuter

Originally powered by two Pratt & Whitney PT6A turbines, the Merlin entered production in 1965. Pressure applied by AiResearch Aviation, who were marketing the aircraft for Swearingen, led to the Merlin being re-engined with Garrett AiResearch TPE331 turboprops, and the improved Metro series soon followed.

To comply with US regulations of the day regarding commuter aircraft, the Metro was initially restricted to a gross weight of 5670 kg (12,500 lb.). Its circular fuselage was derived from that of the Merlin and held 19 passengers.

By 1971, Swearingen had been taken over by Fairchild, with whom the Metro series had been jointly developed and, which had undertaken some sub-assembly work on early production aircraft.

Various improved Merlins and Metros followed, the Metro IIA of 1980 taking advantage of the relaxation in operational weight restrictions, and the Metro III

introducing 746-kW (1,000-hp.) TPE331s turboprops and an extension to its wingspan.

Having sold well, the Metro found customers in the US and abroad. A major boost to the programme came in the 1980s, when the US Air National Guard bought 50 Metro IIIs (C-26As and Bs). Incorporating features of these aircraft, Fairchild then introduced the civil Metro 23 with a 7484-kg (16,500-lb.) all-up weight.

Left: This example is operated by the Swiss airline Crossair. Regional flights are undertaken throughout Europe.

Right: Introduced in later models was the increased wing-span. This allowed the Metro to operate at greater weights as well as higher altitudes, so increasing range and reducing costs.

METRO III

Delivered in 1982, this aircraft operated with Houston Aircraft Leasing. After withdrawal from service, the Metro was passed to Chrysler Management Corporation as a company transport aircraft.

Metro III

Type: twin-engined regional airliner

Powerplant: two 746-kW (1,000-hp.) Garrett Air Research TPE331-11U-601G turboprops

Maximum speed: 555 km/h (344 m.p.h.)

Cruising speed: 513 km/h (318 m.p.h.)

Initial climb rate: 743 m/min (2,440 f.p.m.)

Range: 1149 km (712 mi.)

Weights: operational empty weight 3963 kg (8,719 lb.); maximum take off 6350 kg (13,970 lb.)

Accommodation: two flight crew and 19 passengers

Dimensions: span 17.37 m (57 ft.)
length 18.09 m (59 ft. 4 in.)
height 5.08 m (16 ft. 8 in.)
wing area 28.71 m² (309 sq. ft.)

New features of the Metro III were uprated engines and a stronger wing, associated with the increase in gross weight. There was no increase in fuselage size or passenger accommodation. The aircraft was approved for up to 20 passengers, but in US operations this is limited to 19, since a cabin attendant is carried.

Streamlining the Metro design has played an important part in the aircraft refinement. To this end new Dowty-Rotol supercritical propellers were adopted and the nacelle lines were refined to reduce drag. Another drag-reduction modification allowed the landing gear doors to close after gear extension.

Positioned at the rear of the fuselage is a large cargo hatch. This allows the aircraft to be loaded with a limited amount of baggage. An interesting bonus of positioning the door at the rear is that during commercial flight operations, the aircraft cargo and passengers can be unloaded at the same time.

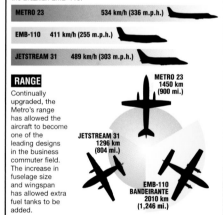

PIONEER AIRLINES

N30693

The forward-mounted passenger door is fitted with integral steps to ease the boarding for passengers. This door is also used by the flight deck crew.

Garrett turboprops are installed on the Metro III. These are equipped with an optional alcohol/water injection system to offer better performance in hot conditions.

The new wing of the Metro III is 3.05 m (10 ft.) longer than that of the original Merlin. To reduce drag, the wingtips are of a conical-chamber design.

With a general increase in the dimensions of the Metro series, the aircraft was fitted with a rear-mounted fillet. Earlier models were equipped with a small rocket pack, to reduce the take-off distance.

First-class performer

■ **MILITARY:** Used as a squadron transport, this Merlin is flown by the Belgian Air Force. The aircraft also provides transport for high-ranking officers.

■ **COMMERCIAL:** Delivered in 1978, this Metro operated with Tavina in Colombia on internal flights. This example was once also operated by British Aerospace Inc.

■ **VIP TRANSPORT:** A substantial improvement was made to South Africa's military transport fleet with the purchase of a Merlin. The aircraft is employed as a long-range VIP transport.

ACTION DATA

MAXIMUM CRUISING SPEED

Equipped with two turboprop engines like similar small regional airliners, the Metro 23 is able to offer an exceptionally high speed mainly because of its streamlined design. Slowest in this field is the Brazilian EMB-110.

METRO 23   534 km/h (336 m.p.h.)

EMB-110   411 km/h (255 m.p.h.)

JETSTREAM 31   489 km/h (303 m.p.h.)

RANGE

Continually upgraded, the Metro's range has allowed the aircraft to become one of the leading designs in the business commuter field. The increase in fuselage size and wingspan has allowed extra fuel tanks to be added.

METRO 23 1450 km (900 mi.)

JETSTREAM 31 1296 km (804 mi.)

EMB-110 BANDEIRANTE 2010 km (1,246 mi.)

PASSENGER CAPACITY

Though not having a passenger load any higher than others within its class, the Metro's design allows a rapid turnaround in between flight operations. With the regular nature of commuter flights, the modest passenger capacity is therefore not a disadvantage.

METRO 23   19 PASSENGERS

EMB-110 BANDEIRANTE   18 PASSENGERS

JETSTREAM 31   19 PASSENGERS

FOKKER

F.VII

● Successful inter-war airliner ● Record flights ● Licence production

▲ By using all
of the experience he had gained
building World War I fighters, Anthony Fokker
was able to develop a world-beating series
of inter-war airliners.

In November 1918, with Germany in a state of collapse, Anthony Fokker fled to his native Netherlands, taking a large number of documents with him. Further intrigue followed. Fokker had been working on designs for a passenger aircraft. Prototypes were flown and it was the first F.II that Fokker's wartime test pilot, de Waal, secretly flew to Holland in 1920. The F.II established Fokker as a manufacturer of practical passenger airliners.

FOKKER F.VII

▼ American customers
Fokker supplied a number of airframes, usually without engines which were fitted locally, to America. This Standard Airlines F.VIIa had a Pratt & Whitney Hornet engine.

▲ Early Swiss airliner
HB-LBO was the first F.VIIa supplied to Switzerland, and was delivered to Balair in 1927. After service with Swissair it was retired in 1948 and later restored to be displayed in a museum.

▼ Tri-motor Bomber
F.VIIb-3ms were licence-built in several countries. Bomber versions were built in Czechoslovakia and Poland.

▲ Red Cross F.VIIa
Although it was originally H-NADP, by World War II this aircraft was in Finnish markings and serialed FE-2.

Famous Fokker ▶
On 9 May 1926 Floyd Bennett flew this F.VIIa-3m, the first F.VII tri-motor, over the North Pole. Purchased by Edsel Ford, it was later displayed in the Ford Museum.

FACTS AND FIGURES

➤ After testing an F.VIIa-3m the US Army bought a small number of US-built tri-motors; most were designated C-2s.

➤ F.VIIs were used by both sides in the Spanish Civil War.

➤ Licence-built F.VIIs included those built in Britain as the Avro Ten.

➤ Perhaps the most famous Fokker F.VII was Southern Cross, which crossed the Pacific non-stop in 88 hours in 1928.

➤ For a 1928 Antarctic expedition an F.VIIb-3m was fitted with floats.

➤ The very first F.VII first flew in 1924 powered by a Rolls-Royce Eagle engine.

PROFILE

From fighters to airliners

By 1923 work had begun on the prototype Fokker F.VII, which was very similar to the F.II and its successors. Powered by a 268.5-kW (360-hp.) Rolls-Royce Eagle engine, it flew in April 1924. This model could carry six passengers and only five were built.

The F.VIIa, which had a smaller wing and bigger engine to improve speed performance, plus an eight-passenger cabin, appeared in 1925. This model

was used by airlines, including KLM, for both passenger and freight services.

When KLM issued a specification for a 10-seat airliner which was able to fly with a failed engine, the result was the F.VIIa-3m. The tri-motored Fokker was destined to become one of the most well-known commercial aircraft in the world. The first F.VIIa-3m made the first flight over the North Pole in 1926, while Charles Kingsford-Smith flew

across the Pacific Ocean in 1928 in an improved F.VIIb-3m named *Southern Cross*. Between 1927 and 1933 the F.VIIb-3m was the world's premier airliner, and licence production was undertaken in seven countries.

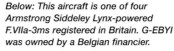

Above: H-NACT was KLM's first F.VIIa. The Dutch company later requested a variant which had more engines to improve safety.

Below: This aircraft is one of four Armstrong Siddeley Lynx-powered F.VIIa-3ms registered in Britain. G-EBYI was owned by a Belgian financier.

F.VIIb-3ms could be fitted with a wide variety of engine types with power outputs of between 149 kW (200 hp.) and 224 kW (300 hp.). In fact, at least 12 types are known to have been fitted.

The F.VIIb-3m had a larger wing than the F.VIIa to increase operating weights. Fuel tanks were located above the cockpit.

The welded steel tube fuselage structure and control surfaces were fabric covered. However, all-metal stressed-skin construction was fast gaining acceptance in the 1930s.

F.VIIB-3M

In Poland, E. Plage and T. Laskiewicz of Lubin built 19 F.VIIb-3ms for the Polish airline LOT. SP-ABK *Krysia* was one of 11 fitted with Wright Whirlwind J5A engines; the remainder were powered by Pratt & Whitney Wasp Juniors.

SP-ABK

For operation in winter conditions, LOT fitted skis to its F.VIIb-3ms. On aircraft with wheeled undercarriages hydraulic brakes were fitted. The fairing above the wheel/ski assembly contained an elastic cord shock absorber.

The usual cabin accommodation in the F.VIIb-3m was two crew and eight passengers, although some companies used a nine- or 10-seat layout. The small plaque under the cabin windows is a board showing the aircraft's route.

As was the case with some of the first F.VII tri-motors, some of the 'big wing' F.VIIb-3ms were conversions from single-engined F.VIIas.

ACTION DATA

ENGINE POWER

The F.VIIb-3m was equipped with three engines and therefore had considerably more power than the contemporary Junkers W.33. The all-metal Ford Trimotor was even more powerful and was destined to replace the Fokker in the US.

F.VIIb-3m	W.33	5-AT-D TRIMOTOR
671 kW (900 hp.)	310 kW (416 hp.)	939 kW (1,260 hp.)

PASSENGERS

Even in single-engined form the F.VII could carry more passengers than the W.33. Three engines not only improved safety, but increased capacity. The Ford Trimotor was a considerable advance and also introduced greater levels of comfort.

F.VIIb-3m — 8 passengers

W.33 — 6 passengers

5-AT-D TRIMOTOR — 13 passengers

RANGE

With a range of engine types available, the F.VII's performance tended to vary according to the powerplant. With three Wright Whirlwind J6 radials, 1200 km (750 mi.) was possible with a maximum fuel load aboard, more than 300 km (200 mi.) better than the Ford Trimotor.

F.VIIb-3m 1200 km (750 mi.)

W.33 1000 km (620 mi.)

5-AT-D TRIMOTOR 885 km (950 mi.)

Fokker tri-motors from three factories

■ **FOKKER-BUILT:** KLM was a prominent user of both single- and three-engined F.VIIs. F.VIIb-3m PH-AFS was sold to Spain and served with the Nationalists during the civil war.

■ **ATLANTIC AIRCRAFT CORPORATION F-10/F-10A:** To overcome American manufacturers' opposition to a foreign design, Fokker set up a US factory. The F-10 was a modified F.VIIb-3m.

■ **POLISH F.VIIb-3m:** This Polish-built No. 211 Squadron aircraft was among a number built as bombers with an open mid-upper turret and bomb racks under the fuselage.

FOKKER

F27 FRIENDSHIP

● Turboprop powered ● Short-field performance ● Licence built

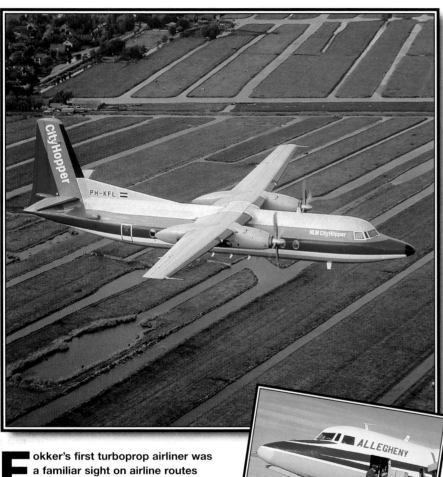

Fokker's first turboprop airliner was a familiar sight on airline routes around the world for 30 years. This medium-range transport appeared on the scene in 1955 when Holland's best-known aircraft manufacturer began selling it to the airlines. Soon after, Fairchild built a version in the United States. The twin-engined, high-wing F27 was noisy and was said to shake like a cement mixer, but it provided affordable and efficient service.

▲ As one of the first turboprop airliners, the F27 was initially regarded with suspicion. However, an excellent capacity plus economical performance made it a successful aircraft.

FOKKER F27 FRIENDSHIP

◀ **Successful sales**
One of the largest operators of the F27 was Air New Zealand. This Mk 500 was delivered in 1977 and served for 15 years.

▼ **Hot and high**
Good short-field performance made the F27 ideal for airlines such as Comair of South Africa.

▼ **Still going strong**
Despite Fokker introducing the more modern F50, the F27 is still in service around the world. This Mk 500 serves with Air UK.

▼ **First into service**
Aer Lingus was the first European airline to operate the F27, starting passenger services in November 1958.

▲ **North American pilgrim**
Pilgrim Airlines operated a pair of F27 Mk 100s on routes in north-eastern USA and into Canada. Praised for their reliability and performance, the aircraft have only recently been retired.

FACTS AND FIGURES

➤ The Friendship was conceived initially as a possible replacement for the venerable Douglas DC-3.

➤ Friendships were purchased by 168 customers in 63 countries.

➤ The first of two F27 prototypes made its initial flight on 24 November 1955.

➤ During the Friendship's era, more F27s were manufactured than any other European airliner.

➤ The prototype for the enlarged Fairchild version took to the air in January 1966.

➤ Production of the F27 ended in June 1986 in favour of the Fokker 50.

PROFILE

Friendly ship of the world's skies

In the early 1950s, Fokker, backed by the Dutch government, began to develop this excellent twin-engined transport. The F27 was a response to a worldwide requirement for an aircraft able to carry 32 passengers over medium distances. Produced by Fokker in Holland and Fairchild in the US, the turboprop-powered F27 went into service in 1958.

Despite early reservations about the safety of a twin-turboprop airliner, the F27

has proved to be one of the safest aircraft in its class. While production was under way, both Fairchild and Fokker developed enlarged versions. The Friendship's passenger capacity was increased from 32 to 40 (as many as 52 in a high-density version), the fuel load was increased and a weather radar was added. In America, the enlarged version was 'stretched' and differed slightly in appearance from the Fokker-built version.

The F27 established a niche as one of the most economical airliners in its class. In some countries the F27 was also employed with great success as a freighter and VIP transport.

Above: One of the many African airlines to operate the F27 is Air Sinai of Egypt, which took delivery of three Mk 500s in the early 1980s. The aircraft pictured crashed in a sandstorm at Cairo airport in 1986.

Left: N334MV is an F27 Mk 500 delivered to Mississippi Valley Airlines in 1980. By 1990 it was based in France after having had several owners.

F27 Mk 300 Friendship

Type: passenger transport

Powerplant: two 1424-kW (1,910-hp.) Rolls-Royce Dart Mk 528-7E turboprop engines, each providing an additional 2.25 kN (506 lb.) of auxiliary thrust

Cruising speed: 428 km/h (266 m.p.h.) at 6100 m (20,000 ft.)

Range: 2010 km (1,249 mi.) with 3050-kg (6,724-lb.) payload and maximum fuel

Service ceiling: 9020 m (29,600 ft.)

Weights: empty 10,257 kg (22,612 lb.); maximum take-off 17,710 kg (39,044 lb.)

Accommodation: two pilots, flight attendant and 40 passengers (standard), or 52 in a high-density layout

Dimensions: span 29.00 m (95 ft. 2 in.)
length 23.50 m (77 ft. 1 in.)
height 8.40 m (27 ft. 7 in.)
wing area 70.00 m² (754 sq. ft.)

FH-227B FRIENDSHIP

Originally delivered to Ozark Air Lines in July 1967, this FH-227 saw service with Delta Air Transport from 1977, and was leased to Air Lesotho for nine months between 1983 and 1984.

Two pilots are seated side by side, with a folding seat for a third crewmember if required. Weather radar, autopilot and instrument landing system aids are available to the flight crew.

F27s and FH-227s are powered by the Rolls-Royce Dart turboprop. The Dart engine went on to power a host of other aircraft and has proved to be highly reliable and economical.

The landing gear is of pneumatically-retractable tricycle type. The nosewheel is steerable and the mainwheels, which retract into the engine nacelles, can be used as airbrakes.

The all-metal fuselage is of a semi-monocoque fail-safe design. The only exception is the nose cap, which is made from glass fibre.

The tailplane is of all-metal structure, except for glass-fibre leading edges to the control surfaces. Goodrich de-icer boots are fitted to the leading edge of the fin and the tailplane.

After establishing a production line for the F27 in the US, Fairchild-Hiller began to develop the aircraft. The FH-227 had a 1.83-m (6-ft.) longer fuselage. In all, 78 were built.

ACTION DATA

CRUISING SPEED

The F27 is one of the most economical aircraft in its class, and of comparable speed to its contemporaries. Top speeds of around 450 km/h were typical of turboprops of this size. The F27 outsold the YS-11 and Herald several times over.

F27 Mk 300	428 km/h (266 m.p.h.)
YS-11A	476 km/h (296 m.p.h.)
HERALD SERIES 200	428 km/h (266 m.p.h.)

PASSENGERS

Dutch-built Friendships were eventually produced with seating for 60 passengers, so that they could compete with larger aircraft like the YS-11. Manufacturers tend to match changes in competing airliners by developing new variants of equal or greater seating capacity, range and fuel economy, but with lower operating costs.

F27 Mk 300 FRIENDSHIP — 52
YS-11A — 60
HERALD SERIES 200 — 56

RANGE

The Mk 300 had an excellent range for a medium-size turboprop, allowing it to fly international flights within Europe. The YS-11A had an even better range performance. The Herald, originally powered by four piston engines, was eventually re-engined with Dart engines.

F27 Mk 300 FRIENDSHIP 2010 km (1,249 mi.)
YS-11A 2110 km (1,311 mi.)
HERALD SERIES 200 1786 km (1,110 mi.)

Friendship through the ages

■ **PROTOTYPE:** PH-NIV was the first Friendship to fly, in 1955. Its excellent performance led to the first orders from Aer Lingus.

■ **F27 TROOPSHIP:** Built for the Dutch air force, these were dedicated military transports. Some have been replaced by Fokker 60s.

■ **F27 Mk 500:** Production of the F27 continued into the 1980s with the improved Mk 500 version, which sold worldwide.

■ **F50:** The F27 was finally replaced on the Fokker production line by the F50, which owed many of its features to the Friendship.

145

FOKKER

F28 FELLOWSHIP

● Small airliner ● Domestic routes ● Twin engined

Like the DC-9 and the BAC 1-11 of the same era, the Fellowship featured a moderately swept wing, twin turbofan engines mounted on the sides of the rear fuselage and a T-tail. It was smaller than both of these types, however, and slower than the DC-9, which also had a longer range. Consequently, it sold in relatively small numbers, and after only a few years in production Fokker switched to a bigger model.

▲ Its small size and reasonable operating costs meant that the F28 appealed to many Third World countries. The aircraft is still widely used from Bangladesh to South Korea.

FOKKER F28 FELLOWSHIP

◀ **Peruvian landing**
AeroPeru operated its F28s on domestic routes, often flying to remote high-altitude airfields.

▼ **F28 in the Far East**
Burma Airways made use of the Fokker F28's excellent hot-and-high performance.

▼ **European service**
Air France no longer uses the F28 on its short-haul routes, preferring more economical aircraft. Other major customers in Europe included TAT, KLM and Linjeflyg.

▲ **Linjeflyg fleet**
Sweden's domestic airline, Linjeflyg, operated an all-Fellowship fleet of 13 Series 4000s.

◀ **Reliable engine**
Like the turboprop F27, the F28 was powered by a Rolls-Royce engine, the Spey Mk 555. It was fitted with a special acoustic liner system to reduce noise.

FACTS AND FIGURES

➤ The Rolls-Royce Spey engine in the F28 also powered military jets like the RAF's Phantoms and Buccaneers.

➤ A freight-carrying version, the Mk 1000C, had an additional large door at the front.

➤ Many military operators, including Argentina's air force, use the F28.

➤ Several versions were built, including the Mk 6000 with a slatted wing and the high-density seating Mk 4000 for Linjeflyg.

➤ The Mk 3000R used water/methanol injection for hot-and-high operations.

➤ By the time the F28 was certified in February 1969, 22 had been ordered.

PROFILE

The great Dutch commuter jet

Developed in collaboration with Shorts of the UK, which supplied the wings, and Germany's HFB and VFW, which built the fuselage sub-assemblies, the Fellowship was powered by two Spey turbofans. It was designed to build upon the success of the turboprop F27 Friendship by offering the ability to carry more passengers at jet speeds over short and medium ranges.

The original Mk 1000 flew for the first time in May 1967

and could carry 65 passengers. The 79-seat Mk 2000 which followed had a slightly longer fuselage, and the Mk 3000 and 85-seat Mk 4000 had new wings and quieter engines. There was also a Mk 6000, which had leading-edge slats for improved take-off performance. This was certified in 1973, but Fokker was unable to find any buyers for this variant.

Germany's LTU was the first customer for the F28, and the last example manufactured was bought by Linjeflyg of

Sweden in 1987. By then Fokker had delivered 241 Fellowships to 59 customers in 39 countries, including a number of air forces.

The standard F28 makes an effective and cheap military light transport or VIP aircraft. It was adopted by the air forces of Argentina (above), Colombia and the Dutch government.

There is a single pressure refuelling point under the starboard wing, near the root.

The swept horizontal tail unit is mounted high on the top of the tailplane and makes use of tough honeycomb sandwich panels and multiple spars.

The Series 5000 and 6000 aircraft feature extended-span wings with full-span, hydraulically operated leading-edge slats.

F28 MK 1000

The Mk 1000 was the original production version. This example was operated by Aviaction before going on to serve with airlines in Ethiopia, South Africa, France and Iran.

The undercarriage is of retractable tricycle type with twin wheels on each unit. The nosewheels are fully steerable and low-pressure tyres are an option on all units.

The nose contains a simple weather radar, for the detection of thunderstorms and heavy cloud, and a Smiths SEP6 autopilot.

The flight deck has side-by-side seating for the pilot and navigator and a tip-up seat for a third crewmember. The six-panel windscreen is electrically heated and de-iced.

The tail unit is of cantilever alloy structure with a hydraulically actuated, variable-incidence T-tailplane. The elevators are hydraulically boosted and there is emergency tailplane actuation.

Two Rolls-Royce Spey turbofans are mounted in pods on either side of the rear fuselage. A six-chute silencing nozzle can be fitted, and the intakes are electrically de-iced.

D-AHLA

AVIACTION

F28 Mk 4000

Type: short- to medium-range twin-engined commercial transport

Powerplant: two 44-kN (9,900-lb.-thrust) Rolls-Royce Spey Mk 555-1P turbofans

Maximum speed: 842 km/h (552 m.p.h.)

Cruising speed: 787 km/h (489 m.p.h.)

Range: 3380 km (2,100 mi.) with maximum load and maximum fuel

Service ceiling: 10,675 m (35,000 ft.)

Weights: maximum take-off 31,523 kg (69,350 lb.)

Accommodation: two crew on flight deck plus a maximum of 85 passengers

Dimensions:

span	25.07 m	(82 ft. 3 in.)
length	29.61 m	(97 ft. 2 in.)
height	8.47 m	(27 ft. 9 in.)
wing area	76.30 m²	(821 sq. ft.)

ACTION DATA

MAXIMUM SPEED

The F28 has a respectable speed, well above that of its German rival the VFW 614, and nearly as quick as the larger, similar-engined BAC One-Eleven. Its service cruising speed is around 780 km/h, allowing improved fuel economy and increased range.

F28 Mk 3000	842 km/h (552 m.p.h.)
ONE-ELEVEN SERIES 200	882 km/h (547 m.p.h.)
VFW 614	735 km/h (456 m.p.h.)

PASSENGERS

For an aircraft of its size the F28 carries a relatively large number of passengers, thanks to its 'wide-body', five-abreast seating with an off-centre aisle. The F28's payload also makes it an attractive light- to medium transport aircraft for military operators.

F28 Mk 3000	65 passengers
ONE-ELEVEN SERIES 200	79 passengers
VFW 614	48 passengers

RANGE

British Rolls-Royce Spey turbofans give the F28 and BAC One-Eleven a useful range, greater than that of the fuel-thirsty VFW 614. Both the One-Eleven and the F28 were capable of flying across Europe, but the VFW 614 was limited to national and regional routes.

VFW 614 1126 km (748 mi.)

F28 Mk 3000 3169 km (1,965 mi.)

ONE-ELEVEN SERIES 200 2410 km (1,495 mi.)

Developments of the Fellowship

■ **FOKKER 70:** Powered by Rolls-Royce Tay turbofans, the 70 was developed to be a market partner for the similar 100. Seating was reduced to 79, and the aircraft first flew in April 1993.

■ **FOKKER 100:** Designed as the successor to the F28, and built on the same production line as its sister model the 70, the 107-seat 100 is flown by, among others, American Airlines.

■ **FOKKER 130:** This promising, larger development of the 100 series had not been built by 1996, when the Fokker company in the Netherlands was declared bankrupt.

FOKKER

F70/F100

● Advanced design ● Regional flights ● Partnership production

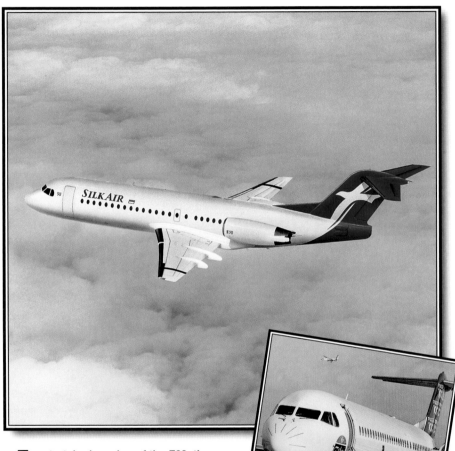

▲ *In the competitive world of civilian airliners, the Fokker aviation company has produced a host of successful designs, all of which have achieved immense sales success.*

A stretched version of the F28, the Fokker 100 flew for the first time in November 1986. It has a longer fuselage seating up to 107 passengers, redesigned wings, Tay engines instead of the F28's Speys, a new cockpit and modernised systems. The Fokker 70 is a shortened version. Using the same wings and engines, it can seat up to 79 passengers. Production of both types ended after Fokker was declared bankrupt early in 1996.

FOKKER F70/F100

▲ **American bird**
Seen wearing a patriotic colour scheme, this Fokker 100 is used for domestic flights within the United States.

▲ **Hungry for success**
Thanks to hard selling by Fokker, the F100 and F70 have been purchased by airlines in many European countries. This particular example serves with the Hungarian airline MALEV.

▲ **Top deck**
A vast range of colour schemes has been adopted by airlines using the aircraft. One of the most attractive is that of Korean Air.

▼ **British operations**
Operating with British Midland Airways for domestic flights, the Fokker 100 has proved itself to be an extremely cost-effective type.

▲ **Partnership in practice**
The soaring costs of developing a modern airliner made Fokker adopt the process by which sections of each aircraft are constructed in various European countries prior to final assembly.

FACTS AND FIGURES

➤ The initial purpose of the Fokker 70 was to replace the ageing F28 Fellowship with a more cost-effective aircraft.

➤ Fokker received their first order for F100s in 1984: 10 aircraft for Swissair.

➤ The first flight of the F100 was accomplished on 30 November 1986.

➤ Fokker gave the go-ahead to develop a short-fuselage variant of the F100 in 1992. This design became the F70.

➤ Launch orders for the F70 came from Pelita and Sempati Air in Indonesia.

➤ Fokker airliners are operated by more than 100 countries worldwide.

PROFILE

Fokker's last jetliner

As a result of a 1992 agreement under which Deutsche Aerospace took a major stake in Fokker, the company planned to develop a range of airliners based on the Fokker 100. This included an 80-seater and a 130-seat stretched version, but only the Fokker 70 materialised.

Quiet and efficient, the Fokker 100 enjoyed reasonable success. American Airlines became the type's biggest operator, with a fleet of 75, and a total of 290 had been ordered by the time of the

company's bankruptcy in 1996.

The Fokker 70 had been less successful, with total orders amounting to 71. However, it had appeared during a recession in the air transport market. It flew for the first time in April 1993 and entering revenue service with Indonesia's Sempati Air in March 1995. It might well have gone on to emulate the success of its larger predecessor had the manufacturer been able to stay in business.

As it is, the existing Fokker airliner fleet will be supported

by a new company, Fokker Aviation. There is a strong possibility that some aircraft will still be flying when the 100th anniversary of the founding of Fokker comes around in 2019.

Above: This Fokker 100 banks away from the camera. The type is widely praised by pilots for its performance.

Below: Only required to operate at medium altitudes for internal flights, the Fokker F100 is proving to be one of the most cost-effective airliners presently flying in Europe's skies.

F100

Type: twin-engined regional airliner

Powerplant: two 44-kN (9,900-lb.-thrust) Rolls-Royce Tay Mk 620-15 turbofans

Maximum speed: 861 km/h (534 m.p.h.) at operating altitude

Range: 1380 km (856 mi.) with maximum load

Service ceiling: 10,670 m (35,000 ft.)

Weights: empty 23,250 kg (51,150 lb.); maximum take-off 41,500 kg (91,300 lb.)

Accommodation: four crew (two flight deck and two cabin attendants) and 107 passengers

Dimensions: span 28.08 m (92 ft. 1 in.)
length 35.31 m (115 ft. 10 in.)
height 8.50 m (27 ft. 10 in.)
wing area 93.50 m² (1,006 sq. ft.)

F100

Operating from its home country of Sweden, Transwede flies to a host of European countries as well as providing numerous internal flights. The aircraft wear a restrained colour scheme.

Only two flight crew are required to operate the F100. Pilots have found it easy to convert to the aircraft after gaining considerable experience on earlier Fokker airliners.

Under the terms of the partnership agreement, MBB of Germany undertook the construction of the mid-fuselage section and the rear tail. Positioned along either side of the fuselage are the usual airliner emergency exits.

A circular-section semi-monocoque light alloy design was used for the fuselage. It provided strength, with an overall saving in weight compared to conventional airliners. Seating for passengers can be adjusted according to the type of flight being undertaken by the airline operator.

A high-set tail, which offers the best handling qualities, has become standard on almost all small regional airlines. A large rudder allows the Fokker 100 to operate from particularly small airfields where ground manoeuvring is restricted. All the controls on the tail are hydraulically boosted.

TRANSWEDE SE-DUB Fokker 100

Equipped with CRT displays, the flight deck is one of the most advanced of the current airliner fleet.

Construction of the wings was contracted-out to Short Brothers in Northern Ireland. Once completed, the sub-assemblies were delivered to Fokker for final assembly.

Positioned on the rear fuselage, the powerplants of the Fokker 100 are Rolls-Royce Tay turbofans. Each engine is equipped with a thrust reverser to reduce the landing run. This is an desirable feature for an aircraft that operates from city airports that may have restricted space. The engines have proved to be extremely reliable.

ACTION DATA

ACCOMMODATION
Operating in the competitive domestic routes market, the F100 is able to accommodate a large number of passengers, but still fewer than the other two aircraft featured. However, fuel efficient engines ensure the cost per passenger is low.

F100 — 107 passengers
A319 — 124 passengers
RJ100 — 128 passengers

CRUISING SPEED
The Fokker F100 is currently one of the fastest aircraft in its class; a high cruising speed is an attractive asset for business passengers. The fastest performer is the Airbus A319.

F100 861 km/h (534 m.p.h.)
A319 903 km/h (560 m.p.h.)
RJ100 801 km/h (497 m.p.h.)

MAXIMUM TAKE-OFF WEIGHT
The more weight that an airliner can lift off the ground, the more profitable it becomes, because the weight translates into freight and passenger revenue. Leader in this field, mainly because of its large size, is the European Airbus A319.

F100 41,500 kg (91,300 lb.) A319 64,000 kg (140,800 lb.) RJ100 44,425 kg (97,735 lb.)

Predecessors of the F100

AÉROSPATIALE CARAVELLE: Holding the distinction of being the first French turbojet-powered airliner, the Caravelle was used for short to medium-haul routes.

BAC 1-11: Once operated by a host of airlines across the world, this elderly British-designed aircraft is still in operation with a number of smaller airlines, for internal flights.

FOKKER F28 FELLOWSHIP: First flying in May 1967, the Fellowship had the capacity to carry a maximum of 79 passengers. Fokker was still receiving orders as late as 1980.

FORD

TRIMOTOR

● Bushplane ● Sightseeing platform ● Restored classic

FORD TRIMOTOR

▲ Air show performer
Trimotors have graced many air shows over the years, often performing amazing stunts. During the barnstorming era, they were used to transport crew for flying circuses around the US.

▲ Scenic survivor
One of the best-known surviving Trimotors is this superb Model 5-AT owned by Scenic Airlines, based at Las Vegas.

Canyon viewpoint ▶
Scenic operated two Trimotors, used by thousands to see the splendours of the Grand Canyon in style.

▼ Airliner progress
Used to illustrate the incredible advances made in aviation technology, in the 1970s this Trimotor donned American Airlines colours to pose alongside a 727.

▲ Crowd puller
The Trimotor is very evocative of the inter-war period, and draws a crowd wherever it goes. The few that still remain change hands for millions rather than thousands of dollars.

One of the great workhorses of aviation, the Ford Trimotor started life as a regular airliner. Although it performed this role outstandingly for a good many years, it had another life as a bushplane, as a sightseeing platform around the Grand Canyon and as a movie star. Today just a handful are left, lovingly restored and cherished by their owners. Its working days are largely over, but for over 65 years the Trimotor has more than earned its keep.

▲ Ground crew
work to fix an engine on a Trimotor, using makeshift platforms. The Trimotor's systems were so simple that maintenance was routinely performed in the field.

FACTS AND FIGURES

➤ One Trimotor was used by a typewriter company for a promotion campaign – dropping 210 typewriters from the air!

➤ In November 1929 a Trimotor was the first aircraft to fly over the South Pole.

➤ Trimotors were fitted with skis and floats to operate in remote areas of the world.

➤ Scenic's Trimotor is so valuable that it is insured for well over a million dollars.

➤ Ford were the first manufacturer to mass produce aircraft on a production line – just as they were with cars.

➤ The high drag factor of the Trimotor's corrugated skin slowed it down in flight.

Ford's 'Tin Goose'

When it first appeared in 1926, the Trimotor was the last word in airliner technology. With the reassuring Ford name behind it, the Trimotor was touted as the safest airliner around. In reality its performance with one engine gone was acceptable but with two out it could not retain altitude.

Some aircraft had rudimentary heating, but for most passengers the Trimotor was freezing cold (or sweltering hot, depending on the weather outside!) and impossibly noisy. Nevertheless,

it was a hit for the airlines until faster and more comfortable types appeared.

This may have spelled the end for lesser types, but the Trimotor was such a good aircraft that it could perform many other tasks. It could carry a good load in its cabin, and its huge wing allowed it to lift off from smaller airstrips. Above all, it was immensely tough, and could take any amount of punishment from rough fields, careless taxiing and the attentions of inexperienced pilots not fully familiar with its

strange flight peculiarities.

A long career in a wide variety of tasks followed, combining to give the Ford Trimotor a special place in the annals of aviation history.

Left: Lovingly referred to as the 'Tin Goose', the Ford Trimotor was built in two major models, the 4-AT and 5-AT. The 4-AT was much smaller and had a humped roof over the flight deck. The 5-AT (illustrated) had an angular roof.

Right: Trimotor's designer, Bill Stout, attempted to put a modernised version back into production during the late 1950s. The resulting Bushmaster 2000 eventually appeared in 1966.

Trimotor 4-AT

Type: passenger transport

Powerplant: three 313-kW (420-hp.) Pratt & Whitney Wasp C-series nine-cylinder radial piston engines

Maximum speed: 259 km/h (161 m.p.h.) at sea level

Cruising speed: 198 km/h (123 m.p.h.)

Range: 708 km (440 mi.)

Service ceiling: 7500 m (24,600 ft.)

Weights: typical empty 3447 kg (7,599 lb.); loaded 5738 kg (12,650 lb.)

Accommodation: flight crew of two side-by-side plus normal seating for up to 15 passengers or (later) 13 passengers plus steward or 1520 kg (3,351 lb.) of cargo

Dimensions:
span	23.72 m (77 ft. 10 in.)
length	15.30 m (50 ft. 2 in.)
height with tail down	3.66 m (12 ft.)
wing area	77.57 m² (835 sq. ft.)

The flight deck has side-by-side seating for two pilots. Although the Trimotor can be flown by a single pilot, the extra set of muscles is useful if an engine is lost, when control forces become almost impossibly high for one person.

Many Trimotors had the seats taken out and were used to haul cargo. In addition to the main cabin, the 5-AT had small holds in the thick inner-wing section, accessed via drop-down doors in the lower wing surfaces.

The whole surface of the Trimotor was skinned in corrugated aluminium. This had good strength, but did little for the aerodynamics. Cruising speed was typically under 200 km/h (124 m.p.h.).

The control cables that connect the stick to the moveable surfaces are external. Just below the flight deck is a rocker arm for the elevator control cables.

Over the years the strut-braced undercarriage of the Trimotor has proved to be immensely strong.

The cabin of the Trimotor typically has seating for around 12 passengers. Entering the Trimotor through the port-side door, the passengers had to contend with a steeply angled floor before they could reach their seats.

TRIMOTOR 5-AT

Perhaps the best-known of the remaining Trimotors is Scenic's aircraft. Unlike other survivors, this has worked all of its life. Until recently it was used to ferry sightseers over the Grand Canyon, but is now used only for promotional and film work, with occasional flights for rich pilots to get a check ride into their logbooks.

LEISURE TOURS

AUSTRALIA

Popular the world over as a pleasure flying aircraft, the BN-2 Islander has a high wing giving good downward vision. This BN-2 operates over Sydney Harbour.

ALASKA

Many of the world's most spectacular natural features can only be appreciated from the air. Tyee Airlines used Beaver floatplanes for sightseeing tours, operating from nearby fjords or lakes. This example is seen flying past the Misty Fjords National Monument near Ketchikan in Alaska. Other companies run tourist trips in the Alps, Himalayas and the Rockies, as well as to other famous landmarks such as Ayres Rock, Victoria Falls and Niagara Falls.

NEW YORK

The only way to fully take in the immensity of the skyscrapers in New York is on an aerial trip. In summer the sky is full of light aircraft and helicopters operating whistle-stop tours of the famous Manhattan skyline.

Flying across the Canyon

Pleasure flying in the Grand Canyon has been popular with tourists since the 1920s. Scenic Airways flew its first tours in 1926 and became famous operating the legendary Ford Trimotor. Now using a range of aircraft, including 20 specially modified Twin Otters, the airline caters for around 300,000 passengers per year. Its flagship Trimotor has a more leisurely life now, only flying occasional VIP trips.

Mt TRUMBULL 2447 m (8,028 ft.)

LAS VEGAS

HOOVER DAM

COLORADO RIVER

GRAND CANYON AIRPORT

HOOVER DAM: After taking off from Las Vegas the passengers are treated to the awe-inspiring view of Lake Mead and the famous Hoover Dam.

THE GREAT SPECTACLE: The Trimotor then descends and flies along the rim of the canyon. The view is indescribable, with sheer walls dropping away from the plane and a myriad of towers rising from the canyon floor. Commentary is provided through headsets.

BACK TO EARTH: At Grand Canyon airport the passengers disembark for a ground's eye view of the canyon before the straight run back to Las Vegas.

GAF

NOMAD

● Rugged and dependable ● Air ambulance ● Short take-off

▲ As well as being a superb flying ambulance, the Nomad seats up to 17 in the 'stretched' N24 variant. The key to the Nomad's performance is its remarkable short-field and rough terrain capability, making it well-suited to a range of operations throughout the Australasian continent.

I n the sprawling expanse of the Australian outback there is only one way a doctor can provide medical help to isolated communities – by air. Fortunately, Australia's Government Aircraft Factory (GAF) produced the twin-engined Nomad, an appealing plane that takes the doctors to the most remote regions. The Nomad short take-off and landing (STOL) aircraft also serves as an ambulance to evacuate patients requiring urgent intensive care.

GAF NOMAD

▲ Accommodation
The Nomad has a capacious cabin, with room for up to 13 passengers or 1685 kg (3,715 lb.) of freight.

▲ Short take-off
High-set wings, powerful turboprops and double-slotted flaps provide the GAF Nomad with its excellent short take-off and landing capability. This is essential for a flying doctor's work.

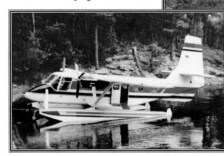

▲ Stretched version
The N24A's fuselage was lengthened by 1.14 m (3 ft. 9 in.) to accommodate 17 passengers and increase the maximum take-off weight to 4263 kg (9,398 lb.).

▲ Floatplane
In 1979 the N22B was certified to operate with floats for flights from lakes.

Flying doctor and air ambulance ▶
A major operator of the Nomad is the Royal Flying Doctor service in Australia.

FACTS AND FIGURES

➤ Australia's Northern Territory Aeromedical Service has flown more than 5,000 medical missions.

➤ The first GAF Nomad transport made its maiden flight on 23 July 1971.

➤ The Australian Customs Service operates radar-equipped Nomad Searchmasters.

➤ The flying doctors are on call 24 hours a day and can be airborne within 10 minutes of receiving an emergency call.

➤ The Nomad was designed specially for operations in Australia's outback.

➤ One N22B Nomad, equipped with floats, has operated as a seaplane and amphibian.

PROFILE

Life-saver of the outback

Developed in the mid-1960s as a light utility transport for civil and military work, the Australian-built Nomad has a rectangular-section fuselage, twin turboprops, a high-set tail, a high wing braced by struts, and pods which contain the retractable landing gear. Intended as an airliner, it has military and law-enforcement uses. And of its many duties, none better suits the Nomad than the difficult task of maintaining a medical lifeline in hard-to-reach locations.

With its short-field landing capability, the Nomad routinely lands at a sheep ranch or on a section of a highway. The speed and load-carrying ability of the Nomad enables it to carry plenty of diagnostic equipment and medicine in addition to a doctor. About 40 per cent of Australians live 500 km (310 mi.) or more away from the nearest full-service hospital, so the Nomad is truly an angel of mercy and a life-saver.

As well as serving numerous civil operators the Nomad has

also found success with the military air arms of Australia, the Philippines, Thailand (as machine-gun-armed gunships), the Indonesian navy and Papua New Guinea.

The manufacturer GAF is now ASTA (Aerospace Technologies of Australia) and production of the Nomad has ended. The last completed airframe came off the production line in 1984, after 170 had been built. Nomads have been retired by the RAAF, but the flying doctor service continues to operate them.

The rough-field capability of the Nomad makes it ideally suited to civil utility, surveillance, agricultural and ambulance missions across Australia's vast and harsh rural expanses.

Nomad N22B

Type: STOL utility transport

Powerplant: two 298-kW (400-hp.) Allison 250-B17B (or 313-kW (420-hp.) 250-B17C) turboprop engines

Cruising speed: 269 km/h (167 m.p.h.)

Range: 1352 km (841 mi.)

Service ceiling: 6400 m (21,000 ft.)

Weights: empty 2150 kg (4,740 lb.); maximum take-off 3629 kg (8,000 lb.) (N22); 3855 kg (8,499 lb.) (N22B); 4263 kg (9,398 lb.) (N24A)

Accommodation: two pilots; 13 passengers (in the N22B) or 17 passengers (in the N24A); several configurations for stretcher-borne medical patients; or up to 1685 kg of medical equipment and personnel

Dimensions: span 16.52 m (54 ft. 2 in.)
length 12.56 m (41 ft. 2 in.)
height 5.52 m (18 ft. 1 in.)
wing area 30.10 m² (324 sq. ft.)

NOMAD N22B

The Government Aircraft Factories Nomad served with the Army Aviation Corps for many years. This N22 was operated by No. 73 (GS) Squadron based at Oakey, Queensland.

The unusually tall tail unit contributes to the remarkable short take-off and landing performance. This can be as little as 200 m (660 ft.) for a N22B taking off fully loaded at 3855 kg (8,499 lb.).

Two American-built Allison 250-B17C turboprops rated at 313 kW (420 hp.) produce a cruising speed of 269 km/h (167 m.p.h.) over a reasonable range.

The spacious cabin can hold 13 troops or, more usually, up to 1685 kg (3,715 lb.) of freight or emergency supplies. Cargo must be tied down as take-offs and landings are very steep.

The Nomad's tough construction and simple layout made it an ideal military utility transport, which in times of conflict could carry 907 kg (2000 lb.) of weapons on underwing pylons.

Army Nomads were painted in this three-colour camouflage scheme when used in the rugged bush-covered areas of Australia in support of ground forces.

The sturdy tricycle undercarriage is housed in streamlined fairings, fitted to struts which brace the high wings.

The flight deck features simple and reliable analogue controls and accommodation for a pilot and co-pilot. The large canopy provides superb visibility.

ACTION DATA

MAXIMUM PASSENGERS

The overall passenger figures reflect the aircraft's similar roles. The smaller Nomad sacrifices some of its payload for better short take-off performance.

NOMAD N22B — 13 PASSENGERS
An-28 'CASH' — 17 PASSENGERS
SKYVAN — 19 PASSENGERS

RANGE

The more modern Nomad and An-28 have a longer range than the veteran Skyvan. These two also have improved performance but lower payloads.

NOMAD N22B 1352 km (840 mi.)
An-28 'CASH' 1365 km (848 mi.)
SKYVAN 1115 km (693 mi.)

MAXIMUM SPEED

The Nomad's simple and rugged construction is not as conducive to speed as that of the streamlined An-28 and the powerfully engined Skyvan. Speed is not a high priority for this type of aircraft.

NOMAD N22B 311 km/h (193 m.p.h.)
An-28 'CASH' 350 km/h (217 m.p.h.)
SKYVAN 327 km/h (203 m.p.h.)

Flying doctor aircraft

BEECH KING AIR 90: A widely used business aircraft which is also operated by the US Army, the King Air 90 is a twin-turboprop 16-seat aircraft with pressurised fuselage.

CESSNA 425: Another popular business aircraft design, the Cessna 425 is powered by two PT6A turboprops. Standard accommodation is for six to eight passengers.

DE HAVILLAND DHA-3 DROVER: Six de Havilland Drovers were used by the flying doctor service. The eight-seat Drover was based on the Dove, but had three Gipsy Major engines.

GULFSTREAM

I COMMUTER

● Executive transport ● Regional airliner ● Navigator trainer

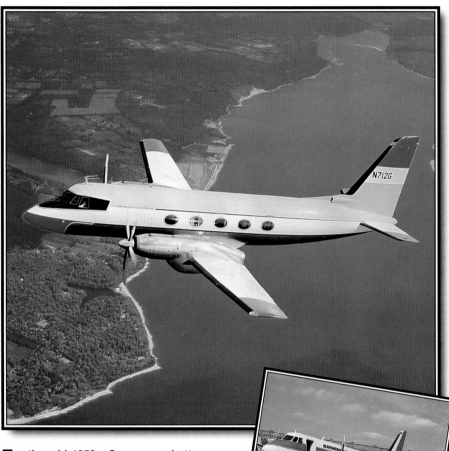

I n the mid-1950s, Grumman – better known as a builder of naval warplanes – ventured into the light turboprop transport field. The Gulfstream was intended as an executive transport, although it was in the same class as small commuter airliners. Grumman manufactured Gulfstreams for more than 11 years for both civil and military use. Later this ship became retroactively known as the Gulfstream I.

▲ As an executive transport, the Gulfstream I is appreciated for its practical performance coupled with a roomy and well-furnished interior, although operating costs are high.

GULFSTREAM I COMMUTER

◀ American Eagle
Although more expensive to operate than its rivals, the Gulfstream I was found ideal for use as a feeder/regional transport. This stretched example operates within the United States.

High performance ▶
Entering a market comprised mainly of converted World War II bombers, the Gulfstream offered better performance and economy.

Intruder trainer ▶
Fitted with the nose of an A-6, this TC-4C was used to train future bombardier/navigators for the US Navy; six students and one instructor were carried.

▲ European sales
Most sales have been in North America, but a few examples have operated in Italy.

Sound design ▶
Comparison of the American Gulfstream I in the background and the G-1C in front reveals a longer fuselage and the addition of two cabin windows.

FACTS AND FIGURES

➤ The Gulfstream had a fairly smooth flight test programme and was cleared for commercial operations on 21 May 1959.

➤ The prototype completed its first flight on 14 August 1958.

➤ Grumman manufactured 200 examples between 1959 and 1969.

➤ Although not a big success with airlines, the Gulfstream was ideal for use as an executive and government transport.

➤ Grumman used the first Gulfstream as a company transport for 40 years.

➤ Austria, Germany and Nigeria used the type as a government transport.

PROFILE

Grumman's executive liner

Grumman developed its G-159 Gulfstream to take advantage of the availability of the reliable Rolls-Royce Dart engine, which was already performing well on the Vickers Viscount airliner.

The Gulfstream became a superb executive transport, filling a gap that had opened when corporations sought to retire used transports of World War II vintage. Business leaders in need of efficient transport admired the Gulfstream for its practical performance coupled with roomy and well furnished, but not over-ostentatious, accommodation. Pilots enjoyed

the Gulfstream for its snappy performance and excellent handling qualities.

The Gulfstream was fairly expensive for an aircraft in its class and was less successful when Grumman sought to sell it overseas. A number of these aircraft were adopted for government use in various countries, including an executive transport for the US Coast Guard and bombardier-navigator trainers for the US Navy.

The Gulfstream became the Gulfstream I when its name was taken over by a series of jet transports built by a new

company formed by Grumman executives. Today, several dozen Gulfstreams are providing good service, four decades after the aircraft was created.Grumman's close association with the US Navy resulted in a bizarre modification to the Gulfstream's airframe. Grafted onto the nose was an A-6 Intruder nose, complete with avionics. Its purpose was to train future A-6 crews.

Left: Incorporating a fuselage extension of 3.25 m (10 ft. 8 in.) allowed a maximum of 37 passengers to be carried; otherwise, the aircraft was basically unaltered.

Above: British operations of the Gulfstream are restricted to executive flights for various companies. This example operates from Birmingham International Airport.

Gulfstream G-1

Type: twin-engined commuter or executive transport

Powerplant: two 1484-kW (1,990-hp.) Rolls-Royce Dart Mk 529-8X turboprop engines

Maximum cruising speed: 556 km/h (345 m.p.h.)

Certificated altitude: 9145 m (30,000 ft.)

Maximum ceiling: 11,245 m (36,900 ft.)

Range: 838 km (520 mi.) with payload

Weights: empty 10,747 kg (23,643 lb.); maximum take-off 16,329 kg (35,924 lb.)

Accommodation: 14 to 18 passengers in executive configuration or a maximum of 24 passengers as a commuter airliner

Dimensions:
span	23.88 m (78 ft. 4 in.)
length	22.96 m (75 ft. 4 in.)
height	7.01 m (23 ft.)
wing area	56.70 m² (610 sq. ft.)

GULFSTREAM G-1

A number of Gulfstream Is have been operated by commuter airlines in Europe. This example was operated for a number of years by Italian airline TAS.

Accommodation for the passengers could be adjusted to suit the requirements of the operator. In executive configuration 10 people were carried, but on regional feeder airline routes a high-density seating arrangement of 24 passengers could be installed.

For cargo operations, the fuselage could accommodate a maximum of 2753 kg (6,057 lb.). Loading was accomplished through a large door on the port side of the fuselage, positioned just aft of the wings.

The tall tail of the Gulfstream bestowed excellent stability, while its all-metal cantilever construction proved extremely reliable.

I-TASO

Seated side by side, the flight crew enjoyed excellent visibility from the flight deck. This was mainly because of the detailed research that Grumman undertook in its design.

Adopting an already proven engine design, two Rolls-Royce Dart turboprops were installed. Driving Rotol four-bladed constant-speed propellers, they were reliable and remained the powerplant for the entire production run.

The hydraulic-powered undercarriage included twin wheels on all three units. The main gear retracted forward into the engine cowlings, and the nose unit retracted forward below the flight deck.

Although intended only as a short-range feeder airliner, the Gulfstream I was fitted with a toilet compartment with hot and cold water. A hydraulically operated self-contained air-stair forward of the main cabin was also installed, providing easy boarding for passengers and crew and allowing a rapid turn-around.

ACTION DATA

MAXIMUM CRUISING SPEED

Despite being a 40-year-old design, the Gulfstream offers high speed. This is mainly due to a proven engine coupled with a fuselage that is exceptionally clean, when compared to the EMB-120ER.

G-1C	556 km/h (345 m.p.h.)
1900D	515 km/h (343 m.p.h.)
EMB-120ER	555 km/h (345 m.p.h.)

PASSENGERS

Feeder airliners are often described as spartan, but their main role is maximum capacity for relatively short flights. Set against more modern designs such as the 1900D, the G-1 is well equipped. Later Gulfstream models had increased capacity, accomplished by a fuselage extension.

G-1C 24 PEOPLE

1900D 19 PEOPLE

EMB-120ER 30 PEOPLE

RANGE

Range is considered to be the Gulfstream's main fault; the modern commuter market has been swamped with more advanced designs which are constantly being refined to operate more efficiently. New turboprop engines not only have lower fuel consumption but are also quieter.

G-1C 838 km (520 mi.)

EMB-120ER 1575 km (1,870 mi.)

1900D 2778 km (1,720 mi.)

Dart-powered derivatives

■ **CONVAIR 600:** Entering service in November 1965, this variant was the last of the series powered by Rolls-Royce Dart engines.

■ **DOUGLAS DC-3:** This classic airliner is seen here with experimental Dart engines fitted, although the conversion was not a success.

■ **FOKKER F27 FRIENDSHIP:** This German design utilising Dart engines has achieved sales in both military and civilian versions.

■ **HANDLEY PAGE HERALD:** Designed to fill similar requirements to the Gulfstream, this British aircraft also employed Dart turboprops.

HAMC

Y-11/Y-12

● Light transport ● Agricultural roles ● Short take-off and landing

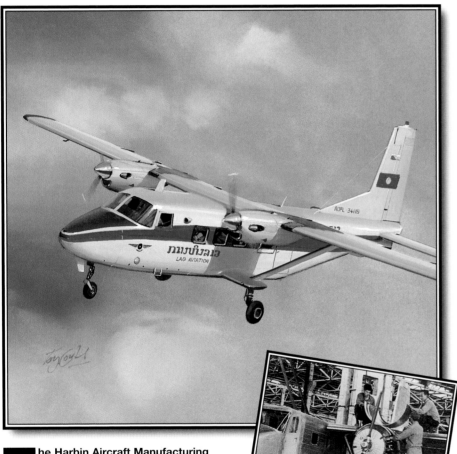

The Harbin Aircraft Manufacturing Company (HAMC) started work on the Y-11 in the early 1970s after several years of building copies of the Soviet Mi-4 helicopter and Il-28 light bomber. Similar in configuration to the Pilatus Britten-Norman Islander, the aircraft flew for the first time in 1975. The Y-12 which followed had a longer fuselage to increase the payload, plus efficient 375-kW (500-hp.) PT6A-11 engines for improved performance.

▲ Built by the
Harbin Aircraft Manufacturing Company, the Y-11 and Y-12 are marketed abroad by CATIC. Harbin is also responsible for licence-built AS 365 Dauphin helicopters.

HAMC Y-11/Y-12

◀ **Military applications**
Y-12s have been delivered to the air forces of Cambodia, Eritrea, Mauritania, Peru, Sri Lanka, Tanzania and Zambia.

▼ **Civil airliner**
In China, the upgraded Y-12 is flown by five airlines, and by February 1996 101 had been built.

▼ **Paradrop mission**
Military configured Y-12s can seat up to 15 paratroops or carry an equivalent cargo load. Maximum payload of the improved Y-12 (IV) approaches 2000 kg (4,400 lb.).

▼ **Agricultural application**
After conversion to the agricultural role, this Y-12 will carry a 1200-litre (317-gal.) chemical hopper, four wing and two stub wing dispensers.

◀ **Y-12 predecessor**
Prior to the first flight of the Y-12 in 1982, HAMC produced the piston-engined Y-11.

FACTS AND FIGURES

➤ With 17,000 employees, Harbin currently constructs doors for the British Avro RJ series of airliners and freighters.

➤ The original Y-11 carried Chinese Zhuzhou HS6A radial powerplants.

➤ For very steep landings and rough-field operations, the Y-11 has a tail bumper.

➤ The first customer for the Teledyne Continental-powered Y-11B was Flying Dragon Aviation, based in China.

➤ For geophysical survey, the Y-12 (II) carries a long, kinked sensor tail boom.

➤ The Y-12 series has an American-made Bendix/King weather radar.

Harbin's utility transport

Able to carry one or two pilots and seven or eight passengers, the 40 Y-11s built were used mainly for agricultural and forestry work. They were powered by Chinese 213-kW (288-hp.) HS-16 engines, could take off and land in distances of as little as 140 m (460 ft.), and had a top speed of 220 km/h (136 m.p.h.).

Harbin flew the first of two Y-12 Is in July 1982, and the first flight of the Y-12 (II) followed in 1983. This variant features a new wing with integral tanks for 1600 litres (423 gal.) of fuel. Nearly half the all-metal structure is resin-bonded instead of rivetted. Hong Kong Aircraft

Engineering installed Western avionics and cabin furnishings in the sixth aircraft for greater appeal to foreign customers. The first Y-12 was exported to Sri Lanka in 1986, and nearly 100 more have followed to 18 other countries since then.

The main user of the type is the CAAC (Civil Aviation Authority of China), which may end up buying as many as 200. There is also a Y-12 (IV) version, powered by twin Pratt & Whitney Canada PT6A-27s, which incorporates winglets, a strengthened undercarriage and other improvements. Military variants are operated by Sri Lanka, Iran, Peru and Paraguay.

Below: More than 40 examples of the Y-11 were built before production switched to the Y-11B with US-built engines.

Above: HAMC currently produces the Y-12 (I) and the Y-12 (IV) with higher operating weights, modified wings, strengthened landing gear and seating for 19 passengers.

Y-12 (II)

This profile represents a typical example of a civilian Y-12 (II). By 1996 there were 55 of this variant in service around the world, mainly employed as utility transports and small-capacity airliners.

Y-12 (II)

Type: utility transport

Powerplant: two 507-kW (680-hp.) Pratt & Whitney Canada PT6A-27 turboprops

Maximum speed: 292 km/h (181 m.p.h.) at 3000 m (10,000 ft.)

Endurance: 5 hr 12 min

Range: 1340 km (830 mi.) at 250 km/h (155 m.p.h.)

Service ceiling: 7000 m (23,000 ft.)

Weights: maximum take-off 5300 kg (11,660 lb.)

Accommodation: crew of two, 17 passengers, 16 paratroops or 1700 kg (3,740 lb.) of cargo

Dimensions:
span	17.24 m	(56 ft. 7 in.)
length	14.86 m	(48 ft. 9 in.)
height	5.58 m	(18 ft. 4 in.)
wing area	34.27 m²	(369 sq. ft.)

Housed within the small cockpit are a pilot and co-pilot. Dual controls are standard and the instruments are thoroughly conventional and well laid out. Interesting features are the four-way adjustable crew seats, providing much needed comfort during longer flights.

All NAMC Y-12s are powered by proven Pratt & Whitney Canada PT-6 turboprops. These engines have established a solid reputation for being powerful and reliable and have been fitted to countless different aircraft types over the years. On the Y-12, they are rated at 507 kW (680 hp.) each.

Approximately 17 passengers can be accommodated in the main cabin with three-abreast seating. Alternatively, the entire cabin can be used for cargo, with a large double-hinged freight door similar to that seen on the de Havilland Canada Twin Otter, making access considerably easier.

Mounted at the very tip of the fin is a large anti-collision beacon, which provides a visual cue for other aircraft, particularly in poor weather.

Flying at relatively low altitudes does not require a pressurised cabin, so large square windows are a standard fitment on the Y-12.

The single mainwheels are fixed and are mounted on small sponsons projecting from the fuselage. For greater rigidity, large struts are attached between them and the wings.

External differences between the Y-11 and Y-12 include a large ventral fin fitted to the newer variant, plus slightly larger tail surfaces in general. The entire unit is of all-metal construction and the rudder features horizontal ribs for greater structural strength.

ACTION DATA

CRUISING SPEED

Although a decent aircraft in its own right, and blessed with exceptional STOL ability, the Y-11 is slower than designs such as the Do 228 and Let L-410.

Y-11	164 km/h (102 m.p.h.)
L-410UVP-E	380 km/h (236 m.p.h.)
Do 228-200	428 km/h (265 n.p.h.)

SERVICE CEILING

As a light utility transport, the Y-11 is ideal, being simple and sturdy. It cannot fly at as high an altitude as the Do 228; however, the German type is not really capable of short take-offs and landings. The poorer ceiling of the Y-11 is partly a consequence of the lower power of its piston engines.

Y-11 — 4030 m (13,200 ft.)
L-410UVP-E — 6320 m (20,700 ft.)
Do 228-200 — 8535 m (28,000 ft.)

PASSENGERS

Both European types, the Czech L-410 and the German Do 228 were designed as feeder liners and are thus more advanced and quieter, with greater passenger capacity than the small Chinese twin. Despite its lack of capacity, the Y-11 excels in being a low-cost and reliable utility transport.

Y-11 — 8 passengers
L-410UVP-E — 19 passengers
Do 228-200 — 19 passengers

An ever-growing family

■ **HARBIN (HAMC) SH-5:** China still believes in long-range flying-boats. The impressive SH-5 fulfils a variety of roles, mainly anti-submarine warfare and search and rescue.

■ **HARBIN Z-5:** Essentially a copy of the Soviet Mil Mi-4 'Hound', this versatile helicopter was produced until 1979 and continues to serve in huge numbers in civil and military versions.

■ **HARBIN Z-9 HAITUN:** Derived from the French AS 365 Dauphin, the Z-9 has been in production since the mid-1980s. Current versions feature a substantial amount of local content.

HAMILTON

H-45/H-47 METALPLANE

● Monoplane transport ● All-metal construction ● Twenty-nine built

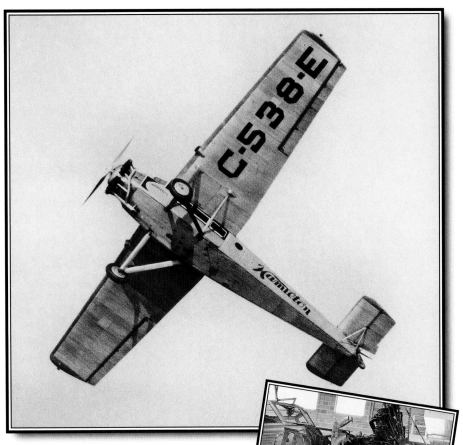

B uilt by the Hamilton Metalplane Company of Milwaukee, Wisconsin, the Metalplane reflected the innovative spirit of aviation pioneers in the 1920s. When two H-45s joined Northwest Airways in September 1928, they introduced unimagined levels of comfort and modernity. Leather-covered wicker seats were nothing new, but cabin heaters and a 'comfort station' (toilet) were revolutionary. They were also the first all-metal airliners in US service.

▲ Most of the 29 Metalplanes built were sold to US operators, although a handful were exported to Canada and Panama. Single examples went to France and Italy.

HAMILTON H-45/H-47 METALPLANE

◀ Northwest service
Northwest's Metalplanes were first employed as mail carriers. Passenger services followed, including flights to Canada.

▲ Company demonstrator
NC538E (No. 24) was one of nine Metalplanes in the Northwest fleet, after having served as a sales flight demonstrator for Hamilton.

▲ Pioneering rail-air services
One of Northwest's early successes was the September 1928 establishment of co-ordinated rail-air services. Here, a Hamilton takes on cargo from a Chicago, Rock Island and Pacific train.

▼ Northwest H-45s
Aircraft 20 and 21 were H-45s powered by the Pratt & Whitney Wasp radial engine. They were in service long after the introduction of H-47s.

▲ In all weathers
Ski-equipped H-47s were the only aircraft able to operate from Chicago during the winter without having the runways cleared of snow.

FACTS AND FIGURES

➤ One Hamilton, used by a Panamanian airline, was taken on charge by the USAAC during World War II as a UC-89.

➤ The Metalplane could be fitted with a pair of Hamilton metal floats.

➤ The first Metalplane was the H-18, which had a rounded fuselage and open cockpit.

➤ A famous Arctic explorer, Carl Van Eissen, was killed in a Metalplane in the early 1950s.

➤ H-47s were nicknamed 'Silver Eagles'; those with floats were 'Silver Swans'.

➤ Most Metalplanes were built by the Hamilton Metalplane division of Boeing.

Forgotten pioneer metal airliner

Aviation pioneer Thomas F. Hamilton, assisted by others including James S. McDonnell (later of McDonnell Douglas fame), was responsible for the Hamilton Metalplane, a genuinely revolutionary aircraft which pointed the way to the future, changing the very face of air transport.

The first Hamilton Metalplane of 1925 was a one-off and carried only six people, but the bigger, more powerful H-45s and H-47s were the best airliners of their class. Northwest Airways and other carriers used

them on diverse routes in varying conditions, even in severe winter weather, when they were ski-equipped.

The Metalplanes were pleasant to fly and their cabins were, by the standards of the day, spacious and comfortable. Northwest dubbed them 'Silver Streak' and used them in the world's first co-ordinated rail-air service for passengers and express mail. Metalplanes were deemed economical by airline companies and continued to provide excellent service until World War II, by which time

The little-known Metalplane was an important type in the Northwest fleet. Nine were operated in all, between 1928 and 1941. By this time, the more advanced Douglas DC-3 had entered widespread service.

Douglas DC-3s and other newer aircraft were on the scene.

At least one Metalplane has survived and been restored to airworthy condition.

Northwest, the first and largest operator of the Metalplane, used the type to inaugurate the airline's first international service in 1935, over the border to Winnipeg, Manitoba in Canada.

The Metalplane's wings were wired to take a landing light on both the port and starboard wings.

H-45 Metalplane

Type: all-metal monoplane airliner

Powerplant: one 298-kW (400-hp.) or 336-kW (450-hp.) Pratt & Whitney R-1340 Wasp nine-cylinder radial engine

Maximum speed: 222 km/h (138 m.p.h.)

Cruising speed: 185 km/h (115 m.p.h.)

Range: 1086 km (675 mi.)

Service ceiling: 3962 m (13,000 ft.)

Weights: empty 1315 kg (2,893 lb.); loaded 2449 kg (5,388 lb.) (empty 1650 kg (3,638 lb.); loaded 2608 kg (5,750 lb.) with 336-kW (450-hp.) engine)

Payload: 620 kg (1,364 lb.) (454 kg (1,000 lb.) with 336-kW (450-hp.) engine)

Dimensions:
span	15.57 m (51 ft. 1 in.)
length	10.62 m (34 ft. 10 in.)
height	2.62 m (8 ft. 7 in.)
wing area	33.44 m² (360 sq. ft.)

The H-45 was powered by a 298-kW (400-hp.) or 336-kW (450-hp.) Pratt & Whitney R-1340 Wasp nine-cylinder radial engine. Performance was greatly enhanced in the H-47, which was fitted with an R-1690 Hornet of 410 kW (550 hp.). At least one H-47 was fitted with a 391-kW (525-hp.) Wright Cyclone.

Two pilots crewed Northwest's Metalplanes seated in a cockpit behind the engine. The cabin boasted wicker seats (between six and eight), and was heated and featured a toilet; both were innovative features.

NC-7522

When first built, the H-45 was priced at $23,200, later raised to $24,500. The H-47 was as much as $26,000. Hamilton was purchased by Boeing in 1928.

The fixed undercarriage on the Metalplane was supported by two 'doughnut' low-pressure tyres. Wheelbrakes were a standard fitting (together with a metal propeller and an inertia-type engine starter).

H-47 METALPLANE

NC7522 was the last of two Wasp-engined and seven Hornet-engined Metalplanes delivered to Northwest Airways. Allocated the fleet number 28, it formed part of Northwest's 'Silver Streak' Hamilton fleet.

Although not the first example built in the US, Hamilton's Metalplane was the first all-metal airliner to enter service in the US, beating Ford's Trimotor by several months. The use of an Alclad corrugated duralumin skin and a cantilever wing were major innovations.

ACTION DATA

PASSENGERS

The Hamilton Metalplane was one of a number of monoplane airliner types of the inter-war period. Eight-seat passenger cabins were typical. Once more powerful trimotor designs appeared, like the F.VII/3m, take-off weights increased.

H-47 METALPLANE	8 passengers
F.VIIa	8 passengers
TEN	8 passengers

MAXIMUM SPEED

Compared to the two European designs, the H-47 had a healthy top speed of over 200 km/h. An aircraft's performance was a major area of competition between US manufacturers in the 1930s. For this reason, the Metalplane was soon outperformed on major routes by the Ford Trimotor and relegated to feederlines.

H-47 METALPLANE	222 km/h (138 m.p.h.)
F.VIIa	185 km/h (115 m.p.h.)
TEN	185 km/h (115 m.p.h.)

RANGE

The H-47's range was comparable to that of the F.VIIa at around 1100 km (700 mi.). The Avro Ten had a comparatively short range, some 500 km (290 mi.) less than that of the American and Dutch designs. Once trimotor aircraft like the Ford Trimotor and Fokker F.VII/3m entered service, longer routes were possible.

H-47 METALPLANE 1086 km (675 mi.)
F.VIIa 1160 km (720 mi.)
TEN 655 km (410 mi.)

Northwest's inter-war airliners

■ STINSON DETROITER: Northwest had four of these aircraft, the first enclosed cabin biplane airliners used by a commercial airline. In 1927, they inaugurated a Twin Cities-Chicago service.

■ FORD 5-AT TRIMOTOR: The first 'Tin Goose' was delivered to Northwest in 1927. It seated between 12 and 14 passengers and used three 313-kW (420-hp.) engines.

■ SIKORSKY S-38: In order to provide Duluth, Minnesota (on Lake Superior) with a service, Northwest used two S-38 amphibians, including NC303N, from 1930.

■ LOCKHEED 10 ELECTRA: Northwest was the first airline to put the Electra, the first truly modern airliner, in service, taking delivery of the prototype in 1934.

HANDLEY PAGE

HERALD

● Turboprop airliner ● Cargo carrier ● Military transport

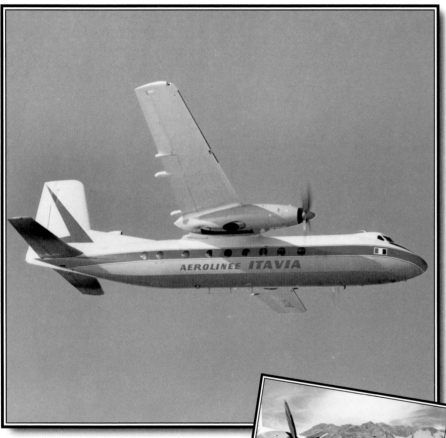

AEROLINEE ITAVIA

Originally designed as a four-piston-engined airliner, the Herald came into its own when fitted with two of the excellent Rolls-Royce Dart turboprops. Built to compete with the Fokker F27 in both the civil and military markets, the Herald did not achieve the sales that its safe and durable performance deserved. However, over 40 years after entering service it still undertakes regular cargo flights around the UK.

▲ *During 1959*
the Herald underwent proving
flights throughout Asia, Australasia and South
America. It operated from rough strips in the
Himalayas, to the amazement of the locals.

HANDLEY PAGE **HERALD**

◀ **Dart power**
Designed with four
piston engines, the
Herald soon adopted
the more efficient Rolls-
Royce Dart turboprops.

◀ **Robust flight deck**
The two-pilot flight
deck was designed
with a 'military' feel
with substantial
controls and switches.

▲ **Foreign sales**
The Herald was aggressively marketed abroad,
especially in Commonwealth countries. This
example was bought by Air Manila in 1966.

▲ **Military service**
In 1963 the Royal Arab Air Force received
the first of its two Heralds. Despite Handley
Page's best attempts few Heralds were sold
to military customers.

▲ **Highlands and islands**
BEA found the Herald's
performance ideal for its
short-haul Scottish routes.

◀ **Cross-Channel routes**
BAF operated the Herald on
routes between Southend
and the Continent.

FACTS AND FIGURES

➤ The original version was fitted with four Alvis Leonides Major piston engines and was called the H.P.R.3.

➤ Early Dart-engined Heralds were priced at £250,000 each.

➤ In 1959 the Herald completed a 55000-km (34,000-mile) demonstration tour of South America.

➤ In March 1960 a Herald undertook emergency relief flights after severe flooding in regions of North Africa.

➤ The H.P.R.8 was a high-capacity car ferry version that was never built.

➤ At least 12 Heralds remain in use after more than 35 years of service.

Forty years of the Herald

The Herald has led a varied life. Three impressive demonstration tours in 1959 took the new-look turboprop aircraft all around the world, proving its worth in places as far apart as the Caribbean and Australia.

With orders increasing the signs looked good until one of the prototypes crashed en route to the SBAC air show at Farnborough. This dented confidence in the aircraft and sales declined.

Despite the setback, Handley Page developed the aircraft into the 'stretched' Series 200. With increased capacity this version entered service with airlines all around the world and proved that the faith the company had in the aircraft was not unfounded by building up an enviable reliability and safety record.

Channel Express still operate a fleet of cargo-configured Heralds in the UK and find these veteran aircraft to be ideally suited to the task.

Above: G-ARTC had its fuselage lengthened to Series 200 standard. In an attempt to capture military sales it is seen demonstrating a paratroop drop.

Right: Built to operate in any conditions, the Herald was very durable and strong with steady flying characteristics.

Herald Series 200

Type: medium-range passenger and cargo transporter

Powerplant: two 1570-kW (2,100-hp.) Rolls-Royce Dart 527 turboprops

Cruising speed: 428 km/h (265 m.p.h.)

Initial climb rate: 590 m/min (1,935 f.p.m.)

Range: 1786 km (1,100 mi.)

Service ceiling: 8505 m (28,000 ft.)

Weights: empty 11,703 kg (25,747 lb.); maximum take-off 19,504 kg (68,655 lb.)

Passengers: maximum of 56

Dimensions:

span	28.88 m	(94 ft. 9 in.)
length	23.01 m	(75 ft. 6 in.)
height	7.34 m	(24 ft.)
wing area	82.31 m²	(886 sq. ft.)

HERALD SERIES 200

Air UK operated a small fleet of Heralds in the 1980s, flying charter and scheduled flights in the UK and Europe.

Each Dart engine drives a Rotol fully-feathering constant-speed auto-coarsening metal propeller. The four-bladed airscrew has a diameter of 3.66 m (12 ft.).

The Herald was one of the strongest aircraft of its era. It had a fail-safe reinforced wing which proved its worth when an early Herald lost an engine which separated from the wing. Only the strength of the wing saved the aircraft from destruction.

Similar to the F27, the Herald's main undercarriage retracted into the engine nacelles. The high wing caused the legs to have a particularly stalky appearance.

The cockpit was designed for a two-man crew. The controls were robust, unlike the more delicate layout of its rivals the HS. 748 and the F27 Friendship.

The original Alvis Leonides piston engines were soon replaced by two Rolls-Royce Dart 527 turboprops, an engine which remains in use today.

Originally conceived as a 36-seater, its capacity was increased to accommodate 44 passengers when turboprop power was adopted. A further stretch allowed 56 seats in the Series 200.

Flying controls were entirely conventional. Control surfaces are of all-metal construction with associated trim tabs.

G·APWE

ACTION DATA

CRUISING SPEED

The more streamlined F27 had the highest speed of these three contemporary aircraft. Although the Herald was slower, its Dart engines were very efficient at normal cruising speed. Its wider fuselage created more drag but allowed a larger passenger load.

HERALD SERIES 200	428 km/h (265 m.p.h.)
F27 Mk 200	480 km/h (298 m.p.h.)
An-24 'COKE'	450 km/h (279 m.p.h.)

PASSENGERS

The improved Series 200 Herald could carry up to 56 passengers, which was at least six more than its rivals. The Herald and F27 competed directly for sales, with the Herald's larger capacity being a major selling point. However, the F27 generally outsold the Herald.

HERALD SERIES 200	56
F27 Mk 200	48
An-24 'COKE'	50

RANGE

One area where the Herald was inferior to the F27 was range. A fully laden Herald did not have the reach to connect cities in Europe to the degree the F27 could. The An-24 was also a good aircraft, which suffered from a lack of range. It was generally employed on short regional routes.

HERALD SERIES 200 1786 km (1,100 mi.)

F27 Mk 200 1926 km (1,195 mi.)

An-24 'COKE' 550 km (340 mi.)

Twin-turboprops of the 1960s

■ **ANTONOV An-24 'COKE':** First delivered to Aeroflot in 1962, the An-24 was designed as a rugged short-to-medium range transport for operations from a wide variety of airfields.

■ **FOKKER F27 FRIENDSHIP:** Of all the twin turboprops developed in the 1950s and 1960s the F27 is undoubtedly the most successful. It sold in significant numbers all around the world.

■ **NORD N 262 FRÉGATE:** Once regarded as a natural DC-3 replacement, the N 262 sold in relatively small numbers. A military version is still in service with the French navy.

HAWKER SIDDELEY

HS.748

● Sixty-seat airliner ● STOL capability ● Turboprop twin

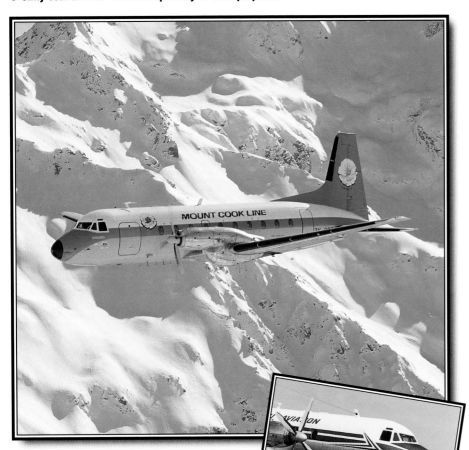

▲ Many smaller airlines have bought the HS.748 and operate it from short or rough airstrips. Larger airlines have used them on feeder routes into major hubs, where their rugged durability is appreciated.

Becoming a common sight on some of the world's more difficult short- to medium-haul routes, the HS.748 survived as a sound design through periods of great upheaval in the British aircraft industry. HS.748s were also built under licence in India, where the Series 2 standard aircraft was especially appreciated for its improved hot-and-high performance. Almost 40 years since its first flight, the HS.748 continues in limited airline service.

HAWKER SIDDELEY HS.748

Dart power ▶
Open nacelle inspection doors reveal the Rolls-Royce Dart RDa.7 Mk 531 turboprop fitted to an Andover CC.Mk 2 military HS.748 variant.

▲ Early customers
Aerolineas Argentinas was the second airline customer of the HS.748. Skyways Coach-Air in the UK also took Series 1 aircraft.

North American operations ▶
Buyers for the HS.748 were even found in the lucrative American market. Most carriers flew passengers into larger airports to meet major airline connections.

▼ Highlands and Islands
British Airways used its HS.748s on Scottish routes, where airports with short runways are common.

▲ Avro heritage
The HS.748 was originally, but only briefly, an Avro design. This very early aircraft carries Avro company titles and livery.

FACTS AND FIGURES

➤ Avro, which began design of the HS.748 in 1959, was absorbed by Hawker Siddeley in 1963 and became part of BAe in 1977.

➤ By the end of production in 1989, a total of 379 HS.748s had been built.

➤ Hindustan Aeronautics built the aircraft under licence in India.

➤ BAe used the HS.748 as the basis for its Advanced TurboProp, ATP, which was later marketed as the Jetstream 61.

➤ The HS.748 has been successfully converted for the fire-bombing role.

➤ The RAF Queen's Flight used six HS.748s as Andover CC.Mk 2s.

PROFILE

International STOL success

In 1957 a misguided British Government announced that the RAF would require no more new manned aircraft as guided missiles were the weapons of the future. Manufacturers of military types therefore sought new product lines and, to this end, Avro decided to develop a twin-turboprop machine as a cheap competitor to the Fokker F.27.

After producing 18 Series 1 machines, Avro switched production to the Series 2, which had more powerful developments of the Dart engine. After reorganisation it was Hawker Siddeley who put the new aircraft into production and developed the Series 2A, 2B and military versions.

Series 2A machines were further improved by the addition of even more powerful 1700-kW (2,280-hp.) Dart RDa.7 Mk 532-2L engines and the provision of a large freight door aft of the wing. Extended wingtips were introduced, plus other detail changes in 1979, to produce the Series 2B, now under the British Aerospace banner.

HS.748s will continue to fly with airlines who appreciate their low cost and dependability.

Series 2 HS.748s were favoured by airlines working out of hot-and-high airfields. Increased engine power from Dart RDa.7 Mk 531s gave better take-off performance.

HS.748 Series 2A

Type: twin-turboprop short-/medium-range airliner

Powerplant: two 1700-kW (2,280-hp.) Rolls-Royce Dart RDa.7 Mk 535-2 turboprops

Maximum cruising speed: 462 km/h (286 m.p.h.)

Initial climb rate: 393 m/min (1,290 f.p.m.)

Range: 1,891 km (1,176 mi.) with maximum fuel and provision for 370-km (230-mi.) diversion

Service ceiling: 7600 m (25,000 ft.)

Weights: maximum take-off 20,182 kg (44,400 lb.)

Accommodation: 40 to 58 passengers

Dimensions:
span	30.02 m	(98 ft. 6 in.)
length	20.42 m	(67 ft.)
height	7.57 m	(24 ft. 10 in.)
wing area	75.35 m²	(811 sq. ft.)

HS.748 SERIES 2

The Series 2 was the most successful production version. Some Series 2 aircraft featured the 1425-kW Dart RDa.7 Mk 531; others were fitted with the Mk 533-2 of 1570 kW.

A circular section was chosen for the fuselage, since it produces a very strong structure.

Extended wingtips are fitted to Series 2B aircraft. These improve take-off and range performance.

The 748s wings are set at seven-degrees dihedral and have an all-metal, two-spar fail-safe structure.

Three crew and 40 to 58 passengers are carried. The seats are arranged in pairs on either side of a central gangway.

Electrically operated flaps and powerful engines produce the HS.748's excellent short-field performance.

Black pneumatic de-icer boots cover all leading edges. These break off the ice by flexing.

Four-bladed Dowty Rotol propellers are standard on all HS.748s.

The maingear retracts forwards to lie in the lower section of the engine nacelles.

A rear door serves the passenger cabin and can be equipped with a power-operated entrance stair. The crew enter through the freight door ahead of the wings.

Bahamasair
C6-BEE

ACTION DATA

ACCOMMODATION

Considering its exceptional STOL performance, the large passenger load of the HS.748 is remarkable. Its Japanese competitor, the NAMC YS-11, never equalled the British aircraft's popularity and few remain in service.

HS.748 SERIES 2A	58 passengers
YS-11A	60 passengers
F.27 FRIENDSHIP	52 passengers

TAKE-OFF DISTANCE

With its superb short-field and hot-and-high performance, the HS.748 was a versatile and rugged workhorse for smaller airlines. Some variants of the F.27 also had good hot-and-high performance, but their STOL capability was inferior.

HS.748 SERIES 2A	1006 m (3,300 ft.)
YS-11A	1110 m (3,640 ft.)
F.27 FRIENDSHIP	1250 m (4,100 ft.)

RANGE

Long range is important for airliners. While the YS-11 has largely disappeared from service, both the HS.748 and F.27 have been developed into more advanced versions. Interestingly, the Fokker 50 has proved far more attractive to airlines than the BAe ATP or Jetstream 61.

HS.748 SERIES 2A 1,891 km (1,175 mi.)
YS-11A 2110 km (1,300 mi.)
F.27 FRIENDSHIP 1705 km (1,060 mi.)

HS.748 Avro ancestors

■ **ANSON:** Entering airline service in 1935, the Anson saw extensive wartime operations with the RAF. After the war it was again a favourite of the airlines.

■ **YORK:** Using the wings, tail unit, engines and undercarriage of the Lancaster bomber, 45 Yorks were built for airliner use. Skyways was also an early user of the HS.748.

■ **LANCASTRIAN:** Victory Aircraft in Canada modified a Lancaster B.Mk III for transport duties in 1942, and Avro adopted this as the basis of a long-range airliner.

■ **TUDOR:** The Tudor suffered a troubled career, plagued by crashes and changing requirements. It proved most successful during the Berlin Airlift.

163

HAWKER SIDDELEY

TRIDENT

- Three-engined airliner
- 727 competitor
- de Havilland design

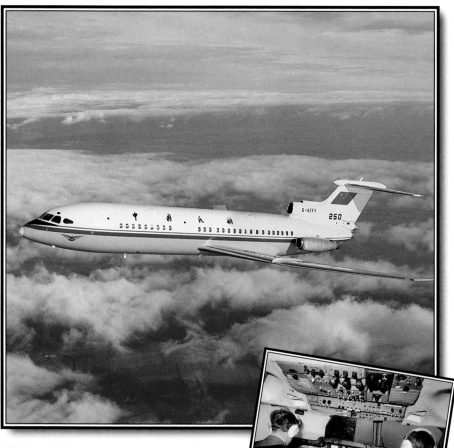

▲ *The Trident first flew in January 1962, and on entering BEA service in April 1964 it became the airline's first jet transport. The Trident managed to fend off rival designs from both Bristol and Avro.*

The Trident design was produced to meet a British European Airways (BEA) specification. In its original form it was to be powered by three Rolls-Royce Medway turbofans, be able to carry 111 passengers and have a range of more than 3300 km (2,050 mi.). But after ordering 24 in 1958, BEA changed its requirements. As a result, the aircraft had less-powerful Rolls-Royce Spey engines and could carry 97–103 passengers only 1500 km (930 mi.).

HAWKER SIDDELEY TRIDENT

Tri-jet power ▶
The Hawker Siddeley Trident, shown here in its prototype form, was powered by three Rolls-Royce Spey 512 turbofans: one mounted on either side of the rear fuselage and the third buried in the tail.

▲ Trident in China
A total of 33 Trident 2E short-to-medium-range transports were purchased by CAAC, the national airline of the People's Republic of China. A number of these were later used by the Chinese air force.

▲ Iraqi orders
The Trident proved successful with airlines that could not afford or could not obtain Boeing's 727; Iraqi airlines for example bought the 1E model.

▲ British European Airways
The Trident had excellent low-speed handling, thanks to Krueger leading-edge flaps, spoilers and large double-slotted trailing-edge flaps.

Trident production ▶
Although not a great success, the Trident kept the Hawker Siddeley factory at Hatfield busy for 20 years.

FACTS AND FIGURES

- ➤ The Trident was originally called the de Havilland DH.121 and then the Hawker Siddeley HS.121.
- ➤ In all, 117 Tridents were built, the last main users being British Airways and CAAC.
- ➤ The first DH.121 Trident I (G-ARPA) made its maiden flight on 9 January 1962.
- ➤ The Trident 3 had a 'fourth engine' fitted; this was principally an auxiliary power unit (APU), but which added 23.3 kN of thrust.
- ➤ An innovation available on the Trident was a 'hands-off' autoland system.
- ➤ Tridents were to be built by Airco, a consortium including Fairey and Hunting.

PROFILE

Britain's tri-jet challenger

The Trident design was started by de Havilland, but by 1964, when the aircraft entered service with BEA, the company had been taken over by Hawker Siddeley. More significantly, though, Boeing had introduced the 727. This was also a tri-jet, but the 727's more powerful JT8D engines enabled it to carry up to 189 passengers over a distance of nearly 4000 km (2,480 mi.).

The result was inevitable. While Boeing went on to sell more than 1800 727s, Hawker Siddeley produced just 117 Tridents, most of them for BEA.

Succeeding Trident variants introduced more powerful engines, longer wings, enlarged fuel capacity and slight increases in passenger loads. Trident 1s and 2Es were delivered to BEA, and a handful of other airlines bought a total of 15 Trident 1Es. Cyprus Airways and the Civil Aviation Authority of China (CAAC) bought the Trident 2E.

A longer variant, the Trident 3B, could carry up to 180 passengers in a high-density seating arrangement on short-haul routes, and two still-heavier Super Trident 3Bs were built for the CAAC. The early decision to restrict range and payload, however, meant that the Trident never caught up with its rivals.

A surprising customer was America's Northeast airlines, which chose the Trident over the aircraft's US rivals.

Following the merger of BEA and BOAC (British Overseas Airways Corporation), the Trident 3 went on to serve in large numbers with British Airways.

The Trident 1E model introduced a superior increased-span wing with leading-edge slats.

Originally designed to incorporate the Rolls-Royce Medway engine, the Trident only ever flew under Rolls-Royce Spey 512 power.

Northeast was the Trident's sole American operator.

The Trident 3E version was boosted during take-off by a Rolls-Royce RB.162-86 mini-turbojet. This was mounted in the rear fuselage below the rudder and above the third engine's exhaust.

Like the Boeing 727 and the Soviet Tu-154 and Yak-40 of the same era, the Trident had three engines and a high-set, all-metal T-type tail unit.

TRIDENT 1E

As well as serving with Northeast airlines in the United States, the Trident 1E variant was operated by the national airlines of Kuwait, Iraq, Pakistan, and by Air Ceylon and Channel Airlines.

The long-span Trident 1E introduced accommodation for a high-density seating arrangement of up to 139 passengers.

An innovative feature of the Trident was its baggage hold, the forward portion of which could be pressurised for the carriage of animals.

The Trident's third engine was buried in the rear fuselage with an intake above the fuselage, and exhaust nozzle in the tail-tip.

The Trident's heavy-duty twinwheel nose landing gear was manufactured in the US by Lockheed.

Trident 2E

Type: three-engined short- to medium-range commercial transport

Powerplant: three 53.2-kN (11,970-lb.-thrust) Rolls-Royce Spey 512-5W turbofans

Maximum speed: 972 km/h (602 m.p.h.)

Economic cruising speed: 959 km/h (595 m.p.h.)

Range with typical payload: 3910 km (2,425 mi.)

Range with maximum fuel: 5726 km (3,550 mi.)

Weights: basic operating 33,250 kg (73,150 lb.); maximum take-off 65,090 kg (143,198 lb.)

Accommodation: up to 139 passengers

Dimensions:
span 29.90 m (98 ft.)
length 34.98 m (114 ft. 9 in.)
height 8.23 m (27 ft.)
wing area 135.70 m² (1,460 sq. ft.)

ACTION DATA

CRUISING SPEED

The Trident 2E had a very similar top speed to its competitors. Speeds in the 950-975 km/h bracket were the norm for airliners of this size in the 1960s, when designing an airliner speed was less important than accommodation.

TRIDENT 2E	959 km/h (595 m.p.h.)
727-200	964 km/h (598 m.p.h.)
Tu-154 'CARELESS'	975 km/h (605 m.p.h.)

PASSENGER SEATS

The Tu-154 was one of the largest tri-jet airliners produced and could carry more passengers than the Trident 2E. The Trident 3 addressed this problem and could carry 180 passengers. The Boeing 727-200 had slightly lower passenger loads.

TRIDENT 2E	115 passengers
727-200	145 passengers
Tu-154 'CARELESS'	154 passengers

RANGE

These three aircraft had very similar ranges. Range varies according to the ratio of fuel load weight to passenger load weight. Successive versions with higher gross weights tend to have shorter range unless they are modified to carry more fuel as well as a bigger payload.

TRIDENT 2E 3910 km (2,425 mi.)
727-200 4040 km (2,505 mi.)
Tu-154 'CARELESS' 3900 km (2,420 mi.)

Disaster at Heathrow

Until the bombing of the Pan Am 747 over Lockerbie, the crash of a BEA Trident 1 on 16 June 1972 was Britain's worst air disaster.

1 TAKE-OFF: At 16.09 the BEA Trident codenamed 'Papa India' took off from runway Two-Eight Right at Heathrow, with Captain Stanley Key at the controls.

2 CLIMB: As the aircraft banked left to climb, turbulence in thick clouds buffeted the Trident's fuselage.

3 STALL: Flying at 162 knots (190 m.p.h.), the Trident's nose began to rise to an unacceptable angle. As speed decreased the nose was pushed up further still, and Captain Key suffered heart failure.

4 IMPACT: At 16.11 the Trident smashed into the ground, six and a half kilometres (four miles) from Heathrow. All 118 people on board were killed in the crash, which was eventually attributed to the poor health of the pilot.

ILYUSHIN

IL-14 'CRATE'

● Eastern Bloc service ● Licence production ● Military transport

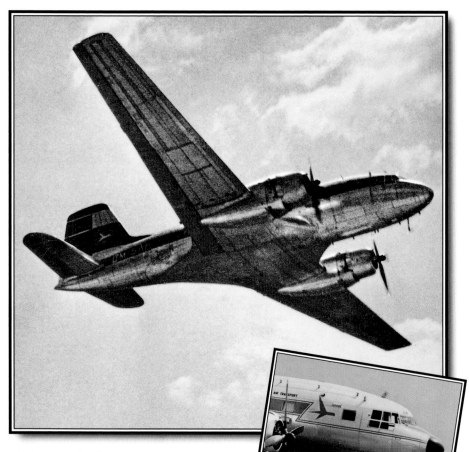

A ppearing in 1950, the Il-14 fulfilled the Soviet Union's requirement for a reliable transport for airline and military service. Developed from the problematic Il-12, the Il-14 was a much improved aircraft and was purchased by many Eastern Bloc countries. Licence production was successfully carried out in Czechoslovakia and East Germany, and a small number still remain in both military and civilian service.

▲ In 1943
Ilyushin began developing a transport aircraft to replace the Li-2. The resulting Il-12 and Il-14 equipped civilian and military organisations for the following two decades.

PHOTO FILE

ILYUSHIN IL-14 'CRATE'

◀ Piston power
At a time when Western airlines were entering the turboprop era with aircraft like the F27, piston-powered Il-14s were still being produced for Eastern Bloc airlines.

Secret missions ▶
A specialised Elint version, reportedly allocated the NATO codename 'Crate-C', was operated by some WarPac countries as well as by the USSR.

Pressurised comfort ▶
Avia of Czechoslovakia built the Avia-14 Super version. This featured a pressurised cabin, circular windows and removable wingtip fuel tanks for extended range.

▲ Romanian 'Crates'
Romanian airline TAROM operated 18 Il-14s, the majority of which were built by VEB Flugzeugwerke in Dresden.

Photo survey ▶
Fitted with a glass nose and an in-built darkroom for film processing, the Il-14FK was used for mapping and survey work.

FACTS AND FIGURES

➤ Total Il-14 production of all versions was about 3200; 2200 examples were built at the USSR's Khodinka factory.

➤ More than 100 examples of the Il-14 are estimated to be still flying.

➤ The first prototype, piloted by V.K. Kokkinaki, took to the air on 15 July 1950.

➤ Freighter versions of the Il-14 were loaded through a large 2.2-m (7-ft.) door on the side of the fuselage.

➤ The Il-14 was the first Soviet post-war aircraft to be widely exported.

➤ President Nasser of Egypt and the Shah of Iran were presented with luxury Il-14s.

PROFILE

Successful Soviet post-war propliner

Ilyushin's Il-14 was a successful attempt to solve the underlying deficiencies of the earlier Il-12. The 'Crate' had a number of improvements, including a new wing design and a strengthened fuselage.

In 1950 all transports were propeller-driven, and the Convair 340 and Martin 404 were demonstrating that a practical, twin-engined aircraft with tricycle landing gear was of great value. In fact, the Il-14's exhaust system, which had twin stacks that crossed over the wing and culminated in ejector nozzles at the trailing edge, was copied from the Convair. The American aircraft also influenced the design of the Il-14's anti-icing system.

During the 1950s and 1960s the Il-14 was the backbone of transport operations in the USSR and those of Soviet allies. In the USSR it was designed to do everything from transporting civil passengers to dropping paratroops and carrying out electronic intelligence-gathering missions for the Soviet air force.

Il-14s were licence-built by East Germany, which manufactured the aircraft at the Dresden State Aircraft Factory, and by Czechoslovakia, which produced the aircraft under the name Avia-14. More than 40 years after this enduring aircraft entered service, a number of Il-14s are still used on both passenger and cargo routes.

Left: Hungarian airline Malév operated a mixed fleet of VEB Il-14s and Ilyushin-built Il-14Ms, which were approximately one metre (3 ft.) longer and had additional capacity.

Above: Unlike its predecessor the Il-12, the 'Crate' handled well even if one engine failed.

Il-14M 'Crate'

Type: passenger and cargo transport

Powerplant: two 1417-kW (1,900-hp.) Shvetsov ASh-82T radial piston engines driving four-bladed AV-50 propellers

Maximum speed: 430 km/h (267 m.p.h.) at 2400 m (7,872 ft.)

Cruising speed: 300 km/h (186 m.p.h.)

Range: 1500 km (937 mi.) with maximum payload

Service ceiling: 7400 m (24,272 ft.)

Weights: empty 12,700 kg (28,000 lb.); maximum take-off 18,000 kg (40,000 lb.)

Accommodation: (typical) two pilots, radio operator, loadmaster and provision for 24, 28, 32 or 36 passengers in various models and configurations; maximum payload of cargo version 3300 kg (7,275 lb.)

Dimensions:
span	31.70 m (103 ft. 11 in.)
length	22.31 m (73 ft. 3 in.)
height	7.90 m (25 ft. 9 in.)
wing area	100 m² (997 sq. ft.)

Normal operating crew comprised two pilots and, aft of a semi-bulkhead, a navigator and radio operator. A flight engineer could be accommodated in a jump-seat. A cargo and baggage compartment was situated between the flightdeck and the passenger cabin.

The ASh-82T engine was developed from the wartime M-82 powerplant, which was itself a Soviet-built Pratt & Whitney R-1830 radial. This version had improved fuel efficiency and an exhaust system copied from the American Convair 240 airliner.

When the Il-14P entered service with Aeroflot it was fitted with 18 seats in pairs on the port side and singularly on the starboard side. This capacity was later increased to 24. The stretched Il-14M could carry up to 36 passengers in high-density configuration.

The newly designed square-topped fin and rudder gave a pronounced handling improvement over the Il-12 thanks to a 17 per cent increase in area.

POLSKIE LINIE LOTNICZE LOT SP-LNH

The undercarriage was hydraulically operated, with the double-wheeled main units retracting forwards into the engine nacelles.

To help rectify the deficiencies of the Il-12, Ilyushin designed an entirely new wing. Built with three spars and a straight taper on the trailing edge, it was far more aerodynamically efficient.

IL-14P 'CRATE'

Polish airline Polskie Linie Lotnicze followed up its purchase of five Il-12s by ordering 16 Il-14s in 1954. Nine were licence built in East Germany and one was a Czech-built Avia-14.

ACTION DATA

MAXIMUM SPEED

The Il-14 was more streamlined than the Il-12B and was fitted with a more powerful version of the ASh-82 engine, giving it greater performance. Western designs of the time, like the Convair 240, were far more advanced than their Soviet counterparts.

Il-14M 'CRATE'	430 km/h (267 m.p.h.)
Il-12B 'COACH'	407 km/h (252 m.p.h.)
CV 240	538 km/h (334 m.p.h.)

POWER

Fitted with an engine based on a wartime radial design, the Il-12 and Il-14 did not have the power of the Pratt & Whitney R-2800-powered 240. This series was the pinnacle of piston-engine design.

Il-14M 'CRATE'	Il-12B 'COACH'	CV 240
2834 kW (3,800 hp.)	2297 kW (3,550 hp.)	3579 kW (4,800 hp.)

PASSENGERS

Although originally designed to carry only 18 passengers, later versions of the Il-14 could hold up to 36 passengers in a high-density configuration. The more powerful 240 could carry the largest load.

Il-14M 'CRATE'	36
Il-12B 'COACH'	28
CV 240	40

The Il-14's Western rivals

■ **CONVAIR 440 METROPOLITAN:** The 440 was the last piston-powered Convair airliner, and more than 160 CV 440s were built.

■ **CURTISS C-46:** After the Japanese surrender in 1945 many ex-military C-46s were bought by civilian operators around the world.

■ **DOUGLAS DC-3:** A pre-war design, the DC-3 was built in huge numbers during World War II and continues to serve with civilian users.

■ **MARTIN 4-0-4:** Entering service at roughly the same time as the Il-12, the Martin series was overtaken by the onset of turboprop airliners.

ILYUSHIN

IL-18 'COOT'

● 1950s airliner design ● Licence-built in China ● Pioneering turboprop

PHOTO FILE

ILYUSHIN IL-18 'COOT'

▲ **Traditional cockpit layout**
The cockpit was well designed.
The object in the centre is a
weather radar scope.

▲ **China service**
Il-18s continued in service with
China's CAAC airline until the
early-1980s, flying throughout
the country including Tibet.
Serviceability was poor for the
aircraft's last few years in China,
resulting in a number of crashes.
About 100 Il-18s were exported
from the total of 800 built.

▲ **Flying with the fleet**
When Aeroflot was split up, the remaining Il-18s
were inherited by new carriers. They are still
operated by companies like Rossiya and SPAIR.

▲ **Polish airlines**
Most Warsaw Pact nations had Il-18s in their
national fleet. LOT, the Polish national carrier,
retired its last examples in the early-1980s.

Dnepropetrovsk ▶
Regional flights in the Soviet Union were the
mainstay of the Il-18's work. This aircraft was the
first to arrive at Dnepropetrovsk's new airport.

As the first (and largest) post-war
aircraft construction project
undertaken by the Ilyushin Design
Bureau, the piston-engined Il-18 was an
attempt to give Russia a much-needed
long-range airliner with the minimum of delay.
A second Il-18 was built in 1953 as a modern
75-seat passenger airliner. Powered by four
turboprops, the Il-18 was later adapted to a
military role as the Il-38 ASW aircraft, and
also for signals intelligence work.

▲ If any aircraft could be said to
have brought air travel to the masses in
Eastern Europe, it was the Il-18.
Operators found that the large turboprop,
dismissed as obsolete in the jet age, was
actually very profitable due to its much
lower operating costs and fuel economy.

FACTS AND FIGURES

➤ The type had carried over 250 million
passengers by 1981 and clocked up
14 million flight hours.

➤ The first 20 Il-18s used the Kuznetsov
NK-4 turboprop engine.

➤ In the 1970s, the Il-18 was still Aeroflot's
second most numerous airliner.

➤ The Il-18's flight deck crew numbered
five – two pilots, a navigator, a radio
operator and a flight engineer.

➤ From the early-1970s a number of Il-18s
were converted to freighters.

➤ African operators such as Air Guinea,
Air Mali and Air Mauritania also used Il-18s.

PROFILE

Turboprop liner for the USSR

During the 1950s, Aeroflot decided, despite its still largely unmodernised infrastructure with many outlying airfields remaining in the 'dirt strip' category, to modernise its civil airliner fleet. The Il-18 was one of the results of this planning.

The specification that led to the Il-18 consequently called for a good rough field capability as well as cabin pressurisation and seating capacity for up to 75 passengers. Ilyushin opted for a conventional, single-fin/rudder

design powered by four turboprop engines and utilising a tricycle landing gear, the resulting aircraft bearing a superficial resemblance to the Bristol Britannia and DC-7. The prototype flew on 4 July 1957.

Five development aircraft proved little need for modification before production commenced and the Il-18 entered service with the Soviet state airline on 29 April 1959. Further models were produced including the Il-18V, which accommodated up to 100 passengers and which

began flying with Aeroflot in 1961. Four years later the Il-18D appeared. This, the last Il-18 production model, featured a reconfigured fuselage interior to take up to 122 seats, greater fuel capacity and uprated engines. In total, at least 800 Il-18s were built for Soviet and foreign airline use, plus the military role.

Below: Due to the US trade embargo and cash shortages, Cubana, the Cuban national carrier, relied heavily on its Il-18s despite their age. This Il-18D, featuring uprated avionics, was still operating in 1986.

Above: Despite the age of the design, Il-18 production only ceased in 1979 after 565 Il-18Ds had been built.

Electro-thermal engine de-icing was fitted as standard, and each engine had two SG-12 starter/generator systems. The main gear retracted forwards into the inboard engine nacelle.

Il-18D 'Coot'

Type: long-range turboprop airliner

Powerplant: four 2983-kW (4,000-hp.) Ivchenko AI-20M turboprops

Maximum speed: 685 km/h (388 m.p.h.)

Range: 3700 km (2,295 mi.) with maximum payload

Service ceiling: 9250 km (30,000 ft.)

Weights: empty 27,980 kg (62,678 lb.); maximum take-off 64,000 kg (93,500 lb.)

Accommodation: 110 in high-density seating

Dimensions:
span	37.40 m	(122 ft. 8 in.)
length	35.90 m	(117 ft. 9 in.)
height	10.17 m	(33 ft. 4 in.)
wing area	140 m² (1,506 sq. ft.)	

IL-18 'COOT'

Still in limited service in Russia, the Il-18 was widely exported and many were sold to China before the Sino-Soviet split in 1960. They were operated by the national airline CAAC, which was split into smaller airlines in 1992.

In later years, Il-18s had a more complete avionics fit, including autoland (an automatic landing instrument). All versions contained the 'Emblema' weather radar in the nose and a Decca Flight Log navigation system.

Fuel was stored in 20 bag-type tanks in the wings, stretching from the wingroot to the ailerons.

Originally, Kuznetsov NK-4 engines were fitted, but these were replaced by Ivchenko AI-20s. The Il-18D (first introduced in 1964) was powered by AI-20Ms, which had about five per cent more power. The large 4.5-m (14-ft. 9-in.) propellers could be put into reverse pitch to give braking assistance on landing.

All flight controls were manual, connected by cables. Hydraulic boosters were fitted to the ailerons and elevators, and there was a spring tab on the rudder.

Five crewmembers were usually seated in the flight deck.

The first Il-18s seated 75 passengers in six-abreast seating. By deleting the unpressurised cargo hold the Il-18D increased this capacity to 110 to 120 passengers.

Cargo and luggage were stored in a rear hold. The only access to this was from outside the aircraft.

ACTION DATA

PASSENGERS

With the additional space produced by removing the rear cargo bay, the Il-18 could carry 110 passengers, albeit in Soviet-style seating which was noticeably spartan by Western standards. Early versions had 95 seats.

Il-18D 'COOT' 110 passengers
BRITANNIA 92 passengers
DC-7C 105 passengers

RANGE

Turboprops are efficient engines, operating well at high altitude and giving a good compromise between the speed of jets and the economy of pistons. The following range figures are with maximum payload.

Il-18D 'COOT' 3700 km (2,295 mi.)
BRITANNIA 6869 km (4,259 mi.)
DC-7 5810 km (3,602 mi.)

PRODUCTION

The largest country in the world also had the largest airline, and the Il-18 was produced in quantity. The Britannia and DC-7 could not compete with the new jet-powered airlines.

Il-18D 'COOT'	BRITANNIA	DC-7
800	74	337

Ilyushin airliners across the world

■ Il-12 'COACH': A Soviet equivalent to the C-47, the Il-12 was used by Aeroflot from 1947 and was also exported to Poland and China.

■ Il-62 'CLASSIC': The Il-62 was the only jet apart from the VC-10 to have four rear-mounted engines. It is still widely used.

■ Il-86 'CAMBER': The first four-engine wide-body Soviet jet, the Il-86 is still widely used on international routes by the airline ARIA.

■ Il-96 'CAMBER': Modifications to the Il-86 resulted in the Il-96, with a new wing and engines and advanced 'glass' cockpit displays.

ILYUSHIN

IL-62 'CLASSIC'

● Long-range airliner ● Rear-mounted four-jet layout

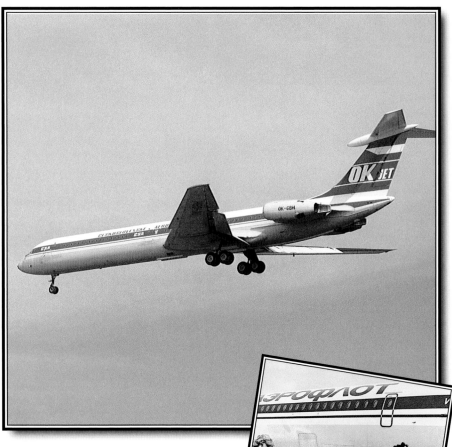

When the Ilyushin Il-62 was revealed to the world in 1962, this long-range airliner looked like a possible Soviet equivalent to the Boeing 707 and Vickers VC10. Until then, the USSR had never excelled at providing comfort and safety in a commercial transport, but the Il-62 met a high standard and served Moscow and its allies well. Although now obsolescent and costly to operate, many Il-62s still fly today.

▲ The Il-62M
served as a main component of the old Soviet airline Aeroflot and its successors. In the former Aeroflot, the aircraft set records for large payloads and speeds with an all-female flight crew.

ILYUSHIN IL-62 'CLASSIC'

▼ **Four at the front**
The Il-62 cockpit seats as many as four or five crew, including pilot, co-pilot, navigator, radio operator and flight engineer.

▲ **Four at the back**
Only the VC10 and the Il-62 share the four engines on the rear fuselage layout. This configuration allows the wing design to be clean and efficient, and reduces cabin noise to some extent.

Sheremetyevo ▶
The international airport at Moscow, Sheremetyevo, is still the main port of call for most Il-62s. Although newer replacements are now arriving, Il-62s remain in use with airlines such as Orbi and Aerovody.

◀ **To Asia**
The Il-62 serves many destinations in central Asia and the Far East. This example is seen at Subang airport in Malaysia; Aeroflot Il-62 services to this destination, via Delhi, began in 1970.

▲ **Still going strong**
Cubana is one of the last civil operators of the Il-62 outside the former USSR, with a few Il-62MK variants still in service.

FACTS AND FIGURES

➤ The first Il-62 flew in January 1963, powered by Lyul'ka AL-7 turbojets while awaiting delivery of NK-8-4 turbofans.

➤ The first scheduled Aeroflot service with an Il-62 took to the air on 10 March 1967.

➤ A total of 244 Il-62s had been delivered when production ended in 1990.

➤ When Germany was unified, the Luftwaffe flew former Interflug Il-62s until replacing them with Airbus A310s.

➤ The Il-62MK has a redesigned structure and undercarriage.

➤ The Il-62 closely resembles the proposed British 'Super VC10' of 1958.

PROFILE

Ilyushin's classic airliner

The Ilyushin Il-62 was developed as a long-haul jetliner for Aeroflot, primarily to replace the turboprop-powered Tupolev Tu-114. With its T-tail and pairs of side-by-side turbofans on the rear fuselage, the Il-62 resembles Britain's VC10.

Given the NATO reporting name of 'Classic', Il-62s have been continuously upgraded to keep pace with rapid improvements in technology elsewhere. Better thrust reversers, improved seats,

triplex inertial navigation and revised nacelles aimed at noise reduction are among the changes. Improved (Il-62M) and strengthened (Il-62MK) models, both with Soloviev engines replacing Kuznetsov NK-8-4 turbofans, carry passengers in Russia and allied nations.

Some surviving Il-62s serve as military transports and one aircraft transports the Russian president in his travels. But although the big Ilyushin was a genuine pioneer in its early

The vast majority of Il-62s served with Aeroflot. Following the break-up of this airline they have been seen in many colours, including that of Aeroflot's main successor, ARIA (Aeroflot Russian International Airlines). Even so, many continued to fly in the old Aeroflot colour scheme for several years after the airline's demise.

days, it has has become geriatric and increasingly difficult to maintain. As a result, many former Il-62 operators have taken advantage of the break-up of the USSR to acquire considerably more advanced aircraft like the Airbus A310 and Boeing 767 from the West.

Il-62M 'Classic'

Type: long-range airliner

Powerplant: four 107.8-kN (24,250-lb.-thrust) Soloviev D-30KU turbofans

Cruising speed: 900 km/h (558 m.p.h.)

Range: 8000 km (4,760 mi.) with maximum payload and reserves

Service ceiling: 11,440 m (37,500 ft.)

Weights: empty 69,400 kg (152,680 lb.); loaded 165,000 kg (363,000 lb.)

Accommodation: provision for flight crew of five; typically 186 passengers, with 72 in forward compartment and 114 in rear

Dimensions:
span	43.20 m	(141 ft. 8 in.)
length	53.12 m	(174 ft. 3 in.)
height	12.35 m	(40 ft. 6 in.)
wing area	282.2 m²	(3,036 sq. ft.)

IL-62MK 'CLASSIC'

Linhas Aereas de Angola is one of the last African operators of the Il-62. They fly two of the Ilyushins on various routes including Luanda to Moscow and Havana.

The last Il-62s featured revised engine nacelles, giving reduced emissions and noise, although they could never meet the latest international noise abatement regulations.

The large bullet fairing improves airflow over the tail surfaces at high subsonic speeds.

A strengthened undercarriage on the IL-62MK is capable of supporting much greater all-up weights.

The Il-62M differs from earlier versions by the addition of an extra fuel tank in the fin, as well as completely revised avionics.

Il-62s have received several avionics upgrades. Many now have a triplex inertial navigation system, and the flight control system can be modified to permit operation in extremely bad visibility conditions.

The galley is located in the centre of the fuselage between the passenger compartments.

The Soviets were never as concerned with comfort as Western airlines, but later versions of the Il-62 have revised cabin layouts, giving increased passenger comfort.

During trials, the rear-engined high-tail layout caused the aircraft to have slender control margins at low speeds, so the wing was redesigned in production aircraft to give more lift.

LINHAS AEREAS DE ANGOLA

D2-TIG

The cabin seats up to 195 passengers in the Il-62MK version, in six-abreast layout with a central aisle. Up to 25 tons of cargo can be stored in containerised underfloor baggage holds.

Some Aeroflot Il-62s have an enlarged dorsal spine containing extra communications gear.

The Il-62M is fitted with the Soloviev D-30KU turbofan instead of the earlier Kuznetsov engine. Thrust reversers are fitted to the outer engines only.

The long-range jet pioneers

■ BOEING 707: First of the modern four-jet airliners, the Boeing 707 entered service in the late 1950s. It revolutionised air transport, bringing the benefits of long-distance jet travel to more people than ever before.

■ DOUGLAS DC-8: The Boeing's great rival first entered service in 1959. Stretched many times over a long career, the DC-8 grew to seat 259 passengers in its final variants. It can still be seen around the world, primarily as a freighter.

■ VICKERS VC10: Designed to operate from 'hot and high' airfields, the sleek VC10 was a better performer than the 707 and DC-8. But operating costs were higher, and so it was not as great a commercial success as its American rivals.

ACTION DATA

PASSENGER LOAD

Seats in Russian aircraft are generally crowded more closely together than is the practice on Western scheduled flights; the reduced seat pitch allows for extra passengers to be carried, but in less comfort. The Tu-154 tri-jet carries almost as many passengers as the Il-62, but has a much smaller range.

Il-62M 186 Passengers

Tu-154 180 Passengers

VC10 152 Passengers

ILYUSHIN

IL-86/96 'CAMBER'

● Modern airliner design ● Hi-tech redesign ● International services

F irst flown in December 1976, the Il-86 started operating scheduled services with Aeroflot four years later. Range fell short of the intended 3600 km when carrying a 40000-kg payload or 4600 km with maximum fuel. As a result, fewer than 100 Il-86s had been delivered before the Il-96 appeared as a replacement in 1988. Although externally similar and having the same fuselage diameter, the -96 was a completely new design and incorporated several advanced features.

▲ With seating for 350 passengers in a 3+3+3 seating arrangement, Aeroflot and Ilyushin had expected the Il-86 to revolutionise Soviet air transport. Unfortunately, the aircraft's range was far less than expected.

ILYUSHIN IL-86/96 'CAMBER'

▲ Il-86 prototype
Five years after development was announced, the first Il-86 was rolled out.

▲ Redesigning the 'Camber'
In an effort to solve the shortcomings of the Il-86, Ilyushin decided to redesign the aircraft. Although the resulting airliner, the Il-96, looks similar to the earlier 'Camber', it is, in fact, an almost completely new design.

▲ Aeroflot service
About 100 Il-86s were delivered to Aeroflot and fly high-density international routes.

▼ Increased capacity
The Il-96M, which has seating for a maximum of 375 passengers, has been test flown.

▲ Il-96 certification
As the Il-96 retained some of the Il-86's features, the new aircraft's test programme was reduced by 750 hours. Ilyushin had hoped that certification would be received in 1990, but it was not granted until 29 December 1992.

FACTS AND FIGURES

➤ Genrikh V. Novozhilov announced the Il-86 at the 1970 Paris air show, after the retirement of Ilyushin himself.

➤ Originally, the Il-86 was to be an Il-62 with a wider fuselage and improved wing.

➤ Huge electrical pulses de-iced all of the Il-86's leading edges.

➤ Many Soviet airports had to be upgraded to make their passenger handling facilities compatible with the Il-96.

➤ A freighter version, the Il-96T, can carry 92,000 kg (202,400 lb.) of cargo.

➤ Ilyushin has proposed the Il-96MK variant, powered by NK-93 ducted propfans.

Success through adversity

In addition to being the first Soviet wide-body airliner and the first to have its engines in wing-mounted nacelles, the Il-86 also introduced a novel boarding system. To overcome the poor facilities at many Soviet airports, passengers could board the Il-86 through doors at ground level, stow their coats and hand baggage, and then climb internal stairs to the cabin.

The improved Il-96, which flew for the first time in September 1988, replaced the original NK-86 engines with

PS-90s. It also introduced new structural components and used composite materials to reduce airframe weight. The wings are bigger and less sharply swept, and large winglets at the tips reduce drag.

Conventional doors located on the passenger deck level give access to the cabin. Up to 300 people can be accommodated in an all-tourist arrangement, or 235 in a three-class configuration.

Ilyushin intended to produce a range of Il-96 derivatives, including 200- and 375-

passenger models and a double-deck version with 550 seats. However, recent efforts have focused on installing Western avionics and engines to make the aircraft more attractive to airlines around the world.

Below: Carrying a Russian registration number, this Il-86 serves with the Latvian airline Transaero. The airline operates two Il-86s.

Above: Aeroflot accepted its first Il-86 on 24 September 1979, but did not start operations until 1981, with a proving flight to East Germany.

Il-96-300 'Camber'

Type: wide-bodied airliner

Powerplant: four 156.9-kN (35,300-lb.-thrust) Aviadvigatel PS-90A turbofans

Cruising speed: 850–900 km/h (525–558 m.p.h.)

Take-off run: 2600 m (8,525 ft.)

Range: 9000 km (5,570 mi.) with 30,000-kg (66,000-lb.) payload

Service ceiling: 12,000 m (39,360 ft.)

Weights: empty 117,000 kg (257,400 lb.); maximum take-off 216,000 kg (475,200 lb.)

Accommodation: 235 passengers in three classes or a maximum of 300

Dimensions: span 60.11 m (197 ft. 2 in.)
length 55.35 m (181 ft. 6 in.)
height 17.57 m (57 ft. 7 in.)
wing area 391.6 m² (4,214 sq. ft.)

ACTION DATA

PASSENGERS
Even though the Il-86 has a respectable passenger load, its poor operating economies and unconventional passenger loading prevent it from competing effectively with comparable Western types, such as the 767-300 and A300-600.

Il-86 'CAMBER' — 350 passengers
767-300 — 290 passengers
A300-600 — 375 passengers

TAKE-OFF RUN
For maximum operational flexibility, airlines require aircraft that have good field performance so that they can operate from smaller international airports. With its older technology engines the Il-86 trails behind.

Il-86 'CAMBER' 2600 m (8,525 ft.)
767-300 2560 m (8,400 ft.)
A300-600 2280 m (7,480 ft.)

RANGE
The Il-86 was intended to have a range of 4600 km (2,850 mi.), which was considerably less than the Boeing or Airbus models. In-service reports suggest that even this figure has not been achieved, with Interflug, the former East German airline, quoting a range of only 2500 km (1,550 mi.) in its sales publications. The Il-96 attempts to rectify this problem.

Il-86 'CAMBER' 4600 km (2,850 mi.)
767-300 7408 km (4,600 mi.)
A300-600 6759 km (4,190 mi.)

IL-96-300

CCCP-96000 acted as the first Il-96 prototype, flying from Khodinka on 28 September 1988 and appearing at the Paris air show the following year. The -300 designation refers to the nominal seating capacity.

A six-screen glass cockpit replaces the conventional instruments of the Il-86. Unlike contemporary Western designs, Ilyushin has retained a flight engineer in the cockpit.

With its Aviadvigatel PS-90A turbofans, the Il-96 has a far better range than the Il-86. Fuel is contained in the wings and fuselage centre section, with a maximum capacity of 148,260 litres (39,170 gal.).

Abandoning the Il-86 wing entirely, Ilyushin designed a modern advanced wing of supercritical section for the Il-96. This included range-increasing winglets. The use of new technology has allowed Ilyushin to aim for a lifetime of 60,000 hours.

Neither the two-section rudder nor elevators have trim tabs. The Il-96M has a shorter tailfin, as the aircraft's lengthened fuselage provides increased directional stability.

A Triplex fly-by-wire system transfers pilot inputs to the control surfaces. The Il-96's tail surfaces have a higher aspect ratio and altered profiles, compared to those of the Il-96. They also have composite leading and trailing edges.

One of the few real similarities between the Il-96 and Il-86 is the four-unit undercarriage.

The Il-96 has a shorter fuselage than the earlier aircraft, with fewer seats and a greatly revised interior. The Il-86's unusual system of internal stairs for passengers has been discarded.

Airliners by Ilyushin

Il-14 'CRATE': A refined development of the Il-12 'Coach', the Il-14 was originally built as an 18- to 26-seat airliner. A stretched 24- to 28-seat variant was produced as the Il-14M. Several examples remain airworthy, most flying as freighters.

Il-18 'COOT': This four-engined turboprop first flew in 1957. It was Ilyushin's response to an Aeroflot requirement for a 75- to100-seat medium-range transport. This aircraft flew VIP/staff transport duties with the Democratic and Popular Republic of Algeria.

Il-62 'CLASSIC': Very similar in appearance to the British Vickers VC-10, the Il-62 first flew in 1963 and was capable of accommodating a maximum of 186 passengers. A range of 6700 km was possible with maximum payload.

JUNKERS
F 13

● Civil aviation pioneer ● All-metal airframe ● Lufthansa service

▲ The F13 brought air
travel to people all over the world, not just
in Europe. These passengers flew on the first
service by the Brazilian airline Varig in May 1927.

When it first flew on 25 June
1919, the F 13 was the world's
first all-metal commercial
transport. It was the embodiment of
everything scientific genius Hugo Junkers
had learned in years of aviation
pioneering, and Lufthansa instantly saw it
as an aircraft worth having. For a single-
engine machine, the F 13 was given a big
job – and performed it with just the right
mix of muscle and elegance.

JUNKERS F 13

Lufthansa on skis ▶
*The adaptability and strength of the F 13 was
a classic mark of all Junkers designs. Well
able to operate in the harshest of conditions,
more than 40 F 13s were converted to use
either float or ski undercarriages.*

◀ Modern lines
*The profile of the F 13 was remarkably modern,
especially when, like this Varig-owned example, it was
fitted with the later square-topped tail. This shape of
tail was to reappear on the classic Ju 52 transport and
on late-World War II Junkers bombers and fighters.*

Built like a tank ▶
*The F 13's massive, chunky wing showed that
all-metal construction was in its infancy in the
1920s, but the toughness this created
contributed to the airliner's long life.*

▼ Stopping for fuel
*This F 13 and its partner, a Fokker
F.III, would not have taken long to
replenish. The entire fuel load of
one of these aircraft would be less
than a modern Lufthansa Airbus
needs to simply get off the ground.*

▲ Floatplane adventure
*This F 13 was owned by a Norwegian, Miss Gidsken
Jacobsen, and flown by Birger Johnsen. It was destroyed
in a crash after its engine fell out while at about 1000 m
(3,000 ft.) above Balestrand. Fortunately, no one was hurt.*

FACTS AND FIGURES

➤ 322 F 13 aircraft (originally called J13)
were manufactured in 11 years.

➤ In 1919, an F 13 broke the world altitude
record by carrying eight people to a
height of 6750 m (22,140 ft.).

➤ Lufthansa at one time operated no fewer
than 55 F 13s.

➤ The last F 13 in service was finally
retired by Varig Airlines in 1948.

➤ The Deruluft airline began F 13 flights to
Russia, between Leningrad, Riga and
Konigsberg, in 1928.

➤ F 13s served with operators in at least
28 countries around the world.

PROFILE

The world's first all-metal airliner

Hugo Junkers wanted to dispense with the cumbersome struts and wires that held the wings of an aircraft to the fuselage during the era of World War I. The monoplane F 13 resulted from his studies. Adopted quickly by Lufthansa, the F 13, with its characteristic corrugated sheet-metal skin, was virtually indestructible. It was eventually

flown on all continents, with a conventional wheeled undercarriage, with floats as a seaplane, and even with runners for ice and snow.

Most remarkably, passengers in the F 13 travelled in comfort, in a closed, heated and ventilated cabin. Its seats were fitted with safety belts, and the F 13 was the first commercial aircraft to have more than one

set of controls so that two pilots could relieve each other on long flights.

Junkers later built bigger and better airliners, but the F 13 was the ship which began a great revolution. Even when it was being retired, few other aircraft measured up to the F 13 in performance or efficiency.

Early all-metal aircraft designs like the F 13 were never pretty to look at. Nevertheless, the aircraft was a favourite with its crews, and F 13s frequently received female names.

F 13

Type: six-seat passenger transport

Powerplant: one 156-kW (210-hp.) Junkers L-5 piston engine (early versions: 138-kW (185-hp.) BMW IIIa piston or 119-kW Mercedes D.IIIa)

Maximum speed: 170 km/h (105 m.p.h.)

Range: 644 km (400 mi.)

Service ceiling: about 7000 m (23,000 ft.)

Weights: empty about 1500 kg (3,300 lb.); loaded 2495 kg (5,489 lb.)

Accommodation: two pilots, four to six passengers

Dimensions: span 17.70 m (58 ft. 3 in.)
length 20.50 m (31 ft. 6 in.)

The F 13's exhaust pipe appeared in various positions, including this prominent mounting in front of the canopy.

The four- to six-passenger cabin was a novel feature for the early 1920s, but compared to modern-day planes it was very noisy and spartan.

The first F 13s may have had an advanced structure, but most retained a traditional two-blade wooden airscrew.

F 13

The F 13 stretched the world's horizons. The first all-metal airliner flew to China from Germany via Moscow.

The original tail of the F 13 had an old-fashioned shape, but it was built with the same advanced metal construction as the fuselage and wing.

Most aircraft were powered by the 156-kW (210-hp.) Junkers L-5 engine, but Mercedes and BMW powerplants were also used. They all gained a reputation for reliability and the need for minimal maintenance.

The prototype F 13 had an open cockpit for both pilots, but production machines had enclosed cockpits, much to the relief of all who had to fly them.

All F 13s except the floatplanes carried a rear tailskid rather than a tailwheel.

ACTION DATA

MAXIMUM SPEED

Airliners were a completely new concept in 1919 and 1920. Many were adaptations of military designs, like the DH.4, and as such had very good performance. But they offered far less passenger comfort than machines like the Junkers, which was designed as a passenger carrier from the start.

F 13	170 km/h (105 m.p.h.)
DH.4	200 km/h (124 m.p.h.)
F.II	150 km/h (93 m.p.h.)

PAYLOAD

F 13	DH.4	F.II
up to 6 passengers	3 passengers	5 passengers

The advantage of designing an aircraft as a passenger carrier was that payload space could be optimised. The DH.4 was larger and much more powerful than either the Junkers or the Fokker, yet it could carry fewer paying customers.

RANGE

The early airline routes were between the capital cities of western Europe, and the range of the Junkers was adequate for most journeys. It was not as good as the high-winged Fokker monoplane, however, which had been designed by Reinhold Platz to carry passengers non-stop between Berlin and Moscow.

F 13	DH.4	F.II
644 km (400 mi.)	700 km (434 mi.)	1200 km (744 mi.)

The first commercial travellers

■ **ENDURANCE TEST:** The first airline services used minimally converted open-cockpit World War I bombers. Exposed to the elements, passengers had to wrap up very well.

■ **WEATHER PROTECTION:** The amazing thing about the Junkers F 13 was that it offered passengers a fully enclosed environment, allowing them to travel in normal clothing.

■ **ENCLOSED COCKPIT:** Unlike many other aircraft of the period, Junkers pilots were protected, since the aircraft had a fully enclosed, if sparsely equipped, cockpit.

■ **TRAVEL IN STYLE:** It might not have matched a limousine of the period, but the cabin of the F 13 offered passengers plenty of comfort and a fine view through large side windows.

JUNKERS

W.33/W.34

● Single-engined civil transport ● F.13 development ● War service

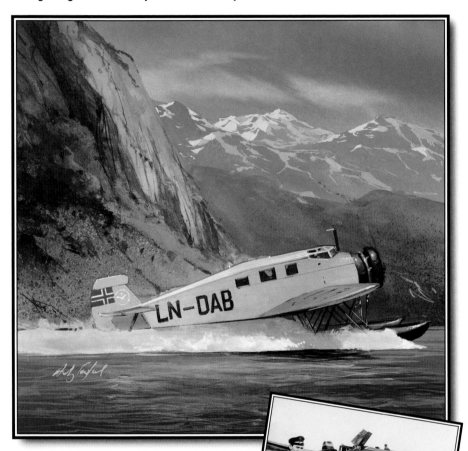

O ne of the most advanced civil aircraft of the period, the Junkers W.34 set the standard in inter-war design. Intended for use as a cargo, mail and utility transport, this product of the forward-thinking Dr Hugo Junkers had a relatively brief, but bright, career. Developed in 1926 and bearing the distinctive lines associated with many Junkers aircraft, it was designed to replace the Junkers F.13 of 1919. It also served with the Luftwaffe until 1945.

▲ In a demonstration of the type's reliability, Lufthansa W.33 D-1167 Bremen made the first East to West non-stop transatlantic flight by a single-engined aircraft on 12/13 April 1928.

JUNKERS W.33/W.34

◀ Record breaker
W.33s and W.34s established a number of world records, including a duration record of 65 hours and 25 minutes set in July 1928. This reputation for reliability prompted Lufthansa (with 15 W.33s and at least eight W.34s) and a number of overseas airlines to purchase the aircraft.

Exported to Finland ▶
The K.43 was a three-seat reconnaissance bomber version built in unknown quantities in Sweden. Examples were exported to Colombia and Finland. This aircraft wears wartime markings.

▼ Canadian fire-bomber
Re-engined with a Pratt & Whitney Wasp, this W.34f was still in service in the early 1960s.

▲ Luftwaffe service
Both types saw German air force service and performed training and liaison duties until 1945.

Swedish-built K.43 ▶
Unmarked, having just left the factory, this K.43 can be identified by its dorsal machine-gun for self-protection and its extra cabin windows.

FACTS AND FIGURES

➤ The W.33 was first flown in 1926; in total 199 were produced, powered by Gnome-Rhone or Junkers engines.

➤ The W.33 and W.34 prototypes were converted from Junkers F.13s.

➤ A total of nearly 1800 W.34s was built in Sweden and Germany.

➤ A single Junkers W.33 is currently on display at the Henry Ford Museum in Dearborn, Michigan.

➤ Junkers W.34s were often used as VIP transports for very high-ranking officials.

➤ The prototype W.33, owned by Junkers, was named Schildkrähe (Hooded Crow).

German utility on land or water

An ordinary-looking aircraft, yet one that inspired transport aircraft design in the 1930s, the Junkers W.34 (and its alter-ego the W.33) was a superb monoplane that appeared on the scene at the right time. Earlier utility transports, dating back to the beginning of aviation, were hopelessly outmoded. This Junkers design, of sturdy construction, with a single wing and a clean shape (except for

bracing on the tail), represented the future. Although with their corrugated skinning they lacked aerodynamic elegance, these aircraft were immensely sturdy and capacious flying machines.

The designation W.33 was applied to the aircraft powered by an in-line engine, usually the Junkers L-5, but the designation was changed to the better-known W.34 with the installation of a radial powerplant. The aircraft was

Above: NX7465 Queen of the Air *was a W.33 registered in the United States in the 1930s.*

available with wheel or float landing gear.

A total of 199 W.33s was built, and W.34s saw extensive service with the Luftwaffe from its formation until the end of World War II. In military service, in addition to their use as transports, these aircraft made fine navigation trainers. The freighter versions had a large compartment which was accessed via the side door.

Below: Like this example of a W.34, many W.33s and W.34s were built with open cockpits.

The principal difference between the W.33 and W.34 was the type of powerplant fitted. While the former had a liquid-cooled Junkers L-5 in-line engine, the W.34 was fitted with one of a number of different types of air-cooled radial motor.

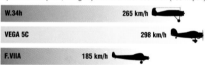

W.34F

Many W.33s and W.34s, like this Canadian-registered example, were exported. CF-AQB flew with Pacific Western Airlines. Float-equipped examples had an enlarged rudder and dorsal fin to maintain flight stability.

W.34h

Type: utility transport and communications aircraft

Powerplant: one 492-kW (660-hp.) BMW 132 radial piston engine

Maximum speed: 265 km/h (164 m.p.h.)

Range: 900 km (560 mi.)

Service ceiling: 6300 m (20,700 ft.)

Weights: empty 1700 kg (3,740 lb.); maximum take-off 3200 kg (7,040 lb.)

Accommodation: pilot and pilot/navigator in enclosed cockpit, plus up to 740 kg (1,628 lb.) of freight or up to six passengers

Dimensions:
span	17.75 m	(58 ft. 3 in.)
length	10.27 m	(33 ft. 8 in.)
height	3.53 m	(11 ft. 7 in.)
wing area	43 m²	(463 sq. ft.)

The first W.34 was powered by a 313-kW (420-hp.) Gnome Rhône Jupiter radial engine. Later examples used various motors, including Siemens, BMW and Bristol engines. In Canada, Pratt & Whitney Wasps were sometimes used.

The W.33 and W.34 were cantilever, low-wing monoplanes with the corrugated metal skin that was becoming a Junkers trademark. The earliest examples had an open cockpit.

Intended primarily as a freighter, in airline service these aircraft could also be fitted with up to six seats. In this role cabin windows were often included in the fuselage.

Worldwide service with airlines was followed by other roles, such as aerial photography and crop dusting. Using floats, the W.34 was popular for flying into inaccessible regions (in Colombia, for example). In Canada, aircraft like this one were used as fire-bombers.

ACTION DATA

MAXIMUM SPEED

Although the Fokker F.VIIa was powered by the same Jupiter engine as some versions of the W.34, its extra weight reduced its top speed considerably. Lockheed's Vega established an excellent reputation for speed, being capable of almost 300 km/h (185 m.p.h.).

W.34h	265 km/h
VEGA 5C	298 km/h
F.VIIA	185 km/h

SERVICE CEILING

With the motor installed, the size of the Fokker hampered its performance. It was not until the enlarged tri-motored variants appeared that this improved. The W.34 had the best ceiling capability of the three aircraft, although the Lockheed Vega was not far behind.

W.34h 6300 m (20,700 ft.)
VEGA 5C 5790 m (19,000 ft.)
F.VIIA 2600 m (8,500 ft.)

RANGE

Both the Vega and F.VIIa had a better range than the W.34, despite the latter's record-breaking flights in the late 1920s. However, all three aircraft were still capable of flights of around 1000 km (600 mi.). The Fokker and Lockheed had 30 per cent more range, partly due to greater fuel capacity.

W.34h 900 km (560 mi.)
VEGA 5C 1165 km (720 mi.)
F.VIIA 1160 km (715 mi.)

Junkers inter-war civil transports

■ **G.31:** Flown in 1926, this tri-motored airliner was an enlarged development of the G.24, itself an extension of the F.13 design.

■ **G.38:** Only two of these remarkable four-engined airliners were built. They could accommodate 34 passengers.

■ **Ju 60:** A high-performance single-engined monoplane, the Ju 60 was intended to compete with the Lockheed Orion. Two were built.

■ **Ju 86:** The first twin-engined passenger and freight aircraft designed to employ diesel engines, the Ju 86 was used by airlines and the Luftwaffe.

JUNKERS

G.38

● 34-passenger luxury airliner ● Largest landplane of its time

▲ It was like nothing else in the skies, but despite its size and appearance the G.38 was a practical airliner. It was not fast, but its massive wing gave the huge machine good take-off and landing ability.

Built in Dessau, the Junkers G.38 was a giant monoplane airliner with four engines, fixed undercarriage and a biplane tail – and windows in its wings. This amazing flying machine was the product of an easier, happier era of luxury air travel. Inside were upholstered lounge seats, a hat rack and two toilets. In Lufthansa colours, it gave top-quality catered service in the pre-war 1930s.

JUNKERS G.38

▲ Dwarfed
A light aircraft like the Junkers A.50 could almost land on the massive 44-metre wing of the G.38, which was the biggest in the world.

◀ Wing seats
The wing was so thick that the engines could be reached in flight. Two three-seat cabins were actually housed in the leading edge.

▲ Engine change
Changing an L8 engine was a complex affair, using cranes and pulleys and a lot of sweat.

▼ Flaps down
With its effective high-lift flaps, the G.38 had a short take-off run and a very low stalling speed.

◀▲ Lufthansa's pride ▶
The G.38 was the world's largest landplane and was a monument to the ingenuity of Junkers. It generated great interest in its services to Rome, London, Stockholm and many cities in Germany.

FACTS AND FIGURES

➤ The first flight of the Junkers G.38 took place on 6 November 1929.

➤ Lufthansa changed the second G.38's engines twice after receiving delivery.

➤ A single Junkers G.38 served with the Luftwaffe in 1939 for transport duties in Norway and the Balkans.

➤ The second G.38 was destroyed by RAF bombers at Athens on 17 May 1940.

➤ The first G.38 was modified to be the same standard as the second.

➤ Japan's copy of the G.38, the Ki-20, was destroyed by American bombing at the start of the war, along with a Ju 52.

PROFILE

Luxurious giant from Junkers

Even the landing gear of the G.38 was a unique piece of engineering. It carried two main wheels on tandem mountings, with a compressed air braking system powered by a diesel engine mounted in the wing.

No feature of this behemoth of air commerce was more impressive than the large windows which made up the leading edge of the wings. Inside each wing, adjacent to the fuselage, was a compartment which housed three passengers in comfort. Remaining passengers in the Junkers G.38 occupied a fuselage, typically ribbed with corrugated metal, which gave them every

luxury – even a smoking lounge. When the 'Deutschland', the first of the two G.38s to be built, was shown to German airline officials, they knew it would be successful on long-distance routes. But the airline career of the magnificent G.38 was brief. The first example crashed in 1936 and was written off. After war was declared, the second, which had been named after President Hindenburg, was taken over by the Luftwaffe and

participated in the 1940 parachute assault on Norway. Six Mitsubishi Ki-20s, bomber versions of the Junkers G.38, were built in secret in Japan between 1931 and 1936. Designated Type 92 Super Heavy bomber, they had nine guns and a five ton bombload, and may have been intended for an attack on Singapore.

A small buffet and kitchen area was located at the top of the forward fuselage.

The nose area housed the navigator, radio operator and one or two engineers. Later, two or three passengers were allocated nose seats, which offered a superb view.

G.38

D-APIS was the second G.38, entering Lufthansa service in July 1932. It served in this role until 1939, when it was taken over by the Luftwaffe.

The captain and first officer occupied the flight deck.

The 'President von Hindenburg' originally carried the serial D-2500, converting to the D-APIS registration shown here in 1934. In Luftwaffe colours it carried the serial GF-GG.

The wing contained a large number of separate fuel tanks. Baggage was stored in compartments behind the two leading-edge cabins.

Hatches in the galley gave access to the wings and engines.

The tail unit of the second aircraft was extensively modified, having three fins and rudders.

The biggest change to the second aircraft was the installation of Junkers Jumo diesel engines, giving a significant increase in range.

The huge undercarriage spats were later removed, as they were found to make little difference to performance.

Passengers in the rear cabin sat in 13 rows of two. In the original configuration, the cabin just behind the cockpit could have beds fitted.

A second toilet was fitted at the rear of the cabin, behind the smoking compartment.

G.38

Type: long-range transport

Powerplant: four 559-kW (750-hp.) Junkers Jumo 204 12-cylinder horizontally opposed diesel engines

Maximum speed: 210 km/h (130 m.p.h.)

Range: about 2000 km (1,200 mi.)

Service ceiling: 5800 m (19,000 ft.)

Weights: empty 14,900 kg (32,780 lb.); loaded 25,488 kg (56,074 lb.)

Accommodation: seven/eight crew; 32 or 34 passengers (26 in main cabin, and three in each of two wingroot cabins); occasionally two passengers in the fuselage nose

Dimensions: span   44.00 m (144 ft. 4 in.)
length   23.20 m (76 ft.)
height   7.00 m (23 ft.)
wing area 294 m² (3,163 sq. ft.)

ACTION DATA

MAXIMUM SPEED

The G.38 was not the fastest of aircraft even when new, being capable of only a stately 210 km/h (130 m.p.h.) at best. At that, it was marginally better than the contemporary British H.P.42, but both were to be left far behind within five years by new-generation airliners like the classic Douglas DC-3.

G.38	210 km/h (130 m.p.h.)
DC-3	370 km/h (229 m.p.h.)
H.P.42	204 km/h (126 m.p.h.)

RANGE

The diesel engines which powered the G.38 were fairly efficient for their time, and together with the massive fuel storage capacity of the huge wings they gave the big Junkers airliner a very good range. The immense drag of the Handley Page's biplane wings meant that on long-distance flights it had to stop for fuel far more frequently.

H.P.42 805 km (500 mi.)

DC-3 2400 km (1,500 mi.)

G.38 2000 km (1,200 mi.)

PAYLOAD

Although it was the world's biggest landplane, the G.38 could not carry as many passengers as the H.P.42 when the British airliner was used on European routes. When fitted with a luxury interior, however, the Handley Page only carried about 20 passengers. The DC-3 had a smaller load, but it could carry its passengers faster and over greater distances.

H.P.42 38 passengers

DC-3 21 passengers

G.38 34 passengers

The rise of Lufthansa

■ **AMALGAMATION:** Formed in 1926, Lufthansa combined the assets of early German private airlines like Deruluft, which pioneered the Berlin–Moscow route.

■ **ABOVE THE WEATHER:** The three-engined 10-seater Rohrbach Roland could fly at 5000 m (16,000 ft.), and in 1927 was used for trials across the Alps.

■ **ATLANTIC PIONEER:** Lufthansa led the way from Europe to South America. The South Atlantic sector was flown by long-range Dornier flying-boats.

■ **JUNKERS WORKHORSE:** From 1932, the reliable Junkers Ju 52 was used with great success on Lufthansa's European and Asian routes.

■ **CONDOR:** Entering service in 1938, the Focke-Wulf Fw 200 Condor was the most advanced airliner developed in Europe before World War II.

JUNKERS

Ju 52

● Three-engine transport ● 60 years of service ● Operated worldwide

With it's corrugated metal skin and ugly exterior, the Ju 52 won no beauty contests, but this aircraft was loved: when a Ju 52 was restored by Lufthansa recently, the sight touched the hearts of airline pilots who had flown it long ago. Although designed as a pioneering airliner, the Ju 52 was also a military aircraft, serving the Luftwaffe as a bomber, transporter, trainer and minesweeper.

▲ A Luftwaffe pilot refuels his Ju 52 during the Norway campaign in 1940. The dependable trimotor carried German forces throughout the war, proving reliable and sturdy in appalling conditions.

JUNKERS Ju 52

▲ French Junkers
The Ju 52 was built in France as the AAC.1 Toucan. In the early 1950s it was used as a bomber in Indochina.

▲ Makeshift bomber
Before World War II the Ju 52 was pressed into service as a bomber. A strange feature was the retractable 'dustbin' for the ventral gunner.

▼ Indestructible transport
Junkers had a reputation for making strong aircraft, and none came tougher than the Ju 52.

Post-war survivor ▲
Ju 52s are still flying today, a testament to their outstanding design. The Swiss air force flew three on transport tasks for years, although in their later life they were employed as film stars rather than serious military types.

Airliner success ▶
Before World War II the Ju 52 established itself as one of the world's top airliners, and sold around the world. Even British Airways operated the type.

FACTS AND FIGURES

➤ The Ju 52/3m (MS), or *Minensucher*, carried an enormous magnetised metal hoop to detonate mines at sea.

➤ Ju 52s were manufactured in France, Hungary and Spain after the war.

➤ The Junkers was fondly known to airmen as Tante Ju ('Auntie Ju').

➤ Although it looked similar, the Junkers Ju 52 was almost one-third larger and heavier than the Ford Trimotor.

➤ The Ju 52 was derived from a successful single-engine aircraft.

➤ Lufthansa has a Ju 52 that has been restored to its 1930s appearance.

PROFILE

'Auntie Ju': still proudly flying

The Junkers Ju 52 was one of the most important aircraft in European aviation history. In the world of aerial commerce the Ju 52 became the backbone of Lufthansa during the 1930s, operating from Norway to South America. For its time, the Ju 52 gave passengers a stylish experience and a level of comfort that had previously been impossible.

War changed the Ju 52. Intended as a servant, it became a soldier. The Junkers trimotor was used as a bomber in early fighting, but became best-known as a military transport. Again and again, in the early days of fighting which were so successful for Germany, elite paratroopers leaped from the Ju 52 to make lightning assaults from Oslo to Crete. It also operated extensively in North Africa, and on the Eastern Front the Ju 52 was the Luftwaffe's most valuable transport asset.

The Ju 52 was equally at home on floats or skis as it was on wheels. This Swedish aircraft was used on airliner duties around the Scandinavian coastline.

Today, the few airworthy Ju 52s are priceless treasures of aviation. At air shows they give us the sounds, feel and smell of an earlier time when great aircraft performed pioneering feats.

To improve engine cooling without increasing drag, the Ju 52's outer engines were fitted with narrow-chord cowlings. In Ju-Air service they are painted royal blue.

Ju 52/3mG4e

HB-HOP was one of three Ju 52s delivered to the Swiss air force in 1939. When withdrawn from service in 1981 the aircraft was acquired by Ju-Air, which operates charter flights to help raise funds for the aviation museum at Dübendorf.

In civil trim, the Ju 52 can carry 17 passengers, though in military use 19 fully-equipped paratroopers or two tons of cargo was the standard payload.

In their military careers, Swiss Ju 52s performed a number of tasks. Paratroopers used the same door as the passengers to exit.

JU-AIR **HB-HOP** **A-703**

In its time, the Ju 52 has been powered by a variety of engines. The Ju-Air machine has the most common fit: three BMW 132 radial engines each delivering 392 kW (525 hp.).

The Ju 52 featured a conventional fixed undercarriage. Although the track was somewhat narrow, the large and fairly soft tyres meant that the aircraft could cope with rough fields.

Professor Hugo Junkers was one of the pioneers in the construction of all-metal aeroplanes. His aircraft were readily identified by their corrugated metal skin, which was used to stiffen the structure against torsion.

The Ju-Air trimotors retain the natural metal finish worn during their Swiss military service, along with Swiss national markings on the tail.

ACTION DATA

MAXIMUM SPEED

The Ju 52 first flew in single-engined form a month before the H.P.42. Although smaller, it was a generation ahead of the lumbering British biplane. But the Junkers was soon to be outclassed in turn by the classic DC-3.

Ju 52
290 km/h (180 m.p.h.)

H.P.42
160 km/h (126 m.p.h.)

DC-3
333 km/h (205 m.p.h.)

RANGE

The early 1930s saw the performance of commercial aircraft leap ahead tremendously. The Ju 52 had the range to fly between Europe's major cities non-stop, and proved immensely popular with airlines all over the Continent. The later DC-3 could eclipse all airliners of the time.

H.P.42
800 km (500 mi.)

DC-3
3400 km (2,100 mi.)

Ju 52
1290 km (800 mi.)

PAYLOAD

Air transport was expensive, and only a small number of people could afford to travel the skies. Nevertheless, demand soared in the 1930s, and aircraft carried two and three times as many passengers as their equivalents of only five years before.

H.P.42
4 crew and 38 passengers

Ju 52
3 crew and 17 passengers

DC-3
4 crew and 21-32 passengers

Versatile 'Tante Ju'

■ **AIRLINER:** The Ju 52 first rose to prominence as a 17-seat airliner. This aircraft flew the first Berlin-London service in 1932.

■ **SPANISH BOMBER:** During the Spanish Civil War the Ju 52 flew both transport and bomber missions. It could carry six 90-kg (200-lb.) bombs.

■ **NORWAY CAMPAIGN:** Nearly 600 Ju 52s took part in the invasion of Norway, where the type performed well on snow-covered airfields.

■ **MEDITERRANEAN TRANSPORT:** The Ju 52 is perhaps best-remembered for the attack on Crete, during which 174 of the type were lost.

■ **FLYING AMBULANCE:** One vital job assigned to the Ju 52 was the rapid evacuation of wounded soldiers away from the battle area.

LEARJET INC.

LEARJET

● The first great 'biz-jet' ● Bill Lear's classic design

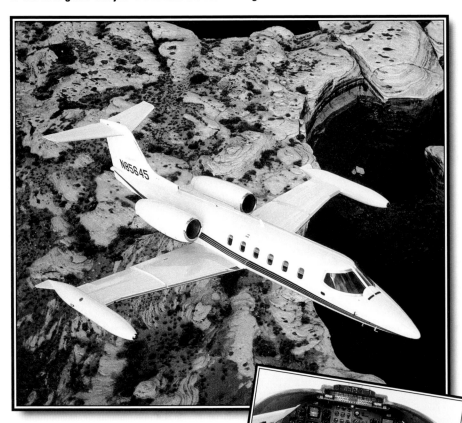

A sports coupé of the skies, the Learjet handles like a fighter (indeed, its sleek design is based on that of a Swiss fighter) and gives speed and luxury to business travellers. One of the most streamlined aircraft ever, the Learjet flies today in dozens of countries, not solely as an executive jet but also on military and scientific assignments. The Learjet is economical as well as speedy in getting small numbers of people quickly from one location to another.

▲ *Millionaire William P. Lear developed the Learjet from a single-seat fighter design for the Swiss air force. Since then the original Learjet has spawned an entire family of advanced business jets.*

PHOTO FILE

LEARJET INC. LEARJET

▲ The Learjet family
Over the years the Learjet family has grown in number, and the aircraft in size. Note the increasing difference in length between the Learjet 24 (top), Lear 25 and Lear 35 in this picture.

▲ Eye in the sky
Its high cruising altitude and long endurance make the Learjet an ideal photo-survey aircraft. This Brazilian Learjet carries a special camera pack for the task.

◀ Mile-high style
While Learjets have always been a little on the small side, passengers can be carried in luxury and privacy exceeding that of any standard airliner.

▼ Special missions
The Japanese Air Self-Defence Force operates four converted Learjet 36As, called U-36As. They are packed with sophisticated radars and electronic jamming equipment.

Learjets around the world ▶
The early versions of the Learjet were fast, but short-legged. As Learjets grew in size, new engines and advanced wing designs gave the latest generation truly intercontinental range.

FACTS AND FIGURES

➤ The company making the Learjet has changed names seven times in 30 years.

➤ Eighty Learjets serve in the US Air Force as the C-21A.

➤ Golf celebrity Arnold Palmer flew a Learjet around the world on a goodwill journey in 1976.

➤ Sources say this executive jet has appeared in more movie and television films than any other aircraft.

➤ The original Learjet 23 of 1963 carried five passengers in its small interior; today's Learjet 60 can carry up to nine in a spacious 'stand-up' cabin.

PROFILE

The pocket rocket

The Learjet is one of the few aircraft named after a man, William Lear, who recruited designers to try features of a Swiss fighter on a revolutionary business jet. The goal was speed and luxury in business travel, and Lear achieved it. The aircraft provides the very best for hundreds of corporate jet owners.

A super ship to fly, the Learjet boasts pilot comfort, simple controls and easy handling. This familiar aircraft

Throughout its life the Learjet has been known the world over simply as the 'Lear'.

has a razor-like wing and twin engines out back; some models use winglets which poke up to improve the flow of air, affording better fuel consumption.

Although it is small enough to be very personal and can fly to and from the shortest of runways, the Learjet has global reach, able to cross oceans and

cruise at high altitude.

A few nations adapted this corporate jet for military work, giving the Lear patrol duties. But to most users Learjet means civilian journeys with speed, luxury and convenience.

All modern Learjets, such as the Learjet 31 and Learjet 60, are fitted with distinctive upturned winglets. These improve the aerodynamics and increase range.

Learjet 35/36

Type: long-range executive transport

Powerplant: two Garrett TFE-731-2-2B turbofan engines offering 15.57 kN (3,500 lb.) thrust each

Maximum speed: 850 km/h (528 m.p.h.) at 12,495 m (41,000 ft.)

Range: 5015 km (3,116 mi.) with four passengers and fuel

Service ceiling: 13,715 m (45,000 ft.) normal, but maximum operating altitude in excess of 15,000 m (49,200 ft.)

Weights: empty 4152 kg (9,154 lb.); loaded 8500 kg (18,739 lb.)

Payload: two pilots, eight passengers and 480 kg (1,058 lb.) of luggage

Dimensions: span 12.04 m (39 ft. 6 in.); length 14.83 m (48 ft. 8 in.); height 3.73 m (12 ft. 3 in.); wing area 23.53 m² (253 sq. ft.)

LEARJET 55 'LONGHORN'

The Model 55 Learjet was the first version to feature winglets. It was dubbed the Longhorn, as the winglets resembled the horns of longhorn cattle.

Despite all the changes that have occurred to the shape of the Learjet over the years, its long, slender nose has remained a constant trademark.

Winglets – developed by a NASA engineer named Richard Whitcomb – are now found on many aircraft, but when they first appeared on the Learjet 'Longhorn' they were revolutionary.

The Learjet was the aircraft which popularised the term 'biz-jet' (short for business jet), and it opened up the global market for such aircraft.

The Learjet 55 was powered by Garrett TFE-731 turbofans. This very versatile engine could also be found on many other 'biz-jets'.

Production of the Learjet 55 ended in 1992 after 147 had been delivered. It has been succeeded by the even larger Learjet 60.

The Learjet 55 'Longhorn' was introduced in 1979. It was not the greatest-selling Learjet version, but paved the way for even more advanced designs.

'V'-shaped ventral fins were first seen on the Learjet 55C. They helped make the aircraft more stable in flight and have since been added to all subsequent Learjet designs.

ACTION DATA

PASSENGER LOAD

The original Learjet was very much the sports car of the executive jet world. Although small and compact, it was an immediate success. However, succeeding jets cater more to the corporate market, and can generally carry more passengers.

LEARJET 35 UP TO 8
CITATION II UP TO 10
MODEL 125-800 UP TO 14

MAXIMUM SPEED

Speed and luxury were Bill Lear's aims, and he achieved them with the Learjet, one of the fastest non-military aircraft flying today.

LEARJET 35	850 km\h (528 m.p.h.)
CITATION II	713 km/h (443 m.p.h.)
MODEL 125-800	840 km/h (522 m.p.h.)

SERVICE CEILING

The Learjet has superb altitude performance, being able to cruise higher than any other civil aircraft except Concorde. Flying at such heights it avoids all weather problems and can keep clear of congested air routes. However, care needs to be taken: the gap between maximum and minimum flying speeds at 15,000 m (49,200 ft.) can be as low as 90 km/h (56 m.p.h.), and it is possible to fall into a high-speed stall from which recovery can be difficult.

LEARJET 35 13,715 m (45,000 ft.)
CITATION II 7600 m (24,930 ft.)
MODEL 125-800 10,000 m (32,800 ft.)

A 30-year success story

■ **LEARJET 23:** When Bill Lear unveiled the first Learjet in 1963, the small yet speedy aircraft was soon dubbed the 'pocket rocket'. Note the large cabin windows.

■ **LEARJET 35/36:** The best-selling Learjets have been the Model 35 and 36. The latter is heavier, but both are identical from the outside. This is a military target-towing version.

■ **LEARJET 55:** The Lear 55 was a radical departure in Learjet design. Gone were the familiar wingtip fuel tanks; in their place came special drag-reducing winglets.

■ **LEARJET 60:** It resembles the Lear 55, but today's long-range Learjet 60 is a larger and far more advanced business jet. First flying in 1990, it is the ultimate Learjet.

LET

L-410 TURBOLET/610

● Czech twin-turboprop ● Huge Aeroflot orders ● Rough-field capability

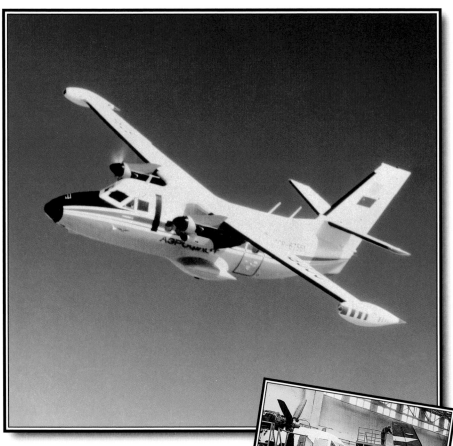

F lown initially in April 1969, the L-410 was one of the first aircraft designed solely by LET. The company had been established in 1950 on the site of the old Avia factory at Kunovice, and had graduated to transport aircraft after building military trainers, air taxis, gliders and agricultural aircraft. LET has built more than 1,000 L-410s, many of them for the Soviet Union, and, in December 1988, it flew the first prototype of the 40-seat L-610.

▲ LET found
that orders for the L-410 were slowing down by the early 1990s, after the loss of Aeroflot as its most important customer. The aircraft still serves in some numbers, however.

LET L-410 TURBOLET/610

▼ Introducing the UVP
In 1977, LET flew the first prototype of the L-410UVP. The aircraft had a slightly extended cabin and longer wingspan.

▲ Multi-blade technology
Five-bladed propellers by the famous Czech manufacturer, Avia, were introduced on the L-410UVP-E from 1984.

▼ Soviet backbone
L-410UVP-Es formed the backbone of Aeroflot's feederliner fleet and are still in service.

▲ First of the 610s
Similar in configuration to the L-410, the L-610 is, in fact, a completely new design. It has seats for 40 passengers.

◀ Hungarian mystery
This Hungarian L-410UVP carries a civilian registration and an unusual equipment fit. A bubble observation window is located at the rear of the flight deck, with unidentified blister fairings on the rear fuselage. The aircraft is most likely equipped for some form of geophysical survey or exploration.

FACTS AND FIGURES

➤ In 1991, LET began deliveries to satisfy an Aeroflot requirement for 600 L-610s, but financial problems intervened.

➤ Neither cabin pressurisation nor air conditioning is fitted to the L-410.

➤ At the end of 1992, LET had 50 unsold L-410s after Aeroflot cancelled orders.

➤ As an ambulance, the L-410 carries six stretchers, five seated patients and a medical attendant.

➤ An aerial photography L-410 for Hungary had a non-retractable nosewheel.

➤ The L-610 has been designed to replace the An-24 and Yak-40.

PROFILE

Czech-built feederliner

LET built only 31 of the initial L-410A model, with Pratt & Whitney PT6A engines, before switching to the L-410M. This used locally built Walter M-601 turboprops. Most of the 110 produced were delivered to Aeroflot, and the Czech army also used a small number.

The M-601B engine with water injection was used for the L-410UVP, which has longer wings, revised control surfaces and improved performance in hot-and-high conditions. More than 500 were built and, from 1986, the UVP-E introduced a bigger, 19-seat cabin and five-bladed propellers.

Aeroflot was the main customer for the L-410 and, in 1977, the Soviet airline asked for a bigger aircraft with more seats. The specified Motorlet M-602 engine would not be ready in time, so Aeroflot proposed a four-engined model with M-601s, only to change its mind again later.

The prototype L-610, with two M-602s, eventually flew in December 1988. LET then decided to build a version for the Western market with General Electric CT7 engines. It flew for the first time in December 1991, but the programme has subsequently been delayed.

Below: In the event of an engine failure, a bank-control surface pops up automatically ahead of the aileron on the side with the running engine, to reduce lift on that wing.

Above: Although by far the largest operator of the L-410, Aeroflot was not alone in its use of the Czech workhorse.

L-410UVP-E

Type: twin-turboprop regional airliner

Powerplant: two 559-kW (750-hp.) Motorlet Walter M-601E turboprops

Maximum cruising speed: 380 km/h (236 m.p.h.) at 4200 m (14,000 ft.)

Range: 1380 km (855 mi.) with maximum fuel at 4200 m (14,000 ft.)

Service ceiling: 6320 m (20,700 ft.)

Weights: empty 3985 kg (8,767 lb.); maximum take-off 6400 kg (14,080 lb.)

Accommodation: 19 passengers

Dimensions:
span	19.98 m	(65 ft. 6 in.)
length	14.42 m	(47 ft. 4 in.)
height	5.83 m	(62 ft. 9 in.)
wing area	35.18 m²	(379 sq. ft.)

L-410UVP-E TURBOLET

Aeroflot employs its L-410UVP-E aircraft alongside An-28s for internal services. The harsh and variable Russian climate led the airline to specify an operational range of -50°C (-58°F) to +50°C (122°F).

A maximum of 19 passengers are carried by the L-410UVP-E. The cabin is heated by engine bleed air and includes a wardrobe and toilet. Heating, and stowage for bulky winter clothing are especially important in Russia.

Although the earlier L-410 models had Pratt & Whitney engines, later variants such as the L-410UVP-E have indigenously-designed Motorlet Walter M-601E turboprops and Avia propellers.

An extra 200 litres (53 gal.) of fuel are carried in each wingtip tank. These tanks are optional fittings, but L-410s are never seen without them. Navigation lights are carried on the tanks and the starboard tank sometimes holds a powerful landing light.

The structure of the L-410 is almost entirely of metal. Unusually for a modern type, although the elevators and rudders have a metal structure, they are fabric-covered.

Alternative roles for the L-410UVP-E include aerial photography, ambulance duties, firefighting and parachute dropping. In the latter role, up to 18 parachutists and their jump master are carried. In the passenger role, the rear fuselage is occupied by a baggage compartment.

CCCP-67551

АЭРОФЛОТ

ACTION DATA

ECONOMIC CRUISING SPEED
Among these types, the L-410UVP-E offers the highest cruising speed; a useful feature in a feederliner which earns its keep by transporting passengers from smaller airports to important hubs.

L-410UVP-E	365 km/h (266 m.p.h.)
Do 228-212	333 km/h (206 m.p.h.)
An-28 'CASH'	335 km/h (208 m.p.h.)

TAKE-OFF RUN TO 10.7 M (35 FT.)
Although LET designed the L-410 for rough-field operations, it has only moderate STOL (Short Take-Off and Landing) performance, especially when compared to the PZL Mielec/Antonov An-28.

L-410UVP-E	685 m (2,250 ft.)
Do 228-212	793 m (2,600 ft.)
An-28 'CASH'	410 m (1,350 ft.)

RANGE
Dornier's Do 228-212 offers excellent range and good operating economics. It is commonly used across Western Europe and in America, but has yet to break into the Eastern European market, which is still dominated by the L-410. The An-28 is now built only in Poland.

L-410UVP-E 1380 km (855 mi.)
Do 228-212 2148 km (1,330 mi.)
An-28 'CASH' 1365 km (850 mi.)

Post-war civil designs from LET

■ L-200A MORAVA:
This twin-engined four-/five-seat light business and taxi monoplane first flew on 8 April 1957. More than 1000 were built in three versions; the L-200D entered production in 1962. Power came from two 156.5-kW (210-hp.) M-337 in-line piston engines.

■ Z-37 CMELAK: Flown in prototype form on 29 June 1963, this agricultural aircraft has also found applications as a mail and cargo transport during the winter months. An M-462RF radial of 234.7 kW (315 hp.) powered the aircraft, production of which ended in 1975. Around 600 were built.

■ Z-37T AGRO TURBO:
A turboprop-powered Z-37, the Agro Turbo is built by Zlin as the Z-137T. Powered by a Motorlet Walter M-601Z rated at 365 kW (490 hp.), the aircraft has found sales in at least six countries. New features include a 1000-litre/900-kg (264-gal./1,980-lb.) hopper.

LOCKHEED

1, 2 & 5 VEGA

● High-speed monoplane ● Wooden monocoque ● Diverse roles

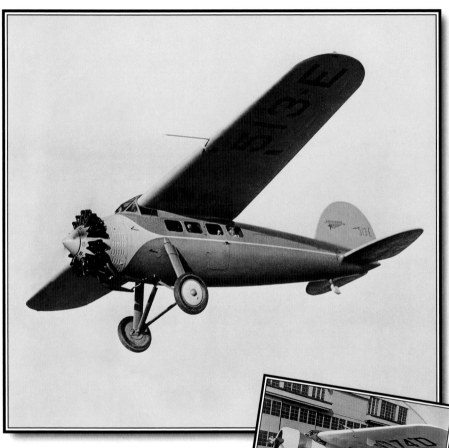

Although his first enterprise, the Loughead Aircraft Manufacturing Company, had failed, Allan Loughead did not give up. Convinced that wooden monocoque construction, as used in the Loughead S-1, had potential, he re-hired Jack Northrop and raised enough capital to found the Lockheed Aircraft Company in 1926. Its first aircraft, the Vega, was an immediate success as an airliner and set numerous records.

▲ *Corporate and private transport was one role tackled by the Lockheed Vega. Others were air ambulance, military transport and floatplane transport.*

LOCKHEED 1, 2 & 5 VEGA

▼ **Still flying in 1955**
Built in 1929 as a Vega 1, this float-equipped aircraft was modified to Vega 2D standard with a Wasp Junior engine.

▲ **Vega on skis**
Equipped for the colder climates of Norway, this Vega has skis fitted in place of wheels. Other ski-equipped Vegas were operated in Canada.

▼ **First trans-Arctic flight**
X3903 was only the fourth Vega 1 off the production line. On 15 April 1928 it took off on a historic flight from Alaska to Spitzbergen – the first ever crosing of the Arctic. In November it made an equally impressive trans-Antarctic flight.

▲ **Army Air Corps Vega**
The US armed forces' first Lockheed type was this Y1C-12 (DL-1), acquired for evaluation as a staff transport.

American airliner ▶
Transcontinental and Western Air Inc. (part of what later became TWA) operated this Vega 5C as a faster alternative to the larger, but slower, Ford Trimotor.

FACTS AND FIGURES

➤ Vegas were used to support American exploratory expeditions to both the Arctic and Antarctic regions.

➤ A Vega 5 made the first non-stop Los Angeles–New York flight in August 1928.

➤ In 1980, six Vegas remained extant; at least one was still airworthy.

➤ Jack Northrop chose the 'Vega' name, starting the tradition of naming Lockheed aircraft after stars and planets.

➤ The USAAC Y1C-12 (DL-1) flew a total of 999 hours before retirement in 1935.

➤ The last Lockheed-built Vega was used by the USAAC as a UC-101 until 1942.

PROFILE

Lockheed's first design

Below: This early production Vega has an uncowled Pratt & Whitney Wasp radial. Cowlings were often fitted later and increased top speed.

Above: In US airline service the Vega was used for passenger-carrying mail services. Although smaller than other airliners, it was considerably faster.

With its wooden fuselage, wooden internally-braced cantilever wing (as pioneered by Fokker) and a 149-kW (200-hp.) Wright Whirlwind nine-cylinder radial engine, the first Vega 1 had an unhappy fate.

Bought by newspaper owner George Hearst, it was entered in the 1927 Oakland to Hawaii air race. First flown on 4 July, the aircraft left Oakland, with seven other machines, on 16 August. It was never seen again. Despite the strange disappearance,

Lockheed went on to build 128 Vegas. A number were employed by US and Latin American airlines or as private transports. Others posted a number of speed, distance and altitude records between the late 1920s and mid-1930s.

The main production variant was the Vega 5 of 1928, which carried five or six passengers. In all, 35 were built, a few with floats. A Pratt & Whitney Wasp engine rated at between 306 and 336 kW replaced the Whirlwind. In July 1929, the

Detroit Aircraft Corporation bought Lockheed and developed a modernised Vega 5 as the DL-1. Two Vegas entered service with the USAAC and at least one flew with Republican forces in the Spanish Civil War as a transport and light bomber. A number are preserved.

Vega 1

Type: high-speed cabin monoplane

Powerplant: one 149-kW (200-hp.) Wright Whirlwind J5 Series air-cooled radial piston engine

Maximum speed: 217 km/h (135 m.p.h.)

Cruising speed: 190 km/h (118 m.p.h.)

Initial climb rate: 259 m/min (850 f.p.m.)

Range: 1450 km (900 mi.)

Service ceiling: 4570 m (15,000 ft.)

Weights: empty 748 kg (1,646 lb.); loaded 1315 kg (2,893 lb.)

Accommodation: one pilot and up to four passengers

Dimensions:
span	12.49 m	(40 ft. 11 in.)
length	8.38 m	(27 ft. 6 in.)
height	2.55 m	(8 ft. 4 in.)
wing area	25.55 m²	(275 sq. ft.)

VEGA 5

NC288W was flown by Varney Air Transport Inc. (later Continental Airlines) which was founded in the Rocky Mountains area in the early 1930s, with four Vegas, each equipped to carry nine passengers.

Exceptionally strong wing construction was a feature of the Vega. The wings were internally braced, removing the need for struts, and of cantilever design.

Lockheed's wooden monocoque construction methods were pioneered by company designer Jack Northrop (later a manufacturer in his own right).

U.S. AIR MAIL

VARNEY AIR TRANSPORT INC

VAT

US AIR MAIL
VARNEY AIR TRANSPORT INC
LOCKHEED
A.M. ROUTE 29

NC 288W

Vegas were fitted with a wide variety of engines. As the aircraft grew in size and capacity, more horsepower was required. Most engines were conventional radial designs, although at least one airframe was fitted with a diesel motor.

Most early Vegas were initially equipped to carry four passengers, though airlines made their own modifications. This aircraft and others in the Varney fleet were able to hold nine people. More powerful engines were fitted to cope with the extra weight.

ACTION DATA

MAXIMUM SPEED

The Lockheed Vega, as a high-speed monoplane mail plane, had a healthy speed advantage over its contemporaries like the Junkers W34h and the de Havilland DH.84. Both those aircraft were five/six-seat commercial types of the 1920s and 1930s. British commercial design was lagging significantly behind that of the US during this period. European civil design, while including monoplanes, was not producing aircraft equivalent to US types.

VEGA 5B	300 km/h (186 m.p.h.)
W34h	265 km/h (164 m.p.h.)
DH.84	206 km/h (128 m.p.h.)

POWER

The Lockheed was able to reach higher top speeds with a less powerful engine than the Junkers W34h. Its wooden construction would have accounted for this, the Junkers being a heavier, all-metal design. The Dragon was a twin-engined aircraft, but even the combined power of its engines was only just over half that of the single-engined Vega.

VEGA 5B	W34h	DH.84 DRAGON Mk I
335 kW (450 hp.)	492 kW (660 hp.)	194 kW (260 hp.)

RANGE

Although it carried less fuel than the W34h, a more economic engine gave the Vega a better range than its German rival. Both types had a greater range than the de Havilland Dragon. That type was limited to a very modest 740 km (458 mi.), less than two-thirds of the range of the Vega.

W34h
900 km (558 mi.)

DH.84 DRAGON Mk I
740 km (458 mi.)

VEGA 5B
1170 km (725 mi.)

US commercial types of the 1930s

■ **BOEING 247:** A revolutionary design at a time when American airliners were mainly heavy biplanes, the 247 was a mostly metal monoplane.

■ **CURTISS T-32 CONDOR:** This 15-seater from the early 1930s was built with seating and sleeping accommodation, and sold well.

■ **FORD TRI-MOTOR:** Built by Ford in 1926, after its acquisition of the Stout Metal Airplane Company. Large numbers were built until 1933.

■ **VULTEE V-1A:** An eight-seat airliner, the V-1A was powered by a Wright R-1820 Cyclone and served with American Airlines.

LOCKHEED

10 ELECTRA

● All-metal design ● Twin-engined airliner ● Military versions

To many people, the Lockheed 10 Electra is known only as the aircraft in which Amelia Earhart disappeared. This unfortunate incident overshadows the career of a machine that was important in the development of passenger services with several US airlines during the 1930s. Most significantly, one of the greatest aviation engineers ever, Clarence 'Kelly' Johnson, the designer of the SR-71, was introduced to Lockheed via his work on the Electra.

▲ With the gradual passing of the airmail service, airline flights became accessible to more people, although they were still mostly for the rich. Lockheed's sleek, all-metal Electra was typical of the new breed of airliner in 1930s.

PHOTO FILE

LOCKHEED 10 ELECTRA

On the flightdeck ▶
This 1930s photograph's caption claimed that the cockpit was equipped with 'every device known to science'.

▼ Museum piece
A US-registered Electra photographed at the Ontario Air Museum in 1966. Some Model 10s remain in airworthy condition.

▼ Wartime service
Several civilian Electras were impressed into Royal Air Force service. This machine joined No. 24 Squadron in April 1940.

▼ Northwest Electra
Very early aircraft were delivered with the prototype-style windscreen, but these were modified in service.

Flying on ▶
Many smaller airlines used Electras after the war. Provincetown-Boston Airlines were the last company to fly a scheduled Electra service in the early 1970s.

FACTS AND FIGURES

➤ Lockheed was part of the Detroit Aircraft Corporation until Robert Gross took the company over in 1932.

➤ A forwards-raked windscreen was fitted to early production aircraft.

➤ Lockheed used the name Electra again in 1957, this time for its Model 188 turboprop.

➤ The Electra was the first product of the 'new' Lockheed and the company's first twin-engined aircraft.

➤ Amelia Earhart's aircraft had more powerful engines and extra fuel capacity.

➤ Britain's Prime Minister used an Electra to fly to Germany in 1938.

Pioneering all-metal airliner

The head of the Lockheed Aircraft Corporation, Robert Gross, planned a 10-seat, all-metal, single-engined airliner. Before work began, however, market research indicated that a twin-engined machines would sell better and so the design of the Electra began.

In October 1934 the US Government banned single-engined aircraft from carrying passengers at night or over rough terrain, leaving Lockheed perfectly placed to pick up airline orders. The Model 10 helped the airlines through this difficult period, as most were quite new to passenger transport since airmail had previously been their main business.

Before the Electra was delivered to the airlines, it was wind-tunnel tested at the University of Michigan, where it was touched by the hand of genius. 'Kelly' Johnson was working as a professor's assistant and recommended a few changes to the airframe. Eventually, all of these

Above: A 1986 flight for a gleaming Electra. Johnson's twin-fin layout became a feature of subsequent Lockheed designs.

modifications were adopted with great benefit to the design, and Johnson joined Lockheed.

In addition to the commercial version, a number of military models were built. Many found their way to South America and flew until the 1970s.

Above: South American Model 10 operators included the Brazilian state airline Varig. While some Electras were delivered pre-war, most South American aircraft were war-surplus or second-hand US civilian machines.

10-A Electra

Type: short-range light transport

Powerplant: two 336-kW (450-hp.) Pratt & Whitney Wasp Junior SB radial piston engines

Maximum speed: 325 km/h (202 m.p.h.) at 1525 m (5,000 ft.)

Cruising speed: 306 km/h (190 m.p.h.)

Initial climb rate: 347 m/min (1,140 f.p.m.)

Range: 1305 km (809 mi.)

Service ceiling: 5915 m (19,400 ft.)

Weights: empty 2927 kg (6,439 lb.); maximum take-off 4672 kg (10,278 lb.)

Accommodation: flight crew of two, plus 10 passengers

Dimensions:
span	16.76 m	(55 ft.)
length	11.76 m	(38 ft. 7 in.)
height	3.07 m	(10 ft. 1 in.)
wing area	42.59 m²	(458 sq. ft.)

10-A ELECTRA

Northwest received the first production Electras. Operators and passengers were pleased with the aircraft's 306-km/h (190-m.p.h.) cruising speed, which was much faster than that of previous airliners.

Northwest was the first airline to place Electras in to service. The original forwards-raked windscreens were replaced by Northwest engineers. Aircraft were also given this Johnson-inspired modification on the production line.

A single aisle separated two rows of five seats. There were no overhead luggage bins and the cabin was very basic, although the windows did have curtains.

When the Electra was introduced into service it was the only US aircraft with complete metal skinning. The Electra was one of the first truly modern airliners.

All Electras, except for 18 Wright-engined 10-Bs for the US Coast Guard, were Pratt & Whitney powered, usually fitted with the Wasp Junior engine.

When retracted, the wheels of the main undercarriage were left partly exposed. The tailwheel was not retractable.

Lockheed felt that a slow, safe landing speed was important for commercial operations. To achieve this, split flaps were installed along the inboard wing trailing edge.

Northwest took a risk by introducing Electras into service early. On 7 August 1934 an Electra crashed, just four days before the award of an Approved Type Certificate.

During initial wind-tunnel experiments, small endplate fins were added to the conventional tail. Johnson recommended that twin fins and rudders would be more suitable and these were adopted.

ACTION DATA

MAXIMUM SPEED

Douglas and Boeing produced slightly larger airliners than the Electra, taking orders away from the Model 10. Although the DC-2 had 60 per cent more power, it was barely faster than the Electra.

10-A ELECTRA	325 km/h (202 m.p.h.)
DC-2	338 km/h (210 m.p.h.)
247D	322 km/h (200 m.p.h.)

PASSENGERS

While the capacity of the Electra was initially adequate, airlines soon required more seats. This meant that the Douglas design, especially as the DC-3, replaced the Electra in many companies.

10 ELECTRA	10 passengers
DC-2	14 passengers
247D	10 passengers

RANGE

Although it was designed to operate over shorter routes, the Electra could fly further than the larger Boeing 247D. It could not match the DC-2's range however, but this was a much larger aircraft, developed very closely with the airlines and therefore suited perfectly to their range and capacity requirements.

10 ELECTRA 1305 km (810 mi.)

DC-2 1609 km (998 mi.)

247D 1199 km (745 mi.)

Lockheed twin-tails

■ **XC-35:** This heavily modified Electra was used for testing cabin pressurisation techniques in 1937.

■ **12 ELECTRA JUNIOR:** The Electra was judged to be too large for feeder services and therefore this six-seat aircraft was built.

■ **14 SUPER ELECTRA:** Although designed to compete with the DC-2/3, the 14-seater Super Electra was still too small.

■ **18 LODESTAR:** A far more successful design than the Model 14, 625 of these 18-seat aircraft were built.

LOCKHEED

18 LODESTAR

● Based on the Electra ● Extensive military use ● Corporate aircraft

Lockheed's Model 14 Super Electra had a disappointing debut as Lockheed's then largest commercial design. Its high running costs resulted in slow sales. One early customer, Northwest Airlines, even withdrew its Model 14s from use after barely two years' service. Production was suspended and a redesign carried out, during which the new Model 18's fuselage was lengthened to accommodate two more rows of seats.

▲ *Compared*
to the Lockheed 14 Electra on which it was based, the Lodestar was slightly longer, allowing a few more seats and hence a lower operating cost.

LOCKHEED 18 LODESTAR

▼ Record-breaker
In the years immediately before World War II, mail delivery by air became well established in the United States. In 1940 a Lodestar flew the mail route between California, and Florida in just over nine hours.

▲ Flying the flag in war
BOAC acquired 38 Lodestars. During World War II, these aircraft were operated on services to Scandinavia, Malta, Africa and the Middle East.

Thoroughbred design ▶
Cruising at altitude, SE-BZE, in the livery of the Swedish Linjeflyg, displays the elegant lines of the Model 18 Lodestar. After the end of World War II, only a small number of Lodestars remained in regular use as airliners.

◀ Howard 350s and LearStars
Howard and Lear were among the companies which modified Lodestars into comfortable executive aircraft.

Post war service ▶
After wartime service as glider tugs and troop transports, surplus military Lodestars were snapped up by individuals and small enterprises and converted back into airliners. Some served on in this role into the 1960s and 1970s.

FACTS AND FIGURES

➤ During World War II, the British Overseas Airways Corporation (BOAC) operated 38 Lodestars on paramilitary duties.

➤ The first Lodestar was an ex-Northwest Airlines Model 14 rebuilt by Lockheed.

➤ The Lockheed Ventura wartime bomber was derived from the Lodestar.

➤ Kawasaki built 121 Ki-56s derived from a stretched version of the Model 14 and very similar to the Lodestar.

➤ In New Zealand, Lodestar airliners were converted into crop-dusters.

➤ Air forces to operate Model 18s included the SAAF, RCAF, RAF, RAAF and RNZAF.

PROFILE

Improving on the Electra

To disassociate the new Model 18 from the old Model 14, the new machine was named the Lodestar. Though the prototype had the wing, tail assembly and engines of the Model 14, production aircraft introduced a raised tailplane, a modified wing trailing edge and a choice of engines – Pratt & Whitney Hornets, Twin Wasps or Wright Cyclones. Lodestars entered service in March 1940 with Mid-Continent Airlines, the type seating either 15 or 18 passengers, depending upon whether or not a cabin attendant and galley were included.

The Model 18-07 offered operating costs close to those of the rival Douglas DC-3. Some aircraft with bench-type seating installed were able to carry as many as 26 people. However, despite these features, Lodestars sold in only small numbers in the US. Foreign orders, on the other hand, were more readily forthcoming, South African Airways becoming the largest civil operator with 29.

The US Navy ordered the first military Lodestars in 1940, as R5Os, but it was the USAAF that amassed the largest fleet during World War II, including impressed and new aircraft.

Post-war, Model 18s were outdated as passenger carriers and of limited use as freighters, though a significant number were converted for use as corporate transports.

Below: Handling problems, resulted in the trailing edge of the wing being extended, blunting the clean profile of the original Model 14 Electra.

Above: Even in the Southwest Pacific, Lodestars were to be seen in post-war civilian use. Trans-Australia Airlines operated the type on regional services shuttling passengers and mail between major cities.

Model 18-07 Lodestar

Type: medium-range airliner and civil transport

Powerplant: two Pratt & Whitney S1E2-G nine-cylinder radial engines

Maximum speed: 351 km/h (218 m.p.h.)

Initial climb rate: 296 m/min (970 f.p.m.)

Range: normal 2895 km (1,795 mi.); maximum 5150 km (3,193 mi.)

Service ceiling: 6220 m (20,400 ft.)

Weights: empty 5103 kg (11,227 lb.); normal loaded 7938 kg (17,464 lb.)

Accommodation: two pilots and up to 18 passengers

Dimensions:
span	19.96 m	(65 ft. 6 in.)
length	15.19 m	(49 ft. 10 in.)
height	3.6 m	(11 ft. 2 in.)
wing area	51.19 m²	(511 sq. ft.)

The Lodestar flight deck was virtually identical to that of the Electra. The two pilots sat side-by-side, though compared to the DC-3, the cockpit was narrow and cramped. Once the 'oscillating control' problem had been solved the aircraft proved well mannered in the air, with few vices.

Compared to the Model 14 Electra, from which it was derived, the Lodestar had a lengthened fuselage in order to accommodate extra seating and hence make the aircraft more appealing to airlines by increasing the revenue per mile. Maximum capacity was 18 passengers.

Early flight trials revealed elevator nibbling, so an attempt to cure the problem was made by splitting the elevators and adding servo trim tabs. The problem was eventually eliminated by raising the tail section a few centimetres, thus taking it out of the wing turbulence.

Different powerplants were offered for the Lodestar, the most numerous in use being the Pratt & Whitney Twin Wasp series. Wright Cyclones were also optional, though they lacked the refinement of the Pratt & Whitney engines.

Extending the trailing edge of the wing also helped eliminate the control problem. Large slotted Fowler flaps mounted inboard of the engines gave the Lodestar exceptional short take-off and landing ability.

LODESTAR I

BOAC operated no fewer than 38 Lodestars for nearly seven years after their first delivery in March 1941. Despite their quasi-civilian role, a camouflage scheme was adopted for their dangerous wartime flights.

ACTION DATA

MAXIMUM SPEED

Pratt & Whitney engined Lodestars were slower than rival airliners in the late 1930s and the type never proved as popular in service as the Douglas DC-3. Boeing's Stratoliner was fastest of all, due in no small part to it being a four-engined design.

18-07 LODESTAR	351 km/h (218 m.p.h.)
DC-3A	370 km/h (229 m.p.h.)
SA-307B STRATOLINER	396 km/h (246 m.p.h.)

MAXIMUM TAKE-OFF WEIGHT

Having roughly the same seating capacity as the DC-3, the Lodestar was considerably lighter on take-off, though it was not able to carry as much cargo as the Douglas design.

18-07 LODESTAR	DC-3A	SA-307B STRATOLINER
8709 kg (17,464 lb.)	11,430 kg (25,146 lb.)	19,050 kg (41,910 lb.)

RANGE

In its day, the Model 18 Lodestar had an excellent range and this resulted in the type being employed on routes between the United States and the West Indies. It is ironic that the DC-3 had the shortest range of all, yet proved to be the most popular of the three in service.

18-07 LODESTAR 5150 km (3,193 mi.)
SA-307B STRATOLINER 3846 km (2,385 mi.)
DC-3A 2400 km (1,488 mi.)

Model 18s in the US armed services

LOCKHEED LODESTAR: Some 36 commercial Lodestars were acquired by the USAAF and pressed into service with the designation C-56. Many served until 1945.

LOCKHEED R5O-1: First order for military Model 18s came from the US Navy. The aircraft of the initial batch were used as staff transports and all were powered by Wright R-1820 engines.

LOCKHEED R5O-4: Four R5O-4 variants, destined for the USN, were diverted to the Coast Guard and entered service in 1942. They were used on administrative flights until 1946.

LOCKHEED

L-100 HERCULES

● Civil C-130 derivative ● Long service ● Still in production

Commercial Hercules have been in service almost as long as the C-130. Though initially dogged by poor sales through having to compete with cheaper freight conversions of older passenger types, the L-100 series remains in production after 30 years. By 1995, 115 had been delivered, mostly to civil operators around the world, though at least 21 have gone to air forces. Successive 'stretches' have culminated in the popular L-100-30.

▲ *Although built in limited numbers compared to the military Hercules, the L-100 has seen service in as many countries, especially on freight charters and humanitarian relief work.*

LOCKHEED L-100 HERCULES

◄ **Rough field expert**
Having cut its teeth on demanding military tasks, the Hercules design allowed civil users the same flexibility to operate from unprepared sites.

▼ **Early production for Delta**
Delta Air Lines was an early L-100 customer in 1966. Like a number of early production aircraft, N9268R was later converted to L-100-20 standard and in 1974 became an L-100-30.

▲ **Asian airlifter**
Merpati Nusantara of Indonesia flies this L-100-30 with cabin windows for passenger service.

▼ **L-100-30 in Africa**
Air Gabon flew this Dash-30, delivered in 1985, which has been leased to TAAG Angola Airlines.

◄ **Many owners**
Most early model L-100s soon changed ownership. This aircraft was with Southern Air Transport when it crashed in 1970.

FACTS AND FIGURES

➤ The latest proposed version is the L-100J – a civil variant of the updated and re-engined C-130J Hercules II.

➤ A twin-engined civil Hercules, the L-400, was suggested in the 1980s.

➤ First operator was Alaskan Airlines in March 1965, with a leased L-100.

➤ US operator Southern Air Transport has a number of L-100s configured for oil slick dispersal operations.

➤ A proposed L-100-50 with a further 6.1-m fuselage 'stretch' was abandoned.

➤ Three L-100-30s transported 50,000 Javan families during Indonesian transmigration.

PROFILE

'Herky Bird' for commercial operators

Having successfully introduced the C-130A into USAF service, Lockheed perceived a need for an aircraft for civil operators with large or heavy cargoes to carry over medium and long distances. On 21 April 1964 a prototype Model 382 (essentially a C-130E with its military equipment and underwing tanks removed) took to the air.

This and the Model 382B (the first version known as the L-100) sold in only limited numbers. Lockheed then 'stretched' the

fuselage, since commercial operators needed more space as their cargoes tended to lack the density of typical military loads. The resulting L-100-20 was some 2.54 m (8 ft. 4 in.) longer and had uprated engines. It flew in 1968.

Freight airlines that had been unprepared for an aircraft with the Hercules' lifting capacity were now being offered a 150.26 m³ (5,306 cu. ft.) hold volume. Sales were encouragingly better; some Model 382B operators even converted their aircraft to Dash-20 standard.

The top-selling commercial Hercules has been the L-100-30 (Model 382G). It introduced another 'stretch', this time by 2.03 m (6 ft. 8 in.), providing 171.5 m³ (6,056 cu. ft.) of hold space. Between its first flight on 14 August 1970 and 1995, 78 were built; production continues.

Southern Air Transport is the largest L-100 operator, with one Dash-20 and 14 Dash-30s. SAT flew para-military duties with L-100s during the Vietnam War and today operates freight charters worldwide.

L-100-30 Hercules

Type: medium- to long-range transport

Powerplant: four 3362-kW (4,510-hp.) Allison 501-D22A turboprops

Cruising speed: 580 km/h (360 m.p.h.)

Initial climb rate: 579 m/min (1,900 f.p.m.)

Range: 2935 km (1,820 mi.) with a 23,014-kg (50,600-lb.) payload

Ferry range: 7435 km (4,600 mi.)

Service ceiling: 10,060 m (33,000 ft.)

Weights: empty 33,685 kg (74,107 lb.); loaded 70,307 kg (154,675 lb.)

Dimensions:
span 40.42 m (132 ft. 7 in.)
length 34.35 m (112 ft. 8 in.)
height 11.61 m (38 ft.)
wing area 162.16 m² (1,745 sq. ft.)

This colourful L-100-20 entered service with TAAG Angola Airlines in late 1979. In June 1986 it was damaged beyond repair in an accident in Dondo, Africa.

L-100-30 HERCULES

C-GHPW was delivered to Pacific Western Airlines in December 1978. In 1983 PWA leased the aircraft to Northwest Territorial Airways, with whom it carried the name *Capt. Harry Sorensen.*

Like the C-130, the L-100 family is powered by Allison's reliable and widely used T56 turboprop, driving a Hamilton Standard fully reversible four-bladed propeller. Known in civil guise as the Allison 501, this turbine design dates from the 1950s. Next-generation C-130Js (and L-100Js) will have entirely new and more efficient Allison AE 2100 engines driving six-bladed propellers.

Lockheed's factory in Marietta, Georgia undertook the first Hercules 'stretch', creating the L-100-20.

As on military C-130s, the L-100 offers the ease of loading and unloading provided by the rear cargo ramp. The first Dash-30s were delivered to Saturn Airways in late 1970, specifically to fly powerplant sets (three Rolls-Royce RB.211 turbofan engines) for the Lockheed TriStar airliner from the UK to California.

Most commercial Hercules are configured for a freight role and are therefore fitted with a minimal number of cabin windows. However, the L-100-30 may be fitted with seating for up to 100 passengers, along with a galley and toilets.

Initial L-100 models omitted the standard military external fuel tank fit. The extra 5300 litres (1,400 gal.) of capacity that each of these tanks supplies was soon perceived as an asset by operators flying over longer routes, and the tanks were later offered as an option.

Such was the success of the stretched L-100-30 in commercial use that Lockheed offered the longer fuselage on the military Hercules. The C-130H-30 is 4.57 m (15 ft.) longer than the standard C-130H, with 40 per cent more internal capacity.

L-100 air freight around the globe

ALASKAN AIRLIFTER: Alaskan Airlines was the first customer for the L-100, the type later serving in the oil exploration support role with various airlines. Built to a military specification, 'Herks' can operate in all weathers.

ENGINES FOR THE TRISTAR: The first L-100-30s were delivered to Saturn Airways for a specific task – the delivery of Rolls-Royce engines from the UK to the US for fitment to new L-1011 TriStar wide-body airliners.

FAMINE RELIEF: Another well-known L-100 role has been famine relief flights (along with military C-130s), especially in Africa. Such life-saving flights often have to be made to rough unprepared airstrips in all weathers.

ACTION DATA

RANGE

Antonov's An-8 was designed for similar roles but appeared before the Hercules and was, at the time, a unique design. However, as a twin-engined aircraft it lacked the lifting capacity and range of the US type. The An-12 added two more engines and carried over twice the load, but with half the range capability.

L-100-20 HERCULES 2472 km (1,503 mi.)

An-8 'CAMP' 2280 km (1,410 mi.)

An-12BP 'CUB' 1450 km (900 mi.)

LOCKHEED

CONSTELLATION

● Long-range airliner ● Last of the great piston transports

T he Lockheed Constellation had style. With its triple tail, porpoise-shaped fuselage and elliptical wing, the Constellation was queen of the skies in an era when airline passengers were pampered shamelessly. The Connie's accommodations were lavish. Stewardesses in elegant attire were under orders to spoil the customer. Even the strong, distinctive purr of four colossal R-3350 engines reinforced a passenger's sense of well-being.

▲ Aircraft of the Constellation's generation represented a huge advance in passenger comfort, being able to cruise high above most of the bad weather while retaining the sumptuous pre-war service.

LOCKHEED CONSTELLATION

▲ Ultimate 'Propliner'
The L-1649 Starliner represented the pinnacle of piston-engined airliner design. Sadly, these magnificent aircraft had their careers cut short by the arrival of the early jets, such as the Boeing 707.

▲ Baggage pannier
Many Constellations carried the Speed-Pak, an extra pannier attached to the aircraft's belly to hold extra baggage and cargo.

Sophisticated lady ▶
Lockheed workers swarm over a Constellation. The aircraft was a technological marvel, with extremely complex systems.

▼ Complicated cockpit
The Connie's flight deck was a mass of dials and switches, mostly concerned with the engines.

▲ Polished performer
Early Constellations carried a polished metal finish. Similar to the heavy bombers of the time, this finish gave the Constellation better range and speed performance as a coat of paint would add drag as well as weight to the aircraft.

FACTS AND FIGURES

➤ Eastern Air Lines Super Constellation services began in December 1951.

➤ Military Super Connies served as cargo and VIP transports, airborne radar stations and reconnaissance craft.

➤ The L-1049D was a cargo version with two large loading doors.

➤ Only 43 of the 'ultimate' L-1649A Starliners, which were late competing with the Douglas DC-7C, went into service.

➤ TWA's 1957 8850-km (5,500-mi.) non-stop Starliner polar service to London from San Francisco lasted 18 hours 32 minutes.

PROFILE

Constellation spanning the globe

Based on the triumphant Constellation which emerged from World War II, the longer and bigger Lockheed L-1049 Super Constellation became the top airliner of the propeller age.

The Super Constellation, which first flew on 13 October 1950, could seat 95 passengers compared with the 60-seat capacity of the original model. Wright, manufacturer of the engines, worked with Lockheed to power the upsized 'Super' with a new R-3350 known as a turbo-compound. Once this truly beautiful craft began earning its keep with the airlines, it marked a high point in piston-engine transport. The Super Constellation flew millions of miles well into the 1980s.

The L-1049G, fondly called the 'Super G', was an advanced model. But the ultimate expression of the Constellation's class and quality was the Lockheed L-1649A Starliner, a Super Connie with longer-span wings, stretched fuselage, and even more powerful turbo-compound engines. The Starliner was the last word in luxury travel in the late 1950s, but its days were to be numbered by the introduction of the first jet airliners.

Air France was among the many top airlines which operated the Constellation on its prestige routes, flying the big airliner on transatlantic and other long-range services.

The tall, stalky undercarriage, curved fuselage and distinctive triple tail made the Constellation one of the most recognisable aircraft of its time.

L-1049E Super Constellation

Type: long-range civil transport

Powerplant: four 2435-kW (3,165-hp.) Wright R-3350-972TC18DA-1 turbo-compound radial piston engines

Maximum speed: 590 km/h (370 m.p.h.) at 5670 m (18,000 ft.)

Range: 7950 km (5,000 mi.)

Service ceiling: 7225 m (23,700 ft.)

Weights: empty 34,665 kg (76,500 lb.); loaded 60,328 kg (133,000 lb.)

Accommodation: flight crew of three; two to four flight attendants; 95 to 109 passengers in various configurations

Dimensions:
span	37.49 m	(123 ft.)
length	34.54 m	(113 ft. 4 in.)
height	7.54 m	(24 ft. 7 in.)
wing area	153.29 m²	(1,650 sq. ft.)

L-1049G SUPER CONSTELLATION

Constellations were a familiar sight around the world in the late 1940s and 1950s. The L-1049G Super Constellations of TWA were among the first airliners to offer non-stop transatlantic crossings.

Constellations were designed for long-range operations, and the extra fuel carried in large wingtip tanks gave the Super Constellation true intercontinental capability.

The banana-shaped fuselage of the Constellation was a builder's nightmare. The passenger section in later Super Constellations was made cylindrical for ease of manufacture.

Originally carrying around 60 passengers, the Constellation's capacity grew with each new model. By the end of Lockheed's 13-year manufacturing run the Starliner was carrying more than 100 passengers across the Atlantic.

The Constellation flew long distance with a flight crew of five: pilot, co-pilot, flight engineer, radio operator and navigator.

The L-1049G was the first Constellation to employ weather radar, essential for these transatlantic airliners.

The L-1049G Super Constellation was powered by 18-cylinder Wright turbo-compound engines developing some 2423 kW (3,150 hp.).

The Constellation's wing was based upon the design of the P-38 Lightning fighter, but was enlarged and strengthened, as was appropriate for a large transport.

ACTION DATA

RANGE

It was the development of bombers during World War II which made intercontinental flight a possibility, and by the early 1950s airliners were carrying full passenger loads non-stop across the Atlantic, and with one stop across the Pacific. The Super Constellation was the ultimate long-range piston-engined airliner, and it inaugurated the non-stop polar route from San Francisco to London.

STRATOCRUISER 7400 km (4,600 mi.)

SUPER CONSTELLATION 7950 km (5,000 mi.)

DC-7C 7500 km (4,660 mi.)

History of the Constellation

MODEL 49 CONSTELLATION: Flying eight years after the DC-3, the Model 49 was snapped up by the wartime US Army as a transport. Over 100 were ordered by airlines after the war.

MODEL 749 CONSTELLATION: More powerful engines and extra tanks gave this improved Constellation greater range. Many were acquired by the US Air Force and the US Navy.

MODEL 1049 SUPER CONSTELLATION: Stretched by nearly 6 m (20 ft.) and powered by turbo-compound engines, the Super Constellation was the biggest and fastest airliner of its time.

MODEL 1649 STARLINER: The ultimate Connie was a superb performer, but was too late to challenge the DC-7C. However, both were soon made obsolete by the new jets.

LOCKHEED

L-1011 TRISTAR

● Wide-body 'Whisperliner' ● Medium-/long-range tri-jet

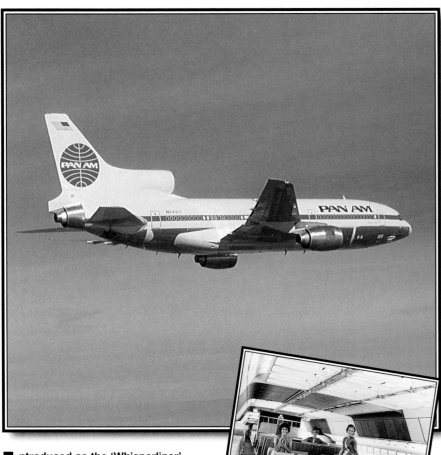

I ntroduced as the 'Whisperliner' because of its quietness, the TriStar was the great rival of McDonnell Douglas' DC-10 tri-jet. With its Rolls-Royce RB.211 fan engines, it promised superb fuel economy and long range. Financial problems for Rolls-Royce and Lockheed almost caused the TriStar to fail before it flew, but it overcame these problems to become a superb airliner, well liked by passengers and pilots.

▲ The TriStar was designed at the end of the 1960s, when airlines wanted 'wide-body' fuselages with twin-aisle seating. Comfort was much better than in older narrow-bodies like the DC-8.

LOCKHEED L-1011 TRISTAR

▲ Delta launches the TriStar
Delta, one of the world's largest airlines, was a launch customer for the L-1011. It is a credit to the aircraft that Delta is still operating more than 50 examples of the tri-jet after over a quarter of a century in service.

▲ Wide body
Although the L-1011 looks similar to the DC-10, its third engine is buried in the rear fuselage rather than being mounted in the fin, as in the Douglas aircraft.

▼ Loading the hold ▶
Even though no dedicated TriStar freighter has been built, the basic airliner has a large cargo capacity.

▲ Tanker TriStar
In service with No. 216 squadron RAF, the TriStar has been a great success. Unlike its great rival, the DC-10, the TriStar has not been adopted by the US armed forces.

Needle nose ▶
The probe on the front of this test TriStar is a special 'gust boom' which measures air movement very accurately to check the aircraft's behaviour in turbulence.

FACTS AND FIGURES

➤ TriStars were originally priced at $14.3 million in the early 1970s, which is about the same price as an F-16 today.

➤ L-1011s are also operated by Saudia, Royal Jordanian and Cathay Pacific.

➤ The last TriStar was rolled out of Lockheed's Palmdale plant in 1983.

➤ Eastern Airlines and TWA received the first deliveries of L-1011s in April 1972.

➤ The RAF bought six TriStars from British Airways for £60 million in 1983.

➤ Lockheed built 250 TriStars; the first was rolled out in November 1970.

PROFILE

Lockheed's 'Whisperliner'

Designed as a medium-haul 250-seat airliner for American Airlines, with the emphasis on fuel economy and low maintenance, the TriStar almost fell victim to the financial problems of its manufacturer. Lockheed managed to pull itself together, and in 1966 the TriStar was born. It was marketed very aggressively by Lockheed, in ferocious competition with the longer range DC-10. By March 1968 the TriStar was selling well, with 118 delivered

to Eastern Airlines, TWA and Delta. But just when sales looked good, disaster struck again as Rolls-Royce almost collapsed, stopping engine deliveries. After more financial dealings the supply of engines resumed and TriStars began selling again, but a large number of DC-10s had been sold in the meantime.

Range was improved in the L-1011-100 and -500, with more fuel tanks added, a wingtip extension and an active control

Like many major airlines, British Airways has now replaced its TriStars with newer aircraft.

system to reduce drag, but the aircraft never quite caught up with the DC-10. A small number were converted to tanker/transports for the Royal Air Force, and many still fly with airlines around the world.

Compared to a DC-10, the TriStar has a short fuselage and the wing is set further back, making it easily recognisable.

The undercarriage retracts into two large bays in the fuselage, just inside the wingroots.

L-1011-500 TriStar

Type: long-range commercial transport

Powerplant: three 222.42-kN (49,900-lb.-thrust) Rolls-Royce RB.211-524B turbofans

Cruising speed: maximum 973 km/h (603 m.p.h.) at 9000 m (29,000 ft.); economy cruise 890 km/h (552 m.p.h.) at 10,500 m (34,000 ft.)

Range: 11,286 km (7,000 mi.) with maximum fuel; 9905 km (6,140 mi.) with maximum passenger and baggage load

Service ceiling: 13,200 m (43,300 ft.)

Weights: empty 111,311 kg (244,884 lb.); maximum 228,615 kg (502,942 lb.)

Accommodation: three flight crew; typically 24 first-class and 222 economy-class passengers

Dimensions:
span	50.09 m	(164 ft.)
length	50.05 m	(164 ft.)
height	16.87 m	(55 ft.)
wing area	329 m²	(3,540 sq. ft.)

L-1011-500 TriStar

The L-1011-500 was a long-range version of the TriStar, which was flown by British Airways on non-stop routes from London to New Orleans, Calgary and Edmonton. This aircraft was sold to the Royal Air Force in 1983, and now operates as a military tanker/transport.

The crew consists of a pilot, co-pilot and flight engineer. Cockpit noise levels are very low in the TriStar. An emergency escape hatch is fitted in the cockpit roof.

The wing has very large leading-edge slats, flaps, ailerons and outboard spoiler/speedbrakes. The wing of the 500 model contains very large fuel tanks, with a capacity of 34,000 litres (8,890 gal.).

The main cabin area typically seats up to 246 passengers in two classes, nine abreast in tourist class. Maximum load is 330, carried in a high-density 10-abreast economy layout.

A forward galley is located just behind the cockpit.

The 500 series TriStar uses the RB.211-524 series turbofan engine. The RB.211 was consistently upgraded, mainly to compete with the Pratt & Whitney JT9-D in the Boeing 747, and it remains a highly efficient and quiet engine.

The Pratt & Whitney auxiliary power unit is located in a bay under the third engine feed duct.

Cowlings for the third engine are removable for maintenance access. A rear cabin door is fitted just ahead of the tailplane.

TriStar 500

British airways

G-BFCB

ACTION DATA

MAXIMUM SPEED

The TriStar was designed to take off from relatively short runways with a full payload. To achieve this it has an efficient aerodynamic shape, an effective wing and three excellent engines. These have the added benefit of making the big Lockheed design one of the fastest airliners around.

DC-10-40 **922 km/h (572 m.p.h.)**

L-1011-500 TRISTAR **973 km/h (603 m.p.h.)**

A300B4-200 **917 km/h (569 m.p.h.)**

RANGE

The TriStar was originally designed to fly the Chicago–Los Angeles route, but the 5000-km (3,100-mi.) range was insufficient for international users. Later models have greatly improved performance. The Model 500 has true intercontinental range, to match long-range variants of its great rival, the DC-10.

A300B4-200 6500 km (4,030 mi.)

DC-10-40 11,685 km (7,245 mi.)

L-1011-500 TRISTAR 11,286 km (7,000 mi.)

PASSENGER LOAD

Long-range TriStars are four metres shorter than the standard variants, which reduces maximum passenger load from around 400 to 330. Passengers are seated 10 abreast in the high-density layout, although six abreast in first class and nine abreast in economy is a more normal configuration.

A300B4-200 **320 single-class high-density**

L-1011-500 TRISTAR **330 single-class high-density**

DC-10-40 **380 single-class high-density**

The wide-body generation

■ **BOEING 747:** First of the wide bodies, the epoch-making Boeing 747 'Jumbo Jet' is still the largest airliner in the world, over 30 years after its first flight. Most 747s are used on long-range high-density routes.

■ **McDONNELL DOUGLAS DC-10:** Smaller than the 747, the DC-10 was designed, like the TriStar, to fly somewhat shorter transcontinental routes than the 747. Longer range variants soon appeared which competed with the large Boeing jet.

■ **AIRBUS A300:** Europe's highly successful Airbus is the progenitor of a whole family of jets which compete with the Americans on all types of journey, from short-hop high-density flights to non-stop ultra-long-range routes.

LOCKHEED

ER-2

● Research ● Ecological monitoring ● Sensor platform

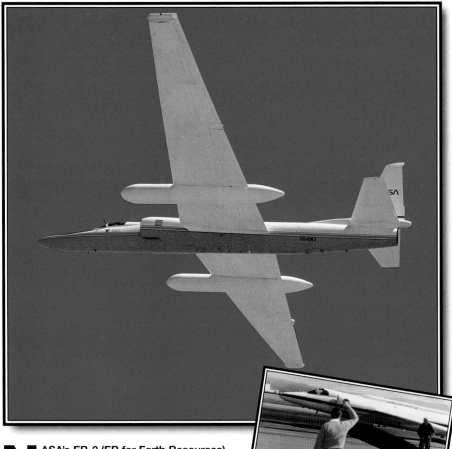

NASA's ER-2 (ER for Earth Resources) is a peaceful version of the Cold War's U-2 spyplane. The nuclear stand-off between the West and the Soviet Union made it necessary to use high-flying reconnaissance aircraft, but the airframe became a less sinister tool when NASA began using it. ER-2s have been vital in recent years for monitoring the hole in the ozone layer, and for performing tasks that would otherwise be carried out by satellites.

▲ NASA operates just three ER-2 survey platforms, and all are based at NASA's experimental facility at Moffett Field. NASA-Ames has also operated civilian versions of the earlier U-2 aircraft.

LOCKHEED ER-2

▲ Narrow body
The TR-1 fuselage assembly is a narrow structure, a shape optimised for low drag in high-altitude flight.

▲ NASA's special missions master
The ER-2 is operated specifically by a unit of NASA known as the High Altitude Missions Branch.

▲ Training variant
Prospective NASA research pilots become accustomed to the unusual handling characteristics of the ER-2 in the USAF's tandem two-seat Lockheed U-2RTs of the the 9th Reconnaissance Wing.

▲ Multi-mission cockpit
Essentially similar to the military TR-1A, the ER-2's cockpit contains various sensor displays.

Foreign detachments ▶
As well as operating in the USA, NASA U-2s and ER-2s were often detached to Norway.

FACTS AND FIGURES

➤ One of NASA's three original U-2 pilots was a Briton, Ivor Webster, who trained for spy flight missions in the RAF.

➤ In 1980 an ER-2 studied volcanic eruptions from Mount St Helens.

➤ Two TR-1s were originally given to NASA and redesignated ER-2.

➤ Extra cameras used by NASA included Wild-Heerbrug RC-10 s with six- and 12-inch focal lengths.

➤ A third ER-2 (formerly a TR-1A of the 9th SRW) is now in service with NASA.

➤ The military TR-1 was used as a precision electronic reconnaissance aircraft.

PROFILE

NASA's civilian spyplanes

To most of the world the Lockheed U-2, manufactured at the top-secret 'Skunk Works', is remembered for being the spyplane shot down over Russia in 1960.

Originally, NASA (National Aeronautics and Space Administration) and its predecessor had only one connection with this Cold War spook, also called the 'Black Lady': NASA's civilian research was originally the 'cover story' for CIA spy flights in the U-2. But with the 1971 Earth Resources Satellite Technology programme (later called Landsat), NASA began operating

two U-2Cs (joined by the improved ER-2 model in 1983) for genuine, peaceful research using sensors and infra-red cameras. The U-2s complemented the satellite in providing a better understanding of the planet we live on, for example, measuring the chlorophyll content of vegetation. The ER-2 model carried most of its sensors in two 'superpods', one under each wing.

Although the U-2 is a difficult aircraft to fly, pilots appreciate this type of work because they are using a one-time clandestine weapon of war for a purpose that benefits mankind.

Above: ER-2s wear NASA's standard civilian-style paint scheme of upper surface gloss white with pale grey undersides and lateral blue stripe. The white paint scheme helps to prevent the systems overheating in strong sunlight.

Above: Lockheed ER-2s are useful to NASA because of their high ceiling. ER-2s regularly fly at heights of up to 24,000 m (78,740 ft.) and have a range of nearly 5000 km (3,100 mi.).

U-2R

Type: single-seat high-altitude strategic reconnaissance aircraft

Powerplant: one 75.02-kN (16,880 lb.-thrust) Pratt & Whitney J75-P-13B turbojet engine

Cruising speed: 740 km/h (460 m.p.h.) at 19,810 m (65,000 ft.)

Operating altitude: 19,810 m to 21,335 m (65,000 to 70,000 ft.)

Maximum altitude: 24,000 m (78,740 ft.)

Range: 4365 km (2,712 mi.)

Weight: maximum take-off 18,733 kg (41,300 lb.)

Payload: (NASA U-2C) 658 kg (1,450 lb.) of sensors; (ER-2) 1361 kg (3,000 lb.) of optical, thermal and electronic sensors

Dimensions: span 31.39 m (103 ft.)
length 19.13 m (62 ft. 9 in.)
height 4.88 m (16 ft.)
wing area 92.90 m² (1,000 sq. ft.)

ER-2

Shown below is one of NASA's three ER-2 single-seat high-altitude earth resources aircraft, based at Moffett Field in the United States and detached to Bodø in Norway.

The ER-2's ultra-high-aspect ratio wings are similar to those of a glider, enabling the aircraft to act almost as a powered sailplane when at high altitude. They also make the aircraft probably the most difficult aircraft in the world to land, and several U-2 and TR-1 pilots have died in crashes after losing control just before touchdown.

The long nose is hollow and can hold whatever equipment is suitable for the ER-2's particular mission profile. Further space is provided by the 'Q-bay' behind the pilot.

On take off the ER-2 jettisons its wing-mounted outrigger wheels, later coming in to land gently on one of its wingtip skids.

The Lockheed U-2 series are the world's largest single-engined production aircraft, propelled by an enormous Pratt & Whitney J75 engine.

The cockpit is fully pressurised to withstand high-altitude missions and contains a single space-suited pilot.

Long, detachable 'superpods' are built under the wings and contain various different missions sensors.

A small composite tailwheel is housed in the rear fuselage, and outrigger wheels on the wings are used for extra balance.

ACTION DATA

SERVICE CEILING

In their assigned roles, whether it be ozone research or monitoring, these aircraft operate on the fringes of the atmosphere. The pilots all wear suits very similar to those used by astronauts in space.

ER-2
21,335 m
(70,000 ft.)

M-55 GEOFIZICA
21,500 m
(70,540 ft.)

MiG-25R 'FOXBAT'
21,000 m (69,000 ft.)

RANGE

Long range is useful in a survey aircraft (and in spyplanes), as data needs to be collected over large areas. The MiG-25 is designed to evade defences by flying at high speed over the target. This means shorter range and much higher fuel consumption.

ER-2
4365 km
(2,712 mi.)

M-55 GEOFIZICA
4965 km
(3,085 mi.)

MiG-25R 'FOXBAT'
1865 km (1,159 mi.)

ENDURANCE

Long wings mean large fuel tanks can be incorporated, and with a single engine running at low power settings both the ER-2 and M-55 can cruise for hours. The MiG-25R was designed to fly very fast but not to stay in the air for long periods.

ER-2	M-55 GEOFIZICA	MiG-25R 'FOXBAT'
12 hours	6½ hours	3 hours

Environmental missions

OZONE RESEARCH: When detached to Norway, the ER-2's prime task is the continued monitoring of the upper atmosphere's ozone levels.

BIOLOGICAL RECONNAISSANCE: NASA has employed the sophisticated monitoring gear of its ER-2s to record a population boom in a species of moth which was destroying crops on the American coast.

VOLCANIC MONITORING: The ER-2 was also successfully used to monitor the activity of Washington State's Mount St Helens during a period of eruptions in 1980.

MARTIN

2-0-2/4-0-4

● Twin-engined airliner ● Still in service ● Military use

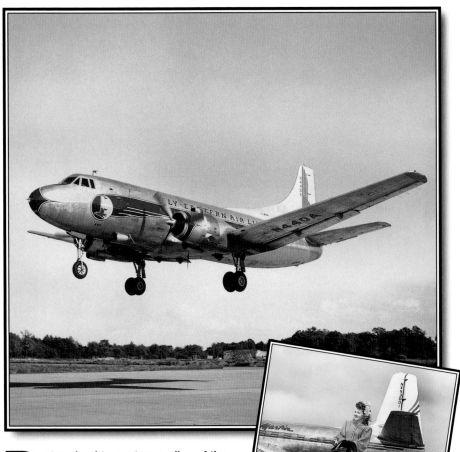

Determined to capture a slice of the lucrative post-war airline market, the Glenn L. Martin company built the twin-engined Model 2-0-2. The aircraft was the company's first attempt at producing a machine tailored for the civil market since the Clipper flying-boats, and ultimately proved unsuccessful. An improved variant, the 4-0-4 entered service in 1951 and most of these flew on into the mid-1960s.

▲ A twin-engined airliner/transport, the 2-0-2/4-0-4 was externally very similar to the Convair 240, though it never achieved the same commercial success as its great rival.

▼ **Survivors**
A handful of 2-0-2s were passed on to small operators in the 1960s. This example was still flying in 1985 with Proair.

▲ **Problematic airliners**
Northwest was the only major airline to buy the 2-0-2 and in service they were not popular, being plagued by mechanical and structural problems.

◀ **First of the few**
Two prototypes were built and the second was distinguished by the greater dihedral (upward sweep) of its wings. Certification was given in mid-1947.

▼ **South American sales**
Among the few operators that actually purchased 2-0-2s was Linea Aeropostal Venezolana, which used it on its Latin American routes.

◀ **Thwarted production**
Production of the 2-0-2 variant was under way in earnest by 1947, though it was soon clear that many airlines wanted much larger, faster aircraft. Orders were cancelled and only 47 aircraft were built.

FACTS AND FIGURES

➤ After one aircraft crashed, killing all on board, Northwest Airlines promptly disposed of its remaining 2-0-2s.

➤ In March 1950, the larger and much improved 4-0-4 was announced.

➤ Eastern Airlines and TWA purchased a total of 103 of the improved variant.

➤ A pressurised version of the 2-0-2, known as the 3-0-3, was ordered by United Airlines, but later cancelled.

➤ One aircraft was converted into an executive transport for Frank Sinatra.

➤ Two aircraft, known as RM-1Gs, were delivered to the US Coast Guard.

PROFILE

Martin's postwar commercial

Nearly forgotten today, the Martin 2-0-2 and 4-0-4 might have been excellent aircraft, and in some ways deserved to succeed, but were plagued by numerous setbacks. The first 2-0-2 prototype flew in November 1946 and six customers immediately ordered the type. However, the market collapsed in 1947 and only Northwest Airlines actually purchased 2-0-2s. These aircraft proved troublesome in service. One was lost during a storm in

1947. Another was seriously damaged and cracks in the wings revealed a major flaw in the design. Martin addressed the problem but the airlines were unconvinced and only 24 of this variant were built.

The 4-0-4 of 1950 looked similar but featured a pressurised fuselage and was somewhat larger. These proved more popular, with two major airlines, Eastern and TWA, acquiring them. Some 4-0-4s serve into the late 1990s, flying charters in the Caribbean.

Above: Although similar in appearance, the 4-0-4 shared few components with its predecessor and featured a pressurised cabin. Compared to the 2-0-2 this variant was a success, with 103 built.

Right: Howard Hughes' TWA was an important customer for the Martin airliner, leasing a dozen 2-0-2s built from surplus parts before acquiring 4-0-4s. Several of these have been preserved.

4-0-4

Type: short/medium-range transport

Powerplant: two 1790-kW (2,400-hp.) Pratt & Whitney R-2800-CB16 radial engines

Maximum speed: 502 km/h (311 m.p.h.)

Cruising speed: 448 km/h (277 m.p.h.)

Initial climb rate: 580 m/min (1,900 f.p.m.)

Range: 1738 km (892 mi.) with maximum payload

Service ceiling: 8840 m (29,000 ft.)

Weights: empty 13,211 kg (29,064 lb.); maximum take-off 20,366 kg (44,805 lb.)

Accommodation: maximum of 40 passengers

Dimensions: span 28.42 m (93 ft. 3 in.)
length 22.73 m (74 ft. 7 in.)
height 8.66 m (28 ft. 5 in.)
wing area 80.27 m² (864 sq. ft.)

4-0-4

Having reached the end of their careers with major airlines such as TWA, Martin 4-0-4s were passed on to smaller operators. Marco Island Airways flew this colourful example on its Caribbean routes.

On the 4-0-4 the standard crew for most flights was three, consisting of a pilot, co-pilot and navigator, though sometimes a fourth member was carried.

Despite a common external appearance, the 2-0-2 and 4-0-4 were structurally completely different aircraft. The 4-0-4 featured a larger, pressurised fuselage which proved more comfortable for both passengers and crew. Not surprisingly, the aircraft sold better than its unpopular predecessor.

The all-metal vertical tail followed contemporary fashion in having a very large dorsal spine which stretched nearly halfway down the fuselage. The tail unit was of all-metal stressed-skin construction and all control surfaces were powered. The aircraft was generally pleasant to fly and had few vices.

The rather stalky tricycle undercarriage featured a single steerable nosewheel and double main units. All three units retracted forward for flight.

Among the improvements introduced on the 4-0-4 were uprated engines. The twin Pratt & Whitney R-2800 18-cylinder Twin Wasp radials featured turbo superchargers for better performance at high altitude.

Retractable steps were built in to the rear fuselage, dispensing with the need for a bulky, cumbersome staircase. This saved time and also enabled the aircraft to fly into airfields where ground support equipment was minimal.

ACTION DATA

CRUISING SPEED

Compared to their 1930s predecessors, the post-war generation of commercial twins could fly higher and faster, though the Soviet Il-14 Crate was slower and somewhat less efficient than Western rivals such as the Martin 4-0-4 and Convair 440.

4-0-4 448 km/h (277 m.p.h.)
IL-14 M 300 km/h (186 m.p.h.)
CV-440 483 km/h (300 m.p.h.)

PASSENGERS

Although a capacity of 40 passengers may not seem impressive today, it was good back in the 1940s. Despite being excellent aircraft these designs were quickly superseded by larger types on major routes and ended up as regional airliners.

4-0-4 40 PASSENGERS
IL-14 M 'CRATE' 36 PASSENGERS
CV-440 52 PASSENGERS

RANGE

A notable quality of the 4-0-4 was its superb range. This made it ideal for regional services across the United States and flights to the Caribbean islands. The similar Convair 440 proved more popular, despite its poor range with maximum payload. The Il-14 had a reasonable range by comparison, but was costly to operate.

4-0-4 1738 km (892 mi.)
IL-14 M 'CRATE' 1034 km (640 mi.)
CV-440 739 km (285 mi.)

Rivals in the post-war market

■ **BOEING 377 STRATOCRUISER:** With its 'double bubble' fuselage the 'Strat' was the most prestigious airliner of the late 1940s.

■ **CONVAIR 240:** Also known as the 'Convairliner', this was the aircraft that beat the Martin 2-0-2 for airline orders.

■ **DOUGLAS DC-3:** In the austere, immediate post-war market, the DC-3 was an attractive buy for many commercial airlines.

■ **DOUGLAS DC-7B:** Ushering in a new era in air travel, were larger four-engined airliners such as the DC-7. Pan-American was a major user.

MCDONNELL DOUGLAS

DC-9

● Short- to medium-haul airliner ● Worldwide service ● New developments

MCDONNELL DOUGLAS **DC-9**

◀ High-altitude cruise
Fitted with a long, clean swept wing, the DC-9 has economic, high-speed cruise capabilities. By mounting the wing low down the designers ensured the wing spars passed beneath the cabin floor.

Canadian colours ▶
Air Canada is typical of the airlines which have used the DC-9 to develop jet services on short- to medium-haul routes. The aircraft has proved efficient and reliable.

◀ Long Beach line-up
DC-9s await delivery from the McDonnell Douglas Long Beach plant. Several airlines bought the DC-9, but ultimately it lost out to the Boeing 737.

▼ DC-9 in Britain
As newer MD-80/90-series machines and other aircraft take its place, the DC-9 is becoming a less common sight around Europe.

▼ Soldiering on
Some older DC-9s require anti-noise and pollution modifications if they are to remain in service.

The Douglas DC-9 is among the most familiar aircraft in the world. More than 700 short- to medium-range DC-9s, together with later-generation derivatives which bear 'MD' (for McDonnell Douglas) designations, ply the world's airways. The DC-9 is often compared with the more numerous Boeing 727 and 737, but it began its career two years earlier than these aircraft. The pilots who fly the DC-9 regard it as the best aircraft in its class.

▲ Since its launch in April 1963 the DC-9 has continued the tradition of the DC-3, giving reliable and cost-effective service to operators around the world.

FACTS AND FIGURES

➤ Delta Airlines placed an order for DC-9s in April 1963, before the first aircraft had flown.

➤ The prototype for the DC-9 series made its initial flight on 25 February 1965.

➤ About 740 DC-9s remain in operation, most of them on US airline routes.

➤ Most DC-9s were offered in freight, convertible and passenger/freight configurations.

➤ Only about 100 DC-9s still fly routes within Europe.

➤ Although the DC-9 is narrow-bodied, Douglas gave it a wide-body look interior.

PROFILE

Setting new standards

With its low wing, a distinctive T-tail and twin engines astride the rear fuselage, the Douglas DC-9 established a winning design formula. The DC-9 was the first short- to medium-range jetliner to enter regular service, and over three decades of passenger flying it has amassed a fine record for both service and safety.

The original DC-9 design was manufactured in several versions with different dimensions, runway capabilities and passenger capacities. It is one of the most popular airliners in the world and the basic design has paved the way for the more advanced MD-80/90 series, which is based on the original DC-9 configuration.

Since its first income-earning passenger flight with Delta Airlines on 8 December 1965, the DC-9 has remained popular with crews and passengers. The aircraft has responsive controls and is fairly inexpensive to maintain and operate. Many of the oldest DC-9s are still in service, and, with modifications to make them quieter, are likely to continue to fly for many years to come.

Right: When Pratt & Whitney developed the more powerful JT8D-15 and JT8D-17 turbofans, McDonnell Douglas produced the larger 139-seat DC-9 Series 50.

Below: A McDonnell Douglas DC-9 Series 40 development airframe flies over the Queen Mary. The first Series 40 aircraft was delivered in 1968.

DC-9 Series 30

Type: short- to medium-range airliner

Powerplant: two 62.3-kN (14,018 lb.-thrust) Pratt & Whitney JT8D-7 turbofan engines

Maximum speed: 926 km/h (575 m.p.h.)

Maximum cruising speed: 821 km/h (510 m.p.h.)

Range: 2775 km (1,724 mi.) at long-range cruising speed of 821 km/h (510 m.p.h.)

Service ceiling: 10,180 m (33,400 ft.)

Weights: empty 24,011 kg (52,935 lb.); maximum take-off 44,450 kg (97,995 lb.)

Accommodation: two pilots, flight engineer and 105 passengers; 115 passengers may be carried with limited facilities

Dimensions: span 28.47 m (93 ft. 5 in.)
length 36.37 m (119 ft. 4 in.)
height 8.38 m (27 ft. 6 in.)
wing area 92.97 m² (1.000 sq. ft.)

DC-9 SERIES 30

In the 1970s Douglas developed versions of the Series 30 with more powerful JT8D engines, higher weights and auxiliary fuel tanks. These models were popular with European charter airlines.

Although only one main passenger entrance and exit door is available, two additional exits, above the left side wingroot, are available in an emergency. Each exit is equipped with an inflatable emergency escape chute.

Douglas produced the DC-9 to compete with the BAC One-Eleven, which was selling very well in the United States. The machines looked very similar, although the rear fuselage area was different. In the One-Eleven this area tapered, while in the DC-9 it was of near constant diameter, allowing five-abreast seating throughout the whole cabin length. This meant that the DC-9 could carry more passengers and offered greater flexibility than the One-Eleven.

To ease passenger loading at poorly equipped airports, a retractable airstair is fitted in the forward cabin doorway. This is the only passenger entrance.

A narrow, swept wing is efficient but produces high landing speeds. For good field performance the wing is equipped with leading-edge slats and large flaps.

Mounting the engines on the rear fuselage helps to keep cabin noise to a minimum and also allows a short undercarriage to be used. This was important as the DC-9 had to fly from less-developed airports with limited ground handling equipment.

The rear-mounted engines dictate the use of a high-set tail, or 'T-tail', which keeps the control surfaces clear of the jet blast. The tailplane of the DC-9 is all-moving for trim and has elevators for pitch control.

ACTION DATA

MAXIMUM CRUISING SPEED

Boeing's Model 737 was slightly faster than the DC-9, but it flew two years later and initially had an uphill struggle to win orders from the Douglas jet. Speed over short sectors is important to reduce journey times for passengers.

DC-9 SERIES 40	903 km/h (561 m.p.h.)
MODEL 737-200	927 km/h (576 m.p.h.)
ONE-ELEVEN SERIES 500	871 km/h (541 m.p.h.)

PASSENGER LOAD

Both the DC-9 and 737-200 were developed into variants which could accommodate more passengers than shown here. The BAC One-Eleven had reached its maximum capacity with the Series 500 and having inspired the DC-9, it lost out to it.

DC-9 SERIES 40	125
MODEL 737-200	130
ONE-ELEVEN SERIES 500	119

MAXIMUM RANGE

Learning from the experience of short- to medium-haul airliners already in service, Boeing was able to develop an aircraft more suited to the emerging needs of the market. Its 737-200 offered appreciably better range than the DC-9 Series 40, but was fitted with a similar number of seats.

DC-9 SERIES 40 2710 km (1,684 mi.)

MODEL 737-200 4075 km (2,532 mi.)

ONE-ELEVEN SERIES 500 3458 km (2,149 mi.)

DC-9s in many colours

■ **DC-9 SERIES 20:** This special 'hot-and-high' variant, used only by SAS, combined the short fuselage of the Series 10 with the long-span wings and more powerful engines of the Series 30.

■ **DC-9 SERIES 30:** With its 115-seat capacity, long-span wings giving efficient cruise and powerful engines in sound-treated nacelles, the Series 30 outsold all other DC-9 models.

■ **C-9 SKYTRAIN II/NIGHTINGALE:** USAF and US Navy aircraft have been used in the aeromedical, transport and VIP transport roles. Two passenger/cargo aircraft were supplied to Kuwait.

McDonnell Douglas

DC-10

● Wide-body transport ● Medium- and long-range tri-jet

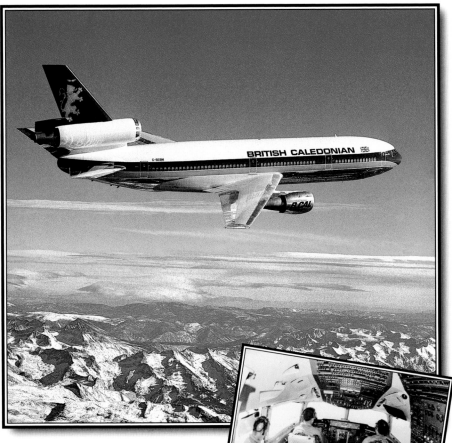

O ne of the original three wide-body aircraft (the others being the Lockheed TriStar and the Boeing 747), the McDonnell Douglas DC-10 is a giant of air commerce. The aircraft has lived down an early tainted reputation to become a stalwart of the world's passenger routes and the inspiration for a family of jets which continues today with the state-of-the-art MD-11.

▲ Compared to the Boeing 747, the DC-10 has a roomy cockpit which is much appreciated by its crews. The majority of those with experience of all three first-generation wide-bodies prefer to fly the DC-10.

McDonnell Douglas DC-10

▼ Air Force tanker
Using the DC-10 airframe, McDonnell Douglas produced the KC-10 Extender for the US Air Force. This versatile aircraft can transport huge cargoes and refuel other aircraft in flight.

▲ Prototype tri-jet
The prototype of the DC-10 lifts off from Long Beach on its maiden voyage. Despite a series of early crashes, the DC-10 matured as a world-beating airliner.

▼ Flying saloon
The wide-body fuselage of the DC-10 allowed designers of aircraft interiors to provide spacious bars for first-class passengers.

▲ Global travel
In the long-range Series 320 version, the DC-10 could span the globe. Air New Zealand used it for a round-the-world service.

Best-seller ▶
The DC-10 proved very attractive to a wide range of airlines who wanted a prestige wide-body airliner without the huge capacity of the Boeing 747.

FACTS AND FIGURES

➤ The DC-10 was originally designed to enter a US Air Force competition for a military heavy-lifter, eventually losing out to the massive Lockheed C-5 Galaxy.

➤ The third engine mounted in the tail is supported by just four forgings known as 'banjo rings' – each weighs only 204 kg (250 lb.).

➤ DC-10 customers could choose between the GE CF6 engine or the PW JT9D.

➤ The Series 15 had more powerful engines for take off at 'hot-and-high' airports.

➤ Thanks to some well-publicised crashes, early DC-10s acquired an unearned reputation for unreliability.

PROFILE

Trans-oceanic tri-jet

When it first flew in 1970, the DC-10 was a brave step into the unknown. The three huge turbofans which powered it were themselves a new concept, and the tri-jet configuration, with one engine held high on the tail, was equally novel. Airlines flocked to the new design, and Douglas seemed to have scored a runaway success.

Success soon turned to tragedy when a spate of catastrophic accidents seriously damaged the aircraft's reputation. The name DC-10 became a household name for all the wrong reasons. However, the faults which had caused the crashes were fixed and the aircraft started to claw back its otherwise excellent reputation.

The airlines kept buying the DC-10 because it was so good, and since then it has shown exemplary performance, reliability and economy. Now in the twilight of its career, many still serve on passenger and cargo-hauling duties, while the tri-jet configuration and basic design goes on in production as the MD-11, a radically upgraded and modernised version.

In Germany both Lufthansa and Condor were staunch supporters of the DC-10's abilities.

Hugely powerful engines are needed to haul the DC-10 and its load into the air. Federal Express aircraft use the General Electric CF6 turbofan.

DC-10 Series 30

Type: long-range airliner and freighter

Powerplant: three 227.52-kN (48,100-lb.-thrust) General Electric CF6-50C high-bypass turbofans

Cruising speed: 920 km/h (570 m.p.h.)

Range: 7500 km (4,270 mi.) with max. payload

Service ceiling: 10,810 m (35,465 ft.)

Weights: operating empty 121,200 kg (2267,200 lb.); maximum loaded 263,000 kg (559,000 lb.)

Passengers: up to 405 passengers maximum; 323 passengers in typical two-class configuration; 293 passengers in three classes

Dimensions:
span	50.40 m (161 ft. 4 in.)
length	55.50 m (181 ft. 5 in.)
height	17.70 m (58 ft.)
wing area	367.70 m² (3,921 sq. ft.)

DC-10-10FC

The DC-10-10FC is a specialised freight version with a huge door in the side of the cabin. Rapid delivery specialists Federal Express bought a fleet to whisk parcels across America and around the world on a 24-hour delivery service.

The cabin of the DC-10 is 41.45 m (136 ft.) long, and together with the underfloor cargo areas allows the DC-10F to carry an astonishing 80,000 kg (176,370 lb.) of cargo on long-haul flights. The load is usually mounted on pallets, 30 of which can be carried in the main cabin alone.

Two pilots and a flight engineer fly the DC-10, although a freight version also carries loading specialists.

The DC-10 differed from other tri-jets in having its third engine built into the tail rather than the rear fuselage.

Long-range versions of the DC-10 weigh considerably more than the short-range versions and consequently need an extra undercarriage leg to support the extra weight. This is located between the two mainwheels.

Federal Express has a huge fleet of parcel-carrying aircraft, ranging from small Cessna lightplanes to the monster DC-10 and MD-11.

ACTION DATA

CRUISING SPEED

Although the tri-jets are less powerful than the 747, having only three engines in place of four, they are only marginally slower than the big Boeing jet.

MODEL 747-200	980 km/h (610 m.p.h.)
L-1011 TRISTAR	925 km/h (575 m.p.h.)
DC-10	920 km/h (570 m.p.h.)

CAPACITY

By widening the fuselage to allow passengers to be seated eight, nine or even 10 abreast, the first generation of wide-body jets doubled the number of passengers that an aircraft could carry.

MODEL 747-200	365 passengers
L-1011 TRISTAR	280 passengers
DC-10	300 passengers

RANGE

Although often used for medium- and even short-haul work, the DC-10 comfortably outranges the preceding generation of jets. Only the larger 747 with its bigger fuel load has better long-range performance.

L-1011 TRISTAR 4700 km (2,920 mi.)
MODEL 747-200 8000 km (4,970 mi.)
DC-10 7500 km (4,660 mi.)

Douglas dynasty

■ **DOUGLAS DC-2/DC-3 (1930s):** These were the first stressed-skin airliners. Built in huge numbers, they were the foundation of modern air transport.

■ **DOUGLAS DC-4/DC-6/DC-7 (1950s):** A logical development of the DC-3, these four-engined airliners introduced long-range capability.

■ **DOUGLAS DC-8 (1959):** The highly successful DC-8 was, in stretched form, the world's largest airliner until the arrival of the Jumbo Jet.

■ **McDONNELL DOUGLAS DC-9 (1965):** The DC-9 and its advanced successors are some of the quietest and most economical short-haul airliners in service.

McDonnell Douglas

MD-80

● Medium-range airliner ● DC-9 successor

▲ McDonnell Douglas has persisted with its highly successful T-tail, rear-engine airliners. The MD-80 series has sold well around the world, despite fierce competition from Boeing and Airbus.

Beginning life as the DC-9, this twin-engine airliner quickly became popular on short- to medium-haul routes. It sold well to carriers worldwide and was developed into various different series with configurations tailored to customer requirements, this usually being achieved by ever-longer fuselage 'stretches'. When the Douglas Aircraft Company was restructured in 1983, the DC-9 Series 80 became the 'new' MD-80.

PHOTO FILE

McDonnell Douglas MD-80

▲ Sales success
The MD-80 has sold well in the U.S., where American Airlines ordered more than 100 in the 1980s as part of the largest order ever placed for commercial aircraft.

▲ Unducted fan
In the 1980s, as oil prices rose, fuel economy became a major consideration for airlines. McDonnell Douglas tested the MD-UHB, featuring an unducted fan engine which proved to be efficient and quiet.

▲ Ever-changing design
The original DC-9 design was so sound that it spawned the subsequent MD-80, MD-90 and MD-95 series. Simple structural stretches and improved engines have kept design costs low and yet still produced world-beating airliners. The last 30 years have shown that it is the ultimate 'rubber airplane'.

▲ Economic performer
Aéropostal of Venezuela flies the 165-seat MD-83, which has a cost per seat-mile rate 12 percent lower than its twin- and tri-jet competitors.

Island-hopper ▶
A highly-durable airframe is vital for high-intensity routes. Multiple take-offs and landings test durability, and the MD-81 passes with flying colors.

FACTS AND FIGURES

➤ In April 1985, McDonnell Douglas signed an agreement with China to have MD-82s assembled in Shanghai.

➤ The larger MD-80 series can carry 26,276 litres (5780 gal.) of fuel.

➤ The MD series has sold particularly well for domestic flights in the U.S.

➤ In 1989, the company tested an MD-80 with ultra-high-bypass (UHB) engines.

➤ When it entered service, the MD-83 was the most fuel-efficient airliner in its class.

➤ The MD-90 Trunkliner is license-built in China, with specially modified landing gear for better rough-field performance.

The ever-changing "rubber" airliner

Part of the "family" of McDonnell Douglas airliners, the twin-engine DC-9 (redesignated the MD-80 in 1983) was intended to serve short- to medium-haul routes and complement the long-range Douglas DC-8. Making its first flight on 25 February 1965, the DC-9 was in competition with the French Caravelle and British BAC One-Eleven. When it was 'relaunched' as the MD-80, the aircraft's main competitor was the Boeing 737, production of the earlier French and British rear-

engine airliners having stopped. Douglas had progressively stretched the DC-9's fuselage to allow space for more seats and extended the wingspan in the DC-9 Series 20, 30, 40 and 50.

Powered by re-fanned Pratt & Whitney JT8D-200 series turbofans, which offered more thrust yet were much quieter, the early MD-80s had a fuselage stretched by another 15 feet and a wing of greater span and chord than the Series 50.

The MD-80 began flight tests on 18 October 1979. The early

model was followed by the MD-81 and four more series models up to the MD-90, some of these later aircraft, reverting to a shorter fuselage and incorporating state-of-the-art systems, being intended to replace the old DC-9.

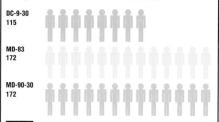

Left: The DC-9-80 was relaunched as the MD-80 in 1983. All subsequent aircraft in the series have adopted the 'MD' prefix.

Right: The launch customer for the MD-80 was Swissair, which received its first aircraft in 1980. It was known then as the DC-9-81.

MD-87

Finnair has long been a staunch McDonnell Douglas customer and was the first operator of the MD-87 in November 1987. The short-fuselage MD-87 can accommodate up to 130 passengers.

Following the success of the DC-9, the MD-80 series continues with rear-mounted engines, allowing a clean wing design. Its competitors, Boeing and Airbus, both use wing-mounted engines.

The MD-87 was the first of the MD-80 family to be fitted with an EFIS 'glass' cockpit and a head-up display, making the pilot's life much easier.

To reduce development and testing costs, the same wing is used throughout the MD-80 series. The wing is an all-metal two-spar structure with riveted spanwise stringers. The wing trailing edge is fiberglass.

The main fuselage section has a galley at the end of each cabin, one toilet at the front and two at the rear. Three cargo doors to the underfloor holds are on the starboard side.

The most distinctive feature introduced in the MD-87 is the new re-sculptured aerodynamically-efficient tail and an extended low-drag tailcone.

A two-man crew is all that is needed to fly an MD-87; traditional flight engineer's tasks are automated.

Power from the earliest DC-9 up to the MD-87 has been provided by continuously refined and upgraded versions of the excellent JT8 turbofan engine.

FINNAIR OH-LMA md-87

ACTION DATA

PASSENGER LOAD
The MD-83 and MD-90-30 both used the same stretched fuselage with a much increased passenger capacity than earlier models. The latest member of the family, the MD-95, will have a shorter fuselage comparable to that of the DC-9 Series 50.

DC-9-30 115

MD-83 172

MD-90-30 172

NOISE
As well as being more fuel-efficient, modern turbofans are much quieter in order to comply with strict noise regulations, especially for night operations. The DC-9 is noisy by today's standards, the MD-83 was one of the quietest airliners of the 1980s, and the even newer MD-90 with its IAE V2500 turbofans is quieter still.

DC-9-30 Maximum | MD-83 Medium | MD-90-30 Lowest

RANGE
The original DC-9 could hold less fuel than the "stretched" MD-83 and MD-90-30. More efficient engines and modifications to the wings have given the MD-83 and MD-90 much better fuel economy, allowing them to fly farther on the same amount of fuel.

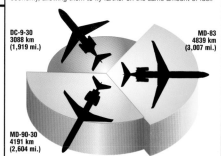

DC-9-30 3088 km (1,919 mi.)

MD-83 4839 km (3,007 mi.)

MD-90-30 4191 km (2,604 mi.)

From DC-9 to MD-95

■ **DC-9 SERIES 50:** The Series 50 was the last version of the original DC-9 series and seated up to 139 passengers. Ninety-six Series 50s were built up to April 1981. Other features included new brakes and redesigned thrust reversers.

■ **MD-80:** Originally called the DC-9-80 'Super Stretch', the MD-80 family includes five different versions that are able to carry varying numbers of passengers over differing ranges. Structural and avionics improvements were also made.

■ **MD-90:** Intended as an advanced-technology follow-on to the MD-80, a major change was the adoption of the considerably more efficient and quieter IAE V2500 turbofan engines in place of the ageing Pratt & Whitney JT8Ds.

■ **MD-95:** This new version combines the short fuselage of the MD-87 (comparable to the DC-9-50) with the wing of the MD-80 and the avionics of the MD-90. New BMW Rolls-Royce BRT715 engines power the aircraft.

McDONNELL DOUGLAS

MD-90

● Turbofan engines ● Medium-range airliner ● Advanced technology

T he McDonnell Douglas MD-90
appeared in the 1990s as a high-
technology airliner to replace
ageing DC-9s and to compete with the
successful Boeing 737. The MD-90 has
enjoyed a respected commercial flying
career, which is now being shortened by
Boeing's 1997 purchase of the McDonnell
Douglas company. The MD-90 is being
discontinued to enable the firm to focus
solely on the 737 in this class.

▲ Despite using some of the
most advanced commercial aviation technology
available, the MD-90 order-books have been revised
downwards after initial interest in the design.

PHOTO FILE

McDONNELL DOUGLAS MD-90

◄ **Sound design**
The MD-90 has the same
fuselage length as the earlier
designed MD-80. This greatly
reduced the cost of the aircraft.

Graceful performer ►
Banking away from the camera, an MD-90
displays its long elegant wingspan.

◄ **Delta direct**
An order for 50 examples from Delta
Airlines and an option for a further 115
has now been significantly reduced by
the operator. Responding to this, Boeing
has decided to cancel the MD-90.

World market ►
Although resembling
many other twin-
engined airliners, the
MD-90 was most
notable for its use of
IAE V2500 turbofans.

◄ **Desert star**
Flying with Saudi
Arabian Airlines these
aircraft are occasionally
used as VIP transports
for Saudi royalty.

FACTS AND FIGURES

➤ The prototype for the MD-90 series
completed its maiden flight on
22 February 1993

➤ Assembly of the first production MD-90
began at Long Beach, California.

➤ The MD-90-30T Trunkliner is fitted with a
modified strengthened undercarriage.

➤ Shanghai Aircraft Manufacturing Factory
(SAMF) was scheduled to build the
MD-95. This deal has been cancelled.

➤ China is seeking at least 130 examples
of the MD-90.

➤ Up to 20 MD-90s were to be assembled
in China for its domestic market.

The MD-90, last of the DC-9 family

The low-wing, twin-engined MD-90 jetliner owes its elegant heritage to the successful Douglas DC-9/MD-80 series that are familiar on world airline routes. Thus, the MD-90's exterior has a familiar look, but on the inside this aircraft is different. The advanced-technology MD-90 uses new engines, power management system, cockpit instruments, and avionics.

The MD-90 (and the planned MD-95) were the most successful commercial aircraft conceived by McDonnell Douglas in California. Airline executives find them efficient and economical.

Passengers enjoy their quiet comfort. Pilots like the digital 'glass cockpit.' A robust career seemed in store when the manufacturer showed off the latest design at the Paris air show in 1991. Also promising were plans for co-production in China, where earlier MD-82/83 variants had already been manufactured for the Chinese airline market.

However, Boeing purchased McDonnell Douglas in 1997 and announced that, in order to allow it to concentrate on its 737 series, the much-admired MD-90 would be discontinued. However, the MD-95 is to remain in limited production.

Left: In an effort to increase sales, McDonnell Douglas undertook a world tour with the MD-90.

Above: The long fuselage of the MD-90 allows the aircraft to carry up to 172 passengers in relative comfort. Airline operators have praised the design and capabilities of the type.

MD-90-30

Type: twin-engine, medium-range airliner

Powerplant: two 111.21-kN (25,020-lb.-thrust) IAE V2525-D5 turbofan engines

Maximum speed: 844 km/h (523 m.p.h.) at 6960 m (23,000 ft.)

Maximum cruising speed: 809 km/h (502 m.p.h.) at 10,670 m (35,000 ft.)

Initial climb rate: 885 m/min (2,900 f.p.m.) at sea level

Range: 4200 km (2,604 mi.) with 153 passengers and fuel reserve

Service ceiling: 12,100 m (39,700 ft.)

Weights: empty 40,007 kg (88,015 lb.); maximum take-off 70,760 kg (155,672 lb.)

Accommodation: two pilots (flight deck); maximum of 172 passengers (standard 153), plus flight attendants

Dimensions:
span 32.87 m (1017 ft. 10 in.)
length 46.51 m (152 ft. 7 in.)
height 9.33 m (30 ft. 7 in.)
wing area 112 m² (1,205 sq. ft.)

MD-90

Operated by Japan Air System, this is one of seven MD-90s that wear an elaborate and highly colourful paint scheme designed by the noted motion picture director Akira Kurosawa.

With its tail adapted from the larger MD-87 the new MD-90 used a host of components from other airliners. This allowed the purchase cost of the aircraft to be greatly reduced.

Pilots have found that, with the latest advanced flight controls, the performance of the aircraft is superb. The flight deck is fitted with electronic flight instruments and a complete full-flight management system. All this information is displayed to the pilots via two large cathode-ray tube displays.

The increased fuselage length allowed the total number of passengers to be increased to a maximum of 172. For general commercial flights however, this number is reduced to 153. Situated below the main fuselage deck is the larger lower-deck space for cargo and luggage.

As airline needs evolve, McDonnell Douglas intended to produce other MD-90s including variants with quieter engines and more fuel-efficient engines. Though interest in the MD-90 was promising further developments are now unlikely.

Retained on the MD-90 were the long slender wings from previous McDonnell Douglas airliners. Offering exceptional performance at high altitude, while allowing the aircraft to use relatively small airports, the design was a major breakthrough.

Internationally developed and manufactured, the V2500 turbofan engine represented one of the most advanced and fuel efficient jet powerplants for the time. The engine is a product of Pratt & Whitney in the USA and Rolls-Royce of Great Britain.

PROUD HERITAGE

Small wonder: Designed as a smaller companion to the DC-8, the McDonnell Douglas DC-9 (pictured below), entered service in the 1960s. The aircraft remains in use for short-haul routes and as a cargo carrier for courier operators.

'Stretched potential': Realising the requirement for a larger medium-range airliner, McDonnell Douglas developed the DC-9 with improved engines into the MD-80 (below). The aircraft operates around the world on domestic flights.

Customer demand: The go-ahead to develop the MD-95 (below) was given in July 1994. The aircraft is now the sole survivor of the company's airliner series remaining in production. The MD-95 will be fitted with Rolls-Royce engines.

Still going strong

■ **AV-8B HARRIER II:** With its unique abilities the Harrier II has seen extensive combat in recent conflicts, proving to be a capable attack platform.

■ **C-17 GLOBEMASTER III:** Fast becoming the standard transport aircraft within the USAF, the C-17 has served in Afghanistan and Iraq.

■ **MD-11:** Long-range coupled with a wide fuselage body are just two of the features that have allowed the MD-11 to become a success.

■ **MD 520N:** Representing a complete departure from normal helicopter design, the MD 520N has become an instant best seller.

McDONNELL DOUGLAS
MD-11

● Successor to the DC-10 ● Electronic 'glass' cockpit ● Long range

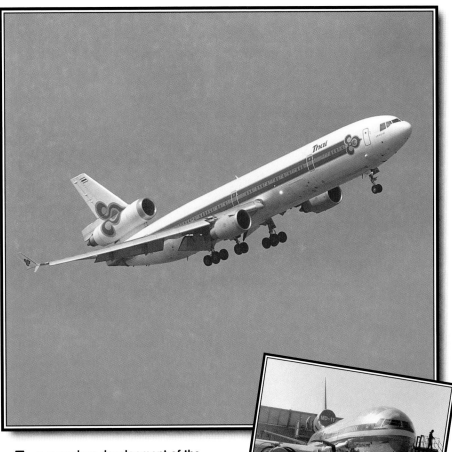

As a modern development of the DC-10, McDonnell Douglas was certain the MD-11 would be highly successful. An all-digital flightdeck and new levels of passenger comfort made the aircraft attractive at a time when many airlines were looking to renew their fleets. Early deficiencies in range and the ailing fortunes of McDonnell Douglas, however, have robbed the MD-11 of the success it deserves.

▲ It is not known whether the MD-11 will survive as an airliner following the merger of McDonnell Douglas and Boeing. It is in direct competition with the Boeing 747, 767 and 777 wide-bodied airliners.

▲ Six-screen cockpit
Each member of the flightcrew has three screens, which display all flight information in multi-colour.

▼ Shiny tri-jet
Development MD-11s and those of American Airlines fly in a polished natural-metal finish.

▲ On the way to Taipei
Taipei-based China Airlines received the 100th MD-11 to come off the McDonnell Douglas Long Beach production line. At least 10 companies in America and Europe supply major components for the MD-11.

▼ Delta MD-11 at Gatwick
Although MD-11s belonging to American Airlines are familiar visitors to the UK, those operated by Delta Air Lines are rare. This Delta MD-11 was seen at Gatwick in 1997.

▲ MD-11 in Hong Kong
Hong Kong has become a centre of MD-11 operations with several Far Eastern airlines. The Pacific Rim is experiencing a huge growth in air transport, especially of cargo, and MD-11Fs are likely to play an important part.

FACTS AND FIGURES

➤ The first flight of the MD-11 was made on 10 January 1990 and five aircraft were used in the flight-test programme.

➤ The MD-11 is 5.66 m (18 ft. 7 in.) longer than the DC-10 and has about 50 more seats.

➤ In mid-1997 McDonnell Douglas was clearing a final backlog of orders.

➤ Specially converted, second-hand MD-11s are proving to be exceptionally useful in the pure-freighter role.

➤ In all-freight configuration the MD-11 has a maximum payload of 93304 kg.

➤ Federal Express is updating a number of DC-10s with MD-11 cockpit systems.

PROFILE

Douglas' last commercial aircraft?

During the mid-1980s McDonnell Douglas depended on sales of its wide-bodied MD-11 to keep the company alive as a supplier of large commercial aircraft. Unfortunately, early problems and the uncertain financial position of McDonnell Douglas meant that few orders were forthcoming.

Easy to distinguish from the DC-10, the MD-11, with its upturned winglets, introduced advanced engines and offered improved range, fuel efficiency and comfort. But when McDonnell Douglas was taken over by the Boeing empire, the future of its aircraft initially looked bleak. When details of the merger were finalised however, it became clear that Boeing were obliged to keep the basic MD-11 design alive.

Although the type is providing excellent airline service and new commercial customers would be easy to find, Boeing will probably develop the aircraft into a next-generation tanker-transport, possibly to replace the USAF's ageing fleet of KC-135 Stratotankers. In this way, competition with Boeing's established long-range airliners will be avoided.

By late-1997 Japan Airlines (JAL) was operating a fleet of 10 MD-11s. JAL gives its aircraft unusual names, with the MD-11s being known as the 'J Bird'. A total of 183 MD-11s were ordered worldwide and are likely to serve for many years.

The large fin gives the MD-11 excellent stability in the horizontal axis. A dual-section rudder provides directional control.

In common with most contemporary airliners, the MD-11 features range-extending winglets. Those of the MD-11 extend above and below the wingtip.

MD-11

A number of airlines received the MD-11 and the majority are very pleased with its performance. From its inception, the aircraft faced stiff competition from Airbus Industrie and Boeing airliners.

With a maximum internal width of 5.71 m (19 ft. 9 in.) the cabin allows nine-abreast seating. Plans for a twin-engined, small-fuselage derivative, the MD-20, have been abandoned.

Modern technology allows long-range operation of the MD-11 with only two flightcrew. Two observers may also be accommodated in the cockpit.

Customers may specify either Pratt & Whitney PW4460 or General Electric CF6-80C2D1F turbofans. Plans to develop a Rolls-Royce Trent 650-powered version were abandoned.

Composite materials form a significant part of the MD-11 airframe, including most of the control surfaces, engine inlets and other nacelle components, and wing/fuselage fillets.

One or two optional fuel tanks, each of 7472 litres (1,974 gal.), can be fitted in the forward, underfloor cargo hold. This extra fuel is carried at the expense of freight, but extends the MD-11's range considerably.

A centre fuselage undercarriage leg, as fitted to later DC-10s, spreads aircraft weight more evenly on runways and allows greater take-off weights.

The MD-11 has less sweepback on its tailplane and a more efficient aerodynamic design than the DC-10. In addition, 7571 litres (2,000 gal.) of fuel are carried in a trim tank.

MD-11

Type: long-range airliner

Powerplant: three 266.9-kN (60,042-lb.-thrust) Pratt & Whitney PW4460 or 273.57-kN (61,542-lb.-thrust General Electric CF6-80C2D1F turbofans

Maximum speed: 945 km/h (586 m.p.h.) at 9450 m (31,000 ft.)

Range: 12,569 km (7,793 mi.) with 323 passengers

Weights: operating empty 131,035 kg (277,500 lb.); maximum take-off 273,289 kg (602,500 lb.)

Passengers: up to 410 passengers maximum; 323 in typical two-class configuration; 293 in three-class configuration

Dimensions: span 51.77 m (169 ft. 6 in.)
length 61.24 m (200 ft. 10 in.)
height 17.60 m (57 ft. 7 in.)
wing area 338.90 m² (3,648 sq.ft.)

ACTION DATA

PASSENGERS
Although the MD-11 can seat 410 passengers in a single-class layout, 323 in a two-class layout is more realistic. The TriStar offers a similar capacity, but the Il-96 seats only 235 in a mixed layout.

MD-11	410 passengers
Il-96-300	300 passengers
L-1011 TRISTAR 100	400 passengers

MAXIMUM SPEED
Speed is important for an airliner as passengers want the shortest possible journey time. A programme of improvements has increased the efficiency of the MD-11 by reducing drag and increasing power, thereby giving an impressive speed performance.

MD-11	945 km/h (586 m.p.h.)
Il-96-300	900 km/h (558 m.p.h.)
L-1011 TRISTAR 100	925 km/h (574 m.p.h.)

THRUST
Modern, powerful and efficient turbofans give the MD-11 long range and good field performance. Early plans to offer a Rolls-Royce Trent 650-powered version were abandoned as the perceived demand did not warrant the financial investment necessary.

MD-11	Il-96-300	L-1011 TRISTAR 100
821 kN (180,123-lb.-thrust)	624 kN (140,375-lb.-thrust)	561 kN (126,203-lb.-thrust)

Tri-jet design

HAWKER SIDDELEY TRIDENT: In 1957 de Havilland began the design of the Trident to meet airline requirements for a 965-km/h (600-m.p.h.) short-haul airliner.

LOCKHEED L-1011 TRISTAR: Designed to match the requirements of American Airlines for a short- to medium-haul airliner, the Tristar was powered by Rolls-Royce engines.

McDONNELL DOUGLAS DC-10: Aimed at the same American Airlines specification as the Tristar, the DC-10 had a very similar configuration.

TUPOLEV Tu-154 'CARELESS': This medium- to long-range transport seats up to 167 passengers and remains in widespread service, especially in former Soviet countries.

NORTH AMERICAN

SABRELINER

● T-39 development ● Many still in service ● High performance

Having successfully built the T-39 for the US military, North American went on to produce the aircraft as the Sabreliner, or Sabre as it was often known, as one of the earliest biz-jets. From the initial Sabreliner 40, the company produced a series of improved variants which culminated in the Sabreliner Series 65, a turbofan-powered, 10-passenger executive transport equipped with a supercritical wing for transcontinental range.

▲ *Originally selling in considerable numbers, by the late 1960s the Sabre/Sabreliner was suffering a drop in sales because of the greater efficiency of turbofan-engined rivals.*

PHOTO FILE

NORTH AMERICAN SABRELINER

▼ **Final Sabre**
The last of the Sabre series in production was the TFE731-3-powered, transcontinental Sabre 65.

▲ **Taller, re-engined 75A**
With greater cabin height and more efficient engines, the Model 75A was built until 1982.

Civil T-39A ▶
Initially, North American offered the Sabreliner Series 40. It was basically a civilian-certified version of the T-39A.

▲ **40 and 60**
Two extra cabin windows distinguish the Series 60 from the Series 40.

Sabreliner into the 1980s ▶
This converted Series 60 was the prototype of the early 1980s Series 65.

FACTS AND FIGURES

➤ Production of the Sabreliner ceased at Rockwell's El Segundo plant on the day the facility's lease expired.

➤ A number of civilian-specification Sabreliners were used by the US Navy.

➤ The shortened Sabre designation was officially adopted in 1970.

➤ A simplified version of the Series 40, the Sabreliner Commander, was available for US $995,000 in 1971.

➤ Sabre production rights were passed to the Sabreliner Corporation in 1983.

➤ Sabreliner Corp's plans to produce an advanced Series 85 with Agusta failed.

PROFILE

North American executive dream

North American was quick to realise the potential of its military T-39 as an executive transport for the civilian market. The company had no civil marketing experience, however, and secured a tie-up with the Remmert-Werner group for finishing, distribution and marketing facilities.

North American became North American Rockwell in September 1967, trading under this title for a while before becoming Rockwell

International. The newly named company established a Sabreliner Division to continue Sabre production, which eventually ceased with the last Series 65 on 1 January 1982.

Evolution of the Sabreliner saw the aircraft develop into a 10-seater when the Series 40 was stretched by 0.96 m (3 ft. 2 in.) to become the Series 60, and sales remained high until more modern turbofan-powered aircraft appeared in the early 1970s. Rockwell responded with

the Series 75A, powered by General Electric CF 700 2D-2 turbofans, and later with the Garrett-powered Series 65, but the popular Sabreliner had reached the end of its development cycle.

A new wing of supercritical type allowed the Series 65 to cruise efficiently at high speeds.

A major boost for the Model 75A came from the Federal Aviation Administration (FAA), which ordered 15 for flight inspection duties. An expected Sabreliner order from the US Coast Guard failed to materialise.

All tail surfaces were of cantilever construction. The main structural material was light alloy, and the Sabreliner continues to maintain an excellent reputation for structural integrity.

Sabreliner 60

Type: eight-ten seat, twin-engined business jet

Powerplant: two 14.68-kN (3,303 lb.-thrust) Pratt & Whitney JT12A-8 turbojets

Maximum speed: 906 km/h (563 m.p.h.) at 6550 m (21,490 ft.)

Range: 3239 km (2,013 mi.) with maximum fuel, with four passengers, baggage and 45 min reserves

Service ceiling: 13,715 m (45,000 ft.)

Weights: empty equipped 5103 kg (11,250 lb.); take-off 8877 kg (19,570 lb.) with four passengers

Accommodation: 10 passengers, or 1135 kg (2,304 lb.) of freight with the seats removed

Dimensions:
span	13.61 m	(44 ft. 8 in.)
length	14.30 m	(46 ft. 11 in.)
height	4.88 m	(16 ft.)
wing area	31.78 m²	(342 sq. ft.)

SABRELINER 65

Seen in the markings of the Acopian Technical Company, this aircraft was the last of the 76 Sabre 65s built. The names Sabre and Sabreliner were both applied to the series.

Full blind-flying equipment was a standard feature of the Model 65's two-crew cockpit. A comprehensive range of avionics, including weather radar, was also available.

A maximum of ten passengers enjoyed the comfort of the Sabreliner's pressurised and air-conditioned cabin. All seating layouts included provision for a galley and toilet.

Unusual 'rounded triangular' windows were a feature of all Sabreliner models except for the Series 70/75 aircraft. The lengthened cabin of later aircraft incorporated five windows.

Rockwell gained certification for the Series 60 and 75A aircraft to fly from gravel runways after the nosewheel leg had been fitted with a special gravel deflector.

Garrett AiResearch TFE731-3-1D turbofans considerably improved the efficiency of the Sabreliner. Each engine was fitted with a hydraulically-actuated thrust reverser for improved landing performance.

ACTION DATA

ECONOMIC CRUISING SPEED

Several US manufacturers found a ready home market for executive jets in the 1960s and 1970s. When it initially entered the market, the Sabreliner was one of the highest performing types, but other manufacturers were quick to catch up.

SABRELINER 75A 772 km/h (480 m.p.h.)

MODEL 1329-25 JETSTAR II 811 km/h (504 m.p.h.)

GULFSTREAM II-B 777 km/h (483 m.p.h.)

PASSENGERS

In its lengthened Series 75A form, the Sabreliner could carry a maximum of ten passengers, although eight or nine was more realistic for maximum comfort. The Gulfstream II-B was a larger contemporary of the Sabreliner 75A.

SABRELINER 75A 10

MODEL 1329-25 JETSTAR II 10

GULFSTREAM II-B 19

RANGE

Even with the unusual CF 700 turbofan, featuring a turbojet core and rear-mounted fan, the Sabreliner 75A was unable to match the range of its US rivals. The other types were larger, heavier, more complex machines, and correspondingly were more costly to operate, however.

SABRELINER 75A 3174 km (1972 mi.)

GULFSTREAM II-B 6025 km (3,744 mi.)

MODEL 1329-25 JETSTAR II 4818 km (2,994 mi.)

Biz-jets of the 1960s

■ **ROCKWELL JET COMMANDER 1121:** Following first deliveries in 1965, the Jet Commander design was taken over by IAI.

■ **DE HAVILLAND DH 125:** Work began in 1961 on what was to become a huge sales success. This aircraft is still in production.

■ **LEARJET 23:** As the first model in a long line of highly successful biz-jets, the Model 23 had several features from a Swiss fighter project.

■ **MBB HFB 320 HANSA:** This unusual German design first flew in 1964, but was not as successful as its US and British contemporaries.

NORTHROP

GAMMA

● All-metal monoplane ● Airmail hauling ● Single pilot

▲ *Ultra-modern for the period, the Northrop Gamma brought new standards to aircraft design. With its record-breaking flights, the Gamma was admired everywhere it was exhibited.*

he beautiful Northrop Gammas of the early 1930s began as mail-carriers, but performed many duties. In an age when biplanes were made of wood and fabric, Jack Northrop's flying machines were silvery monoplanes constructed of metal. The Gammas were custom-built, and (except for a batch sent to China) each was different. Conceived in peacetime, later versions of the Gamma did see combat in China.

NORTHROP GAMMA

▼ **Great Gamma**
Though not designed for air racing, the Gamma achieved a good reputation during the 1930s and set many inter-city records. This increased orders for the aircraft across the USA.

▲ **Wheel covers**
Huge fairings were placed over the wheels, leading to a more streamlined design.

▼ **Wing design**
The Northrop Gamma utilised one of the most efficient wings of its time. Northrop knew more about airfoils and strength than any manufacturer of the period.

▲ **Ellsworth's Gamma**
This example was equipped for a flight across the Antarctic, but was damaged before the attempt.

◀ **Airline operations**
Trans World Airlines flew the Gamma as an Experimental Overweather Laboratory aircraft, allowing information to be collected for future overseas routes. Mail was also carried within the fuselage.

FACTS AND FIGURES

➤ In 1933 Frank Hawks flew the *Sky Chief* from Los Angeles to New York in 13 hours 27 minutes, averaging 291 km/h (180 m.p.h.).

➤ Gammas influenced the design of later military planes, including the Dauntless.

➤ Howard Hughes flew a Gamma from California to New Jersey in nine hours.

➤ Forty-nine aircraft in the Gamma series were delivered to the Chinese government as light bombers.

➤ The Gamma lost out to North American's BC-1 as a military trainer.

➤ Variants of the Gamma were used as research aircraft in Great Britain.

PROFILE

Gamma's golden era

Jack Northrop (who broke away from Douglas to form his own company in 1933) spent a lifetime creating advanced aircraft, from his all-metal Gammas of the 1930s to the flying wings that evolved into today's B-2 bomber. The first two Gammas were built for celebrated pilot/adventurers Frank Hawks and Lincoln Ellsworth. Hawks used his ship, called the *Texaco Sky Chief*, to set distance records; Ellsworth, with Bernt Balchen, carried out dramatic explorations of the Antarctic.

Other Northrop Gamma aircraft were built to serve military missions and to carry mail. One Gamma became an Overweather Experimental Laboratory, contributing immensely to scientific knowledge of flight at high altitude. Yet another Gamma was flown to a distance record by Howard Hughes after having been raced by famous aviatrix Jacqueline Cochran.

The record-breaking flights by Gammas were all accomplished in the civilian world, but the majority of the Gammas built were military. Unfortunately, the Gamma bombers of the Chinese air force proved of little use when Japan invaded China.

Above: This Gamma was fitted with a Curtiss V-1570 Conqueror engine for the pioneering aviatrix Jacqueline Cochran. Unfortunately, this aircraft was destroyed in a crash in Texas.

Above: The Gamma's all-metal skin sparkles with the reflections from the sun. The type brought with it new advances in aircraft design.

Gamma 2A

Type: high-speed monoplane

Powerplant: typically (Gamma 2A) one 585-kW (785-hp.) Wright Whirlwind GR-1510 14-cylinder air-cooled radial driving a three-bladed propeller, or (Gamma 2B) one 373-kW (500-hp.) Pratt & Whitney Wasp SD nine-cylinder radial driving a two-bladed propeller

Maximum speed: 399 km/h (247 m.p.h.) at 2135 m (7,000 ft.)

Cruising speed: 354 km/h (219 m.p.h.) at 2135 m (7,000 ft.)

Range: 4025 km (2,495 mi.)

Service ceiling: 7130 m (23,400 ft.)

Weights: empty 1588 kg (3,494 lb.); loaded 3175 kg (6,985 lb.); max. take-off 3460 kg (7,612 lb.)

Dimensions:
span 14.63 m (48 ft.)
length 9.07 m (29 ft. 9 in.)
height 2.67 m (8 ft. 9 in.)
wing area 33.72 m² (363 sq. ft.)

GAMMA 2D

This Gamma was operated by Trans World Airlines. The type offered customers the means to carry a small number of passengers or mail at high speed across the United States.

The two cargo compartments were situated behind the engine. Hatches were positioned on top of the fuselage to provide access to the cargo. If passengers were carried seats were fitted to the fuselage sides in these sections. On most flights only mail was carried. The pilot's cockpit was situated under a simplified sliding canopy; visibility was adequate, although landing required a fair degree of experience.

To increase the performance of the aircraft the wheels were housed in large streamlined trousers, from which only about one third of each wheel protruded. Other variants of the Gamma were equipped with large floats.

The most revolutionary feature of the Gamma was its wing design, made of metal and incorporating a full multi-spar construction. The centre-section was built integrally within the fuselage, while the outer panels were bolted to the centre-section.

AIR EXPRESS
NC13758
TWA
NC13758
17

ACTION DATA

MAXIMUM SPEED

The Gamma had exceptional performance and many of the type established aviation records because of their high speed. Northrop's Delta used a similar layout to the Gamma but compared to other aircraft of the period, the Gamma was revolutionary.

GAMMA 2A	399 km/h (247 m.p.h.)
ORION 9	354 km/h (219 m.p.h.)
DELTA 1D-5	352 km/h (218 m.p.h.)

OPERATIONAL RANGE

In operation as a mailplane and small airliner, range was vital for the Gamma's future. Its ability to cover huge distances compared to its rivals gave Northrop aircraft sales success.

ORION 9 1205 km (747 mi.)
GAMMA 2A 4025 km (2,495 mi.)
DELTA 1D-5 2655 km (1,646 mi.)

SERVICE CEILING

By employing a sophisticated wing design, Northrop's Gamma was able to obtain a considerable altitude advantage over the Orion 9 and Delta 1D. Operating at a higher altitude meant the Gamma had reduced fuel consumption yet offered exceptional range.

GAMMA 2A 7130 m (23,400 ft.)
ORION 9 6705 m (22,000 ft.)
DELTA 1D-5 6095 m (20,000 ft.)

Numerous Northrops

■ **ALPHA:** Despite its ungainly appearance and fixed landing gear, the 1930 Alpha may be regarded as the first 'modern' airliner.

■ **BETA:** The Beta sporting monoplane was the first aircraft to exceed 322 km/h (200 m.p.h.) with its Wright Whirlwind radial engine.

■ **DELTA:** The United States Coast Guard operated a version of the Delta airliner as a transport for the Treasury Secretary.

■ **MODEL 8A:** The Northrop-designed but Douglas-produced A-17A was operated briefly by the USAAF before being sold to the RAF.

PIPER PA-31

NAVAJO

● Business aircraft ● Commuter airliner ● Twin-engined safety

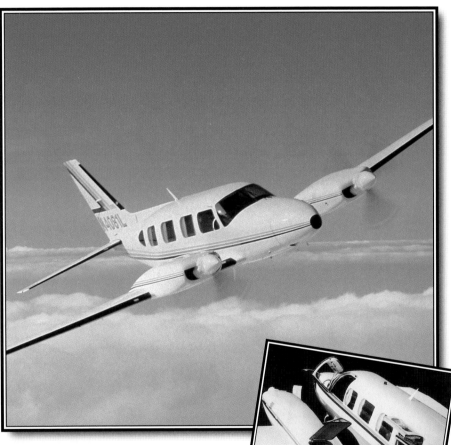

As the first of a new series of large twin-engined executive aircraft, Piper's PA-31-300 Navajo was also aimed at the commuter airline and corporate markets. The Navajo family includes the Turbo Navajo, Navajo C/R, Pressurised Navajo and Navajo Chieftain. Each model in the series is available in standard, commuter or executive versions with differences in seating arrangements and interior cabin layouts.

▲ With its PA-31, Piper produced an aircraft which was universally popular. 'Customer friendly' features included the provision of baggage stowage space in the rear of the engine nacelles.

PIPER PA-31 NAVAJO

◀ **Clean design**
Each of the slim engine nacelles is positioned well forward of the low-set straight wings.

▼ **Built-in stairs**
For easy cabin access at poorly equipped airfields, the Navajo features a 'Dutch' door at the rear of the cabin; the top half hinges upwards and the lower half, with built-in steps, hinges downwards.

Freight version ▶
Removal of the Navajo's seats allows it to fly as a light freight transport. Here an assorted cargo is secured by webbing straps to strongpoints on the aircraft's floor.

▼ **Instrumentation**
Full blind flying instruments and night flying capability are common to all variants of the PA-31. This aircraft is finished in the standard Piper scheme.

▼ **Pressurised Navajo**
Changes from the initial Navajo design are evident in this picture of the pressurised version. There are fewer windows, a smaller windshield and an elongated nose.

FACTS AND FIGURES

➤ The pressurised version of the Navajo was designated the PA-31-425. A total of 258 was built.

➤ The prototype Navajo first flew on 30 September 1964.

➤ A total of 1824 Navajos was built and production ended in 1972.

➤ Introduced in 1973, the PA-31-350 Navajo Chieftain had a longer fuselage; 1942 examples were manufactured.

➤ The Navajo was the design basis for all of Piper's subsequent large twins.

➤ The Navajo has a main cabin cargo capacity of 6 m³ (211 cu. ft.).

PROFILE

Piper's big business twin

Piper introduced the Navajo in 1964 as an addition to its range of business twins which included the Apache, Aztec and Twin Comanche. With a pair of 224-kW (300-hp.) Lycoming IO-540 piston engines and greater capacity than previous models, the streamlined Navajo provided seating for up to eight passengers, although the standard layout held six.

Aimed primarily at the business market, the Navajo has been successfully employed as a third-level commuter airliner

and for air taxi operations. Various versions of the Navajo were produced, including the Turbo Navajo which had turbo-supercharged engines (whose propellers counter-rotated to cancel out engine torque).

A pressurised version, the PA-31P, was first flown in 1968, followed in the early 1970s by the Navajo Chieftain, later just called the Chieftain, which had a fuselage extension of 0.61 m and seating fitted for up to 10 passengers.

In 1969 the Navajo range was extended with the first

flight of the PA-31T Cheyenne, basically a turboprop version of the PA-31P. Certificated in 1972, it became Piper's first turbine-engined business aircraft and allowed Piper to compete with the Beech King Air. A number of Navajos also serve with air forces around the world.

Below: Argentina was one of several military customers, including a number elsewhere in South America, for variants of the PA-31.

Above: Basically similar to the standard Navajo, the PA-31 Navajo C/R introduced counter-rotating propellers and nacelle baggage accommodation.

All versions of the Navajo have the same swept-back cantilever all-metal vertical tail surfaces and variable-incidence tailplane. Trim tabs are installed on the rudder and starboard elevator.

Power comes from two 261-kW (350-hp.) six-cylinder horizontally-opposed air-cooled engines, fitted with Hartzell three-bladed, constant-speed, fully-feathering metal counter-rotating propellers. The engines are turbocharged.

The fuselage is a conventional all-metal, semi-monocoque structure. It has a long nose which can accommodate baggage as well as the undercarriage nosewheel.

In 'Standard Interior Group' configuration the cabin seats six passengers. In 'Commuter Interior Group' configuration, accommodation increases to a maximum of 10 and basic empty weight rises by 39.5 kg (87 lb.). Both configurations offer a choice of nine interior colour schemes.

PA-31-350 CHIEFTAIN

With its 0.61-m (2-ft.) fuselage extension, the Chieftain was a higher capacity version of the Navajo. It was the first aircraft in the series to incorporate the nacelle baggage holds.

FAR WEST AIRLINES

N27906

At the rear of the cabin a 91-kg (200-lb.) maximum capacity baggage compartment is provided. This is especially useful when the optional fuel tanks are installed, since they are accommodated in the baggage space at the rear of the nacelles.

Piper twins

■ **PA-23 AZTEC:** Piper developed the Aztec from its first twin, the PA-23 Apache. The Aztec introduced more powerful engines.

■ **PA-30 TWIN COMANCHE:** A twin-engined variant of the PA-23 Comanche, the PA-30 was powered by two 119-kW (160-hp.) engines.

■ **PA-31T CHEYENNE:** Adding turboprop engines to the Chieftain airframe produced the fast and comfortable Cheyenne.

■ **PA-34 SENECA:** Again, Piper developed a twin from a single-engined design. In this case, the PA-32 Saratoga led to the PA-34.

PIPER PA-34

SENECA

● Traffic monitoring over London ● Radio broadcasting from the air

▲ Providing a 'flying eye' service is an advertising and publicity opportunity for a radio station. It also gives a valuable service to the motoring public allowing better journey planning.

Anyone who has experienced driving conditions in London, or any other large city around the world for that matter, will know of and appreciate the efforts of the 'flying eye' aircraft that circle overhead during the morning and evening peak traffic periods. These aircraft, sponsored by local radio stations, provide a bird's-eye view of the road network below, allowing advice to be given to drivers fighting their way through rush hour traffic.

PIPER PA-34 SENECA

◄ Low-level flying
Much of a typical traffic-monitoring flight is undertaken at low level not only to allow observers a good view of the ground, but also to avoid airliner flight paths.

▼ Police operations
As well as those flights undertaken by radio stations, police forces often employ aircraft of various types (including helicopters) to keep watch on traffic flows.

▲ Twin engines for safety
Two engines give aircraft operating over urban areas an extra safety margin should they encounter mechanical problems. In London, flight regulations ban single-engined fixed-wing types.

▼ Monitoring motorways
As well as urban road networks, 'flying eyes' keep an eye on the motorways that feed them.

▲ Current 'flying eye'
The current Capital Radio aircraft, a Grumman Cougar, is appropriately registered G-FLII.

FACTS AND FIGURES

➤ The Seneca remained in production in 1997 as the PA-34-220T Seneca IV, with styling and other changes.

➤ Piper's Seneca has been built under licence in Poland and Brazil.

➤ In 1996, the standard equipped price for a Seneca IV was $459,900.

➤ The Seneca handles well on take-off as it has 'handed' propellers to counteract engine torque.

➤ The PA-34's avionics allow instrument flying; weather radar may be fitted.

➤ Senecas have a conventional light alloy semi-monocoque fuselage.

PIPER PA-34 SENECA

PROFILE

London's 'flying eyes'

As single-engined aircraft are prohibited from operating over London, twin-engined types are chosen for the 'flying eye' role. Popular types include the Piper PA-34 Seneca six/seven-seat cabin monoplane.

First announced in 1971, the design was essentially a twin-engined derivative of the well-known Cherokee Six. In 1975 a number of modifications were made, resulting in the Seneca II. Major differences were the introduction of turbocharged engines and changes to the controls to improve low-speed handling, an important

consideration during traffic monitoring. The Seneca does not have a monopoly on such operations, however. Other twin-engined types are equally useful in the role, including the varied products of Cessna and other manufacturers.

A typical operation is that undertaken by Cabair Group on behalf of Capital Radio over

London. Based at Elstree Aerodrome, north of London, the 'flying eye' aircraft, a Grumman American GA.7 Cougar (which replaced a PA-34 Seneca), takes to the air during the morning and evening 'rush hours' to provide up-to-the-minute traffic reports to Capital Radio's in-car listeners stuck in London's traffic.

Above: Appropriately registered G-FLYI, this Seneca was employed as the Capital Radio Flying Eye traffic-monitoring aircraft, adorned with the London radio station's name and logo.

Above: Piper's Seneca has been a popular aircraft in the company's range. Based on the single-engined Cherokee Six, it was developed over a relatively short period and sold well.

PA-34-200T Seneca II

Type: six/seven-seat cabin monoplane

Powerplant: two 149-kW (200-hp.) Continental TSIO-360-E flat-four piston engines

Maximum speed: 362 km/h (225 m.p.h.) at 3660 m (12,000 ft.)

Maximum cruising speed: 352 km/h (219 m.p.h.) at 6100 m (20,000 ft.)

Economic cruising speed: 306 km/h (190 m.p.h.) at 7620 m (25,000 ft.)

Range: 1640 km (1,019 mi.) at 6100 m (20,000 ft.)

Service ceiling: 7620 m (25,000 ft.)

Weights: empty 1289 kg (2,842 lb.); maximum take-off 2073 kg (4,570 lb.)

Dimensions:
span	11.86 m	(38 ft. 11 in.)
length	8.72 m	(28 ft. 7 in.)
height	3.02 m	(9 ft. 11 in.)
wing area	19.39 m²	(209 sq. ft.)

PA-34-200 SENECA

Until recently, Capital Radio's Flying Eye was this aircraft, G-FLYI. More than 4500 PA-34s were built by Piper, including the turbocharged variants of the Seneca II and Seneca III, the latter with 164-kW engines.

As well as a flight crew of two and a broadcaster, most 'flying eye' traffic monitoring aircraft carry radio equipment to allow radio broadcasts from the air. The radio signal from the aircraft must be 'beamed' from the aircraft to the radio station and then out to the listeners below.

Gaudy colour schemes are often applied to aircraft engaged in this role as a means of advertising the sponsoring organisation. Corporate names are often applied in large letters on the undersurfaces of the wing.

Originally equipped with normally-aspirated Continental IO-360 air-cooled, flat-six engines, the Seneca was later re-equipped with turbocharged powerplants to improve performance.

The retractable tricycle landing gear fitted to the Seneca was based on that used on the single-engined Cherokee Lance.

As many twin-engined cabin monoplanes are six- or seven-seaters, radio stations using such aircraft for 'flying eye' work often offer seats to members of the public interested in seeing their home town from a different perspective.

'Personalised' out-of-sequence aircraft registrations are a common feature of corporate aircraft. They act as a low-cost means of advertisement for the aircraft's operators.

ACTION DATA

RANGE

Various types of aircraft are used in the traffic reporting role. While the Cessna 172 has a similar range at sea level to the larger twin-engined design, the Bell JetRanger helicopter has a much shorter range. Helicopters are favoured by police forces.

PA-34 SENECA II 1012 km (629 mi.)
172 SKYHAWK 963 km (598 mi.)
MODEL 206B-3 JETRANGER III 676 km (420 mi.)

ECONOMIC CRUISE SPEED

A high economic cruising speed allows an aircraft to cover its patrol area quickly, though traffic monitoring is of necessity carried out at fairly low speeds to guarantee good visibility. High cruise speeds also allow aircraft to reach their monitoring areas quickly after take-off.

PA-34 SENECA II 306 km/h (190 m.p.h.)
172 SKYHAWK 160 km/h (99 m.p.h.)
MODEL 206B-3 JETRANGER III 214 km/h (133 m.p.h.)

MAXIMUM TAKE-OFF WEIGHT

The six/seven-seat Seneca has a maximum take-off weight of just over two tons, while the four-seater Cessna 172 is limited to just over one ton. While the Cessna 172 would be a cheaper aircraft to operate, it lacks the versatility and comfort of the Seneca.

PA-34 SENECA II 2073 kg (4,570 lb.)
172 SKYHAWK 1156 kg (2,549 lb.)
MODEL 206B-3 JETRANGER III 1451 kg (3,199 lb.)

Piper twins in diverse roles

■ **AIRCREW TRAINER:** This PA-23 carries the colours of Greek airline Olympic. Twin-engined types are often used by airlines in a training role.

■ **BUSHPLANE:** Mounted on floats, this Aztec has been modified for use in the Pacific Northwest region of the United States.

■ **MINERAL SURVEYING:** Fitted with a magnetometer and other equipment, this Piper is equipped for mineral survey work.

■ **UTILITY TRANSPORT:** Designated UO and, later, U-11 by the US Navy, the PA-23 Aztec was ordered in small numbers as a transport.

219

SAAB
90 SCANDIA

● Regional airliner ● DC-3 replacement ● Piston powered

SAAB 90 SCANDIA

▲ **Piston power**
The original Pratt & Whitney R-2000 engine did not produce enough power. Production aircraft were powered by the bigger R-2180-E1.

▲ **Unveiling the prototype**
After a fairly secret development, the first flight took place in November 1946, with the pilot Claes Smith declaring, 'In contrast to the J 21 fighter, the Scandia behaved exactly as predicted.'

▲ **Vikings of the air**
The only European operator of the Scandia was SAS who named all their aircraft after famous Vikings. This example was called Jarl Viking.

▲ **Export orders**
Some two Brazilian airlines operated the Scandia. This example flew for VASP.

Silver shine ▶
Like many of the classic propliners of the postwar period the Scandia flew in a polished bare-metal finish.

Saab's Scandia delighted pilots and passengers. It was the ultimate small, piston-powered airliner when it made its debut after the end of World War II. Sweden's innovative Saab company had never built an airliner, but it hoped to reap huge profits as the creator of a replacement for the Douglas DC-3. Unfortunately, it was too late for piston power and too early to consign the DC-3 to the aircraft boneyard.

▲ *Production versions of the Scandia could accommodate 24 passengers with a three-abreast seating arrangement as seen above. For high-density routes, 32 passengers could be accommodated in a less comfortable four-abreast layout.*

FACTS AND FIGURES

➤ Despite its great promise, only a total of 18 Scandias, including one prototype, were manufactured.

➤ The prototype for Saab Scandia made its initial flight on 16 November 1946.

➤ The first 12 airplanes were built by Saab, and the last six by Fokker in Holland.

➤ Another Saab 90 was broken into components and used as a ground instruction trainer at Sao Paulo, Brazil.

➤ The final Scandia in service logged 15,683 hours and travelled 3,208,500 miles.

➤ One Scandia was preserved for display at a museum in Brazil in 1975.

PROFILE

Saab's first airliner

A new age of air travel dawned at the end of the Second World War, and aircraft builders hastened to prosper from it. Saab, a new company whose experience was with combat aircraft, developed a conventional and perfectly acceptable short-range transport in the Saab 90 Scandia. The Scandia was offered to any airline that wanted to launch a modern fleet. Except for its tricycle landing gear, the Scandia resembled the DC-3 it was meant to replace.

The Scandia may have been available a little too soon for some countries rebuilding after the war. AB Aerotransport, the carrier that became the Scandinavian Airlines System, ordered a few of these transports, as did Aeroavias Brasil (later VASP).

Both airlines found the Saab 90 to be efficient and popular, and placed second orders. But the Scandia had drawbacks. It was not pressurized, though a pressurized version was planned. And by the time the world was ready for a DC-3 replacement, it was too late for

The prototype conducted extensive demonstration tours in Europe, Africa and later the United States and Latin America. It was also tested as a freight carrier, including an impressive nonstop flight between Albenga and Stockholm.

this piston-powered air plane to make major inroads into the civil transport market.

Each structurally conventional wing held two fuel tanks with a total volume of 29,700 litres (6,512 gal.).

The nosewheel leg was raised an extra 10 cm (4 in.) on production versions to give the propellers extra ground clearance.

The passenger cabin had 16 windows. There were also eight small windows in the cabin ceiling with built-in lamps to illuminate the cabin at night.

90 Scandia

Type: short-range civil transport

Powerplant: two 1,800-hp. Pratt & Whitney R-2180-E1 radial piston engines

Cruising speed: 389 km/h (242 m.p.h.) at 3048 m (10,000 ft.)

Range: 1480 km (920 mi.)

Service ceiling: 7498 m (24,600 ft.)

Accommodation 4 or 5 flight crewmembers and 24 to 36 passengers.

Weights: empty 9939 kg (21,912 lb.); max takeoff 15,966 kg (35,200 lb.)

Dimensions: span 27.99 m (91 ft. 10 in.)
length 21.29 m (69 ft. 10 in.)
height 7.42 m (24 ft. 4 in.)
wing area 85.66 m² (922 sq. ft.)

90 SCANDIA

This Scandia was the second production aircraft and served with SAS until it was sold to Aeroavias of Brazil.

The Scandia would normally fly with a pilot and a co-pilot. Standard equipment included a Sperry A-12 autopilot.

The fuselage could accommodate 24 passengers in three-abreast seating or 36 passengers in a four-abreast arrangement.

This Scandia appears in the markings of Scandinavia Airline System (SAS) which was the only European operator.

Production Scandias were fitted with the 1342-kW (1,800-hp.) Pratt & Whitney R-2180-E1 engine.

The undercarriage retracted forwards into the engine nacelle to facilitate lowering in case of hydraulic failure.

Behind the passenger cabin was a cargo hold with a volume of 24.43 m³ (236 cu. ft.). The lavatory at the rear was fitted with a ceiling window.

The Scandia had a conventional tail layout with a rounded fin and tailplane. This feature resembled the aircraft it was designed to replace – the DC-3.

ACTION DATA

SPEED

The Scandia was much faster than the DC-3, which it was designed to replace. However, it could not match the speed of the more powerful Convair 340. The turboprop airliners that were being developed were faster still and made the Scandia look sluggish.

SCANDIA	389 km/h (242 m.p.h.)
CONVAIR 340	447 km/h (278 m.p.h.)
Il-12	349 km/h (217 m.p.h.)

ACCOMMODATION

Although the Scandia could carry 36 passengers on high-density routes, this arrangement was very cramped. A more usual cabin arrangement would be for 24 passengers in comfortable reclining seats. The Soviet Il-12 carried a similar number of passengers.

SCANDIA	36 passengers
CONVAIR 340	44 passengers
Il-12	32 passengers

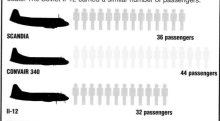

RANGE

Designed as a regional airliner, the Scandia had more than sufficient range for its tasks. The bigger Convair 340 had a much larger fuel capacity and could travel much longer distances. The Il-12 was generally used for domestic flights in the Soviet Union and had similar range to the Scandia.

CONVAIR 340 3219 km (2,000 mi.)
SCANDIA 1480 km (920 mi.)
Il-12 1247 km (775 mi.)

Regional airliners that failed

■ **DOUGLAS DC-5:** The DC-5 first flew in 1939, but the outbreak of World War II reduced the demand for civil airliners. Douglas abandoned the project to concentrate on military production.

■ **CESSNA 620:** This pressurized 8- to 10-seat transport was powered by four Continental engines. It was abandoned when second-hand Convair 440s and Martin 4-0-4s became available.

■ **LOCKHEED 75 SATURN:** The Saturn was an excellent design. However, with many wartime transports becoming available it was not financially viable and the project was scrapped.

■ **AVIATION TRADERS ACCOUNTANT:** This 28-seat twin-turboprop airliner was marketed in the late 1950s. No sales were forthcoming and only one example was built.

221

SAAB
340

● Commercial airliner ● Corporate transport ● Military VIP aircraft

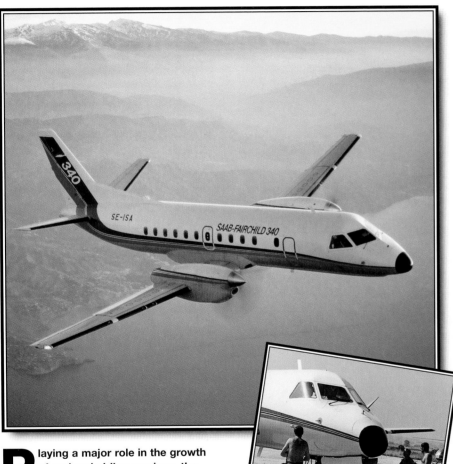

Playing a major role in the growth of regional airline services, the Saab 340 extends passenger flights to markets that could not support a larger aircraft. Feeding major airline hubs, the 350-plus 340s in service make an average of six flights each per day. Around the world that means a Saab 340 either takes off or lands on average every 20 seconds. Each plane can carry a maximum of 37 passengers up to 1500 km (930 mi.).

▲ Since its first flight in 1983 the Saab 340 has been a success, with 280 aircraft delivered by early 1992. Production of the improved 340B continues at approximately 50 per year.

SAAB 340

▼ **Comair sale**
Penetration of the American market was vital to the 340's success. The first customer was Comair, which took delivery of 19 aircraft.

▲ **Propeller economy**
Turboprop airliners are much favoured for their low noise and operating costs. Saab has achieved new levels of fuel economy with the 340 thanks to its low-drag airframe and highly efficient General Electric engines.

◄ **More customers**
By the late 1980s, with Saab running the project alone, the 340 had notched up customers in Asia, Europe, Australasia and America. The 340 prototype leads this formation.

▼ **Advanced wing**
America's National Air & Space Administration designed an all-new, low-drag wing for the 340 when Fairchild were originally involved in the project. The tapered planform wing had a single-slotted, hydraulically operated honeycomb-alloy flap.

▲ **Metal frame**
The new aircraft was largely built of alloys, with selective use of composites and Kevlar.

FACTS AND FIGURES

➤ Fairchild withdrew from the original 340 project after suffering financial difficulties in 1987.

➤ The largest customer for the 340 was American Eagle, which bought 100 aircraft.

➤ The 340 was temporarily grounded due to problems with the CT-7 engines.

➤ An airborne early warning version with a spine-mounted Ericsson radar has been developed for the Swedish air force.

➤ Asian customers include China Southern Airlines and Formosa Airlines.

➤ A Collins APS-85 autopilot and flight control system is fitted as standard.

Short haul in the quiet Saab

Launched in 1980 as a joint development by Saab of Sweden and Fairchild of the USA, the 340 project was later taken over completely by Saab. The first aircraft were delivered to Crossair of Switzerland in 1984. The initial American operator was Comair, and in 1985 the first corporate version was delivered.

In the years since then the 340 has proved a popular choice. It has enabled both established and start-up regional airlines to open up new routes while offering passengers high standards of speed and comfort.

In 1988 the improved 340B was introduced with more powerful engines. The resulting increase in operating weight allowed airlines to provide a better level of service, including, for example, hot meals to be served. Since 1989 this has been the standard model.

Ten years after the 340 entered service, Saab introduced a further upgrade. The 340

BPlus featured a new interior and active noise monitoring and control, using a system of microphones and loudspeakers. This reduced noise by about half. The first BPlus, and the 359th 340, was delivered to American Eagle in 1994.

Crossair of Switzerland have become an established operator of Saab aircraft, having been the launch customer for the Saab 340 and the larger 2000. The 340 has also been successful in the Far East.

The spacious cabin generally has three-abreast seating for up to 37 passengers in 12 rows. There is also provision for a galley, toilet and wardrobe or baggage module. Alternatively, a cargo or combined layout can be adopted.

The wings are constructed from aluminium spars with glass fibre and Kevlar panels and ailerons.

The horizontal stabiliser contains VOR/LOC antenna and the cockpit voice recorder.

340B

Type: regional commercial and corporate transport

Powerplant: two 1394-kW (1,870-hp.) General Electric CT-79B turboprops

Maximum speed: 522 km/h (324 m.p.h.)

Initial climb rate: 624 m/min. (2,048 f.p.m.)

Range: 2414 km (1,500 mi.) with 45-minute reserves and 30 passengers

Service ceiling: 7620 m (25,000 ft.)

Weights: maximum take-off 12,927 kg (28,439 lb.)

Accommodation: 33, 35 or 37 passengers seated three abreast

Dimensions:
span	21.44 m	(70 ft. 4 in.)
length	19.72 m	(64 ft. 8 in.)
height	6.91 m	(22 ft. 8 in.)
wing area	41.81 m²	(450 sq. ft.)

340B

Continental operate the Saab 340 on short-range regional air routes in the United States. The aircraft is also ideal for business and VIP transport roles.

The modern flight deck has seating for two pilots and an observer. The flight attendant has a seat at the front of the cabin.

Two General Electric CT7-9B turboprops with Dowty four-blade reversible propellers provide a maximum of 1394 kW (1,870 hp.) of thrust and 1305 kW (1,750 hp.) for normal take-off. Refuelling points are over the wing and in the wing leading edge.

Located above the wing on either side of the fuselage is an emergency exit door for passengers. The crew's escape hatch is located in the flight deck roof.

Entry to the aircraft is via a single door at the front of the cabin on the port side, using an integral airstair which folds up into the forward fuselage for stowage during flight.

The main undercarriage is of twin-wheel type, retracting forward into the engine nacelle in flight.

Luggage is loaded into a rear fuselage bay via a large square section cargo door which slides upwards to open. All parts of the cabin are fully pressurised.

The tailcone contains discharge valve nozzles to jettison excess fuel prior to landing or in an emergency situation.

ACTION DATA

MAXIMUM CRUISING SPEED

Airlines do not operate turboprops for sheer speed, as regional jets are faster but more expensive to operate. Competition between manufacturers for performance means that all these aircraft are very closely matched in speed.

340B 522 km/h (324 m.p.h.)
EMB-120 504 km/h (312 m.p.h.)
JETSTREAM 41 547 km/h (339 m.p.h.)

PASSENGER LOAD

Passenger capacity is all-important to regional airline operators, as a few empty seats can make all the difference between profit and loss. The Saab is slightly larger than most of its rivals.

340B 35 passengers
EMB-120 BRASILIA 30 passengers
JETSTREAM 41 29 passengers

RANGE

During the design stage Saab aimed the 340 at the US feederliner market as a result of the collaboration with Fairchild. The Jetstream and Brasilia were intended for the business sector and were designed with a shorter range.

340B 2414 km (1,500 mi.)
EMB-120 BRASILIA 1020 km (632 mi.)
JETSTREAM 41 1100 km (682 mi.)

Regional turboprop airliners

■ **ATR-42:** Built by a consortium of Aérospatiale of France and Alenia of Italy, the ATR-42 has been very successful and dominates sales of turboprops in the civil sector.

■ **DHC DASH-8:** The twin-engined counterpart of the Dash-7, the Dash-8 has the notable short take-off performance associated with DHC turboprops and is popular in North America.

■ **LET 610:** Produced in the Czech Republic by LET, the 610 uses General Electric CT-7 turboprops. It is aimed at existing customers of the LET 410 and was purchased by Aeroflot.

■ **AIRTECH CN.235:** Produced by a consortium in Indonesia and Spain, the CN.235 is operated by the military for maritime surveillance and transport and used by civilian customers as an airliner.

SAAB

2000

● 50/58-seat transport ● Swiss launch customer ● 340 derivative

▲ Saab developed a new 50-seater for a fraction of the cost of a totally new design by basing the 2000 on the successful 340 35-seater. Common fuselage and wing cross-sections were used.

On the back of considerable success with its 340 (more than 400 sales worldwide of its 35-seat feederliner), Saab secured an order from 340 operator Crossair of Switzerland in 1988 for 25 new Saab 2000s. As the name suggests, this was designed as an aircraft for the new millennium, but sales were sluggish as other operators chose regional jets over turboprops. Production of the 2000 came to an end in 1999.

PHOTO FILE

SAAB 2000

Swiss Phantom ▶
Crossair joined the growing list of airlines painting their aircraft in promotional colour schemes, with its 'The Phantom of the Opera' Saab 2000.

◀ Six-bladed propellers
Dowty Aerospace's efficient six-bladed propellers are of carbon-fibre sandwich construction. Their multi-blade design allows them to be rotated at reduced speeds, which minimises the 2000's noise footprint.

Saab's feederliners ▶
In this comparative view, some of the major differences between the 340 and 2000 are apparent.

◀ In German service
German associate of British Airways, Deutsche BA, was the second 2000 customer. Operators appreciate the jet-like speed of the type.

2000 prototype ▶
SE-001 was the first Saab 2000, which took to the air on 26 March 1992. Here it is seen on an early flight with its undercarriage extended. An instrumentation probe has been fitted to the aircraft's nosecone.

FACTS AND FIGURES

➤ Construction of large parts of the Saab 2000 was sub-contracted. The rear fuselage was built by Westland.

➤ The 2000's tail was built by Valmet in Finland; CASA built the wings in Spain.

➤ Crossair of Switzerland had the largest 2000 fleet with 25 in service.

➤ Sweden's government lent around US$180 million for Saab 2000 development, to be paid back by 2009.

➤ General Motors took delivery of the first corporate 2000 in October 1995.

➤ By August 1996, 33 Saab 2000s were in service, all but one in Europe.

PROFILE

Fast turboprop 2000

Saab's objective was to combine jet-like speeds with the economy of a turboprop aircraft. A cruising speed of 680 km/h (425 m.p.h.), a climb rate sufficient to take the aircraft to 6100 m (20,000 ft.) in 10 minutes, and cruising altitudes between 5485 m (18,000 ft.) and 9450 m (31,000 ft.) were the principal aims of the aircraft's designers.

Not simply a 'stretch' of the 340, the 2000 incorporates a number of new features. For example, power comes from two Allison AE 2100 turbines, the 2000 being one of the first types to use this new fuel-efficient engine. Each AE 2100 drives a six-bladed Dowty Aerospace propeller.

Features shared with the 340B are the fuselage cross-section and wing section, though the fuselage is naturally longer to accommodate up to 58 passengers. Wing span is increased by 15 per cent; the total wing area is 33 per cent greater. The engines are set further out from the fuselage to reduce cabin noise.

During the design phase, Saab made extensive use of computer-aided design and manufacture (CAD/CAM) to produce a prototype which took to the air for the first time on 23 March 1992, less than four years after programme launch.

The sixth aircraft off the production line was the first to be delivered, in August 1994, and entered service the following month.

Above: SE-004 was the first production example and was later delivered to launch customer Crossair.

Below: The Saab 2000 heralded a new era of fast, quiet turboprops which could compete effectively with jets over shorter sectors.

Most of the Saab 2000's primary structure is of aluminium alloy, like that of the 340B. The fin, propeller blades and cabin floor are of carbon-fibre, however, and limited use of composites is also made elsewhere.

2000

Type: twin-turboprop regional transport

Powerplant: two 3096-kW (4,150-hp.) (flat rating) Allison AE 2100A turboprops

Maximum speed: 682 km/h (423 m.p.h.)

Cruising speed: 594 km/h (369 m.p.h.) at 9450 m (31,000 ft.)

Initial climb rate: 685 m/min (2,250 f.p.m.) at sea level

Range: (at maximum cruising speed with 50 passengers and reserves at 1525-m (5,000-ft.) altitude) 2222 km (1,375 mi.)

Service ceiling: 9450 m (31,000 ft.)

Weights: operating empty 13,800 kg (30,360 lb.); maximum take-off 22,800 kg (50,160 lb.)

Accommodation: flight crew of three or four, plus 50 passengers ('European' configuration) or 58 (high-density configuration)

Dimensions:
span	24.76 m	(81 ft. 3 in.)
length	27.28 m	(89 ft. 6 in.)
height	7.73 m	(25 ft. 4 in.)
wing area	55.74 m²	(600 sq. ft.)

2000

Carrying its test registration SE-018, this aircraft was destined for Swiss operator Crossair. It was finished in a 'Phantom of the Opera' livery to mark the opening of the musical production in Switzerland.

An Ultra Electronics Active Noise Control (ANC) system uses 72 microphones and 36 speakers to monitor and neutralise cabin noise by means of an anti-phase sound field.

Some operators chose to move the cabin rear bulkhead further aft. This allows more space for the galley and wardrobe, which in turn frees cabin space for an additional eight seats, giving a 58-seat capacity.

A six-screen Collins Pro Line IV cockpit instrumentation system is standard. All aircraft also feature a solid-state WXR-840 weather radar and customers may specify turbulence-detecting weather radar.

A single control is used to adjust the Allison AE 2100A engines and their propellers, allowing for simplicity of operation. The engines have been moved outboard to minimise cabin noise.

A 10.2-m³ (361-cu. ft.) baggage hold is located in the rear fuselage, with access gained via a large door on the port side. If the rear bulkhead is moved aft, baggage space is diminished.

Certification of the 2000 was delayed by problems with the Powered Elevator Control System, which was replaced in late 1993. The first deliveries were delayed 18 months.

ACTION DATA

PASSENGERS

Usually flown in a 50-seat layout, the Saab 2000 may be configured with 58 seats. The new aircraft has a considerably greater capacity than Saab's 340B but holds fewer passengers than Jetstream's troubled ATP.

2000	58 passengers
340B	37 passengers
ATP	72 passengers

MAXIMUM SPEED

Passengers and airlines appreciate the benefits offered by an aircraft capable of near-jet speeds, with the economy of a turboprop. Jetstream's ATP (or 61) should have been a direct competitor to the 2000 but failed to offer adequate performance.

2000	682 km/h (423 m.p.h.)
340B	522 km/h (324 m.p.h.)
ATP	502 km/h (311 m.p.h.)

RANGE

Range is another strong point of the excellent Saab 2000. High-tech engines and other modern systems account for the aircraft's fine overall performance. The Saab 340B continues in limited production, while the ATP and its Jetstream 61 derivatives are no longer being made.

2000 2222 km (1,375 mi.)
ATP 1739 km (1,080 mi.)
340B 1732 km (1,075 mi.)

Civil Saab designs

■ **90 SCANDIA:** Conceived during World War II and first flown in 1946, the Scandia entered service in Europe and with VASP in Brazil.

■ **91 SAFIR:** This four-seat cabin monoplane dated from 1945. Around 320 were built for customers in 20 countries.

■ **SAFARI TS:** The late 1960s Safari was originally powered by a 149-kW (200-hp.) Lycoming IO-360 air-cooled piston engine.

■ **340:** Originally conceived in a joint venture with Fairchild (who withdrew in 1985), the 340 35-seater went on to sell in large numbers.

SHORT

SC.5 BELFAST

● Strategic airlifter ● Civilian freighter ● Tactical transport

A British long-range transport with much more potential development than it got, the Short Belfast production line ran to just 10 aircraft before 1970s defence cuts announced its end. The Belfast served with the RAF as a long-range strategic freighter until 1976. After retirement, the small fleet was purchased by the civil carrier HeavyLift, which from 1980 used it on charters to carry outsize loads around the world.

▲ *Another example of wasted development that could have made a winner for British aviation, the Belfast is still seen all over the world in the colours of HeavyLift, the freight specialist.*

SHORT SC.5 BELFAST

▲ Transport Command
Belfasts entered service with RAF Transport Command in 1966 and served for 10 years. No. 53 squadron was the only user. Some were sold to Pan African Freightliners in 1977 after the RAF retired them.

▲ Armour freight
Saladin armoured cars were no problem for the Belfast. The rear ramp door made fast loading of cargo simple.

◀ Built in Belfast
Named after the city where it was built, the Belfast did not keep the factories busy for long. Had the aircraft not been cancelled by the RAF, it may have attracted export orders.

▲ Worldwide lifter
With the capability to refuel in flight, the Belfast gave the RAF the ability to lift large cargoes anywhere in the world. The refueling probe has been removed from the HeavyLift Belfasts, since there is no need for it.

◀ Aircraft carrier
The Belfast could easily swallow up a fuselage from a small airliner. The fuselage was larger than that of the Lockheed Hercules, an interesting fact considering the arguments about the size of the proposed European FLA.

FACTS AND FIGURES

➤ The Belfast stemmed from a March 1957 design study into an aircraft called the Britannic.

➤ The Belfast was the first transport to have an automatic landing system.

➤ The Belfast prototype first flew on 5 January 1964; 10 were built for the RAF.

➤ Up to 10 Land Rovers and trailers or three Whirlwind helicopters could be carried by the Belfast.

➤ HeavyLift has carried Sepecat Jaguar fuselages to India in its Belfasts.

➤ Only two of HeavyLift's Belfasts remain in service today.

PROFILE

Heavy weight lifter from Belfast

HeavyLift Cargo Airlines, based at London's Stansted Airport, was set up in October 1978 specifically to operate Short Belfast freighters. These had recently come up for sale following their retirement from the RAF as an economy measure. Five were initially purchased by HeavyLift, three for mainstream operations and two held in reserve for use as spares.

The RAF's Belfast fleet was purchased to fulfill the shortage of high-capacity transport aircraft that existed in the late 1960s. The Belfast could carry the largest guided missiles, guns

and vehicles of the British army.

Each Belfast has a freight hold 90 feet long and 16 feet wide and the aircraft's high-strength airframe and four turboprop engines enable it to carry loads weighing up to 36,434 kg (80,323 lb.). Loading is accomplished from the rear of the hold via a ramp, often with the aid of an onboard powered winch. Now HeavyLift uses the Belfast's excellent cargo-carrying capacity to transport goods around the world. Despite being a wonderfully reliable aircraft, the 10 RAF aircraft were withdrawn in the late 1970s as

the United Kingdom's worldwide influence dwindled and the need for long-range heavy transport aircraft ended. It is ironic that the Belfast would subsequently have been a highly valuable asset in conflicts such as the Falklands and the Gulf.

Above: The Belfast could also carry 150 troops in the hold, or up to 250 if a temporary upper deck was fitted.

Below: The Belfast showed remarkably benign handling for an aircraft that handled bulkier cargoes than a Boeing 747.

SC.5 Belfast

Type: Long-range freighter.

Powerplant: Four 4124-kW (5,530-hp.) Rolls-Royce Tyne Mk 101 turboprop engines.

Maximum speed: 565 km/h (351 m.p.h.)

Service ceiling: 9144 m (30,000 ft.)

Range: 1609 km (1,000 mi.)

Weights: Empty 104,081 kg (229,460 lb.); loaded 139,008 kg (306,460 lb.)

Dimensions: span 521.11 m (158 ft. 10 in.)
length 41.66 m (136 ft. 8 in.)
height 14.30 m (46 ft. 11 in.)
wing area 245.73 m² (2,465 sq. ft.)

BELFAST C.MK 1

Each of the RAF's Belfasts was given a personal name; XR367 was named *Hercules*. All military Belfasts served with No. 53 Squadron based at Brize Norton in Oxfordshire.

Flight crew in RAF Belfasts consisted of two pilots, a navigator, flight engineer and two loadmasters in the hold. Civil Belfasts have a similar crew configuration.

The excellent Rolls-Royce Tyne engines were so much in demand by the RAF when the Belfast was retired that Rolls-Royce bought five Belfasts and scrapped them just to recover the Tynes. This engine is also used in the Italian G.222 tactical transport.

The Belfast used basically the same wing as the Bristol Britannia. The ailerons were manually actuated through servo tabs, but the spoilers were hydraulically controlled and electrically activated.

The huge hold could also accommodate 10 Land Rovers with trailers, or two Wessex, or three Whirlwind helicopters.

The tail section, with its huge vertical fin, was also derived from the Bristol Britannia.

Unlike the rival An-12, the Belfast had an integral rear loading ramp and door for fast loading of vehicles.

367

XR367

ROYAL AIR FORCE

HERCULES

Belfast military loads

CHIEFTAN TANK: Perhaps the most impressive cargo carried by the Belfast was the Chieftan tank, a very heavy vehicle with a long gun barrel. The Chieftan could not be carried by similar aircraft like the C-130 Hercules.

SALADIN ARMORED CARS: Three Saladins fitted easily in the hold of the Belfast, with the rearmost vehicle facing forward. The weight of the Saladins was no problem, the limiting factor being the size of the cargo bay floor.

TWO WESSEX: With the helicopters' rotor blades removed and the airframes turned tail-to-tail, two Wessex could be fitted into the Belfast. This was an example of just how spacious the hold was given the shape of a Wessex.

ACTION DATA

RANGE

The Belfast was not as long-ranged as had been intended, mainly due to higher than expected drag. This was partly remedied in RAF service by the aircraft having air-to-air refueling provision, which the RAF C-130s did not have until 1982. Had the Belfast been designed from scratch rather than using Britannia parts, range could have been longer.

BELFAST
1609 km
(1,000 mi.)

HERCULES
2467 km
(1,533 mi.)

AN-12
3592 km
(2,232 mi.)

SHORT
SC.7 SKYVAN

● Turboprop commuter ● Square-section fuselage ● Private venture

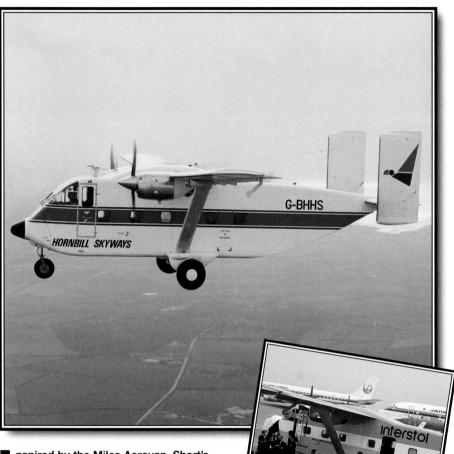

Inspired by the Miles Aerovan, Short's Skyvan filled a niche in the civil market for an aircraft with an uncluttered box-section fuselage with provision for straight-in loading from the rear. Originally equipped with piston engines, the Skyvan was soon re-equipped with turbines. The aircraft sold well, starting a fashion that was followed by other manufacturers and followed up by the Short company itself with the enlarged Short 330 and 360.

▲ Slotted in
among bigger aircraft, the Skyvan became a well-known sight at numerous airports all around the world, providing feeder services for larger airlines.

PHOTO FILE
SHORT SC.7 SKYVAN

▼ Olympic Airways
Greek airline Olympic was an early operator of the SC.7 and used it for short regional flights around Greece.

▲ Belfast's baby
Seen flying over Harland & Wolff's Belfast shipyard, this is the first of two Skyvans produced for Olympic Airways.

Flight testing ▶
Serving from 1979, with NASA's flight test facility at Wallops Island, Virginia, this sole example carried out mid-air retrievals of sounding-rocket payloads, which were used for atmospheric research. The aircraft was nicknamed the 'Ugly Hooker' and has now been retired.

▼ De-luxe travel
The Skyliner was an all-passenger variant which was introduced in 1970. It became the definitive commuter model of the Skyvan.

▲ Parachute training
Withdrawal of the balloon flight from RAF Hullavington left parachutist training to the operators of this example from Luxembourg.

FACTS AND FIGURES

➤ The Skyvan 1 prototype made its first flight from Sydenham, Northern Ireland, on 17 January 1963.

➤ Design of the Skyvan began as a private venture by Short in 1959.

➤ Civil Skyvans were used in Australia, the Middle East and the United States.

➤ When production ceased in 1985 154 Skyvans had been constructed; many are still in use.

➤ The Skyvan's roles included aerial survey, radio relay and fire spotting.

➤ Retractable skis can be fitted to the undercarriage of some variants.

PROFILE

Short's small wonder

Miles approached Short with a proposal that they build a version of the Aerovan, with high aspect ratio wings, called the HDM.106 Caravan. Although Short's purchased the design, they chose not to build it and instead designed a new aircraft along similar lines – the SC.7 Skyvan. This all-metal, beaver-tailed, rear-loading 'box van' aircraft had strut-braced rectangular wings and two Continental supercharged flat-six piston engines. Two prototypes were built, and the first flew on 17 January 1963.

Early interest came from Alaska and Australia, where a reliable, economical aircraft was required. Within a matter of months, however, the prototype had been re-engined with Turboméca Astazou turboprops, which greatly improved its short field performance.

First sales came in 1965, when Aeralpi purchased Skyvans to operate between Milan and the Cortina d'Ampezzo ski resort.

Above: G-ASCN was the first Skyvan. Here it is seen fitted with a production tail unit and Astazou turbine engines.

Below: In flight the Skyvan looked ungainly, yet it proved to be an extremely practical design for light transport and passenger work.

Problems with the 'hot-and-high' capabilities of the Astazou engine led to the adoption of the Garrett TPE331 in 1967. When production ceased in 1985, 154 Skyvans had been built, including military examples.

SC.7 Skyvan 3

Type: light utility transport

Powerplant: two 533-kW (715-hp.) Garrett AiResearch TPE331-201 turboprops

Maximum cruising speed: 327 km/h (202 m.p.h.)

Initial climb rate: 500 m/min (1,640 f.p.m.)

Range: maximum 1115 km (695 mi.); 300 km (185 mi.) with 1814 kg (4,000-lb.) payload

Service ceiling: 6860m (22,500 ft.)

Weights: empty 3331 kg (7,344 lb.); maximum take-off 5670 kg (12,500 lb.)

Accommodation: up to 19 passengers or 2086 kg (4,600 lb.) of cargo

Dimensions:
span	19.79 m	(64 ft. 11 in.)
length	12.22 m	(40 ft. 1 in.)
height	4.60 m	(15 ft. 1 in.)
wing area	34.65 m²	(373 sq. ft.)

With the Skyvan 2 Short introduced an optional weather radar installation contained in a more pointed nose radome (not fitted to this aircraft). The aircraft's controls are laid out for operation by a single pilot.

Garrett AiResearch's well-known TPE331 turboprop transformed the Skyvan's performance at altitude.

Inspired by the stillborn Miles HDM.106 Caravan, the SC.7 had a rectangular wing which produced STOL performance.

Between the prototype and production stages of the Skyvan's development various modifications were made, especially to the tail fins which were repositioned.

N70DA

SUMMIT

Skyvans in the feeder liner role were configured to carry 19 passengers. About a dozen 22-seat Skyliners were produced late in the production run.

At the time of its first flight the Skyvan was a unique design and gained orders worldwide. US operators generally viewed the type as a freighter.

SC.7 SKYVAN 3

Delaware Air Freight bought this Skyvan 3, which was first flown in July 1968, in 1973. The following year Delaware became Summit Airlines Inc. and flew the aircraft until it was sold in 1979.

ACTION DATA

PASSENGERS

Passenger versions of the Skyvan featured de-luxe comfort, but size was a limiting factor. Although other airliners were capable of carrying more passengers, this was in less comfortable conditions.

SC.7 SKYVAN 3	19 passengers
330	30 passengers
L-410UVP	15 passengers

ECONOMIC CRUISING SPEED

The square-section fuselage meant that performance was never outstanding compared to other airliners, like the Let L-410. The Skyvan more than compensated for its lack of speed, however, with its exceptional short take-off and landing capability.

SC.7 SKYVAN 3	278 km/h (172 m.p.h.)
330	296 km/h (184 m.p.h.)
L-410UVP	300 km/h (186 m.p.h.)

RANGE

Despite its ungainly design, the Skyvan had exceptional range, but at the cost of a reduced payload when compared to the later turboprop designs. The demands of expanding air travel forced larger passenger loads at the expense of range performance.

SC.7 SKYVAN 3 1115 km (695 mi.)

330 805 km (500 mi.)

L-410UVP 1040 km (645 mi.)

Small turbine-powered transports

ANTONOV An-28 'CASH': A turboprop development of the An-14, the An-28 entered production in Poland in 1980.

CASA C.212 AVIOCAR: Intended to replace the DC-3, this Spanish design flew in 1971. More than 400 have been built for civil and military users.

HARBIN Y-12: An enlarged version of the Y-11, the Y-12 flew in 1982 powered by PT6A turboprops. Roles include geological survey.

IAI ARAVA: The first wholly IAI-designed aircraft, the Arava 20-seater, flew in 1969 and was produced in military and civil marks.

SHORT

330/360

● Twin-turbine feederliner ● Overseas sales ● Skyvan development

▲ *Short*
always envisaged the United
States as the primary market for the 330 and 360 and
took advantage of changes in the law which allowed
commuter airlines to operate larger aircraft.

With the success of the Skyvan and a perceived need for a larger aircraft in the 'DC-3 replacement' mould, Short embarked on the SD3-30. Originally conceived as a 26-seater, the aircraft was enlarged to take advantage of changed rules in the United States which allowed commuter airliners to carry 30 passengers. The 330, as it became, flew in 1974, and was followed by the 36-seat 360 in 1981.

SHORT 330/360

▲ **In German service**
Few 330s or 360s have seen service in Europe. German company DLT operated a small fleet of the earlier aircraft in the 1970s.

▼ **From the Isle of Man**
With an appropriate registration, the Manx airline's 360 G-ISLE rests on the tarmac before a flight across the Irish Sea to the British mainland.

▼ **330-200**
The Series 200 was introduced in 1985 and had an improved fuel capacity over the earlier 100 variant.

▲ **To the Western Isles**
Now trading under the British Airways name, Scottish airline Loganair has retired its 330s but continues to fly a number of 360s.

Multiple owners ▶
With feeder airlines preferring more modern pressurised types, 330s and 360s have been phased out by many early operators. This Casair 330 was sold after two years and is now owned by Short Aircraft Leasing Ltd.

FACTS AND FIGURES

➤ A number of former feederliner aircraft have had their seats removed and entered service as freighters.

➤ Owned by Bombardier of Canada since 1989, Short no longer builds aircraft.

➤ The 360 entered service with Suburban Airlines of Pennsylvania, USA, in 1982.

➤ Most of the USAF's C-23A Sherpas were transferred to the US Forest Service in 1990; the Air National Guard flies C-23Bs.

➤ Of the 104 Short 360s still in service in late 1996, 54 were based in the Americas.

➤ The Thai army operated two 330-UTT (utility tactical transport) variants.

Short Brothers' last airliner

Powered by the well-known Pratt & Whitney PT6A turbine engine, the SD3-30 was a development of the Skyvan design, and retained the earlier aircraft's square cross-section fuselage and twin tail. The wings and fuselage were longer, however, and the sponsored undercarriage was retractable, which was a major improvement.

The first SD3-30 flew in August 1974 and entered service, as the 330, in 1976 with Time

Air of Canada. This was followed by the 330-200, which had increased fuel capacity. A quick-change version was also offered, along with a military 330-UTT transport (used by the US forces as the C-23).

When US aviation regulations were relaxed again, Short enlarged the 330 to carry 36 passengers. This version was called the 336, later 360. The

first two 360s carried the descriptive registrations G-ROOM and G-WIDE and flew in 1981 and 1982, respectively. The last variant built was the 360-300 of 1987, which had up to 39 seats in an improved cabin and was fitted with an autopilot.

Production ended in 1992, after 139 330s and 164 360s had been built.

Deliveries of production 360s began in 1982. The following year Air UK received two aircraft, G-BLPV and G-BLPY.

The 360's redesigned tail surfaces had several advantages over the twin-tail arrangement of the 330, including reducing drag which thereby increased fuel efficiency. The baggage capacity in the rear of the aircraft was also improved on the later type.

On the 330 the outer wing panels of the Skyvan were used, but the span was increased. The 360's wing panels and bracing struts were strengthened.

360-300

Type: twin-engined feederliner

Powerplant: two 1062-kW (1,425-hp.) Pratt & Whitney Canada PT6A-65AR turboprops

Maximum cruising speed: 400 km/h (248 m.p.h.)

Initial climb rate: 290 m/min (950 f.p.m.) at sea level

Range: 745 km (460 mi.) with maximum payload and typical reserves at maximum cruising speed; 1178 km (732 mi.) with 31 passengers and at a cruising speed of 337 km/h (209 m.p.h.)

Weights: operating empty 7875 kg (17,325 lb.); maximum take-off 12,292 kg (27,042 lb.)

Accommodation: two flight crew and up to 36 passengers; in the freight role up to 3765 kg (8,283 lb.) of cargo

Dimensions:
span	22.80 m	(74 ft. 9 in.)
length	21.58 m	(70 ft. 9 in.)
height	7.27 m	(23 ft. 10 in.)
wing area	42.18 m²	(454 sq. ft.)

360-100

Delivered to Manx airlines in March 1984, the appropriately registered G-LEGS was named 'King Magnus Barefoot (1098-1103)' in 1989. It was later sold to Loganair and operates on commuter flights in Scotland.

As is standard on feederliner aircraft of this size, the Short 330/360 has a flightdeck crew of two pilots.

After problems with the engines originally chosen for the Skyvan, Short selected the proven Pratt & Whitney Canada PT6A turbine for the 330, along with a Hartzell five-bladed propeller.

In addition to the new tail, the 360 featured a stretched fuselage which was 0.91 m (three feet) longer than that of the 330. This was accomplished by inserting a section in the fuselage forward of the wing.

A luggage compartment was situated at the rear of the cabin. On the 330 a loading door was situated below the tail unit.

The 360, originally known as the 336, could carry 36 passengers.

The undercarriage was contained in small sponsons, but was retractable.

The 330's twin fin and rudder were similar to those fitted to the Skyvan, although they were larger. The 360 was a more streamlined design, and the twin fins were replaced by a conventional single swept fin. The 360 also boasted more powerful PT6A engines.

ACTION DATA

MAXIMUM CRUISING SPEED

The shape of the 330/360 was not as aerodynamic as contemporary feederliner designs, and would have contributed to its slow cruising speed. Other major factors which affect speed are wing design and engine power.

360-300	400 km/h (248 m.p.h.)
340B	522 km/h (324 m.p.h.)
Do 328	620 km/h (384 m.p.h.)

PASSENGERS

All three types were designed in Europe but have sold extensively in the USA. A passenger load of 30 to 45 is the most economical configuration in this sector.

360-300	**340B**	**Do 328**
36 passengers	37 passengers	33 passengers

RANGE

Range was the main weakness of the 330/360 once larger types came on to the market, especially in the USA where internal flights tend to be longer than elsewhere. The popular Saab 340 and the Dornier 328 could fly about twice as far as the Short aircraft.

- 360-300 745 km (470 mi.)
- 340B 1520 km (1,120 mi.)
- Do 328 1352 km (840 mi.)

British twin-turbine airliners

■ **BAe JETSTREAM:** This family of feederliner and regional airliner was designed by Handley Page in the 1960s. The J41 has up to 29 seats.

■ **BAe JETSTREAM 61:** Originally known as the Advanced Turboprop, this 72-seat development of the HS.748 has new Pratt & Whitney engines.

■ **HANDLEY PAGE HERALD:** Flown in 1958, the Rolls-Royce Dart-engined Herald could seat 60 in its Series 700 variant. A total of 50 was built.

■ **HAWKER SIDDELEY HS.748:** The Dart-engined 748, designed by Avro, was first flown in 1960 and became Britain's best-selling turboprop.

TUPOLEV

Tu-104/Tu-124

● Based on Tu-16 bomber ● First Soviet jet airliner ● Medium range

▲ When introduced in 1956, the Tu-104 dramatically reduced domestic and international journey times. As the second jet airliner in service in the world, it was the pride of Aeroflot's fleet.

I n May 1954 Western observers first viewed the Tupolev Type 88 prototype and eight pre-production Tu-16 bombers. Analysts were rightly concerned that this bomber was a potential strategic threat. What they did not realise was that within two years a developed version, the Tu-104, would become the world's second jet airliner, upsetting the widely-held belief that Soviet aircraft were inferior to those in the West. The type served with Aeroflot for 25 years.

TUPOLEV Tu-104/Tu-124

Bomber origins ▶
Based on the Tu-16 bomber, the Tu-104 featured modified wing-mounted engine nacelles.

▼ Jet pioneer
The Tu-104 drew much attention when exhibited in the West, being the Soviet Union's first jet airliner.

Export 'Cookpots' ▶
This Tu-124K2 was exported as a VIP carrier for the Iraqi air force. Other users included the East German and Indian air forces.

▼ Visits abroad
In March 1956 the Tu-104 became only the second Soviet civil aircraft type to visit Britain. The Tu-104 was still operating to the UK in the 1970s. This example is seen at Gatwick Airport on an unscheduled service in August 1971.

▲ Sharply swept wing
An early production Tu-104A displays the wing trailing-edge fairings which held the four-wheeled main undercarriage.

FACTS AND FIGURES

➤ The prototype Tu-104, SSSR-L5400, was first flown by Y. I. Alasheyev from the Vnukovo factory on 17 June 1955.

➤ Two demilitarised Tu-16s used for crew training were designated Tu-104G.

➤ In service, the Tu-104 cut the Moscow-Irkutsk flight time by eight hours.

➤ Military use included the Tu-104Sh crew trainer as well as modified civil Tu-104Bs employed in cosmonaut training.

➤ In September 1957 a Tu-104A set three world records for an aircraft in its class.

➤ Two weather research Tu-104s were armed with cloud-seeding rockets.

PROFILE

From bomber to jet airliner

Right: Surprisingly, Czech national carrier CSA was the only export customer for the Tu-104, despite a low cost of £425,000 each.

No other large jet transport aircraft has been placed into production in as little time and for as little money as Tupolev's record-breaking Tu-104. Designer S. M. Yeger was the man tasked with turning a strategic bomber into a passenger aircraft. The main modifications included a new fuselage with pressurisation and environmental control, and a new wing centre-section.

The prototype first flew in June 1955, and the excellence of the design was proved by successful, trouble-free flight trials. When the prototype visited Britain in 1956 it caused a great stir, as it was not only a rival to the Comet but, in several factors, showed technological superiority. After crews had been trained on a Tu-16, the Tu-104 entered service in September 1956. After only 11 aircraft, production was switched to the improved Tu-104A fitted out with a higher capacity, improved interior and more powerful engines. Despite the aircraft's excellent record and low cost, the only export customer was CSA of Czechoslovakia which bought six Tu-104As. Further development led to the Tu-104B with a 1.21-m (4-ft.) stretch to the fuselage, increasing the capacity to 100 passengers.

Based very closely on the Tu-104, the Tu-124 short-haul airliner entered service in 1962 and compiled an impressive service history.

Tu-104B 'Camel'

Type: medium-range jet transport

Powerplant: two 95.13-kW (21,500-lb.-thrust) Mikulin AM-3M-500 turbojets

Maximum speed: 950 km/h (589 m.p.h.)

Economical cruising speed: 770 km/h (477 m.p.h.)

Take-off run: 2500 m (8,200 ft.)

Range: 2650 km (1,645 mi.) (with maximum payload)

Service ceiling: 11,500 m (37,700 ft.)

Weights: empty 44,020 kg (96,845 lb.); maximum take-off 78,100 kg (171,820 lb.)

Accommodation: up to 100 passengers

Dimensions: span   34.54 m (113 ft. 4 in.)
length   40.05 m (131 ft. 4 in.)
height   11.90 m (39 ft. 1 in.)
wing area 183.50 m² (1,974 sq. ft.)

The tail unit was basically the same as the unit fitted to the Tu-16, the major difference being a lower tailplane.

The control surfaces were all manually operated with hydraulic boost for the rudder. A trim-tab was fitted in the rudder and each elevator.

Tu-104A 'Camel'

Aeroflot was the main operator of the Tu-104 and flew all commercial versions of the type. From 1960 a few Aeroflot Tu-104As were converted to Tu-104D standard with luxurious forward cabins fitted with divans.

The Tu-104A was flown by a flight crew of five, consisting of two pilots, a navigator, an engineer and a radio operator.

The fuselage forward of the centre-section held a smaller cabin and on early versions was often fitted out for 16 first-class passengers. A toilet was situated at the front of the cabin.

The wings were lowered from the mid to the low position to accommodate the passenger cabin. They were of anhedral swept design.

Like many early Soviet commercial aircraft, the navigator's position was in a glazed nose compartment.

The most radical difference between the Tu-16 and the Tu-104 was the fuselage, which was pressurised and had environmental control.

The rear cabin was separated from the front cabin by the galley. A wardrobe was situated opposite the rear door and a powder room, washroom and two toilets were situated at the rear.

The wing centre-section reduced the height of the cabin. This area was used on early versions as the galley, with two windows fitted at a higher level.

The retractable tricycle undercarriage had four wheel main units which retracted backwards into trailing-edge wing fairings.

ACTION DATA

CRUISING SPEED

As the world's first commercial jet airliner, the Comet had an excellent cruising speed and halved the travel times of the previous 'prop-liners'. The Tu-104 and the Caravelle were capable of similar speeds, but usually cruised at a more moderate pace to increase fuel economy.

Tu-104A 'CAMEL'	770 km/h (477 m.p.h.)
CARAVELLE III	805 km/h (499 m.p.h.)
COMET 4C	872 km/h (541 m.p.h.)

PASSENGERS

In its original form the Tu-104 carried only 70 passengers but, like the Comet, later versions carried more. By 1960 modified Tu-104As were carrying up to 100 passengers. The medium-range Caravelle could carry more than the original Comet I and Tu-104.

Tu-104A 'CAMEL'	70
CARAVELLE III	80
COMET 4C	101

RANGE

Designed for medium-range domestic or international flights, the Tu-104 and the Comet 4C had a much longer range than the Caravelle. Range was a very important consideration for Soviet designers as aircraft had to cover the vast distances of the interior of the Soviet Union.

COMET 4C 4168 km (2,585 mi.)

Tu-104A 'CAMEL' 4200 km (2,600 mi.)

CARAVELLE III 1845 km (1,145 mi.)

Airliners based on bomber designs

■ **AVRO 691 LANCASTRIAN:** The Lancastrian was a high-speed long-range transport conversion of the Lancaster bomber. The Canadian-built versions could carry 10 passengers.

■ **BOEING 377 STRATOCRUISER:** In 1942 Boeing began developing a transport version of the B-29. The resulting Model 377 flew with both civil and military operators.

■ **TUPOLEV Tu-114:** As a civil counterpart to the Tu-95 'Bear' bomber, the Tu-114 was the largest and heaviest commercial airliner in the world when it appeared in 1957.

TUPOLEV
TU-114 'CLEAT'

● Long-range performance ● World's biggest turboprop airliner

▲ Despite its
ageing appearance compared
to Western jet designs, the Tu-114 was a
superb piece of engineering and remains
the largest civil turboprop ever produced.

W ith its unique combination of
turboprop power and swept-back
wings, the Tupolev Tu-114 'Cleat'
was a flying giant of the 1950s. This famous
transport was the largest, heaviest and
longest-range civil aircraft of its era.
Despite having propellers, it regularly
cruised almost as fast as the newer swept-
wing jets. In many respects, this was a
'jumbo jet', and was the world's heaviest
aircraft before the advent of the Boeing 747.

TUPOLEV TU-114 'CLEAT'

▲ Passenger heaven
Another first for the Tu-114 was
the introduction of four-by-four
passenger seating for 220
passengers, although this
configuration was not commonly
used. Most aircraft seated 170
with a galley and divans.

▲ Long legs
This Tu-114, at Heathrow Airport, shows off its extremely long nose
undercarriage strut. The truck in the foreground gives an indication
of just how massive the Tu-114 was.

Landing approach ▶
Landing was sedate in the Tu-114,
the aircraft touching down at 205
km/h (127 m.p.h.) and stopping in
about 1500 m (4,920 ft.). It needed
about 1700 m (5,575 ft.) to take off.

▼ Low-wing design
To allow the passenger compartment to be as
large as possible the Tu-114 was fitted with a
low-mounted wing. This was the main structural
difference between it and the military Tu-95, which
features a mid-mounted wing.

▲ Big spinner
The Tu-114's huge NK-12 turboprops
featured contra-rotating propellers, which
absorb more power from the engine.

FACTS AND FIGURES

➤ Cabin volume of the Tu-114 was
332 m³ (11,724 cu. ft.), making it by far
the largest airliner of its era.

➤ The Tu-114 was also the world's fastest
propeller-driven aircraft in 1960.

➤ The first of 31 Tu-114s, 'Rossiya' made
its maiden flight on 15 November 1957.

➤ With an area of 64.90 m², the horizontal
tail of the Tu-114 was larger than the
wing of many aircraft.

➤ Tu-114Ds flew the 10,900-km (6,758-mi.)
route from Moscow to Havana.

➤ The Tu-114 won the Grand Prix at the
Brussels World Fair in 1958.

PROFILE

Mightiest of the turboprop airliners

Biggest, fastest and arguably the most impressive turboprop airliner, the Tu-114 'Cleat' gave the Soviet airline Aeroflot a colossal transport able to cover intercontinental distances with ease. Everything about this aircraft was big, new and different. Derived from the military Tu-95 'Bear', the Tu-114 was initially rather restricted in where it could operate in the Soviet Union, as few routes could use an aircraft that carried 200 passengers, and many airfields were too limited for its immense size, weight and long take-off run. Another problem

was that its doors were 5 metres above the ground. Plans for self-contained staircases never materialised, and finding steps that could reach the Tu-114 was a problem whenever it arrived at a new airport.

By the time the 'Cleat' began airline service from Moscow to Khabarovsk on 24 April 1961, becoming the first plane to routinely carry passengers a distance of 6500 km (4,000 mi.), this remarkable aircraft had established 32 records and had even flown Soviet Premier Khruschev on a non-stop Moscow to New York visit. The Tu-114 carried over six

million passengers in its years of Aeroflot service before retiring in 1971. Some were converted to prototype Tu-126 airborne early-warning aircraft.

Below: This Tu-114 duo appeared at Zurich airport in 1967, but more usual destinations were Delhi, Montreal, Tokyo and Conakry in West Africa. The aircraft's impressive range saved stop-over time.

Above: There was nothing like the sound of a Tu-114 landing, with its NK-12s whistling and propellers throbbing. Large flaps were fitted to reduce landing speed.

Tu-114 'Cleat'

Type: long-range airliner and transport

Powerplant: four 11,033-kW (14,784-hp.) Kuznetsov NK-12MV turboprop engines

Maximum speed: 880 km/h (545 m.p.h.) at 7100 m (23,000 ft.)

Cruising speed: 770 km/h (477 m.p.h.)

Range: 6200 km (3,853 mi.)

Service ceiling: 12,000 m (39,500 ft.)

Weights: empty 88,200 kg (194,000 lb.); loaded 179,000 kg (393,800 lb.)

Accommodation: flight crew of five (two pilots, engineer, navigator and radio/radar operator); typically eight or nine flight attendants; typically 170 passengers in three cabins holding 42, 48 and 54; maximum seating of up to 220 passengers

Dimensions:
span	51.10 m (168 ft.)
length	54.10 m (177 ft.)
height	13.31 m (44 ft.)
wing area	311.10 m² (3.347 sq. ft.)

Tu-116

As a parallel project to support the Tu-114, the Tu-116 was a direct civil variant of the Tu-95. This example was used for crew training for the Tu-114.

Windscreen de-icing was by means of electric AC current, but the wing leading edges were de-iced by hot air bled from the engines and the tailfin by a flexible rubber boot.

The powerplant was the same as used on the Tu-95 bomber. The four NK-12 engines were very powerful and drove the Tu-116 to an impressive top speed. The main undercarriage retracted to lie inverted in the rear of the inboard engine nacelles.

The fuselage skin was specially thickened adjacent to the propellers to give protection in case of engine failure. The NK-12 engine and its massive propeller system actually proved very reliable in service. The propellers were electrically de-iced.

The massive swept wing was identical to that of the Tu-95 and had the same main structure of three spars. A single spoiler ahead of the aileron assisted in roll control.

All control surfaces were hydraulically operated, a major innovation in this successor to the B-29-derived designs by Tupolev. The tailplane was of the variable incidence type.

An access tunnel linked the front and main cabins, passing through the skinned-over weapons bay.

The rear fuselage held up to 30 passengers in a two-by-two arrangement. A galley and two toilets were provided.

Inside the NK-12

TURBOSHAFT OPERATION:
A turboshaft engine is basically a jet engine with a turbine at the back that uses the gas produced to drive a propeller at the front through a central driveshaft. It is more efficient than a pure jet engine, and produces much more thrust than a piston engine of equivalent weight, as well as using cheaper fuel.

1 COLD AIR IN: The engine pushes air around the spinner and prop shaft, where it enters the 14-stage axial compressor and is pressurised.

2 IGNITION: The high-pressure air from the compressor has kerosene injected into it after passing through stators and into the combustion chamber.

3 HOT GASES: The kerosene-filled air is ignited electronically in the combustion chamber. The gas produced has enormous energy, and as it burns it rushes through the rear five-stage turbine, spinning both it and the driveshaft. This, in turn, spins the propeller at the front of the engine, via reduction gearboxes.

HOT GAS

DRIVESHAFT

HOT GAS

POWER TURBINE

EXHAUST GAS

Tu-114 MAIN WING SPAR

ACTION DATA

PASSENGERS
In its maximum density configuration, the Tu-114 carried more passengers than a Boeing 707, but a more usual load was around 170 in less cramped conditions. Soviet passengers on internal routes endured much lower standards of comfort than foreigners in jet airliners. However, air travel in the USSR was as cheap as taking a train.

Tu-114 'CLEAT'	220
MODEL 707	189
BRITANNIA	133

TUPOLEV

TU-134 'CRUSTY'

● Medium/short haul ● Long serving ● DC-9 equivalent

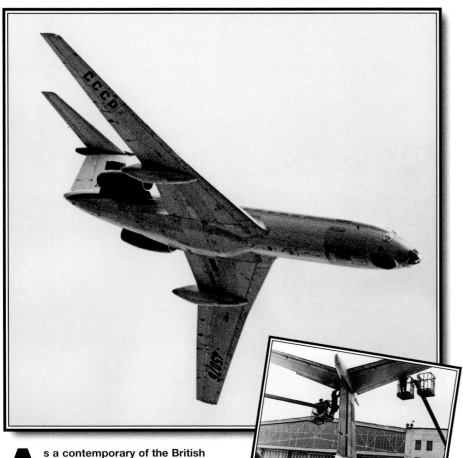

As a contemporary of the British One-Eleven and American DC-9, the Soviet Union developed the Tu-134. Like those aircraft the Tu-134 has twin engines mounted on the rear fuselage and a T-tail, although its wings are more sharply swept. It entered service with Aeroflot in 1967, and nearly 800 were built. According to Tupolev, by the mid-1990s the Tu-134 and the Tu-154 were providing 65 per cent of all passenger transport in Russia.

▲ Although a large number of Tu-134s remain in service after many years, the type is slowly disappearing as former Eastern Bloc airlines re-equip with more efficient Western aircraft.

PHOTO FILE

TUPOLEV TU-134 'CRUSTY'

◄ Military transport
Many Tu-134s have been used for passenger transport and test duties with military agencies. The Bulgarian air force uses this Tu-134A as a transport.

'Crusty' cafe ►
As increasing numbers of Tu-134s are retired, the majority are being scrapped. Others, like this aircraft near Prague, gain a new lease of life serving in roles never envisaged by Tupolev's design team.

◄ African liner
This quasi-military Tu-134A belongs to the Angolan government. Many Tu-134s are finding their way to Third World operators.

Aeroflot original ►
Having been designed to satisfy Aeroflot requirements, the Tu-134 was used in huge numbers by the airline on its vast internal network.

◄ Middle Eastern service
Many of the countries flying Tu-134s were long-term allies of the Soviet regime. This Syrianair 'Crusty' was photographed in 1984. With the break-up of the Soviet Union, spare parts and other support services for older Russian aircraft are increasingly hard to find.

FACTS AND FIGURES

➤ Aeroflot began international service with the Tu-134 in September 1967, flying from Moscow to Stockholm.

➤ Only one Tu-134 prototype was built, flying for the first time in 1963.

➤ Tupolev designers claimed that the aircraft could fly from earth runways.

➤ The existence of the Tu-134 was not revealed until 1964, after 100 test flights had been completed.

➤ Early aircraft had no thrust reversers or auxiliary power unit.

➤ Tu-134s can land automatically and in fog when visibility is down to 50 m (150 ft.).

PROFILE

Soviet stalwart airliner

Known originally as the Tu-124A, the Tu-134 was developed from the earlier aircraft, whose layout was derived from that of the Tu-16 'Badger' bomber. As a result, with its engines carried in the wingroots, the Tu-124 was both inefficient and noisy, and as soon as it entered service work started on its replacement.

First flown in the early 1960s, the Tu-134 was a much improved aircraft. It started flying passenger services with Aeroflot in 1967, and in 1970

the Tu-134A introduced a lengthened fuselage with two extra rows of seats.

The type was also sold to several airlines outside Russia. In the mid-1990s it was still in service with Balkan Bulgarian, Czech, Malev Hungarian and LOT-Polish airlines, as well as Russia's Aeroflot, Samara and Tyumen.

The Tu-134 and early Tu-134As had a glazed nose for the navigator, but from 1971 a radar was installed in the nose. Various passenger layouts have

been used, with typical seating in later models for between 66 and 76. Variants include the Tu-134A3, which has lightweight seats for up to 96 passengers.

Appearing in an ever-changing series of liveries, the Tu-134 has become a reflection of the political turmoil of many Eastern Bloc nations. This aircraft belongs to the national airline of the Czech Republic.

Tu-134 'Crusty'

Balkan Bulgarian airlines was one of the first Tu-134 customers. Six of the early model were delivered and the airline eventually flew a fleet of 16 aircraft. This is an early Tu-134 with a glazed nose.

On early machines the navigator sat in the glazed nose-cone with the RO3-1 weather and navigation radar housed in a radome to the rear of the navigator's compartment.

A 2.10-metre fuselage stretch allowed seating to be increased from the original 64 to 72 passengers, to between 72 and 80 in the Tu-134A. The Tu-134B-3 sub-variant could accommodate 96 passengers.

The incidence of the entire tailplane was altered for trimming, while the elevators were used for pitch control and had their own trim-tabs.

Sharp sweep and pronounced anhedral are distinctive features of the wing. Each wing contains three fuel tanks.

The two large wing fences on each wing help to reduce induced drag by preventing span-wise movement of air flowing over the wing. Reducing drag helps increase wing efficiency and thereby lowers fuel consumption and increases the aircraft's range.

As with all airliners having rear-mounted engines, the tailplane of the Tu-134 was high-set. The leading edge of the fin was de-iced electrically, while the fin was de-iced by hot air.

In common with many Soviet-designed aircraft, the retracted main undercarriage units of the Tu-134 were housed in large aerodynamic fairings behind the trailing edge of the wing.

The pilot and co-pilot sat side-by-side on the flightdeck. On aircraft with solid noses, the navigator was positioned behind the pilot, and the radar was moved into the nose radome.

Pilots relied solely on the wheelbrakes to stop these early aircraft, as no thrust-reversers were fitted.

From their experience with the Tu-104, the Tu-134's designers placed the engines at the rear to keep cabin noise to a minimum. The undercarriage was unusually tall for a rear-engined type to give the Tu-134 rough-field capabilities.

Tu-134A

Type: short- to medium-haul airliner

Powerplant: two 66.69-kN (15,000-lb.-thrust) Soloviev D-30-II turbofans

Maximum cruising speed: 900 km/h (558 m.p.h.)

Climb rate: 888 m/min (2,914 f.p.m.) at sea level

Range: 2000 km (1,240 mi.) with 8215-kg (18,075-lb.) payload or 3500 km (2,170 mi.) with 4000-kg (8,800-lb.) payload

Service ceiling: 12,000 m (39,400 ft.)

Weights: empty 29,000 kg (63,800 lb.); maximum take-off 47,000 kg (103,400 lb.)

Payload: 72 passengers or 80 passengers with reduced baggage space

Dimensions:
span 29.00 m (95 ft. 2 in.)
length 37.10 m (121 ft. 8 in.)
height 9.02 m (29 ft. 7 in.)
wing area 127.30 m² (1,370 sq. ft.)

ACTION DATA

PASSENGERS

Several airliners were developed for the 70- to 80-seat short- to medium-haul market during the mid-1960s. Western designs faced very stiff international competition, but the Tu-134 had no rival for Aeroflot orders.

Tu-134A 'CRUSTY' — 72 passengers
F28 FELLOWSHIP Mk 2000 — 79 passengers
Tu-104A 'CAMEL' — 70 passengers

MAXIMUM CRUISING SPEED

Most passengers prefer to be airborne for as short a time as possible, so a fast, efficient cruising speed is highly desirable. The 'Camel' is the fastest of these three, but it offered little in the way of passenger comfort compared to the quieter Tu-134. The F28 has been developed into the advanced Fokker 100.

Tu-134A 'CRUSTY' — 900 km/h (558 m.p.h.)
F28 — 843 km/h (523 m.p.h.)
Tu-104A 'CAMEL' — 950 km/h (589 m.p.h.)

MAXIMUM RANGE

With its vast size, the Soviet Union demanded longer range from its short- to medium-haul airliners than was available from contemporary Western designs. With its bomber origins the Tu-104A offered outstanding range, but it was a crude airliner. The Tu-134 was a compromise between the Tu-104 and Western types.

Tu-134A 'CRUSTY' 3500 km (2,170 mi.)
F28 FELLOWSHIP Mk 2000 2038 km (1,264 mi.)
Tu-104A 'CAMEL' 4200 km (2,600 mi.)

Western 'Crusty' contemporaries

■ **BAC ONE-ELEVEN:** Some One-Elevens, usually with hush-kitted engines, still remain in service with smaller charter airlines in the UK and abroad. More than 200 aircraft were built, some under licence in Romania.

■ **BOEING MODEL 737:** With a maximum capacity of between 103 and 130 passengers, the 737 was unusual because Boeing opted to position its twin engines beneath the wings rather than at the tail. It has become the world's best-selling airliner.

■ **HAWKER SIDDELEY TRIDENT:** With its three Rolls-Royce Spey turbofans and seating for between 103 and 180 passengers, depending on the variant, the Trident was designed for short- to medium-range, high-capacity routes.

TUPOLEV

TU-144 'CHARGER'

● Supersonic transport ● Concorde competitor ● Technology testbed

F irst flown on the last day of 1968, the Tu-144 was a product of the Cold War competition that saw the Soviet Union and the West repeatedly trying to outdo each other in various areas of aerospace technology. Alongside the space race, supersonic passenger transport was one of the most demanding areas of development, and one where the Soviets were determined to beat the Anglo-French team working on the aircraft that became Concorde.

▲ Before the fuel crises and strict noise regulations of the 1970s, Europe and the USSR were involved in a dramatic race to produce the first supersonic airliner, which the Tu-144 won.

TUPOLEV TU-144 'CHARGER'

Double-delta ▶
This view clearly shows the pronounced double-delta shape of the wing planform, which gave the Tu-144 a much more angular appearance than Concorde. The large air intakes are visible beneath the wing.

▲ Paris disaster
The second production Tu-144, 77102, suffered an inflight break-up during an unplanned violent pitch maneuver while participating in the 1973 Paris Show.

▲ Drooping moustache
For production versions, low-speed handling was improved by adding retractable canards just aft of the flight deck.

▲ Concorde copy
Many features of the Tu-144 were remarkably similar to Concorde, such as the distinctive drooping nose. It was later revealed that the KGB obtained blueprints of the Concorde design.

Afterburning engines ▶
The NK-144A engines fitted to production aircraft were designed by Kuznetsov. Uprated engines, which resulted in the Tu-144D, allowed cruise without afterburner, but never entered service.

FACTS AND FIGURES

➤ The original Tu-144 was smaller than the production version and did not have the high-lift canards fitted.

➤ The prototype first flew on 31 December 1968, beating Concorde by 61 days.

➤ The first Mach 2 flight by an airliner was made by the Tu-144 in May 1970.

➤ It has been alleged that the violent maneuver which led to the Paris crash was to avoid a French Mirage camera ship.

➤ Passenger service began in November 1977 between Moscow and Alma Ata.

➤ Only 102 revenue-making flights were flown before the Tu-144 was retired.

PROFILE

Catching up to the West, supersonically

In its efforts to overtake the West's lead in supersonic transport, the Soviet Union embarked on a concerted campaign of industrial espionage in the early 1960s. At the same time, a flight test program was started using a MiG-21 with a scaled-down version of the Tu-144's wing.

Thanks to the skill of their spies and an incredible amount of work by the design bureau, Tupolev won the race. The Tu-144 flew two months before Concorde, and started scheduled services in December 1975, nearly

five months ahead of its rival. No passengers were carried until November 1977, though, and after at least one had crashed the aircraft was withdrawn from service less than a year later.

Despite its commercial failure, the Tu-144 made a major contribution to the understanding of high-speed aerodynamics. Evidence of that came in the early 1990s, when the U.S. paid for one of the original Tu-144s to be refurbished as a technology testbed. The purpose was to help develop a second-generation supersonic transport.

Tupolev itself had been developing a successor to the 'Charger'. Designated Tu-244, it was intended to carry 300 passengers and have a range of 9173 km (5,700 mi.).

Above: The prototype first flew in late 1968. It differed from production models by having less camber in the wings and no nose canards.

Above: The streamlined shape needed for attaining Mach 2 is evident in the design of the Tu-144. Its similarity to Concorde led to it being nicknamed 'Concordski' in the Western press.

Tu-144 'Charger'

Type: supersonic passenger transport

Powerplant: four 196.31 kN (44,115-lb.-thrust) Kuznetsov NK-144 afterburning turbofans

Maximum speed: 2494 km/h (1,550 m.p.h.)

Cruise height: 17,000 m (55,750 ft.)

Range: 6486 km (4,030 mi.) with 140 passengers at Mach 1.9.

Weights: 84,822 kg (187,000 lb.) empty; 167,376 kg (369,000 lb.) max take-off

Accommodation: 140 passengers typically

Dimensions:
span	94 ft. 6 in.)
length	215 ft. 6 in.)
height	42 ft. 2 in.)
wing area	437.85 m² (4,713 sq. ft.)

Tu-144 'CHARGER'

Aeroflot was the only operator of the Tu-144, making just 102 commercial flights before an accident in 1978 led to retirement.

Production aircraft had redesigned engine nacelles with oblique rectangular inlets similar to Concorde. The intakes were electrically de-iced.

The virtually full-span powered control surfaces consist of four separate elevons on each wing. These act in unison as elevators, or in opposition as ailerons.

The double-delta wings have a leading-edge sweepback of about 76 degrees on the inboard sections and 57 degrees on the main panels. The wing also has a camber on both leading and trailing edges.

During low-speed flight, takeoff and landing the nosecone droops by 12 degrees. A pair of canards also extend in this flight regime to improve the low-speed handling of the aircraft.

The Tu-144 is of largely light alloy construction. Titanium and stainless steel are used in the leading edges and control surfaces. Advanced flight controls and navigation systems are fitted.

Four afterburning Kuznetsov NK-144A turbofans powered the Tu-144. Afterburning was necessary to maintain supersonic cruise.

The Tu-144 had a normal flight crew of three with the two pilots seated side-by-side. The prototype was fitted with ejection seats for the crew, but these were removed in production aircraft.

The main landing gear was a 12-wheel bogie that retracted forward, rotating through 180 degrees to lie inverted in the wing. The long nose gear was based on the unit used in the Tu-114 and retracted forward into the fuselage.

The most common seating arrangement in the Tu-144 was for 11 first-class and 129 tourist-class passengers. The theoretical maximum was 167 passengers.

Aerodynamic features of the Tu-144

CRUISING POSITION: During supersonic cruise the nose is aligned with the fuselage, allowing for an extremely aerodynamic shape. The retractable visor is not transparent, giving the crew very poor forward vision.

LOW-SPEED POSITION: The nose droops by 12 degrees during low-speed flight, take-off and landing to give the pilots much better forward vision. The visor, which is armored to resist a supersonic birdstrike, retracts.

CANARDS RETRACTED: For high-speed flight the double-delta wing provides all the lift the aircraft needs and the rectangular canards, 6 m (20 ft.) long, retract back into the top of the fuselage to give a more aerodynamic shape.

CANARDS EXTENDED: To improve handling of the aircraft at low speeds the canards swing forward to zero-degree sweep, but sharp anhedral. Each canard is fitted with a double leading-edge slat and a trailing-edge flap.

ACTION DATA

SPEED

Of the two supersonic jet transports that have entered service, the Tu-144 was bigger and faster than the Concorde. Concorde, however, was commercially successful for more than 25 years. The DC-10 is a typical subsonic airliner of the time; it takes over twice as long as Concorde on Atlantic crossings.

Tu-144 'CHARGER'	2494 km/h (1,550 m.p.h.)
CONCORDE	2174 km/h (1,351 m.p.h.)
DC-10-30	954 km/h (593 m.p.h.)

TUPOLEV

Tu-204

● New-generation airliner ● Western technology ● Growing orders

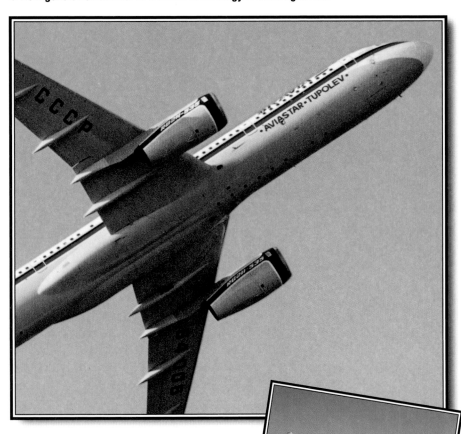

Designed as a replacement for the Tu-154, and flown for the first time in January 1989, the basic Tu-204 was just the first in a planned family of airliners. The different models include versions with Russian and Western engines, and offer various combinations of payload and range. Howver, development has been hampered by lack of funding for flight testing and certification. A version powered by Rolls-Royce engines has achieved growing interest from several airlines.

▲ *Designed in the early 1980s as a successor to the tri-jet Tu-154, this medium-range airliner bears a resemblance to the Boeing 757. Deliveries began in 1992 and the first revenue-earning flight took place in 1996.*

TUPOLEV Tu-204

▼ **Major improvement**
Compared to its predecessor, the Tu-154, the new airliner boasts greater passenger capacity and better fuel economy, making the aircraft more attractive to western airlines.

▲ **Joint venture**
After the collapse of the Soviet Union, Tupolev looked for partners to secure funding for the Tu-204. This led to the creation of BRAVIA (British Russian Aviation), whose markings adorn this example.

▼ **State of the art**
Compared to previous Tupolev airliners, the Tu-204 is an engineering marvel. The wing has a comparatively modest sweep and features winglets which help improve airflow.

▲ **Various powerplants**
As with many modern airliners, different engines can be specified for the Tu-204. Series 100 aircraft are powered by two Aviadvigatel PS-90 turbofans.

First flight ▶
Completed in 1988, the first prototype made its maiden flight in early 1989 from the Zhukhovskii test centre near Moscow, with Andrei Talalakin at the controls.

FACTS AND FIGURES

➤ Development of the Tu-204 was aided by Armand Hammer, a US tycoon who had many contacts inside the Soviet Union.

➤ Two-crew operation is possible, though a third seat for a flight engineer is fitted.

➤ A Tu-204 fuelled by liquid natural gas has been proposed, but so far not built.

➤ A smaller Tupolev design, yet to be flown, the Tu-304 incorporates many features of the larger Tu-204.

➤ BRAVIA has acquired a number of aircraft which are intended for resale.

➤ A maritime version is being considered by the Russian navy to replace the Il-38.

PROFILE

A new airliner for a new era

Above: Versatility has been demonstrated by the introduction of both combi and freighter versions of the Tupolev Tu-204.

Above: Proudly wearing the old Soviet-style Aeroflot colours, the first prototype SSSR-64001 sits quietly at Le Bourget. At that time the airline had intended to acquire 350 examples.

Finally awarded its Russian certificate of airworthiness in December 1994, the standard Tupolev Tu-204 is currently built at the Aviastar plant in Ulyanovsk alongside several other variants. They include the Tu-204-100, -120, and the 204C freighter variant with a large cargo door.

With each successive variant, maximum take-off weight has been increased and more powerful engines have been introduced to compensate.

Further variations include the Tu-224 and 324. These aircraft were designed for trunk route services and feature a shortened fuselage with seating for up to 160 passengers and a range of 7200 km (4,465 mi.).

Russian airline Sirocco Aerospace placed an order for around 200 of the Rolls-Royce RB211-engined aircraft which are known as Tu-204-120s. A dedicated freighter variant is also available and features US avionics and Western cabin furnishings in addition to the British engines, resulting in a truly international aircraft. The first production version of the Rolls-Royce-powered Tu-204 rolled off the line in March 1997.

After a long and turbulent development process, the future of Tupolev's twin-engined medium-range airliner looks brighter than it did several years ago. Massive investment by Western organisations has aided the programme considerably.

Tu-204

First flown in August 1992, this particular aircraft, RA-64006, was the first Tu-204 to be fitted with Rolls-Royce RB211s. It was fitted out by Hunting in the UK before being demonstrated at Farnborough '92.

Up front, the flight deck of the Tu-204 follows modern airliner practice in featuring a digital glass cockpit with TV type multi-function displays. Side-stick control columns, similar to those of the Airbus A340, were originally planned, but were discarded in favour of conventional yokes.

Depending on customer requirements, the cabin layout of the Tu-204 can vary considerably. A maximum of 214 passengers can be accommodated for charter flights, though for scheduled services a total of 184 passengers will normally be carried, comprising 30 in business and 154 in economy/tourist class.

Roughly 18 per cent of the airframe consists of composites. The fuselage also makes extensive use of titanium and aluminium-lithium for greatest possible strength and lowest possible weight.

The tail unit makes the most extensive use of composites, particularly on the moving surfaces. As in the much larger Boeing 747-400, the tail also holds an integral fuel tank.

This Tu-204 wears the markings of BRAVIA (British Russian Aviation), a consortium which was formed in the early 1990s. Through it, the aircraft received the Rolls-Royce engines and the door was opened for development of further variants of this promising Russian design.

Fitted to this variant are two RB211 Series 535 high-bypass-ratio turbofans. These engines are among the most popular on the civil market today and have gained a reputation for being ultra-reliable, fuel-efficient and powerful, not to mention quiet.

Under the cabin floor is the baggage compartment, which runs virtually the entire length of the fuselage, interrupted only by the fuel tanks. For greater payloads, a Tu-204 combi variant is available, in which a section of the normal cabin is reserved for freight.

Tupolev's previous jet airliners

■ Tu-104: This aircraft created a sensation in 1956 when it was the first Soviet jet airliner to appear in the West. It was, however, a crude machine, and performance was not spectacular.

■ Tu-134: An altogether better airliner, the Tu-134 was more refined and had a much lower level of cabin noise than the Tu-104, because of its rear-mounted engines.

■ Tu-154: Similar in concept to the Boeing 727 and Hawker-Siddeley Trident, the Tu-154 became a much-loved airliner in Aeroflot service. It is destined to be around for some time yet.

Tu-204-100

Type: medium-range airliner

Powerplant: two 157-kN (35,320-lb.-thrust) Aviadvigatel PS-90A turbofan engines

Maximum cruising speed: 850 km/h (527 m.p.h.)

Range: 4000 km (2,480 mi.)

Maximum fuel capacity: 40,730 litres (10,760 gal.)

Weights: empty 59,000 kg (129,800 lb.); loaded 103,000 kg (226,600 lb.)

Take-off run: 1450 m (4,760 ft.)

Accommodation: standard accommodation for two crew and 184 passengers, though a third crew member is often carried and passenger seating can be increased to 214

Dimensions:		
span	42.00 m	(137 ft. 9 in.)
length	46.22 m	(151 ft. 7 in.)
height	13.88 m	(45 ft. 6 in.)
wing area	182.40 m²	(1,963 sq. ft.)

ACTION DATA

MAXIMUM CRUISING SPEED

Not quite as efficient as the Boeing 757, the Tu-204 is nevertheless an economical aircraft and has a high cruising speed compared to other Russian airliners. The MD-90 is a modernised version of the 1960s' DC-9 and, not surprisingly, is somewhat slower.

Tu-204-100	850 km/h (527 m.p.h.)
757-200	935 km/h (580 m.p.h.)
MD-90-30	809 km/h (502 m.p.h.)

PASSENGERS

All three of these medium-range airliners are known as 'narrow bodies', in which passengers sit on either side of a single aisle. During the development stage, the Tu-204 was repeatedly stretched to accommodate more passengers; it still carries fewer passengers than the 757, though more than the lengthened MD-90.

Tu-204-100	214 PASSENGERS
757-200	239 PASSENGERS
MD-90-30	172 PASSENGERS

MAXIMUM RANGE

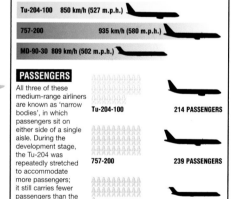

Today, medium-range airliners are capable of flying distances unheard of two decades ago. Though the basic design of the MD-90 is more than 30 years old, in updated form it still has a respectable range. The Boeing 757 is more capable, however.

Tu-204-100 4000 km (2,480 mi.)

757-200 5150 km (3,195 mi.)

MD-90-30 4200 km (3,470 mi.)

VFW-FOKKER

614

● German airliner ● Overwing engines ● Rough-field STOL capability

▲ *A large number of orders were initially received for the 614, but few of these turned into deliveries. Airlines may have considered the aircraft too slow, or perhaps its unusual configuration and the early withdrawal of SNECMA from the project did not give potential buyers confidence in it.*

Focke-Wulf, 'Weser' and Heinkel united as VFW in the mid-1960s to develop the VFW 614 airliner. In 1970 the VFW consortium joined forces with Fokker to produce the aircraft. It flew for the first time in July 1971, and by early 1975 ten operators had expressed their intention to buy a total of 26 aircraft. Two years later, though, only 16 had been ordered, and production ceased at the end of 1977 after just 19 had been built. Only four examples remain airworthy.

VFW-FOKKER 614

▲ **Overwing engines**
Foreign objects were unlikely to enter the engines as they were protected by the wings.

▲ **Flying in France**
VFW-Fokker 614s had short airline careers, with Air Alsace using its jets only from 1976 to 1979.

Prototype number three ▶
After the first prototype crashed, the third aircraft was rushed into service to help with testing.

◀ **Destined for Denmark**
Cimber Air introduced the VFW-Fokker 614 into commercial service in 1975.

Icelandic runway ▶
According to a VFW-Fokker press release, the stones on this unprepared runway were 'fist-sized'. These tests were required for the aircraft to gain certification for rough-field operations. Tests were also undertaken in Saudi Arabia and north and west Africa.

FACTS AND FIGURES

➤ A merger of Focke-Wulf and 'Weser' Flugzeugbau produced VFW in 1963, with Heinkel joining in 1964.

➤ After 1969 Fokker became an equal partner in the company with VFW.

➤ Elevator tab flutter caused the crash of the first prototype in 1972.

➤ Early in 1973 VFW-Fokker had 23 orders for the 614, but only 19 were ever completed; 13 served with airlines.

➤ SABCA and Fairey in Belgium were also involved in production.

➤ MBB now uses its aircraft to test new technologies, including fly-by-light.

PROFILE

Radical airliner design

VFW designed the 614 as a modern version of the DC-3. Originally proposed as the E.614 by the Entwicklungsring division of Focke-Wulf, it could carry up to 44 passengers over ranges of around 600 km (372 mi.).

The most remarkable feature of the design was its overwing engines. Mounted on pylons, they enabled the aircraft to use very short undercarriage legs, which simplified passenger loading and helped to reduce the risk of engine debris ingestion.

Unfortunately, the idea did not prove popular and fewer than a dozen were sold before the manufacturers decided to stop production. The first 614 entered service with Cimber Air in Denmark, and Air Alsace operated three. Another three were delivered to the German air force, which still uses them as VIP transports.

In the mid-1980s one 614 was rebuilt as a research aircraft. It is used by the German aerospace research establishment, the DFW, to investigate new aerodynamics, systems and air traffic control technology. The projected 614-200 version, with a slightly longer fuselage and increased wingspan, would have carried 52 passengers.

Above: With a large flap area and strong undercarriage the VFW-Fokker 614 was destined to become a favourite with STOL operators, but it never happened.

Above: Three aircraft were delivered to the Luftwaffe and remain in service. Only one other VFW-Fokker 614 remains airworthy, operated by MBB.

614

Type: short-haul passenger transport

Powerplant: two 32.4-kN (7,290-lb.) Rolls-Royce SNECMA M45H Mk 501 turbofans

Maximum speed: 735 km/h (455 m.p.h.) at 6400 m (20,000 ft.); maximum cruising speed 722 km/h (448 m.p.h.) at 7620 m (25,000 ft.)

Climb rate: 1026 m/min (3,365 f.p.m.)

Landing run: 631 m (2,070 ft.) from 15 m (50-ft.)

Range: 2500 km (1,500 mi.) with maximum fuel; 667 km (414 mi.) with 40 passengers or 3680-kg (8,096-lb.) payload with fuel reserves for a 277-km (170-mi.) diversion

Service ceiling: 7620 m (25,000 ft.)

Weights: empty 12,200 kg (26,840 lb.); maximum take-off 18,600 kg (40,920 lb.)

Accommodation: 40 to 44 passengers

Dimensions:
span	21.50 m	(70 ft. 6 in.)
length	20.60 m	(67 ft. 7 in.)
height	7.84 m	(25 ft. 9 in.)
wing area	64 m²	(689 sq. ft.)

614

D-BABB was the second VFW-Fokker 614 prototype, flown on 14 January 1972, before the 1 February crash of the first aircraft, which claimed the life of its co-pilot. Its development was otherwise untroubled.

An engine pylon was mounted on each wing, just behind the rear spar at about two-thirds chord. This position left the wing leading edge well ahead of the engine and prevented debris entering it.

Rolls-Royce and SNECMA co-operated in the production of the M45H Mk 501 turbofan. It had been developed to power an Anglo-French strike fighter, but only found this one application.

The all-metal tailplane could be moved as a trimming method. A liquid de-icing system protected the leading edges.

Pilot and co-pilot sat side-by-side with dual controls. An observer could be carried as an option. In addition to the flight crew, two cabin attendants were carried.

Aircraft flying test duties, especially prototypes, are often fitted with large instrumentation booms. These collect a range of data about aircraft attitude and speed.

This forward door served as the main passenger entrance, with an in-built airstair. A cargo door for baggage was mounted opposite.

Massive flap guides were a result of the STOL capabilities of the design. The wing also had two spoilers for in-flight use and six for ground use.

A maximum of 44 passengers could be accommodated. Unfortunately engines mounted alongside the windows resulted in a noisy cabin.

ACTION DATA

MAXIMUM CRUISING SPEED

Some industry experts criticised the 614 for its low speed, although over the short routes for which it was designed this would not have been a problem.

614	722 km/h (448 m.p.h.)
ONE-ELEVEN SERIES 475	871 km/h (540 m.p.h.)
146-100	778 km/h (482 m.p.h.)

TAKE-OFF RUN

Even compared to the BAe 146, the take-off performance of the VFW 614 is remarkable. The 146 was to have been launched at the same time as the 614, but its manufacturers shelved the design after they judged that a market for the type did not exist at that time.

614	830 m (2,720 ft.)
ONE-ELEVEN SERIES 475	1676 m (5,500 ft.)
146-100	1116 m (3,660 ft.)

RANGE

Gaining a number of export orders, the One-Eleven was favoured for its long range, although it could not match the operational flexibility of the 614. Designed to the same philosophy as the 614, the 146 would have benefited from the incorporation of newer technology to produce an aircraft of greater overall capability.

614 2500 km (1,500 mi.)
ONE-ELEVEN SERIES 475 3677 km (2,275 mi.)
146-100 2872 km (1,780 mi.)

VFW aerospace projects

■ **VFW H3:** Typical of the innovative designs of VFW, this three-seat helicopter featured a compressed-air driven main rotor and shrouded propellers for forward flight.

■ **PANAVIA MRCA:** VFW was an early partner in the project that was to produce the Tornado, destined to become one of Europe's most important combat aircraft.

■ **VFW-FOKKER CH-53G:** A 1969 contract for 135 CH-53Gs to equip the German army resulted in VFW-Fokker building the type under licence from Sikorsky.

■ **FOKKER-VFW F.28 FRIENDSHIP:** VFW-Fokker was responsible for building fuselage sections and tail assemblies for the F.28 and contributed greatly to the type's success.

VICKERS

VIKING

● Short-haul airliner ● Based on the Wellington ● RAF service

A s World War II reached its climax in 1945, it became apparent that Britain urgently required an interim transport aircraft for short-haul work. Vickers designed the Viking, which was ideal for the task and could quickly be placed into production since it was based on the Wellington bomber. Vikings saw extensive service with British European Airways and served as transport and training aircraft, known respectively as the Valetta and the Varsity, with the RAF.

▲ *Vikings replaced*
DC-3s serving with a number of British airlines. The Vickers aircraft was one of the first airliners to feature personal steward call-buttons, adjustable headrests and air vents.

VICKERS VIKING

◄ **Viking in production**
Seen flying off the Isle of Wight, G-AGON was the first production Viking. It was used by BOAC's development flight, based at Hurn.

▼ **Export Vikings**
The first overseas customer was Indian National Airways, which named this aircraft Jumna.

▼ **Jet power**
On 6 April 1948 a specially converted Rolls-Royce Nene turbojet-powered Viking took to the air and became the world's first pure-jet transport aircraft.

▼ **Metal wing**
After the first 19 aircraft, stressed-skin metal wings were fitted, as these were easier to maintain.

◄ **Linking Europe**
Originally delivered to South African Airways, G-AMGG was one of 75 Vikings operated by BEA. The Viking was a vital component of BEA's fleet linking Britain to other European countries.

FACTS AND FIGURES

➤ Before the Viking name was chosen, the aircraft was also known as the Wellington Continental and the VC.1.

➤ The prototype first flew from Wisley airfield on 22 June 1945.

➤ British European Airways' Admiral-class Vikings could carry up to 36 passengers.

➤ Four Mk 1 Vikings were operated by the King's Flight on state visits to South Africa in 1947 and Nigeria in 1951.

➤ The RAF operated transport and training variants called Valetta and Varsity.

➤ A number of the 163 Vikings built were still operating charter flights in the late 1960s.

PROFILE

Britain's first post-war airliner

Post-war Britain had a demand for a civil transport aircraft, and before machines such as the Comet could enter service an interim aircraft was required. Vickers proposed the VC.1 (later the Viking), which combined the virtues of the tried-and-tested Wellington wing and Bristol Hercules engine with a new stressed-skin fuselage.

A year after design work began the VC.1 prototype took to the air. After a successful test programme, British European

Airways (BEA) ordered 50 Vikings, with an improved stressed-skin wing, to replace its fleet of DC-3s. BEA operated the first Viking service on 1 September 1946.

In December 1946 icing problems were discovered, and operations were halted for four months. Solutions were found, however, and export sales were won after a successful 64,400-km (40,000-mi.) tour to New Zealand.

In April 1950 disaster nearly struck one of BEA's Vikings, *Vigilant,* when a saboteur's bomb

exploded in the toilet over the English Channel. The strength of the design and the skill of Captain I.R. Harvey ensured the badly damaged aircraft made a safe landing. BEA's Vikings flew more than half a million hours and carried three million passengers before being replaced in 1954.

G-AHOS was one of the earliest Vikings and featured the geodetic wing.

The first 19 Vikings featured fabric-covered geodetic wings and tail. They were replaced by stressed-skin units.

Much of the wing design, including the main spar system, was based on the Wellington. Stressed-skin wings were introduced for ease of maintenance.

Viking Type 610

Type: twin-engined short-haul airliner

Powerplant: two 1260-kW (1,690-hp.) Bristol Hercules 634 piston engines

Maximum speed: 423 km/h (262 m.p.h.) at 3000 m (10,000 ft.)

Initial climb rate: 457 m/min (1,500 f.p.m.)

Range: 2736 km (1,700 mi.) at 338 km/h (210 m.p.h.)

Service ceiling: 7620 m (25,000 ft.)

Weights: empty 10,433 kg (22,936 lb.); maximum take-off 16,400 kg (36,080 lb.)

Accommodation: four crew and up to 27 passengers, or up to 36 passengers in Admiral-class layout

Dimensions:
span	27.20 m	(89 ft. 3 in.)
length	19.86 m	(65 ft. 2 in.)
height	5.97 m	(19 ft. 7 in.)
wing area	81.94 m²	(882 sq. ft.)

VIKING TYPE 610

G-AHPL, *Verdant,* was first delivered to BEA and was later renamed *Lord Anson.* It went on to serve with five other airlines, including Central African Airways.

Power was provided by two Bristol Hercules engines. They were chosen ahead of the Rolls-Royce Merlin because they had greater single-engine performance, and could meet new take-off regulations.

Unlike pre-war airliners, the Viking was designed with passenger comfort in mind. Sound-proofing was introduced to the cabin walls and ceiling, and a leather and moquette finish was applied to the interior.

Icing problems encountered on the tailplane were solved by increasing the flow rate of the de-icing solution.

The functional flightdeck had a central console with throttles, trim wheels, fuel-cock controls and the instrument panel. The wide-angle front and side windscreens were an innovative feature.

ACTION DATA

CRUISING SPEED

Capable of cruising at a higher speed than the ubiquitous DC-3, which it replaced, the Viking reduced travelling time for passengers. The later CV 240 and the the Il-12 'Coach' had more powerful engines, giving greater performance.

VIKING Mk 1B	338 km/h (210 m.p.h.)
CV 240 CONVAIRLINER	432 km/h (268 m.p.h.)
Il-12B 'COACH'	350 km/h (217 m.p.h.)

MAXIMUM PASSENGERS

In maximum passenger configuration the Viking could carry up to 36 passengers. A more typical load was 27, which gave greater passenger comfort. The CV 240 was a larger aircraft and offered more space for passengers and cargo.

VIKING Mk 1B 36 passengers

CV 240 CONVAIRLINER 40 passengers

Il-12B 'COACH' 32 passengers

RANGE

Built to operate British European Airways' services from London to major European cities, the Viking did not require, or possess, long range. The CV 240 and Il-12 were designed to cover the much larger areas of North America and the Soviet Union, and therefore required much greater range to meet the specific needs of customers.

VIKING Mk 1B 837 km (520 mi.)

CV 240 CONVAIRLINER 2880 km (1,800 mi.)

Il-12B 'COACH' 1250 km (775 mi.)

Vickers civil transport aircraft

■ **WARWICK:** Deliveries to British Overseas Airways Corporation (BOAC) started in 1943. Three Warwicks were used on North African routes.

■ **VISCOUNT:** Regarded as a milestone in air transport, the Viscount was the first turbine-powered aircraft to enter revenue service.

■ **VANGUARD:** Following on from the success of the Viscount, Vickers built the larger and faster Vanguard. It entered service on 1 March 1961.

■ **VC.10:** The four-engined VC.10 was built to a BOAC specification for a long-range airliner with good hot-and-high performance.

VICKERS

VISCOUNT

● Short-haul airliner ● World's first commercial turboprop ● Still in service

A revelation when it appeared soon after World War II, the much-loved Vickers Viscount was the world's first true turboprop airliner. With its four Dart turboprop engines, tricycle landing gear and a sumptuous interior which enabled the airlines to treat passengers in comfort, it was a great leap forwards for commercial aviation. Conceived as a short-haul transport for European routes, Viscounts are still flying today after more than 40 years.

▲ *The Viscount went through a phase of being unpopular when jets became fashionable, but it enjoyed a sudden revival in fortune when oil prices and operating costs rose.*

VICKERS VISCOUNT

▲ Two engines only
Viscount pilots liked to perform at Farnborough. One display stunt was a low pass in front of the crowd, with the aircraft only using two engines.

▲ Star of the show
Despite its size, the Viscount put on an exciting performance at the 1955 Farnborough air show in 1955. This display was by a 700 series 59-seat aircraft.

▼ Third World workhorse
The Viscount gave some of its most valuable service to Third World countries in Africa and South America because of its reliability and low operating costs.

▲ Assembly line
The main assembly line at Weybridge normally had 12 aircraft in production at any one time.

▼ German Viscount
Nine Viscounts were operated by Lufthansa, the first arriving in October 1958 at Hamburg. The airline flew its Viscounts to European destinations until the end of March 1971.

▲ Darts modified
The superb Dart turboprop was the main reason for the Viscount's success. This very reliable engine was also fitted to the Fokker F27 and BAe HS.748.

FACTS AND FIGURES

➤ The aircraft was originally named the Viceroy, but this was changed to Viscount when India gained independence in 1947.

➤ The first Viscount prototype made its initial flight on 16 July 1948.

➤ The RAF used Viscounts at its test pilot school and radar establishment.

➤ When the manufacturer delivered the last new-build Viscount in 1964, the production run had reached 444 aircraft.

➤ British World Airways operated the very successful Viscount Freightmasters.

➤ Viscounts survive in service in locations as varied as the Philippines and Zaire.

First turboprop airliner

The Viscount was one of the few successes of the Brabazon committee, established during World War II to oversee the future of British commercial aviation. Early Viscounts carried 47 passengers (32 in the prototype), and used turboprop power to set new standards of performance with British European Airways, Air France, Trans Canada and many others. Very attractive Viscounts were flown by Capital Airlines

of Washington DC, which was later absorbed by United Airlines.

The first improved Viscount offered underwing slipper tanks and more engine power. A 2.82-m (9-ft. 3-in.) cabin stretch and improved structural strength produced the Series 800, with increased power and carrying capacity. The definitive Model 810, produced in the early 1960s, seated 74 passengers.

The Viscount is out of date

today, but still turns heads when seen at airports. A few Viscounts were employed by air forces, including India and Turkey. The last Viscounts flying commercial services in Britain were eventually retired in Autumn 1996.

The Viscount came into its own when flying short inter-city flights, such as the London to Edinburgh route with British European Airways. The expense of flying jets on such routes meant that the Viscount remained a viable airliner even though its performance was much lower than jet 'feederliners'.

The Viscount tailplane had a very pronounced dihedral of 15°, and a distinctive rounded fin profile.

Irving-type ailerons and double slotted flaps were fitted to the wing. The structure was an all-metal frame covered with Alclad, and the wing was thermally de-iced.

Viscount 810

Type: short-/medium-range transport

Powerplant: four 1566-kW (2,100-hp.) Rolls-Royce Dart RDa.7/1 Mk 525 turboprops

Maximum cruising speed: 563 km/h (349 m.p.h.) at 6100 m (20,000 ft.)

Range: 2832 km (1,755 mi.) with no fuel reserve

Service ceiling: 7620 m (25,000 ft.)

Weights: empty 18,854 kg (41,479 lb.); loaded 32,884 kg (72,345 lb.)

Accommodation: two pilots, stewardesses, typically 65 to 74 seats in several configurations; up to 11 tons of cargo in freight configuration

Dimensions:
span	28.56 m	(93 ft. 8 in.)
length	26.11 m	(85 ft. 8 in.)
height	8.15 m	(26 ft. 9 in.)
wing area	89.46 m²	(963 sq. ft.)

VISCOUNT 708

Air France purchased 12 Vickers Viscount 708s, the first of which flew in 1953. This version, with improved Dart engines, could carry up to 48 passengers and was widely exported.

The flight crew consisted of only a pilot and co-pilot, with an optional crew station for a radio operator/navigator.

The original specification for the Viscount assumed that the Dart engine would produce about 600 kW (800 hp.), but final versions produced nearly 1600 kW (12,150 hp.).

The tail unit was of all-metal construction, with spring tabs on all control surfaces.

AIR FRANCE
AIR FRANCE
F-BGNK

Three large underfloor freight holds were accessible from a rear hatch.

The 700 series was different from earlier Viscounts in having a 1.5-m (5-ft.) longer wing and 2-m (6-ft. 6-in.) longer fuselage.

ACTION DATA

MAXIMUM CRUISING SPEED

The Viscount was so much faster than its piston-engined contemporaries that a number of manufacturers looked to re-fitting their aircraft with turboprops. Only the long-serving Convair twins proved at all successful, since by that time smaller, more economical purpose-designed turboprops like the HS.748 were coming into use.

VISCOUNT	563 km/h (349 m.p.h.)
MODEL 580	550 km/h (341 m.p.h.)
HS.748	450 km/h (279 m.p.h.)

RANGE

The Viscount's engines were more fuel-efficient than pistons, but four engines meant that consumption was higher than in smaller twin-engined rivals like the Convair 580 and HS.748, and the Viscount's range suffered slightly.

MODEL 580 3000 km (1,860 mi.)
VISCOUNT 2832 km (1,756 mi.)
HS.748 3200 km (1,984 mi.)

PASSENGER LOAD

Successive stretches to the Viscount airframe saw the passenger capacity rise from a planned 32 seats to as many as 74. When Viscounts began to be retired, they were often replaced by smaller aircraft like the HS.748, which were less capable but, being more modern, were cheaper to run.

VISCOUNT	MODEL 580	HS.748
74 passengers	52 passengers	36 passengers

The turboprop generation

VICKERS VANGUARD: The Viscount's big brother first flew in the late 1950s, but when it entered service the jet had become dominant and sales were disappointing.

LOCKHEED ELECTRA: Similar in concept to the Vanguard, sales of the Electra were also unspectacular. However, it was developed into the long-serving P-3 Orion ASW plane.

BRISTOL BRITANNIA: Best of the Western turboprops, the Britannia entered service on the transatlantic run. But it was soon outmoded by the arrival of the 707 and the DC-8.

TUPOLEV Tu-114: The greatest of the propliners, the Tu-114 used the wings and engines of the mighty 'Bear' bomber to fly further and faster than any other propeller-driven airliner.

ILYUSHIN Il-18: Jets were not as dominant behind the Iron Curtain, and the Il-18 was the most important Eastern Bloc airliner in the 1960s and 1970s, with more than 800 in service.

VICKERS

VANGUARD

● Turboprop airliner ● Economical operation ● Freighter conversions

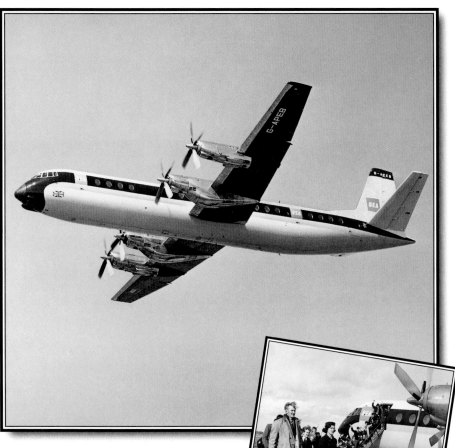

Vickers developed the Vanguard in the late 1950s as a bigger counterpart to the successful Viscount. Its longer cabin could carry up to 139 passengers, nearly twice as many as the Viscount. Unfortunately, it had to compete with the new generation of turbojet-powered airliners designed to serve short- and medium-haul routes. Sales were disappointing and most Vanguards were converted to freighter configuration.

▲ *Although the Vanguard was not very successful, passengers appreciated its quiet cabin and airlines were pleased with its low operating costs. The last freighter version was retired in 1996.*

VICKERS VANGUARD

▼ **Canadian Vanguard**
Air Canada, as Trans-Canadian Airlines, was the only Vanguard export customer.

▲ **Flagship of the fleet**
G-APEA was the flagship of the British European Airways Vanguard fleet. This aircraft was actually named 'Vanguard'.

Wet start ▶
On 20 January 1959 the first Vanguard, known as the Type 950, lifted off from a very wet runway to make its first flight. The fin was neatly blended into the fuselage at this stage, but production machines had a large dorsal fin.

▼ **Looking for customers**
The second Vanguard undertook a demonstration tour of Europe, setting out for Hamburg on 6 March 1959. From Germany the aircraft visited Brussels and Rome, and is seen here in Italy on 4 June 1959. At the end of June it set off for a similar tour of Canada.

▲ **Merchantman**
The Air Bridge company was a major user of the Merchantman freighter conversion. Its overnight flights formed the bulk of the operations, with items such as letters, parcels and newspapers being the most common cargo. The company's last Merchantman was recently retired.

FACTS AND FIGURES

➤ Vickers studied 60 different proposals for their new airliner, including jet-powered and swept-wing designs.

➤ BEA decided that the new airliner would be named Vanguard.

➤ Vickers and BEA argued over whether the aircraft should be high- or low-winged.

➤ Vickers financed the development of the Vanguard and had no assistance from the Government.

➤ BEA's fleet of Vanguards was named after famous warships.

➤ A Vanguard flew from Canada to the UK in 8 hours and 15 minutes.

PROFILE

Airliner to freighter

First flown in January 1959, with much more powerful Tyne engines replacing the Darts that powered the Viscount, the Vanguard could fly further and faster than its smaller predecessor with nearly three times the payload. But, by then, the first medium-range jet airliners were starting to appear.

Turboprops were quieter and more fuel-efficient than turbojets, but at the time fuel was relatively cheap and airports were not subject to the same noise controls as they are in the 1990s. The jets were faster and had greater appeal to

British Airways Cargo operated six Merchantmen; G-APEK had previously flown with BEA as 'Dreadnought'. Airlines in Canada, France, Iceland, Indonesia and Sweden also flew freighter conversions.

passengers, so it was not surprising that the airlines preferred them.

As a result, Vickers sold only 43 Vanguards. Six Type 951s and 14 heavier Type 953s went to British European Airways (BEA), while Trans-Canadian Airlines (TCA) bought 23 of the Type 952. By the mid-1970s all had been retired from passenger service, but many were converted to Cargoliner freighters

in Canada or to Merchantmen in the UK. Journey time is less of a priority for short-haul cargo flights and the Vanguard's quiet engines helped to make it more acceptable on overnight freight services. For these reasons the Merchantman continued to serve into the late 1990s with a handful of specialist cargo airlines.

A crew of three flew the Vanguard, with two cabin attendants.

The area within the wing box structure was sealed to form a fuel tank. The wing tanks held 23185 litres of fuel.

TYPE 951 VANGUARD

British European Airways named this Vanguard 'Euryalus'. The aircraft spent its entire career with the airline.

Part of the original BEA specification was for freight holds with a height of at least 1.22 m (4 ft.). The Vanguard's hold is 1.30 m (4 ft. 3 in.) high.

Large, four-bladed propellers drove the Vanguard. In recent years improved propeller design and multi-blade technology has seen an increase in the popularity of propeller aircraft.

All controls were manually operated and aerodynamically balanced. The Vanguard had a low approach speed.

The Vanguard had large oval windows, like those of the Viscount. These produce a very strong structure and allow the passengers an excellent view.

The distinctive dorsal fin was added to the tail unit to solve minor problems with the airflow around the rudder.

Like the Viscount, the Vanguard's tailplanes were angled upwards to improve directional stability and avoid jet wash from the engines.

Route-proving trials prior to service entry revealed a number of engine problems which delayed BEA services until 1 March 1961.

Long, slender, high-aspect ratio wings gave the Vanguard good range and cruising speed characteristics.

Vickers' airliner designs

■ **TYPE 72 VANGUARD:** Only one of these 23-seat airliners was built. It entered service with Imperial Airways in 1928.

■ **TYPE 610 VIKING:** Offering seating for a maximum of 27 passengers, the Viking was a successful post-war airliner.

■ **TYPE 630 VISCOUNT:** This proved to be Vickers' most successful airliner and served for more than 40 years; 444 Viscounts were built.

■ **TYPE 1150 SUPER VC-10:** Most of East African Airline's VC-10s now fly with the RAF as tanker/transports.

ACTION DATA

MAXIMUM PASSENGER LOAD

With various seating arrangements, between 93 and 139 passengers could be accommodated in the Vanguard. BEA found that the high-density 139-passenger layout, with seats six abreast, was popular on many routes. The competing airliners shown were not able to offer this flexibility, although the Electra was also the subject of many freighter conversions.

TYPE 952 VANGUARD	139
ELECTRA	85
Il-18 'COOT'	120

VICKERS

VC.10

● First rear-engined four-jet ● Short take-off ● Long range

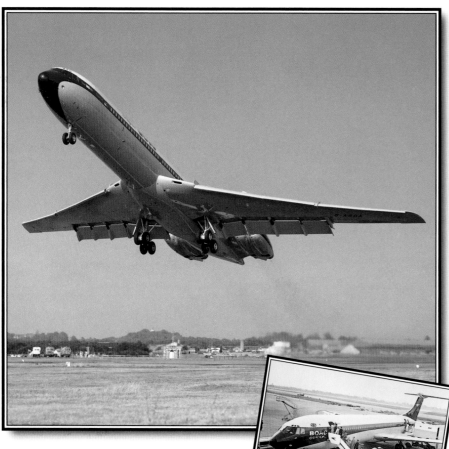

▲ When it entered service with BOAC in April 1964, the VC.10 was the world's first long-range, intercontinental jet airliner with four rear-mounted turbofan engines. It was therefore the first of many airliners with a 'clean-wing' layout.

The Vickers VC.10 was a 'great' of the golden age of the 1960s, when jet-powered air commerce was new and airlines pampered travellers. It was chosen without hesitation by many carriers, including BOAC (British Overseas Airways Corporation), British United and Ghana Airways, with a military version joining the Royal Air Force. In addition, the popularity of the VC.10 led to the successful extended-body Super VC.10 model.

VICKERS **VC.10**

▼ Super VC.10
The stretched Super VC.10 had more powerful Rolls-Royce Conway engines, an additional fuel tank in the fin and extended wing leading edges. It carried more passengers over a longer range, but was not a great commercial success.

▲ Quick development
The design of the VC.10 began in March 1958, with the prototype becoming airborne for the first time four years later in June 1962. Within two years it was in regular service with BOAC.

◀ Tanker conversions
Retired airline VC.10s and Super VC.10s have been converted by British Aerospace as air-to-air refuelling tankers for the RAF. The first nine aircraft had holes cut in the tops of their fuselages to enable fuel tanks to be lowered into their cabins. The VC.10's five fuel tanks each hold 3182 litres.

▼ Spacious cockpit
The roomy cockpit provided accommodation for an airline flight crew of three.

▲ Tri-jet testbed
One of the RAF's 14 VC.10 transports had its two portside Conway engines replaced by a single RB.211 turbofan for flight testing. Large turbofans like the RB.211 gave next-generation airliners greater range.

FACTS AND FIGURES

➤ The Super VC.10 (Type 1151) was able to carry 163 to 180 economy-class passengers.

➤ BOAC introduced the first VC.10s on the London-Lagos route on 29 April 1964.

➤ First flight of the VC.10 prototype was made on 29 June 1962.

➤ When British Airways ended scheduled service in March 1981, VC.10s had carried over a million passengers.

➤ The lengthened Vickers Super VC.10 flew for the first time on 7 May 1964.

➤ The RAF ordered 14 of these Vickers transports for general support.

PROFILE

Britain's last big jet airliner

In the 1960s, when fewer than five per cent of all people in developed Western nations had even been inside an aircraft, the Vickers VC.10 offered a high standard of transportation for the lucky few who flew in it. The VC.10 was largely underwritten by BOAC, the airline since replaced by British Airways, but Vickers' fine servant of the skies appeared in many colours: Ghana Airways leased one to Middle East Airways which stationed the VC.10 in Beirut.

The success of the VC.10

jetliner paralleled faithful service by its military counterpart: RAF VC.10s are still used for long-range troop and VIP transport. A growth version, the Super VC.10, joined BOAC's North American routes in 1965. With greater capacity, the Super VC.10 had a lengthened fuselage, a fuel tank in the fin and more powerful turbojet engines.

All variants of the VC.10 sustained a fine record for reliability and safety; so much so that the RAF purchased a fleet of VC.10 airliners for conversion as air-to-air refuelling platforms.

Below: The only new-build VC.10s to go directly to an overseas airline were two modified Model 1102s supplied to Ghana Airways in 1965.

Above: The first Super VC.10 entered service with BOAC in April 1965, and the 17 production aircraft were operated until 1981. Four new Super VC.10s, with large cargo doors and strengthened floors were built for East African Airways.

Super VC.10

Type: four-engined long-range passenger/cargo jet airliner

Powerplant: four 100.08-kN (23,030-lb.-thrust) Rolls-Royce Conway RCo.43 turbofans

Maximum speed: 935 km/h (580 m.p.h.)

Initial climb rate: 700 m/min (2,300 f.p.m.)

Cruise height: 11,600 m (38,000 ft.)

Range: 7560 km (4,698 mi.) with maximum payload

Weights: empty 66,660 kg (146,960 lb.); basic operating weight 70,479 kg (155,054 lb.)

Maximum payload: 27,043 kg (59,495 lb.)

Dimensions:
span	44.55 m (146 ft.)
length	52.32 m (172 ft.)
height	12.04 m (39 ft.)
wing area	272.4 m² (2,931 sq. ft.)

SUPER VC.10

As the fastest subsonic transatlantic airliner, the stretched fuselage of the Super VC.10 held up to 187 passengers. Its increased fuel capacity gave it a longer range.

The well-equipped flight deck had space for up to four crewmembers.

The spoilers on the top of the wings were used as airbrakes.

The Super VC.10 was powered by four Rolls-Royce Conway RCo.43 turbofan engines, mounted in pairs on either side of the rear fuselage. Thrust reversers were fitted to the outer engines only.

The Super VC.10 had a 4.27-m (14-ft.) longer fuselage, carried a bigger payload and had an additional toilet. The rear passenger door was moved aft of the wing.

The low wings, with 32° of sweep, made extensive use of fail-safe measures, with each aileron divided into two separate sections.

The cantilever, all-metal tail had the tailplane set at the top of the fin, ahead of a large bullet-shaped fairing at the junction. The fin also had an integral fuel tank.

The flight deck was the first to become fully operational with the new Elliott automatic landing system, permitting hands-off landings in restricted visibility.

The inward-retracting main undercarriage units each used four-wheel bogies. It had twin wheels on the forward-retracting, steerable nose unit.

The Super VC.10 had an oval-shaped fuselage of light-alloy, semi-monocoque construction with conventional frames and stringers.

Four-jet transports of the 1960s

■ **ILYUSHIN Il-62:** The first long-range, four-jet transport built in the USSR, the Il-62 remained in production for 30 years, with more than 250 delivered to airlines and military customers. It is longer and heavier than the VC.10, but with a lower top speed (901 km/h/580 m.p.h.) and shorter range (6700 km/4,587 mi.).

■ **McDONNELL DOUGLAS DC-8-50:** First flown in 1958, the DC-8, with its conventional underslung engines, was shorter overall than the VC.10 but could accommodate more passengers. It was not quite as fast as the Vickers' aircraft and did not have the range with maximum payload and reserves.

■ **VICKERS VC.10 C1:** With a standard VC.10 length fuselage, large forward loading door and strengthened cabin floor, the more powerful VC.10 supplied to the RAF in 1966 is still in service more than 30 years later. It is fast, with a maximum speed of 935 km/h (558 m.p.h.) and good range, up to 7560 km (4,154 mi.).

ACTION DATA

MAXIMUM SPEED

The Super VC.10 was the fastest subsonic transatlantic airliner when it entered service with BOAC in 1965. Possessing powerful engines, it is still one of the quickest airliners in the sky.

Il-62 'CLASSIC'	900 km/h (558 m.p.h.)
SUPER VC.10	935 km/h (580 m.p.h.)
DC-8-50	932 km/h (578 m.p.h.)

PASSENGERS

The rear fuselage-mounted engines reduce the interior cabin length available for passenger seating on both the Super VC.10 and Il-62. RAF VC.10 transports have rearward-facing seats for safety.

Il-62 'CLASSIC'	180 passengers
SUPER VC.10	163 passengers
DC-8-50	189 passengers

RANGE

The Super VC.10, with its additional fin fuel tank, has a markedly greater range than either of its 1960s competitors.

Il-62 'CLASSIC'	6700 km (4,154 mi.)
SUPER VC.10	7560 km (4,687 mi.)
DC-8-50	6440 km (3,993 mi.)

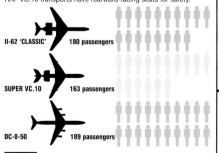

YAKOVLEV

YAK-40 'CODLING'/YAK-42 'CLOBBER'

● First Soviet feeder-liner ● Short take-off capability ● VIP transport

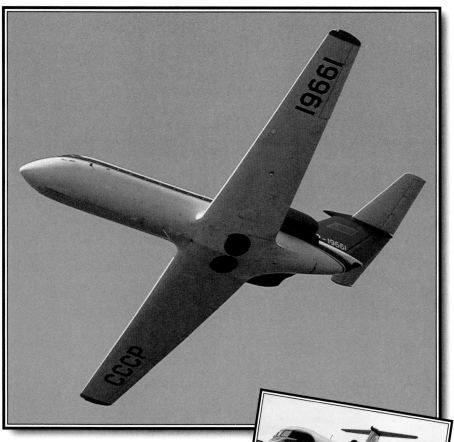

The Yak-40 was designed as a short-range regional transport to replace older piston and turboprop aircraft. It featured a straight wing and accommodated up to 27 passengers, and could take off from small, 700-m (2,300-ft.) grass strips. The Yak-42 was a larger aircraft with a swept wing which significantly improved performance. Both aircraft remain in widespread use in Russia and former Soviet bloc countries.

▲ The Yak-40
was a very useful aircraft for a nation like the USSR, which has its population spread over a massive area. The aircraft could use airfields that Western jets could not.

YAKOVLEV YAK-40 'CODLING'/YAK-42 'CLOBBER'

▼ Oil platform
When Aeroflot split, many Yak-40s went to small regional carriers. This one is used to transport executives of the LUKoil firm.

▲ Slovakian Yak
The Slovak air force operates a small force of Yak-40s, based at Malacky with 32/1 Letka.

◀ Fan test
During a trials programme, this Yak-42E-LL tested the contra-prop D-236 engine. The front propeller had eight blades and the rear propeller six.

Prop nose ▶
This Yak-40 had a Czech M-602 turboprop engine mounted in the nose for test purposes.

◀ Swept fin
The Yak-40 had a curious mixture of traditional and new aerodynamics, with a straight wing for short take-offs and a sharply swept fin for fast cruising. The wing flaps were split, with three on each side.

FACTS AND FIGURES

➤ The prototype Yak-40 flew on 21 October 1966 and entered service in 1968; more than 1,000 had been built by June 1976.

➤ A Yak-42E-LL was used to test the D-236 experimental propfan.

➤ One Yak-40 was fitted with the nose section of a MiG-25R for trials.

➤ The Yak-42F, fitted with a cylinder containing electro-optical sensors, was an Aeroflot Earth survey aircraft.

➤ The Polish air force operates Yak-40s formerly used by the national airline LOT.

➤ The Yak-42 was the longest development project ever carried out by the Yak OKB.

PROFILE

First of the Aeroflot feeder-liners

Left: With flaps and undercarriage down, a Yak-40 lands at a Soviet airfield. The Yak carried on the tradition of the An-2 in operating from the small grass strips found all over the USSR.

Designed to replace the obsolete Li-2 and Il-14 propeller-driven aircraft in Aeroflot service, the Yak-40 was first ordered in 1964. Alexander Yakovlev himself was involved with the project, as was his son Sergei.

To fulfil the role of regional feeder-liner, which made up over half of Aeroflot's passenger requirement, the Yak-40 required a short take-off capability, plus the ability to cruise economically. Initially, it was planned to cruise on two engines and use the third for maximum performance, but the two-engine requirement was soon dropped.

Although mainly seeing civil use as a 27-seat airliner, a few Yak-40s were used as military testbeds. Yak-40s were also sold to many air forces as VIP transports, including those of Ethiopia, Laos and Poland; many are still in service.

Work on the Yak-42 design began in 1972. It had the distinction of using the first high-bypass ratio turbofan in the USSR. The first prototype flew in 1975. It was a much larger aircraft than the Yak-40, seating 120 passengers, but had a protracted development, and did not enter service until 1981.

The ultimate version, the Yak-142, entered service in 1993, and featured advanced avionics, flight-deployable spoilers and a new power unit.

Above: The Yak-42 featured a swept wing and relinquished much of the short-field capability of the Yak-40. High-lift devices meant that it could still use runways as short as 1800 m (5,900 ft.), however.

A small auxiliary power unit is fitted above the air inlet duct for the central engine. This provides air for starting the main engine and for heating the cabin when on the ground. Early Yak-40s had a bullet fairing on the tailplane and fin junction, which was later deleted.

Yak-40

Type: three-engined short-haul feeder-liner

Powerplant: three Lotarev Ivchenko 14.71-kN (3,300-lb.-thrust) AI-25 turbofans

Maximum speed: 600 km/h (372 m.p.h.)

Economical cruising speed: 500 km/h (310 m.p.h.)

Take-off run: 340 m (1,115 ft.) at normal weight

Landing run: 340 m (1,115 ft.) at normal weight

Service ceiling: 8000 m (26,240 ft.)

Weights: empty 9000 kg (20,723 lb.); loaded 13,750 kg (30,250 lb.)

Payload: 2790 kg (6,130 lb.)

Accommodation: 2 crew and 27 passengers

Dimensions:
span	25.00 m (82 ft.)
length	20.36 m (66 ft. 10 in.)
height	6.40m (21 ft. 4 in.)
wing area	70 m² (754 sq. ft.)

ACTION DATA

CRUISING SPEED

The bigger swept-wing Yak-42 had a slower cruising speed than the Western types but it had a similar maximum speed. The swept wing of the Yak-42 gave the aircraft much greater performance than that of the Yak-40. Being jet-powered the Yak-40 and Yak-42 both out-performed the piston-engined aircraft they replaced.

Yak-42	820 km/h (508 m.p.h.)
ONE-ELEVEN SERIES 475	871 km/h (540 m.p.h.)
F-28 FELLOWSHIP	843 km/h (523 m.p.h.)

PASSENGERS

The Yak-42 in standard fit could carry more passengers than the One-Eleven or the F-28. The proposed Yak-42M would have had 156 seats. The Yak entered service much later than the One-Eleven.

Yak-42 'CLOBBER'	121 PASSENGERS
ONE-ELEVEN SERIES 475	79 PASSENGERS
F-28 FELLOWSHIP	50 PASSENGERS

RANGE

The larger Yak-42 could carry 120 passengers more than 1900 km (1,100 mi.). This range was reduced to 1000 km (559 mi.) with maximum payload. Feeder-liners are used for flying passengers between cities in one country rather than between countries, but the size of the former USSR highlighted the Yak-42's lack of range.

Yak-42 'CLOBBER' 1000 km (559 mi.)

F28 FELLOWSHIP 2593 km (1,608 mi.)

ONE-ELEVEN SERIES 475 3001 km (1,860 mi.)

YAK-40

The former Yugoslavian air force, one of many Eastern European air forces to use the type, operated Yak-40s in the VIP transport role. Yak-40s are still in use from Georgia to Sakhalin, and will continue to fly into the next century in the hands of civil operators.

The Yak has a crew of two pilots, with an autopilot fitted for cruising. Grosa-40 weather radar and instrument landing systems are also fitted. The windscreen is electrically heated.

The wing was first produced with 6° of dihedral, but this was later reduced. Each wing was produced in left and right halves, joined at the centreline. The wing skins were chemically milled and assembled by spot-welding, bonding and rivetting. Flaps are set to 15° for take-off and 35° for landing.

The intake mouth for the central (number two) engine is slightly raked back. The main cabin is 6.7 m (22 ft.) long and seats 24 people in a two plus one configuration. The fin leading edge is de-iced with engine bleed air.

The front left cabin door is a service door, with the ventral hydraulic airstair being the main door. This Yugoslavian Yak has its designation written in Cyrillic script.

The Yak-40K had a large upward-lifting cargo door fitted in the port fuselage.

The fuel is contained in integral wing tanks forward of the main spar. The wing leading edge is de-iced by engine bleed air. The wing has manual ailerons, with a tab on the right wing only.

The Lotarev Ivchenko AI-25 turbofan has three low-pressure and eight high-pressure stages with cooled blades. The proposed Yak-40TL would have used two LF 507 engines and no thrust reverser, but it was never built.

Three-engine airliners

■ **BOEING 727:** The world's favourite tri-jet, the Boeing 727 is still employed in large numbers, particularly on American domestic routes. Large numbers of 727 freighters were also sold.

■ **HAWKER SIDDELEY TRIDENT:** One of the few real success stories in British airliner history, the Trident was also produced in Romania under licence and was sold to the Chinese airline CAAC.

■ **LOCKHEED L-1011 TRISTAR:** Now a rare sight at the world's airports, the Tristar was popular with the major airlines in the 1970s because of its low noise and high fuel economy.

■ **TUPOLEV Tu-154:** Still in widespread service and produced in updated form, the Tu-154 was used by Aeroflot and Soviet-bloc nations on international medium-haul routes.

INDEX